Facts about
Germany

SOCIETÄTS**VERLAG**

Table of contents

The country

Natural features	5
The people	10
The states	19
Baden-Württemberg	21
The Free State of Bavaria	25
Berlin	31
Brandenburg	37
The Free Hanseatic City of Bremen	41
The Free and Hanseatic City of Hamburg	44
Hesse	51
Mecklenburg-Western Pomerania	55
Lower Saxony	59
North Rhine-Westphalia	65
Rhineland-Palatinate	69
Saarland	74
The Free State of Saxony	77
Saxony-Anhalt	82
Schleswig-Holstein	86
The Free State of Thuringia	89

History

German history up to 1945	93
From 1945 to the present	112

Government, constitution and legal system

The Basic Law	143
The constitutional bodies	150
Federalism and self-government	159
The legal system	164
Parties and elections	171

The state and its citizens

Internal security	177
Public finance	182
The common good and individual interests	188

Germany and the world

Foreign policy 191
Germany and Europe 210
External security 230
Development policy 233

The economy

Economic system and policy 245
Germany:
an economic hub 252
The labor market 259
Incomes and prices 266
Housing and urban development 270
Environmental protection 277
Energy and raw materials 289
Scholarship and research 295

Economic sectors

Industry and its products 303
Crafts and trades 312
The independent professions 315
Agriculture, forestry and fisheries 318
Commerce 328
Foreign trade 331
Money and banking 336
Traffic and transport 343
Information Technology 350
Fairs and exhibitions 357

The system of a social market economy

Industrial relations 361
Social security 368
The health care system 376
Consumer protection 381

Life in society

Women and society 385
Youth 389
Sports 397
Leisure and holidays 401
Churches and religious communities 408
Mass media and public opinion 412
The press 415
Radio and television 419

Education and training

Schools 425

Vocational training 433

Higher education institutions 437

Adult education 445

Cultural life

Cultural diversity 449

Literature 452

The book trade and libraries 460

Art 464

Architecture and design 470

Museums, collections and exhibitions 477

Theater and music 481

Cinema 490

Germany in figures 497

Index 513

Published by the German Federal Press and Information Bureau

© Societäts-Verlag, Frankfurt/Main, Germany
All rights reserved to texts and pictures
Editorial deadline: July 2000
Project management and chief editor: Dr. Arno Kappler
Translation: Dr. Jeremy Gaines
Production management: Stefan Reichart
Picture research: Christin Schultz, Jürgen Dörr
Cover and layout: Odeon Zwo GmbH, Hanover & Berlin
Charts: Peter Lenz, Wiesbaden
Typesetting and reproductions: Societäts-Druck, Frankfurt/Main
Printers: Westermann, Brunswick
Printed in Germany 2000 on paper bleached free of chlorine
ISBN 3-7973-0752-7

This book appears in German, English, French, Spanish, Portugese, Italian, Turkish, Russian, Polish, Chinese, Japanese, Arabic and Farsi
The contents of this book can be downloaded from the Internet by clicking:
http://www.bundesregierung.de/

The country

Natural features

The Federal Republic of Germany is situated in the heart of Europe. It has nine neighbors: Denmark in the north, the Netherlands, Belgium, Luxembourg and France in the west, Switzerland and Austria in the south, and the Czech Republic as well as Poland in the east. This central location has been more pronounced since 3 October 1990, when Germany was reunited. The Federal Republic is more than ever a link between East and West, but also between Scandinavia and the Mediterranean. As an integral part of the European Union and NATO, Germany is a bridge to the countries of Central and Eastern Europe.

The Federal Republic of Germany covers an area of about 357,000 square kilometers. The longest distance from north to south as the crow flies is 876 kilometers, from west to east 640 kilometers. Its extremities are List on the island of Sylt in the north, Deschka, Saxony, in the east, Oberstdorf, Bavaria, in the south, and Selfkant, North Rhine-Westphalia, in the west. The total length of the country's borders is 3,758 kilometers.

Germany has a population of about 82.1 million, the largest in Europe after the Russian Federation, followed by the United Kingdom (59 million), France (58.6 million) and Italy (57.5 million). In size, however, Germany is smaller than France

	Over 1,000,000 inhabitants		
	Over 500,000 inhabitants	**Berlin**	Federal Capital
	Over 100,000 inhabitants	<u>Bonn</u>	Federal City
	Less than 100,000 inhabitants	<u>Mainz</u>	State Capital

In the North – the red sandstone island of Helgoland with the "Lange Anna"

(544,000 square kilometers) and Spain (506,000 square kilometers).

Geographical features. Germany has an extraordinary variety of charming landscapes. Low and high mountain ranges intermingle with upland plains, terrace country, hilly regions and lakelands as well as wide, open lowlands. From north to south, Germany is divided into five regions with different topographical features: the North German Plain, the Central Upland Range, the terrace panorama of the southwest, the Alpine foothills in the south and the Bavarian Alps.

In the north are dry, sandy lowlands with many lakes as well as heaths and moors. There is also the fertile land stretching southward to the Central Upland Range. These lowland penetrations include the Lower Rhenish Bight, the Westphalian Bight and the SaxonThuringian Bight. The marshes along the North Sea coast extend as far as the geest. Characteristic features of the Baltic Sea coastline are in Schleswig-Holstein the fjords, in Mecklenburg-Western Pomerania the lakes and the counterbalancing coastline.

The main islands in the North Sea are the East Frisian Islands, among them Borkum and Norderney, the North Frisian Islands of Amrum, Föhr and Sylt (and the Halligen), as well as Helgoland in the Helgoland Bight. Situated in the Baltic Sea are the islands of Rügen, Hiddensee and Fehmarn. Some

Monschau, an idyllic little town in the Eifel and a favorite travel destination

parts of the Baltic coast have flat, sandy shores; others have steep cliffs. Between the North Sea and the Baltic Sea lies the low-hill country called "Holsteinische Schweiz" (Holstein Switzerland).

The Central Upland Range divides northern Germany from the south. The central Rhine valley and the Hessian depressions serve as the natural north-south traffic arteries. The Central Uplands include the Rhenish Schist Massif (Hunsrück, Eifel, Taunus, Westerwald, Bergisches Land and Sauerland), the Hessian Mountains, and the Weser and Leine Mountains in western and central Germany. Right in the heart of Germany are the Harz Mountains. Toward the east are the Rhön Mountains, the Bavarian Forest, the Upper Palatinate Forest, the Fichtel Hills, the Franconian Forest, the Thuringian Forest and the Ore Mountains.

Mountains, rivers, lakes, islands:

Mountains:

Zugspitze (Northern Limestone Alps)	2,962 m
Watzmann (Northern Limestone Alps)	2,713 m
Feldberg (Black Forest)	1,493 m
Grosser Arber (Bavarian Forest)	1,456 m
Fichtelberg (Erz Mountains)	1,215 m
Brocken (Harz)	1,142 m

Rivers in Germany:

Rhine	865 km
Elbe	700 km
Danube	686 km
Main	524 km
Weser	440 km
Spree	382 km
Mosel	242 km

Shipping canals:

Mittellandkanal	321 km
Dortmund-Ems-Kanal	269 km
Main-Donau-Kanal (Main-Danube canal)	171 km
Nord-Ostsee-Kanal (North Sea-Baltic Sea canal)	99 km

Lakes and dams:

Lake Constance (German part)	305.0 sq km
Müritz	110.3 sq km
Bleiloch	215 million cubic meters
Schwammenauel	205 million cubic meters
Edertalsperre (Edersee reservoir)	202 million cubic meters

Islands:

Rügen	930 sq km
Usedom (German part)	373 sq km
Fehmarn	185 sq km
Sylt	99 sq km

Krün-Gerold-see Lake with the Karwendel mountains behind

The terrace landscape of the Central Uplands in the southwest embraces the upper Rhine valley with the adjacent mountain ranges of the Black Forest, the Oden Forest and Spessart, the Palatinate Forest with the Haardt, and the Swabian-Franconian terrace country with the Alb.

In a narrow valley between Bingen and Bonn, the river Rhine, the main north-south axis, slices through the Rhenish Schist Massif, whose highland areas are less densely populated than the sheltered wine-growing areas on both sides of the Rhine valley which are very popular with tourists.

The Alpine foothills embrace the Swabian-Bavarian highlands with their hills and large lakes in the south, broad gravel plains, the hilly landscape of Lower Bavaria, and the Danube valley. Characteristic features of this region are the moors, dome-shaped hill ranges and lakes (Chiemsee, Starnberger See) as well as small villages.

The German part of the Alps between Lake Constance and Berchtesgaden is limited to the Allgäu, the Bavarian Alps and the Berchtesgaden Alps. In this Alpine world lie picturesque lakes such as the Königssee near Berchtesgaden and popular tourist resorts such as Garmisch-Partenkirchen or Mittenwald.

Climate. Germany is situated in the moderately cool west wind zone between the Atlantic Ocean and the continental climate in the East. Sharp changes in temperature are rare. There is precipitation all the year round. In the winter, the average temperature is between 1.5°C in the lowland areas and -6°C in the mountains. In the warmest month of the year, July, temperatures are between 18°C in low-lying regions and 20°C in the sheltered valleys of the south. Exceptions are the Upper Rhine Trough with its extremely mild climate, Upper Bavaria with its intermittently occurring warm Alpine wind (Föhn) from the south, and the Harz Mountains, a climatic zone of its own with cold winds, cool summers and heavy snow in winter.

The people

Germany has a population of approximately 82.1 million (including 7.3 million foreigners) and is one of the most densely populated countries in all of Europe (230 people per square kilometer). Only Belgium, the Netherlands and Great Britain have a higher population density (see chart, p. 498).

The population is distributed very unevenly. The Berlin region has been growing rapidly since Germany's unification and presently has more than 4.3 million inhabitants. More than 11 million people (about 1,100 per square kilometer) live in the Rhine-Ruhr industrial region, where towns and cities are so close together that there are no distinct boundaries between them.

Other concentrations are to be found in the Rhine-Main area around Frankfurt, Wiesbaden and Mainz, the Rhine-Neckar industrial region around Mannheim and Ludwigshafen, the industrial area around Stuttgart, and the catchment areas of Bremen, Cologne, Dresden, Hamburg, Leipzig, Munich and Nuremberg/Fürth.

These densely populated regions contrast with very thinly populated areas such as the heathlands and moorlands of the North German Plain, parts of the Eifel Mountains, the Bavarian Forest, the Upper Palatinate, the March of Brandenburg and large parts of Mecklenburg-Western Pomerania.

The western part of Germany is much more densely populated than the eastern part, where less than one fifth of the population (15.3 million) live on roughly 30 percent of the national territory. Of the 20 cities with more than 300,000 inhabitants, three are in the eastern part of Germany.

Nearly one third of the population (about 25 million people) live in the 82 large cities with more than 100,000 inhabitants (see chart, p. 499). But the majority of people in the Federal Republic live in small towns and villages: nearly 6.4 million in municipalities with a population of fewer than 2,000 and

Great fun
for the small
ones –
a merry-go-
round for kids

50.5 million in towns with between 2,000 and 100,000 inhabitants.

The population in the old and new states began to decline in the 1970s because the birthrate was falling. Germany had one of the lowest birthrates in the world in the year 1998: 10.2 births per 1,000 inhabitants per year (in the western part of the country). The population increase after the Second World War was mainly due to immigration. Some 13 million refugees and expellees entered the present German territory from the former German eastern provinces and Eastern Europe.

Wedding –
a special
moment in
life

There was a continuous strong flow of people who fled from eastern to western Germany until the Berlin Wall was erected by the regime in the former German Democratic Republic (GDR) in 1961, which hermetically sealed the border. Beginning in the early 1960s, large numbers of foreign workers came to the Federal Republic of old whose expanding economy needed additional labor which was not available at home.

Regional disparities. The German nation essentially grew out of a number of German tribes such as the Franks, the Saxons, the Swabians and the Bavarians. These old tribes have of course long since lost their original character, but their traditions and dialects live on in their respective re-

The new millennium – greeted on Jan. 1, 2000 in front of the Brandenburger Gate

gions. Those ethnic regions are not, however, identical to the present states (Länder), most of which were only formed after the Second World War in agreement with the occupying powers. In many cases the boundaries were drawn without any consideration for old traditions. Furthermore, the flows of refugees and the massive postwar migrations, but also the mobility of the modern industrial society, have more or less blurred the ethnic boundaries.

Since time immemorial, different characteristics have been ascribed to the various regional groups. Natives of Mecklenburg, for instance, are considered reserved, Swabians thrifty, Rhinelanders happy-go-lucky, and Saxons hardworking and shrewd – traditional observations that are gladly perpetuated to this very day in a spirit of good-natured folkloric rivalry.

The German language. German is one of the large group of Indo-Germanic languages, and within that one of the Ger-

Enjoying summer reading in the garden

manic languages. It is thus related to Danish, Norwegian, Swedish, Dutch and Flemish, but also to English. The emergence of a common High German language is attributed to Martin Luther's translation of the Bible.

Germany has a wealth of dialects. It is usually possible to determine a German's native region from his or her dialect and pronunciation. These dialects differ greatly: If, for instance, a Mecklenburger and a Bavarian or a Baden-Württemberg native were to carry on a conversation in their respective pure dialects, they would have great difficulty understanding each other.

German is also spoken as the native language in Austria, Liechtenstein, most of Switzerland, South Tirol (northern Italy), northern Schleswig (Denmark) and in small areas of Belgium, France (Alsace) and Luxembourg along the German border. The German minorities in Poland, Romania and the countries of the former Soviet Union have partly retained the German language as well.

German is the native language of more than 100 million people. About one in ten books published throughout the world is originally written in German. As regards translations into foreign languages, German is third after English and French, and more works have been translated into German than into any other language.

Curiosity and understanding – the young and old in dialog

National minorities. Germany has signed the "European Council's skeleton agreement for protection of national minorities" for the four national minorities residing in Germany from early times, the Sorbs, Frisians, Danes and the German Sinti and Roma peoples, as well as the "European Charter for Regional or Minority Languages". Both agreements come under German law since 1998.

The Lusatian Sorbs are the descendants of Slavic tribes. They settled the territory east of the Elbe and Saale rivers in the 6th century in the course of the migration of peoples that occurred in the early centuries A.D. The first document in which they are mentioned dates from 631. In the 16th century, under the influence of the Reformation, a written Sorbian language evolved. In addition to the Institute for Sorbian Studies at the University of Leipzig, there are a large number of schools, associations and other institutions which are devoted to the cultivation of the Sorbian language and culture.

The Love Parade at Berlin's "Siegessäule" column

Colorful life at Berlin's "Carneval of the Cultures"

The Frisians are the descendants of a Germanic tribe on the North Sea coast (between the Lower Rhine and the Ems River) and have preserved numerous traditions in addition to their own distinct language. A Danish minority lives in the Schleswig region of the state of Schleswig-Holstein, especially around Flensburg.

The number of Sinti and Roma peoples with German citizenship is estimated at 70,000. The Central Council for German Sinti and Roma, which has received support from the German government since 1982, gives strong voice to the compensation of holocaust survivors, minority rights and the preservation of the Romani language while tackling discrimination and prejudice.

Foreign nationalities. Of the country's approximately 82.1 million inhabitants (1998), 7.3 million are foreigners. They were all glad to come and stay in Germany (see table, p. 499). For decades there were no racial problems. The category of "guest workers", initially consisting of Italians, was extended to include Greeks and Spaniards, and then Portuguese, Yugoslavs and Turks.

Integration within the European Union and the Western world, the dissolution of the East bloc, and the immigration of people from Asian and African countries naturally meant a considerable increase in the number of foreigners of diverse origin in Germany.

The Federal Republic has proved itself to be an open society not only by taking in asylum-seekers and war refugees. It has also always been a champion of the free movement of labor, freedom of occupation and freedom of establishment within the European Union. Approximately 2.7 million German repatriates from the countries of the former East bloc, especially from the territory of the former Soviet Union, have come to the Federal Republic of Germany since 1987; in 1999 they numbered more than 104,916.

Germany's willingness to open its doors to foreigners who have been persecuted on political grounds is unparalleled. The new Article 16a of the Basic Law, like the former Article 16, still guarantees protection from political persecution as an individual basic right. In 1989 the number of foreigners seeking asylum in Germany was 121,318; in 1991 the figure rose to 256,112 and in 1992 to 438,191. At the same time, the proportion of those who could be recognized as genuine victims of political persecution fell to less than five percent. In 1993 some 322,600 asylum-seekers entered Germany. Their number fell significantly when the new legislation on the right of asylum became effective on 1 July 1993: Only 127,210 people sought asylum in 1994, 127,937 in 1995, 116,367 in 1996, 104,353 in 1997, 98,644 in 1998 and 95,113 in 1999. Under the new constitutional amendment in force since 1 July 1993 (the "asylum compromise"), the right of asylum has been focused on its true purpose – the normal state of affairs in other countries – of affording protection to those who actually have been persecuted on political grounds and really do need protection. As a result, foreigners who enter Germany from a safe third country may no longer invoke this basic right. Germany also reserves the right, notwithstanding the Geneva Convention relating to the Status of Refugees, to draw up a list of countries where, according to official sources of information, no one is subject to persecution so that there is, as a rule, no ground for asylum. Nonetheless, anyone whose application for asylum has been rejected may appeal, if necessary right through to the Federal Constitutional Court.

Policy on foreigners and naturalization. More than half of the foreigners residing in Germany have lived here for at

Dispatcher and employees at an international forwarding company

least ten years; almost one third of them have already lived here for 20 years or more. Of the foreigners who have resided here for at least ten years, about 870,000 are under the age of 25. More than two thirds of the children and adolescents were born here.

On 1 January 2000, important regulations contained in the new law reforming citizenship came into effect. Essential aspects:

— In accordance with the law, children born in Germany to foreign parents now receive German citizenship at birth. The prerequisite is that the usual legal residence of one parent has been Germany for the prior eight years and that this parent possesses a residence certificate or has had an unlimited residence permit for the prior three years. When, by virtue of parentage these children acquire another citizenship, they must choose between German and foreign citizenship upon reaching maturity at age 18.

— The law grants a special limited right of citizenship under the same conditions to children who have not reached the age of ten as at 1 January 2000.

— Foreigners may now claim citizenship after eight years (previously 15 years). This claim is dependent on a sufficient command of the German language and acceptance and knowledge of the German constitution. Citizenship for foreign political extremists is excluded by way of a new protective clause. Fundamentally, in order to acquire citizenship, one's previous nationality must be forfeited; exceptions are determined according to law.

— When an individual applies for and acquires foreign citizenship, he or she automatically forfeits German citizenship, regardless of whether or not he or she continues to reside within Germany.

— At the same time, the opportunity to retain German citizenship in such cases of automatic loss has been extended by means of authorization of such retention.

— Emigrants of German origin from Eastern European states are automatically naturalized upon issuance of an appurtenant certificate confirming their special status or presentation of a late repatriate certificate. The separate naturalization process hitherto in place is no longer valid.

The interests of foreigners living in Germany are represented by the Federal Government's Commissioner for Matters relating to Aliens who is concerned with the conception of and individual issues pertaining to policy on foreigners and to this end conducts talks with German and foreign politicians, representatives of the parties to collective bargaining agreements, and other groups within society. In particular, this is the person approached by organizations actively involved in matters pertaining to foreigners. The Commissioner above all supports initiatives to promote the interests of the foreigners permanently residing in Germany. For this reason, the Commissioner is also constantly in contact with the embassies of the countries in which Germany formerly recruited labor and visits these countries and meets with government representatives there to discuss pertinent issues.

One important task of the Commissioner is to disseminate comprehensive and factual information on the history of employment of foreigners in Germany and its economic significance, the origination and development of German policy on foreigners, humanitarian aspects of the actual immigration situation for foreigners and Germans alike, and the political and legal obligations assumed by Germany under international conventions and declarations.

Further information:
- Bundesministerium des Innern
  (Ministry of the Interior)
  Alt-Moabit 101d, 10559 Berlin
  Internet: http://www.bmi.bund.de
  E-mail: posteingang@bmi.bund.de
- Statistisches Bundesamt
  (Federal Statistics Office)
  Gustav-Stresemann-Ring 11, 65189 Wiesbaden
  Internet: http://www.statistik-bund.de
  E-mail: pressestell@statistik-bund.de

The states

The Federal Republic of Germany consists of 16 states known as "Länder" (capitals in parentheses): Baden-Württemberg (Stuttgart), Bavaria (Munich), Brandenburg (Potsdam), Hesse (Wiesbaden), Lower Saxony (Hanover), Mecklenburg-Western Pomerania (Schwerin), North Rhine-Westphalia (Düsseldorf), Rhineland-Palatinate (Mainz), Saarland (Saarbrücken), Saxony (Dresden), Saxony-Anhalt (Magdeburg), Schleswig-Holstein (Kiel) and Thuringia (Erfurt). Berlin, Bremen and Hamburg are city-states.

Germany has always been divided into states, but the map has changed its shape over the centuries. The most important changes in the modern age resulted from the Napoleonic wars at the beginning of the 19th century, the Austro-Prussian War of 1866, the First World War and the Second World War. After the latter, Germany was divided and the country's largest state, Prussia, was dissolved. Most of the states as we know them today were established after 1945, but they have largely retained their ethnic traditions and characteristics and some of the old boundaries.

Until Germany was reunited in 1990, the Federal Republic consisted of eleven states which had been created in the former Western occupation zones and had adopted democratic constitutions between 1946 and 1957.

In the Soviet-occupied zone, which later became the German Democratic Republic (GDR), five states were likewise formed, but these were soon replaced by a centralized administration. After the first free election in the former GDR on 18 March 1990, five new states were created with boundaries largely conforming to those of the period prior to 1952. On 3 October 1990 the German Democratic Republic, and hence the states of Brandenburg, Mecklenburg-Western Pomerania, Saxony, Saxony-Anhalt and Thuringia, acceded to the Federal Republic of Germany. At the same time, Berlin (East) was merged with Berlin (West).

Baden-Württemberg

Population	10.4 million	
Area	35,751 sq km	
Capital	Stuttgart	

State election 1996	
CDU	41.3%
SPD	25.1%
Alliance 90/The Greens	12.1%
FDP/DVP	9.6%
Republicans	9.1%

Extremely diverse landscapes – state-of-the-art industry. Baden-Württemberg has some of the Federal Republic's most scenic countryside. The Black Forest is one of the most popular recreation areas in Germany. Lake Constance, the exceedingly varied valleys of the Rhine, Danube and Neckar rivers, the rugged Swabian Jura, the gentle Markgräfler Land and the striking hilly Kaiserstuhl region in the Upper Rhine Plain (famous for its wine) are popular holiday resort areas. Every year more tourists come to Baden-Württemberg than the state has inhabitants. Baden-Württemberg is an important business and industrial location as well; global companies such as Daimler-Chrysler, Bosch, Porsche, SAP and IBM have their headquarters here. The state's economic strength is manifest, for instance, in the fact that the volume of its exports is nearly equal to that of Spain, Sweden or Singapore and that it exports more than any other German state. This is attributable not only to the productivity of large-scale industry: Hundreds of small and medium-sized businesses manufacture highly specialized products which are in demand all over the world. The people of Baden-Württemberg are born tinkerers – their ingenuity is legend. Thanks to the state's mild climate, cultivation of special crops such as ornamental plants, hops and tobacco is also possible in addition to traditional agriculture.

Investing in the future. In proportion to its gross domestic product, Baden-Württemberg's expenditure for research ranks near the top worldwide; endeavors presently focus on information technology as well as energy and environmental

Mainau Island on Lake Constance

technologies. Biotechnology and especially genetic engineering are likewise playing a key role today: In this area the state's research infrastructure ranks at the top in Germany and in Europe – in terms of both quality and quantity. Biotechnology departments have been established at numerous universities and industry-aligned research institutions, and several hundred firms are active in the field. A high-speed data transmission network links the state's nine universities, 39 Fachhochschulen and roughly 130 research institutions (including the Research Centre in Karlsruhe, the German Cancer Research Centre in Heidelberg, and several Max Planck and Fraunhofer institutes). International private universities opened their doors in Bruchsal and Stuttgart in 1998. There are also a number of vocational colleges as well as universities specializing in art and music. In the field of the humanities, special mention must be made of the German Literature Archive in Marbach on the Neckar River, which among other things houses the literary legacy of most German writers. Scholarship and research have a long tradition here: The University of Heidelberg, founded in 1386, is the oldest university in Germany; the first technical college was founded in Karlsruhe.

Cities worth seeing. Situated in a picturesque basin, the state capital Stuttgart (582,000 inhabitants) enjoys an enviable location. From the "Liederhalle" concert hall to the Wilhelma Botanical and Zoological Gardens, from the airport to the folk festival "Cannstatter Wasen", from the trade fair complex atop the Killesberg to the postmodern New State Gallery, the city offers all the attributes of a modern metropolis.

The distinctive architectural feature of Mannheim (309,000 inhabitants) is the geometrical layout of the city center. Together with its twin city of Ludwigshafen on the left bank of the Rhine in the state of Rhineland Palatinate, Mannheim is an important industrial center, yet with its art collections in the Fine Arts Museum and the Reiss Museum, the State Museum for Labor and Technology as well as its longstanding National Theater it is also a city with a remarkable cultural flair.

Karlsruhe (277,000 inhabitants), seat of the highest German courts – the Federal Constitutional Court and the Federal Court of Justice – has a layout which is just as distinctive as that of Mannheim: 32 streets of the former Baroque Grand-Ducal capital radiate in the shape of a fan from the palace dating from 1715. Favorably situated along major traffic routes, this industrial city has a busy Rhine port.

Freiburg im Breisgau (201,000 inhabitants) with its university dating from 1457, old city gates and Gothic Minster with a delicately articulated spire lies in a picturesque setting between the southern slope of the Black Forest and the Rhine Plain. Heidelberg (139,000 inhabitants) is a tourist magnet famed for its historic city center with the Late Gothic Church of the Holy Ghost, the Old Bridge with the Neckar Gate, the castle and quaint old student pubs.

The landmark of the city of Ulm (116,000 inhabitants) on the Danube River is its Minster with the highest church tower in Germany; the Gothic Town Hall boasts a famous astronomical clock. Other important cities in Baden-Württemberg are Heilbronn (120,000 inhabitants), Pforzheim (118,000 inhabitants), Reutlingen (110,000 inhabitants) and Tübingen (81,000 inhabitants).

Land of philosophers and artists. Nearly a thousand museums (such as the Clock Museum in Furtwangen with its unparalleled collection of Black Forest cuckoo clocks), two state theaters, 150 municipal, independent and private theater festivals, film festivals and the Solitude Palace Academy near

At the Daimler-Chrysler auto factory in Stuttgart's Untertürkheim district

The Gothic cathedral in Freiburg was completed in 1513

Stuttgart: Cultural life finds exceedingly varied forms of expression in Baden-Württemberg. Literary memorials and literature prizes recall the many great figures in Germany's intellectual history who were born here: Friedrich Schiller (1759-1805), Friedrich Hölderlin (1770-1843), Wilhelm Hauff (1802-27) and the philosophers Georg Wilhelm Friedrich Hegel (1770-1831), Friedrich Wilhelm Schelling (1775-1854) and Martin Heidegger (1889-1976).

Today the Stuttgart Ballet, the International Bach Academy and the Center for Art and Media in Karlsruhe are internationally acclaimed. 6,400 music and choral groups as well as 90 amateur orchestras by their very number attest to the joy that many people in Baden-Württemberg derive from music.

Qualified media location. The state is also an important media center and the domicile of major publishing companies; 33 percent of Germany's magazines and 22 percent of its books are published here.

Growth areas such as telecoms, IT, entertainment and multimedia are being systematically developed. The state's qualification as a media hub is attested to by the fact that there are 156 different media-related courses of study available.

Further information:
— Baden-Württemberg, Staatsministerium (Ministry of State)
  Richard-Wagner-Strasse 15, 70184 Stuttgart
  Internet: http://www.baden-wuerttemberg.de
  E-mail: poststelle@stm.bwl.de

The Free State of Bavaria

Population	12.0 million
Area	70,552 sq km
Capital	Munich

State election 1998	
CSU	52.9%
SPD	28.7%
Alliance 90/The Greens	5.7%

Tradition embedded in an earthy nature. The historical term "Free State of Bavaria" indicates that Bavaria is a republican rather than monarchical state. The largest state (in terms of area) and its twelve million inhabitants are proud of their history, which dates back to the 6th century. Nowhere else in Germany are customs preserved as much as if they were part of everyday life as they are here; people wear colorful traditional dress not only during major folk festivals such as the annual Oktoberfest in Munich. Bavaria owes its great tourist appeal to both its rich cultural and historical heritage as well as the charm of its spectacular natural beauty. The Alps with the Zugspitze, Germany's highest peak (2,962 meters), the Alpine foreland with its exquisite lakes such as the Chiemsee and the Königssee, the Bavarian Forest with its national park, the Franconian Jura, the Fichtel Hills, the Steigerwald, the Spessart and many other scenic areas around the state offer tourists incomparably enticing opportunities for rest, recreation and enjoyment of nature. The mountains are a hiker's paradise; the lakes in the Alpine foothills and the new artificial lakes created in Franconia in the course of construction of the Main-Danube Canal invite vacationers to indulge in water sports.

The state is richly endowed with extensive parks such as Schönbusch Park in Aschaffenburg, the Hofgarten in Ansbach and the English Garden in Munich, as well as magnificent palaces, above all the great palaces of the "fairy-tale king" Ludwig II: Linderhof, Neuschwanstein and Herrenchiemsee. The royal residences in Würzburg and Bamberg are likewise

Augsburg: the Renaissance Town Hall and the Perlach Tower, built in the early 17th century by Elias Holl

of imposing beauty, as is the Veste Coburg with its rich collection of copper engravings.

Agriculture and industry. Until 1950, agriculture was the principal economic sector in Bavaria. Over the following decades this primarily agrarian state has come to be a modern industrial and service center. Bavaria is now the number one high tech location in Germany. In scientific, economic and technical matters the free state has a first-class qualification in all major future-oriented segments ranging from information and communication technology, through bio- and gene technology , all the way to medical technology. However, in large parts of Bavaria – not only in the Alpine foreland – farming and forestry still play a key role. Bavarian beer (brewed according to the purity regulations of 1516) is world-famous; the hops used in its production are grown in Bavaria itself. Franconian wine is likewise prized by connoisseurs. Today, approximately 35 percent of the state's gross do-

Regensburg: stone bridges, bridge gatehouse and St. Peter's Cathedral

Schmalensee Lake near Mittenwald with the Karwendel mountains behind

mestic product stems from production industries and well over half from the service sector. The twin cities of Nuremberg (487,000 inhabitants) and Fürth (109,000 inhabitants), linked by Germany's first railway line in 1835, form an industrial region focusing on electrical, mechanical and vehicle engineering, the printing trade and the plastics, toy and food industries. Regensburg (125,000 inhabitants), which has a well-preserved medieval townscape (the Stone Bridge dates from 1146), today lives from automobile manufacturing and the textile, machinery and wood industries. It also has an efficient Danube port. Ingolstadt (114,000 inhabitants) is the site of automobile manufacturing and oil refineries. Würzburg (126,000 inhabitants) boasts not only printing press, electronics and food industries but also the state's three largest wine-growing estates. In eastern Bavaria, glassworks and porcelain manufactories carry on traditional crafts. International trade fairs such as "bauma" and "SYSTEMS" in Munich and the Toy Fair in Nuremberg are famous the world over.

Lifestyle and high tech. The state capital Munich (1.19 million inhabitants) lacks nothing as a major metropolis, yet the city also has its own distinctive atmosphere. In addition to the proverbial sociability to be encountered in the Hofbräuhaus, for instance, both the city and the surrounding region have a vibrant and dynamic economic life: automobile and aircraft industries, electrical and electronics industries, insurance firms and publishing houses. With its renowned universities and other higher education institutions, the Bavarian State Library (with over six million volumes one of the largest libraries in Europe), the Max Planck Institute for Plasma Physics, the nuclear research reactor and many other institutions, Munich is an important center of science and research. Munich is now considered Germany's "Internet capital". As a media location, Munich need not fear measuring up to any standard of comparison in Europe. Its airport is a major international air traffic hub. In February 1998 the new exhibition complex was opened at the former Munich-Riem airport.

Culture and bygone eras. Bavaria spends well over DM 100 million every year to conserve its cultural heritage. Munich boasts not only the Deutsches Museum, which houses the world's largest collection devoted to the history of science and technology, but also many historic buildings and art museums such as the Alte and Neue Pinakothek, Lenbach House and the Schack Gallery. Nuremberg, the city of Albrecht Dürer (1471-1528) and Hans Sachs (1494-1576), preserves some of the finest examples of late medieval treasures in its churches. The National Museum of German Culture is itself worth a special trip to the city. The churches in the Banz and Ettal monasteries, the Vierzehnheiligen basilica and the Wieskirche near Steingaden, which appear in the UNESCO World Heritage List, are outstanding examples of Baroque and Rococo architecture, as is the former residence of the prince-bishops in Würzburg. The latter's staircase, created by Balthasar Neumann (1687-1753) and graced with frescoes by Giovanni Battista Tiepolo, is one of the most beautiful in the world. Rothenburg ob der Tauber, Nördlingen and Dinkelsbühl are virtually open-air museums, linked with other sights by the "Romantic Route". There are 33 permanent stages and 34 open-air stages in Bavaria. Every year the Bayreuth Festival showcases the operas of Richard Wagner, who lived in Bayreuth from 1872 to 1883. Other outstanding festivals include the Munich Opera Festival, the Passau European Festival Weeks, the Ansbach Bach Week and the Würzburg Mozart Festival. Folk music is popular all over Bavaria as well, especially during the many folk festivals such as the "Leonhardi-Fahrt" in Bad Tölz, the Augsburg "Friedensfest", the Würzburg Festival of St. Kilian and the Kiefersfelden jousting tournament. A tradition since 1634 is the Oberammergau Passion Play, which is performed every ten years (most recent performance in the year 2000).

Further information:
— Freistaat Bayern, Bayerische Staatsregierung (Bavarian State Government)
  Franz-Josef-Strauß-Ring 1, 80539 München
  Internet: http://www.bayern.de
  E-mail: presse@stk.bayern.de

Berlin

Population	3.4 million
Area	889 sq km
Capital	Berlin

State election 1999	
CDU	40.8%
SPD	22.4%
PDS	17.7%
Alliance 90/The Greens	9.9%

A capital with a turbulent past. Within just a few centuries, Berlin – today the capital of the Federal Republic of Germany – grew from a fishing village and trading center at a crossing point on the Spree River into the Prussian capital city and royal residence. The town of Cölln was first mentioned in a document dating from 1237. It later merged with its sister city Berlin, profited from Prussia's rise to the rank of a great power, and after the founding of the German Empire in 1871 became the political, industrial, scientific, academic and cultural center of Germany. In the year 1939 the German capital had a population of more than four million. The Second World War unleashed by the National Socialists had catastrophic consequences for Berlin, resulting in the nearly total destruction of the city center and its industrial districts. After the War, the city was divided into four sectors by the victorious powers. In 1948-9, the Soviet Union imposed an eleven-month blockade of the land routes to Berlin in an attempt to bring the people of Berlin (West) to their knees and force the Western Allies to withdraw from the city. This attempt was thwarted by an airlift launched by the Western Allies. To stem the mass exodus of people from the German Democratic Republic (GDR) and the eastern part of Berlin, the GDR communist leadership began construction of the Berlin Wall in 1961. It fell in 1989 when the communist bloc collapsed. On 3 October 1990, the unification of Germany was consummated in Berlin with a state ceremony. Since then, united Berlin has once again been the capital of unified Germany.

As the oppo-
site of the Im-
perial inscrip-
tion on the
Reichstag "To
the German
People",
Hans Haacke
has created
a wooden
trough for the
inner court-
yard bearing
the words:
"To the popu-
lation". The
goal is for the
669 Members
of Parliament
to fill it with
earth from
their con-
stituencies.
Bundestag
President
Wolfgang
Thierse
comments:
"Food for
thought for
German
democracy."

A cultural metropolis in the heart of Europe. Cultural diversity is a long-standing tradition in Berlin. Its museums and collections on the Museum Island – which in March 2000 was included in the UNESCO list of cultural and natural heritages – in the Culture Forum and in the district of Dahlem are renowned the world over, receiving around six million visitors a year. The Philharmonic Hall, three opera houses and many theaters, concert halls and libraries, as well as the Berlin Festival, the International Film Festival and the Berlin Theatre Encounter are further highlights in this European cultural metropolis. Berlin has not only made a name for itself in these classical areas of artistic endeavor, however: For many years it has also been very popular with young

Trial run with one of the turbine rotors in the Siemens gas turbine factory in Berlin's Wedding district.

artists who flock to the German capital from every corner of the globe to enrich the city's lively and progressive cultural scene.

Economic, scientific and academic life. Berlin has undergone a process of radical economic change entailing painful adjustments. Yet its prospects for the future are good: Billions of marks are being spent to improve the infrastructure, alleviate traffic congestion and rebuild the city. As the seat of the Bundestag, the Bundesrat and the Federal Government, as the gateway to the markets of Eastern Europe, and endowed with a first-class infrastructure, Berlin and the surrounding region need not fear measuring up to any standard of comparison. Its outstanding advantage as a business and industrial location is the network of close contacts between research and development, production and marketing. Three universities, four colleges of the fine arts, the European School of

The Photonics Center in the Berlin Adlershof Technology Park

Management, nine Fachhochschulen, some 250 non-university research institutions and a multitude of small and medium-sized technology firms constitute key potential for future economic growth and new jobs. One of Europe's largest integrated technology parks, the Science and Business Technology Centre Berlin Adlershof (WISTA), is being built in the southeastern part of the city. The rising number of firms active in the communications sector and in the area of information technologies are making Berlin a productive and innovative location for the media. Berlin, with its ten daily and four Sunday newspapers, eleven city and twelve advertising magazines, has the largest press selection in Europe. With 210 book publishing companies, Berlin is the second largest publishing city in Germany. It broadcasts 25 regional radio programs.

Berlin has for some years been the scene of the greatest building activity in Germany. Firms such as debis, Sony and ABB have been constructing spectacular office complexes on Potsdamer Platz. The large new federal buildings like the Federal Chancellery and the administration buildings for the Bundestag are nearing completion. The Tiergarten area, which is now largely free of vehicle traffic, is characterized by the reemergence of the embassy district, party headquarters, representative state offices, federal associations of industry and com-

The Federal Ministry of the Interior at the Spreeufer in Berlin

The Bode Museum – on UNESCO's world cultural heritage list since 2000

merce and foundations. The contours of the new Lehrter train station, the future central train station in direct proximity to the government district, are already recognizable. Friedrichstrasse has been transformed into an attractive shopping experience in the center of the city. But in the outlying districts of Berlin as well, cranes are in motion and old buildings are being restored.

Berlin is an important venue for congresses and trade fairs. Events such as the International Audio and Video Fair, the International Green Week Berlin and the International Tourism Exchange make the city an attractive meeting place for over 4.2 million visitors per year.

The capital city settles into its new role. Berlin's development, transforming the city into the capital of Germany, has almost been completed. In accordance with plans and time schedules for moving the German government, the Bundestag and the Bundesrat from Bonn to Berlin, modernization and expansion of the ministerial buildings has almost been fully carried out. The Reichstag building has been converted into the seat of the German Bundestag and was officially opened in April 1999. Its dome is a new landmark in Berlin and open to visitors. In May 1999, the Federal President was elected by the Federal Assembly here. In September 1999, the Bundestag was inaugurated and parliament started to debate here. Since that time, Germany is once again being ruled from its old capital, Berlin.

Further information:
— Berlin, Senatskanzlei (Senate Chancellery)
  Berliner Rathaus, Jüdenstrasse, 10178 Berlin
  Internet: http://www.berlin.de
  E-mail: berlin@t-online.de

Brandenburg

Population	2.6 million
Area	29,479 sq km
Capital	Potsdam

State election 1999	
SPD	39.3%
CDU	26.6%
PDS	23.3%
DVU	5.3%

Prussian heritage. The state of Brandenburg surrounds the German capital Berlin; the state capital Potsdam (130,000 inhabitants) lies southwest of the metropolis. During the Potsdam Conference held at Cecilienhof Palace in the summer of 1945, the political leaders of the United States, the United Kingdom and the Soviet Union made far-reaching decisions concerning the future of Germany.

Potsdam has been linked with Prusso-German history since time immemorial. Beginning in 1157, Albert I the Bear called himself the Margrave of Brandenburg. In 1237, the city of Berlin was founded. In 1640, the Hohenzollern elector Frederick William, later called the "Great Elector", assumed power in Germany's largest electorate. He encouraged Huguenots from France as well as colonists from Holland and Switzerland to settle in Brandenburg, thus stimulating the development of commerce and the craft trades. The 1685 Edict of Potsdam granted the immigrants religious freedom; to this very day the "Dutch Quarter" and the "French Church" in Potsdam

Potsdam – view across the vineyard terraces of Schloss Sanssouci

evoke memories of these warmly welcomed foreigners. In 1701 Elector Frederick III of Brandenburg crowned himself Frederick I, King in Prussia, thus laying the foundations for the Prussian kingdom; the Brandenburg March became part of Prussia. Under the reign of Frederick II the Great (1740-1786) Prussia emerged as a great European power. Frederick II made Potsdam his royal residence and oversaw the evolution of the masterpiece Sanssouci Park with its palaces and other magnificent buildings.

Nature reserves and industrial sites. Compared to other states, Brandenburg is sparsely populated. The Havel and Spree rivers meander through its hilly countryside. Nature conservation is practiced in the numerous nature parks, land-scape reserves and biosphere reserves in areas such as the Uckermark, the Elbtalaue, the Schorfheide and the Spree-wald; in the Lower Oder Valley National Park, nature conser-vation measures undertaken jointly with the neighboring

The main portal of the "Viadrina" European University in Frankfurt/Oder

**Schloss
Rheinsberg**

country of Poland transcend frontiers. In years past, Brandenburg's poor sandy soil led it to be called the "sandbox of the
Holy Roman Empire of the German Nation". Today the backbone of the state's economy is increasingly shifting from agriculture with its traditional crops of rye and oilseed to industries such as vehicle construction, mechanical engineering,
electronics, environmental technologies, the optical industry,
and the energy, food and chemical industries.

Now that visas are no longer required for travel between Germany and Poland, the city of Frankfurt an der Oder (76,000
inhabitants) is acquiring ever greater importance as the place
of transshipment for trade with the countries of Eastern Europe. Since 1991 a German-Polish intergovernmental Commission has been working to promote good neighborly contacts.

"Viadrina" and membrane research. Viadrina University
in Frankfurt an der Oder already existed between 1506 and
1811. Heinrich von Kleist and the Humboldt brothers studied
there. In 1991 the institution was reopened as the European
University Viadrina Frankfurt/Oder; it places special emphasis
on Polish-German cooperation in teaching and research. But
Brandenburg's other universities in Cottbus and Potsdam as
well as its five Fachhochschulen and 15 technology centers also make the region an important center of German research.
Since 1992 the GFZ Potsdam has been engaged in basic research on topics of global significance in the geosciences.
The likewise unique Membrane Research Department of the
GKSS Research Center in Teltow is devoted to the development of high-performance membranes for fields of application such as environmental engineering, materials salvage,
recycling and medicine. The Potsdam Institute for Climate
Impact Research studies today's climate changes as problems
arising from a distorted relationship between mankind and
nature. The Berlin-Brandenburg Academy of Sciences, which
took up its work in March 1993, cultivates not only the natu-

The
Techno-Park
Henningsdorf

ral, biological and social sciences but also the humanities. On its agenda are editions of the works of Jean Paul and Gottfried Wilhelm Leibniz as well as a documentation of medieval stained glass painting in the new states.

Theodor Fontane and Marlene Dietrich. The 19th-century writer Theodor Fontane described Brandenburg's beauty and natural charm in his "Walks in the March of Brandenburg". Approximately 350 palaces and manor houses can be found here; particularly popular tourist destinations in addition to Sanssouci are the palaces in Rheinsberg (which Kurt Tucholsky made the subject of a short novel) and Branitz (with the Prince Pückler Museum). Of the roughly 150 museums and memorials, the Heinrich von Kleist Museum and Research Institution on Kleist in Frankfurt an der Oder deserves special mention.

Cultural festivals take place throughout the year. Well known beyond the state's boundaries are the Rheinsberg Music Days, the concerts in the impressive former abbeys of Chorin and Lehnin, and the Potsdam-Sanssouci Music Festival. A distinctive kind of technical achievement is the world's largest ship elevator in Niederfinow (built in 1934), which enables ships to overcome a 36-meter difference in elevation along the course of the Oder-Havel Canal.

The film city of Potsdam-Babelsberg with its film and television studios, the "Konrad Wolf" Academy of Film and Television, the High Tech Center and numerous firms active in the media sector carries on the tradition of the Universum Film Aktiengesellschaft (Ufa), harking back to the days when stars such as Marlene Dietrich and directors such as Friedrich Wilhelm Murnau, Ernst Lubitsch and Fritz Lang made their famous films here.

Further information:
— Brandenburg, Staatskanzlei (State Chancellery)
   Heinrich-Mann-Allee 107, 14473 Potsdam
   Internet: http://www.brandenburg.de

The Free Hanseatic City of Bremen

Population	668,000
Area	404 sq km
Capital	Bremen

State election 1999	
SPD	42.6%
CDU	37.1%
Alliance 90/The Greens	8.9%

A commitment to tradition. Together with Bavaria, Hamburg and Saxony, the Free Hanseatic City of Bremen is one of the political entities which already existed prior to 1945; after San Marino, it is the second oldest city republic in the world. The Free Hanseatic City of Bremen consists of the city of Bremen (543,000 inhabitants) and the city of Bremerhaven (125,000 inhabitants), which lies 65 kilometers farther down the Weser River. The territory in between the two cities belongs to the state of Lower Saxony.

First mentioned more than 1,200 years ago, namely in the year 782, a bishopric since 787, and endowed with the rights of a free city by Emperor Frederick I Barbarossa in 1186, Bremen joined the Hanseatic League in 1358. With the erection of the statue of Roland in 1404 and the construction of the Town Hall in 1405, the city demonstrated its claim to self-determination. In 1646, Bremen was granted the status of a free imperial city; since 1806 it has called itself the Free Hanseatic City. Bremerhaven was founded in 1827 and elevated to the

Parade of windjammers in Bremerhaven's New Harbor

status of a city in 1851. The state parliament bears the traditional name "Bremische Bürgerschaft"; the state government is called the "Senat", and the president of the Senat is the Minister President of the state. Every year, on the second Friday in February, distinguished German public figures are invited to the historic "Schaffermahlzeit" banquet held by Bremen's maritime community in the Town Hall.

Ports and high tech. Ports and shipping, international trade connections and products of highest quality manufactured by state-of-the-art industries are the foundations of Bremen's economic life. The container terminal in Bremerhaven is Europe's largest interconnected container transshipment facility. Every year, nearly 10,000 ships link Bremen's ports with roughly 1,000 ports all over the world. With an annual volume considerably exceeding one million vehicles (1999 figure), Bremerhaven is Europe's most important automobile transshipment point. The Free Hanseatic City's shipyards stand for quality in shipbuilding. Bremen is also one of the centers of the German food, luxury food and beverage industries: Coffee, chocolate, flour, milk products, spices, fish products and beer are the best-known products. Key components for rockets, satellites and the Airbus are developed and built in Bremen, a hub of the aerospace industry. The electrical and electronics industries as well as high-tech industries likewise play a prominent role in the city's economy. Symbolic of Bremen's expertise in the field of high technology is the 148-meter-high tower of the Center for Applied Space Technology and Microgravity, in which experiments can be conducted under conditions of weightlessness. The Bremen Securities Exchange – which is over 300 years old – and the commodities exchanges handle trading for all of northwestern Germany.

The Universum Science Center in Bremen resembles an open oyster

Key parts of the Airbus are manufactured in Bremen

Marine research and the fine arts. Bremen's university has about 18,000 students; its primary fields of emphasis are engineering and the natural sciences. Leaders in the area of basic research are the Bremen Institute of Applied Beam Technology (BIAS) and the Institute of Shipping Economics and Logistics. The Center for Tropical Marine Ecology and the Max Planck Institute for Marine Microbiology develop modern concepts for marine research. Bremen is also the home of the Alfred Wegener Institute for Polar and Marine Research. The Bremen Academy for Fine Arts and Music, which focuses on design, the fine arts and music, is nationally renowned as well. The beginning of 1997 marked the re-opening of the renovated "Glocke", the concert hall with extraordinary acoustics.

Bremen's sights attract millions of visitors to the city every year: the Market Square with the Renaissance Town Hall, the statue of Roland and the Gothic St. Peter's Cathedral, the famous "Böttcherstrasse" and the historic Schnoor Quarter. The Bremen Free Market, which has been held on the Bürgerweide for over 960 years, is one of Germany's largest fairs.

The Art Gallery, the New Museum Weserburg, the Gerhard Marcks House and the Paula Becker Modersohn House display important works of art. The German Maritime Museum in Bremerhaven boasts impressive collections from all eras of seafaring as well as a number of historic ships in the museum's own port. The Theater am Goetheplatz, the bremer shakespeare company, the annual Bremen Music Festival and the International Music Project Bremen are household names for music and theater aficionados.

Further information:
— Freie Hansestadt Bremen, Senatskanzlei (Senate Chancellery)
  Rathaus, Am Markt 1, 28195 Bremen
  Internet: http://www.bremen.de
  E-mail: webmaster@bremen.de

The Free and Hanseatic City of Hamburg

Population	1.7 million
Area	755 sq km
Capital	Hamburg

State election 1997	
SPD	36.2%
CDU	30.7%
GREENS/GAL	13.9%

Germany's gateway to the world. Hamburg is the second largest German city, the country's principal seaport and its largest overseas trade center. 220 firms from China (including Hong Kong) have offices here, along with 13 from Japan and 65 from Taiwan; all in all, more than 3,000 firms are engaged in the transaction of import and export business in the Hanseatic City. Traditional port-related industries are shipyards, refineries and processing plants for raw materials from abroad. Through a consistent policy of structural change, Hamburg has developed into a thriving service metropolis. Future-oriented sectors such as the civil aviation, microelectronics and communications industries are laying a modern foundation for the future of this attractive site for business and industry.

Founded around the year 811 (as Hammaburg), Hamburg began to flourish as a commercial town in 1189, when it was granted customs and commercial rights. One of the first members of the Hanseatic League, it was the League's main transshipment port on the North Sea. Kings and princes never ruled Hamburg: It was always the citizens themselves who governed the city-state. The devastating fire of 1842, a readiness to continually modernize and World War II spared little of the crowded heart of the old commercial metropolis. Prominent structures include the Late Baroque St. Michael's Church (whose 132-meter-high tower – affectionately called "Michel" – is the city landmark), the 100-year-old Town Hall, and the Chilehaus, an Expressionist brick building dating from the 1920s. A distinctive type of cultural monument is the old

"Speicherstadt" in the port area, a complex of brick ware-houses erected toward the end of the 19th century. It is not, however, individual buildings which lend Hamburg its special flair but rather the expansive panorama afforded by the Alster, a body of water in the center of the city that has been dammed up to form two lakes, and the colorful picture presented by the port and houses along the broad Elbe River.

The green industrial city. Hamburg is Germany's second largest industrial center and the heart of a metropolitan area with a population of four million. It is nevertheless one of the greenest cities in Germany. 40 percent of Hamburg's total area consists of arable land and garden plots, parks and public gardens, woodlands, moors and heaths. Landscape reserves and nature reserves cover 28 percent of the city's area. In addition to the numerous park grounds, there are 240,000 roadside trees. The Ohlsdorf Cemetery is the largest leafy cemetry in the world. As a result of the unification of Ger-

Hamburg's Town Hall was built in 1886-97

Hamburg –
bird's eye
view of the
Binnenalster
Lake, the
heart of the
city and
the port

many and the opening up of Eastern Europe, the port of Hamburg has regained its old hinterland. This enhances the city-state's prospects of once again becoming the hub of trade, services and communications between East and West while being the southernmost metropolis of Scandinavia. There are also new perspectives opening up south of the city center. On the former port premises is Hafen City, a mixed urban district with 6,000 apartments and 20,000 jobs with a direct view of the River Elbe.

The port, one of the largest in the world, spreads out over 75 square kilometers, occupying one tenth of Hamburg's city area. In terms of container transshipment volume, Hamburg ranks second in Europe after Rotterdam. More than 200 scheduled shipping lines offer about 12,000 departures each year from the port of Hamburg to points all over the globe. Every day more than 250,000 people from the surrounding area commute to work in the Hanseatic City. Hamburg is the banking center for northern Germany and one of Germany's largest insurance headquarters. With more than 95 consulates-general and consulates, Hamburg is the world's principal consular city. The Congress Center conveniently located in the heart of the city is one of the most modern and most popular conference centers in Europe. The immediately adjacent trade fair halls further enhance its attractiveness as a venue for important trade exhibitions.

Hamburg is the center of the German media industry. The roughly 9,000 firms active in this sector employ a work force of approximately 60,000 and utilize the services of numerous free-lancers. Their annual turnover exceeds DM 50 billion. In recent years the communications sector has been the city's most rapidly expanding economic sector. The electronic me-

The traditional fish market in Hamburg's Sankt Pauli district

dia are playing an increasingly important role in this development: the city's major radio and television stations as well as the numerous firms engaged in the production of audiovisual and multimedia programs. Hamburg's advertising industry and its award-winning agencies have steadily gained ground as well. Four of the twelve largest German advertising agencies are located here while out of the 25 multimedia agencies with the highest turnovers, nine are represented in Hamburg. In both the German recording market and the newspaper and magazine market, firms headquartered in the metropolis on the Elbe command a market share of up to 50 percent.

Civic pride and a passion for the arts. The mercantile city of Hamburg is and always has been a place of freedom and tolerance and a city with a rich cultural tradition. It was here that Germany's first permanent opera house was established in 1678: George Frideric Handel (1685-1759) staged his first opera ("Almira") in the Hanseatic City. Both Georg Philipp Telemann and Karl Philipp Emanuel Bach lived and worked in Hamburg. One of the city's famous sons was the composer Johannes Brahms (1833-97); the name of Felix Mendelssohn Bartholdy (born in Hamburg in 1809) is likewise closely tied to the city on the Elbe.

Influenced by England and France, Hamburg was a cradle of the Enlightenment in Germany. In 1767, the Deutsches Nationaltheater was founded here, an institution linked with the name of Gotthold Ephraim Lessing ("Hamburgische Dramaturgie", 1767-9), which became renowned especially for its performances of Shakespeare's works. "Minna von Barnhelm" (Lessing) and "Don Carlos" (Schiller) were both performed for the first time here. Friedrich Gottlieb Klopstock (1724-1803) and Matthias Claudius (1740-1815) were Hamburg's "literary institutions" at the time. During the period of reaction in the 19th century, Julius Campe of Hamburg published the works of Heinrich Heine and other "rabble-rousing" writers of the "Young Germany".

After World War II, the directors Rolf Liebermann and Gustav Gründgens gave the opera and theater a modern thrust with a strong international appeal. Unforgotten is the Hamburg-born actor Hans Albers (1891-1960). Today, three state theaters and roughly 35 private theaters enhance the city's cultural profile. In recent years, the Hamburg State Opera and its general musical director Ingo Metzmacher has become a renowned stage for 20th century works. Thalia Theater and the Deutsches Schauspielhaus are becoming top-class theaters in Germany under the guidance of Jürgen Flimm and Frank Baumbauer, with almost regular invitations to the Berlin Theatertreffen. They are also regular recipients of the "Theater of the year" award. The new theater directors Ulrich Khuon (Thalia) and Tom Stromberg (Schauspielhaus) are pushing ahead with the ambitious theater plans of their predecessors.

The three state theater stages are backed up by Kampagnel, the former crane factory in Barmbek which is well suited to experimental international guest performances due to its workshop nature. Especially successful in recent years were the musicals "Cats" and "Phantom of the Opera" by Andrew Lloyd Webber, productions famous far beyond Hamburg's city limits. The Hamburg Ballet under the direction of John Neumeier is internationally renowned. It was here in Hamburg that the graphic artist and painter Horst Janssen (who died in 1995) created his extensive and independent portfolio of works. At the beginning of the 1960s the Beatles embarked on their international career in the Hamburg entertainment district of St. Pauli. Hamburg has recently become the stronghold of Germany's hip-hop culture: Bands such as Fettes Brot, Absolute Beginner and Eins Komma Zwo have reached the top of the charts.

Further information:
— Freie und Hansestadt Hamburg, Senatskanzlei (Senate Chancellery)
Rathausmarkt 1, 20095 Hamburg
Internet: http://www.hamburg.de/StadtPol/welcome.htm
E-mail: Rainer.Scheppelmann@sk.hamburg.de (Pressestelle)

Hesse

Population	6.0 million
Area	21,114 sq km
Capital	Wiesbaden

State election 1999	
CDU	43.4%
SPD	39.4%
Alliance 90/The Greens	7.2%
FDP	5.1%

A future-oriented center of business and industry.
With a population of six million and an area of about 21,100
square kilometers, Hesse is Germany's fifth largest state. Today it is one of the country's major centers of business and
industry and ranks among the most dynamic regions in Europe. Better known than the state capital Wiesbaden is the
international financial center Frankfurt/Main, seat of the
Deutsche Bundesbank and, since 1 January 1999, seat of the
European Central Bank as well. Over 400 commercial banks
are situated here, as is Germany's largest stock exchange.

Political unity since 1945. The region has a turbulent history. In 1848-9, the National Assembly, the first democratic German parliament, convened in St. Paul's Church (which is now
a national monument) in Frankfurt/Main. This democratic beginning failed, however, as a result of the power wielded by
Germany's ruling princes. Prior to Bismarck's wars of unification, the territory which is now Hesse – like many other regions at that time – resembled a patchwork, encompassing

**The skyline
with the
banking
district in
Frankfurt/
Main**

The Baroque cathedral in Fulda was built in 1704-12

four principalities and duchies, an earldom and the free city of Frankfurt. After the Austro-Prussian War of 1866, Prussia absorbed all of this territory except the Grand Duchy of Hesse-Darmstadt. With the "Proclamation No. 2" of 19 September 1945, issued in the IG Farben complex in Frankfurt/Main, the American military government merged Hesse-Darmstadt and most of what had formerly been Prussian territory to form the state of Hesse.

Lush idyllic landscapes and vibrant cities. Geographically the countryside between the Diemel and Weser rivers in the north and the Neckar River in the south has been characterized as a colorful and confusing weave of uplands and depressions. Western Hesse is part of the Rhenish Schist Massif; the iron ore deposits on the Lahn, Dill and Sieg rivers were already exploited during the pre-Christian era. Eastern Hesse is geologically younger; the prevalent Bunter sandstone soil is poor in minerals and unsuitable for cultivation so the east is barren and more sparsely populated. Typical of the region are its volcanic landscapes: Old massifs can be found in the Westerwald, in the Rhön, on the Hoher Meissner and in the Kaufunger Forest. Amidst charming landscapes are the university towns of Marburg (77,400 inhabitants) and Giessen (72,400 inhabitants) as well as the city of Wetzlar (52,800 inhabitants), famous for optics. The Bergstrasse and the Rhinegau are among Germany's best fruit and wine-growing areas. In eastern Hesse lies the bishopric of Fulda (62,300 inhabitants), a Baroque town of considerable historical importance. The state capital Wiesbaden (267,000 inhabitants) is not just an administrative center but also an elegant spa.

Modern industry with a long tradition. Together with the service metropolis Frankfurt (644,000 inhabitants), four branches of industry – the chemical, vehicle, mechanical engineering and electrical industries – have been instrumental in propelling this state to a position of economic strength:

Hesse's per-capita gross domestic product is approximately DM 128,000. With their chemical products, pharmaceuticals, dyes, or special assembly components for the computer industry, firms such as Aventis, Degussa and Rütgers in Frankfurt or Merck in Darmstadt (138,000 inhabitants) are firm fixtures in the world's markets just like the Opel main plant in Rüsselsheim, the Volkswagen plant in Baunatal and the Thyssen-Henschel-Werke (machinery and transport technology) in Kassel (201,000 inhabitants). Teves in Frankfurt produces asbestos-free brake linings used by vehicle manufacturers worldwide; VDO is the world's second largest producer of automobile instruments and electronic regulation and control instruments for vehicle engineering. Honeywell in Offenbach (117,000 inhabitants) produces electronic measurement and control systems for climate control engineering.

Crucial to Hesse's economic success is the state's central location with its many air, rail and waterway traffic junctions. The

The Russian Church at Darmstadt's Mathildenhöhe

Rhine-Main Airport is one of the most important traffic hubs in Europe. With about 62,500 employees it has now become the largest local employer in Germany – and is still growing.
Research scientists and inventors from what is now the state of Hesse laid the foundations for entire branches of industry and new technologies with their trailblazing discoveries and inventions. The Darmstadt chemist Justus Liebig developed the chemical fertilization of agricultural plants around 1840. Gelnhausen physicist Johann Philipp Reis constructed the first electric telephone in 1861. Television and modern communications technology can be traced back to the invention of the electron tube by the Nobel Prize laureate Karl Ferdinand Braun of Fulda. Konrad Zuse, a resident of Bad Hersfeld, developed the first computer.

The International Book Fair and avant-garde art.
Frankfurt, the birthplace of Johann Wolfgang von Goethe, demonstrates a particular devotion to the world of books. The Deutsche Bibliothek (German Library) in Frankfurt, depository for every German-language work to appear in print since 1945, is "Germany's largest bookcase". Internationally outstanding cultural events in Hesse are the world's largest book fair in Frankfurt and the "documenta" art exhibition in Kassel. Famous festivals are held in Bad Hersfeld, Wetzlar, Wiesbaden and in the Rhinegau. Artistic impulses emanate from the Young Literature Forum Hesse. The state's Georg Büchner Prize for Literature is one of Germany's most prestigious literary awards. Hesse offers a wealth of interesting museums and exhibitions: Aside from Frankfurt's "museum embankment" on the Main River and the many other museums in the city, people can visit the Ivory Museum in Erbach, the Brothers Grimm Museum in Kassel, or the Hessenpark Open-Air Museum in Neu-Anspach featuring original reconstructed Hessian houses dating from many different centuries. A truly distinctive type of open-air exhibition are the Art Nouveau grounds of the Mathildenhöhe complex in Darmstadt.

Further information:
— Hessen, Hessische Staatskanzlei (State Chancellery)
  Bierstadter Strasse 1, 65189 Wiesbaden
  Internet: http://www.hessen.de/regierung/homepage.htm
  E-mail: poststelle@stk.hessen.de

Mecklenburg-Western Pomerania

Population	1.8 million	
Area	23,170 sq km	
Capital	Schwerin	

State election 1998		
SPD	34.3%	
CDU	30.2%	
PDS	24.4%	

The "land of a thousand lakes". Mecklenburg-Western Pomerania, situated in northeastern Germany along the Baltic Sea, is sparsely populated (approximately 80 inhabitants per square kilometer) and has a predominantly agrarian character. One of the prime assets of this state dotted with inland lakes (Lake Müritz, with an area of 117 square kilometers, is the largest) is its unspoiled nature: Its exceedingly varied coastline affords sweeping vistas, as do its variegated inland landscapes with their gently rolling hills, broad fields and pastures, and extensive forests.

The two parts of the state, Mecklenburg and Western Pomerania, have different histories. For many years Western Pomerania was largely under Swedish dominion; later, as part of the province of Pomerania, it was under Prussian rule. Mecklenburg, by contrast, was an independent part of the German Empire. After 1701, it was split into two states: Mecklenburg-Schwerin and Mecklenburg-Strelitz. Not until the year 1934 were the two Mecklenburgian states reunited. The state of

Bascule bridge over the Ryck in Wieck, nr. Greifswald

Mecklenburg-Western Pomerania was created after the Second World War as part of the GDR, but shortly thereafter it was dissolved and subdivided into three districts. In 1990, it was reestablished as a state of the Federal Republic of Germany. Today about 1.8 million people live in Mecklenburg-Western Pomerania. The dialect known as Low German (Plattdeutsch) is common in everyday speech.

Historic cities worth a special visit. Striking Brick Gothic architecture distinguishes the state's old Hanseatic cities such as Rostock, Wismar, Stralsund and Greifswald. For centuries the Baltic Sea ports were centers for the transshipment of goods to and from Scandinavia. Rostock and Greifswald are university towns with a long, proud tradition. The capital of Mecklenburg-Western Pomerania is Schwerin (105,200 inhabitants). Its most prominent landmark is the palace, formerly the residence of the grand dukes of Mecklenburg-Schwerin and now the seat of the state parliament of Mecklenburg-

The isle of Rügen – the steep chalk cliffs in the Jasmund National Park

Rostock's
deep-sea port

Western Pomerania. Other particularly noteworthy sights include the Mecklenburg State Theater, the State Museum with its magnificent collection of Dutch and Flemish 17th-century paintings, and the cathedral, which is one of the most outstanding examples of Brick Gothic architecture.

Rostock is the state's largest city (207,400 inhabitants). Its Church of St. Mary has an astronomical clock dating from the 15th century. The city is known for its seaside resort Warnemünde and for the "Hanseatic Port Days". The medieval fortifications of Neubrandenburg (75,900 inhabitants) with the four old city gates have survived the centuries virtually intact.

The economic base. Ten years after the transition from a state-controlled economy to a market economy, the restructuring of Mecklenburg-Western Pomerania's economy is well under way. The most important branches are the shipbuilding industry, the food, luxury food and beverage industries, the construction industry, mechanical engineering, the building materials industry and the wood industry. Mecklenburg-Western Pomerania's seaports continue to figure prominently in the state's economy. The largest of them is Rostock; the port of Mukran on the island of Rügen, which affords swift connections to the countries adjoining the Baltic, is taking on increasing importance as well. A well-developed network of roads and rail lines links the state with its neighbors.

Stralsund:
the old
market,
town hall,
and Nikolai
Church

An autobahn along the coast is currently being improved and extended.

Agriculture plays a more significant role in Mecklenburg-Western Pomerania than in other states. Principal crops are grain, oilseed (rape) and potatoes. 80 percent of the 1.3 million hectares given over to agriculture are farmed by operations with more than 500 hectares.

Tourism is an important economic factor for Mecklenburg-Western Pomerania. In 1999, 3.8 million people visited the state which offers more than 2,000 accommodations with over 130,000 beds. The most famous tourist magnet is Rügen, Germany's largest island (930 square kilometers). Its white chalk cliffs never fail to captivate the beholder. Many visitors are also drawn to the Granitz Hunting Lodge or the Störtebeker Festival. Mecklenburg-Western Pomerania takes particular care to ensure that the steadily growing tourism industry does not become a burden on the environment. 283 nature reserves, 110 landscape reserves, three national parks and two biosphere reserves attest to the importance which the state attaches to nature conservation and environmental protection.

The arts and sciences. Prominent individuals linked with the area that is now Mecklenburg-Western Pomerania include the painter Caspar David Friedrich (1774-1840) of Greifswald, who romantically transfigured the landscape of his homeland in numerous paintings. Writing in the dialect Low German, Fritz Reuter (1810-74) realistically described the region's people and countryside. The aviation pioneer Otto Lilienthal (1848-96) conducted many glider flights here. The sculptor and poet Ernst Barlach (1870-1938) created his lifework in Güstrow. Uwe Johnson (1934-84) produced a literary monument to his native land with his novels and short stories.

Further information:
— Mecklenburg-Vorpommern, Staatskanzlei (State Chancellery)
  Schloßstrasse 2-4, 19053 Schwerin
  Internet: http://www.mv-regierung.de
  E-mail: stk-mv@t-online.de

Lower Saxony

Population	7.8 million
Area	47,338 sq km
Capital	Hanover

State election 1998	
SPD	47.9%
CDU	35.9%
Alliance 90/The Greens	7.0%

Tidal mud flats and heathland. Lower Saxony is the second largest state in Germany (47,338 square kilometers). It stretches from the North Sea island of Borkum to the Harz Mountains; in between lie remote heathland regions, greater metropolitan Hanover and the Hildesheimer Börde with the most fertile arable soil in the Federal Republic. Lower Saxony has about 7.8 million inhabitants. They are joined every year by millions of visitors who seek rest and recreation on the seven East Frisian islands of Borkum, Juist, Norderney, Baltrum, Langeoog, Spiekeroog and Wangerooge, in the Harz Mountains, in the Weser Hills, in the Teutoburg Forest or in the Lüneburg Heath (Germany's oldest nature park) or who wish to keep abreast of the latest developments at the world's two largest trade fairs held in the state capital. Another popular attraction, especially when the apple orchards are in bloom, is the "Altes Land", Europe's largest fruit-growing area. Here, just outside the gates of Hamburg, begins the "wet triangle": the lowlands between the mouths of the Weser and Elbe rivers with the tidal mud flats known as the "Wattenmeer" (Germany's largest nature park), the fishing town of Cuxhaven and the artists' colony of Worpswede. Lower Saxony offers cyclists the most extensive network of cycle paths in Germany.

Home of the "Beetle" – center of alternative energy production. Hanover (516,000 inhabitants), the state capital, is an industrial and service center, seat of a world-famous manufacturer of writing materials and of TUI, Europe's largest tour operator. Each year, the latest developments are

Production hall at the Meyer Wharf in Papenburg

presented at the Hanover Fair, the world's largest industrial fair, and at "CeBIT", the international fair for communications technology. From 1 June to 31 October 2000, Hanover played host to the World Exposition EXPO 2000 with its theme "Humankind – Nature – Technology".

Two thirds of the state's total area is given over to farming; the food industry produces a wide variety of delicacies ranging from Oldenburg smoked ham to honey from the Lüneburg heath. Nevertheless, Lower Saxony cannot be classified as an agricultural state: In addition to traditional industries such as steel, chemicals and shipbuilding, (for example Meyer in Papenburg, who produces luxury liners) it now also has thriving electronics and computer industries. The VW Beetle, made in Wolfsburg, is the most frequently built car in the world; it still rolls off the line in Mexico. Volkswagen AG is the state's biggest company and has manufactured more than 50 million automobiles in Lower Saxony to date. The Volkswagen Foundation is the largest non-governmental foundation for the promotion of science and scholarship in Germany.

Schimmel pianos and Rollei cameras are made in Brunswick (247,000 inhabitants). Brunswick is also the home of the Federal Institute of Physics and Metrology, which determines the exact Central European Time (CET) by radio signal. Video recorders and CD players are built in Peine and in Osterode. The firm MAN in Salzgitter (114,000 inhabitants) manufactures trucks; Wilhelmshaven is the only German deepwater port for supertankers. Natural gas from Lower Saxony satisfies one fifth of the Federal Republic's requirement. Between the Ems and the Elbe rivers, the Lower Saxony Energy Agency is already exploring alternatives for the next millennium:

Goslar's Kaiserpfalz dates from the 11th-12th centuries

Hanover
City Hall
(1901-3)
next to the
Maschteich

electricity generated by wind power, solar power, landfill gas and biomass.

Explorers and inventors, intellect and politics. Diederik Pining of Hildesheim landed in America 19 years before Columbus. Gottfried Wilhelm Leibniz developed the binary system of numeration in Hanover and built the world's first functional calculating machine. Carl Friedrich Gauss of Brunswick invented the telegraph, Robert Wilhelm Bunsen of Göttingen the carbon-zinc battery, Werner von Siemens of Lenthe the generation of electricity by means of a dynamo, and Emil Berliner of Hanover the gramophone. Karl Jatho completed the first successful powered flight at the Vahren-walder Heide in Hanover – three months before the Wright brothers' attempt in the United States. Walter Bruch, also from Hanover, developed the PAL color system for color television.

1961 marked the appearance of the last volume of the "Deutsches Wörterbuch", a comprehensive dictionary of the German language begun in 1838 by the brothers Grimm at the University of Göttingen. In 1837, the brothers Grimm and five other professors – the "Göttingen Seven" – had protested against the sovereign's decision to repeal the constitution. In 1957, the "Göttingen 18", a group that included the Nobel Prize laureates Max Born, Otto Hahn, Werner Heisenberg

**Knochenhauer-
amtshaus
and the
Civic Bar at
Hildesheim's
Marktplatz**

and Max von Laue, warned against the dangers of nuclear rearmament.

Stone witnesses to power. At the turn of the 10th century Hildesheim (105,000 inhabitants) was the center of the Ottonian Empire; in the 12th century Bardowick was the most important hub of trade between East and West. Brunswick grew to become one of the four major metropolises of the Late Middle Ages. At the end of the 16th century Emden boasted more ships than any other port in Europe; in the 18th century Clausthal-Zellerfeld in the Harz Mountains was one of the world's principal industrial centers.

Stone witnesses to the past are everywhere: The 900-year-old church in Idesen is considered the most outstanding ecclesiastical structure of its time in Germany. The world's largest medieval library, where Gotthold Ephraim Lessing and Gottfried Wilhelm Leibniz worked, is located in Wolfenbüttel; Goslar, with its magnificent old townscape, is the site of the Kaiserpfalz, Germany's largest medieval secular building. Brunswick's Herzog Anton Ulrich Museum is the oldest art museum on the European continent. Celle is the home of Germany's oldest theater in which performances are still staged. Notable collections of modern art can be found in the Art Gallery in Emden and the Sprengel Museum of Modern Art in Hanover. A special attraction for archaeology buffs is Hildesheim's Roemer-Pelizaeus Museum, which has a fine collection of ancient Egyptian art. The "Violinale" in Hanover is one of the world's preeminent violin competitions.

Further information:
- Niedersachsen, Niedersächsische Staatskanzlei (Lower Saxon State Chancellery)
  Planckstrasse 2, 30169 Hannover
  Internet: http://www.niedersachsen.de

North Rhine-Westphalia

Population	18 million
Area	34,080 sq km
Capital	Düsseldorf

State election 2000	
SPD	42.8%
CDU	37.0%
FDP	9.8%
Alliance 90/The Greens	7.1%

A European industrial area. Industrial heartland, modern technology center, land of culture and the media: Formerly an industrial landscape dominated by factory smokestacks, winding towers and blast furnaces, North Rhine-Westphalia – with nearly 18 million inhabitants the most populous state – has undergone a profound structural change in recent decades. The land of coal and steel has become a land of coal, steel and promising new industries, an attractive site for domestic and foreign investors not least because of its outstanding infrastructure. The International Building Show Emscher Park has also played a role. Nearly half of its people live in large cities with more than 100,000 inhabitants; at 527 persons per square kilometer, its population density is one of the highest in Europe. The nickname "Kohlenpott" (coal scuttle) is a thing of the past, for the state has long since satisfied the call of the 1960s for "blue skies over the Ruhr".

Nearly 52 percent of North Rhine-Westphalia's land area is given over to farming; 25 percent is woodlands. Nevertheless, the Ruhr, with a population of approximately 4.8 million, is Europe's largest industrial region. Many energy producers and suppliers have their headquarters here. North Rhine-Westphalia is also a prime location for the large-scale power plant industry and the chemical industry.

The creation of the state of North Rhine-Westphalia dates to the time of British occupation after World War II: In 1946, the greater part of the former Prussian Rhine province and the province of Westphalia were merged – and later augmented by the inclusion of the former state of Lippe-Detmold.

Cologne Cathedral and the railway bridge

In 1949, the city of Bonn on the Rhine (305,000 inhabitants) was chosen as the provisional capital of the Federal Republic. After the unification of Germany, Berlin became the permanent capital. The "federal city " of Bonn, based on the Berlin-Bonn law of 1994, is presently on the way to becoming an innovative service center while retaining considerable significance in Germany's political scene: Six government ministries are maintaining their prime administrative functions here as previously. The city also has a big future on an international level as the seat of major political institutions given the location there of three UN organizations, the traditional Rheinische Friedrich Wilhelms University, the not-yet-completed CAESAR Research Center and other major research institutes and rich cultural offerings.

Coal, steel and the media. Today the state's economy has a broader foundation than ever before. Since 1960 the percentage of the work force employed in the coal and steel industry has dropped dramatically: from 12.5 percent to four percent. Only 12 coal mines are still in operation in the Ruhr, four of which are to be closed down or amalgamated with other mines in the coming years. Many new jobs have been created in the media and cultural sector, which has become the sector with the highest annual increases in turnover. In 1996 the media conglomerate Time Warner opened a movie park and movie studio complex in Bottrop-Kirchhellen built at a cost of more than DM 360 million – the largest investment ever made in this sector in Germany. The Academy of Media Arts in Cologne, the Institute for Media Practice and Media Transfer at the Folkwang Academy in Essen and the academy for the media in Siegen are further examples of the endeavors undertaken by the state in this area.

Today about 66 percent of the work force in North Rhine-Westphalia is employed in the service sector. Here the restructuring process has always been conjoined with ecological renewal as well: The state's innovative firms active in the field of environmental protection have made it one of Europe's foremost centers of environmental technology.

North Rhine-Westphalia's bustling economic life is supported by a dense network of autobahns, rail lines and waterways connecting the state's numerous big cities such as Cologne (963,000 inhabitants), Essen (603,000), Dortmund (592,000), Düsseldorf (568,000), Duisburg (523,000), Bochum (393,000), Wuppertal (372,000), Bielefeld (322,000), Gelsenkirchen (284,000), Mönchengladbach (265,000), Münster (264,000), Krefeld (243,000) and Aachen (244,000). The Düsseldorf and Cologne/Bonn airports round out this network; Duisburg on the Rhine has the world's largest inland port.

44 of Germany's 100 largest firms have their headquarters in North Rhine-Westphalia. In addition to industrial giants such as Bayer Leverkusen, E.ON AG or the printing and publishing corporation Bertelsmann, about 685,000 small and medium-sized businesses are engaged in production. Düsseldorf is one of Germany's largest banking centers. Cologne is one of the nation's leading insurance headquarters. With Düsseldorf, Cologne, Dortmund and Essen, North Rhine-Westphalia boasts four internationally competitive trade fair venues. The state generates more than one fifth of all German exports and consumes nearly one fourth of the Federal Republic's imports.

Scholarship, culture and leisure. North Rhine-Westphalia's 52 higher education institutions and trade and technical schools offer professional training for some 500,000 students at 70 locations. A network of technology centers and transfer sites – including ten institutes operated by the Max Planck Society, five run by the Fraunhofer Society, and ZENIT,

Bonn's Art Museum, designed by Axel Schultes in 1993

Power generation of the future: the Energie-Forum-Innovation in Bad Oeynhausen

a center for innovation and technology in Mülheim an der Ruhr – ensures that small and medium-sized businesses are also able to profit from higher education know-how.

Around 13 million people visit the state's 602 museums every year, for example Bonn's Museum Mile, the Wallraf-Richartz-Museum and Museum Ludwig in Cologne, the Düsseldorf State Art Collection and the Folkwang Museum in Essen, the Kunsthalle Bielefeld and the Westphalian Landesmuseum in Münster. The state of North Rhine-Westphalia contributes to the maintenance of more than 80,000 architectural and natural grounded monuments. Prominent representatives of the modern fine arts pursue their work at the academies of art in Düsseldorf and Münster. The state's more than 160 stages ensure cultural diversity and international renown, as do the Ruhr Festival, the NRW Theater Encounter and the Oberhausen Days of Short Films. Pina Bausch and her dance theater are just as well known in New York and Tokyo as they are in their native city of Wuppertal.

Given this wealth of offerings it is no wonder that nearly 13.5 million people (booking 34.7 million overnight stays) come to North Rhine-Westphalia every year – as trade fair visitors, for instance, or as holidaymakers attracted by the unspoiled scenery of the Münsterland with its charming moated castles and by recreational opportunities such as skiing in the Sauerland or windsurfing on one of the state's many artificial lakes.

Further information:
– Nordrhein-Westfalen, Staatskanzlei (State Chancellery)
Stadttor 1, 40219 Düsseldorf
Internet: http://www.nrw.de
E-mail: poststelle@stk.nrw.de

Rhineland-Palatinate

Population	4.0 million
Area	19,849 sq km
Capital	Mainz

State election 1996	
SPD	39.8%
CDU	38.7%
FDP	8.9%
Alliance 90/The Greens	6.9%

In the middle of Europe. The state of Rhineland-Palatinate was formed after the end of World War II, on 30 August 1946, by the French military government. Traditional structures were not taken into account; instead parts of Germany were merged that never before belonged together: parts of the Prussian Rhine provinces, the territory of Hesse on the left bank of the Rhine, and the strongly Bavarian-influenced Palatinate. These regions have become closely knit over time, however, and Rhineland-Platinate has acquired its own identity.

Rhineland-Palatinate has profited greatly from its geographical location. The extensive modernized network of autobahns and federal highways, the convenient rail connections between the cities of Mainz, Kaiserslautern, Trier, Ludwigshafen and Koblenz, the major waterways Rhine and Mosel, as well as the state's proximity to three economically powerful centers – the Rhine-Main, Rhine-Neckar and Rhine-Ruhr regions – have created optimal framework conditions for the development of Rhineland-Palatinate into one of Germany's most dynamic regions.

An old European cultural heartland. The Rhineland was settled by Celts, Romans, Burgundians and Franks. In Speyer, Worms and Mainz, all on the Rhine, stand the great imperial cathedrals of the Middle Ages. Construction of the oldest synagogue in Germany (built in the Romanesque style) began in Worms in 1034. It was in Worms, too, at the Imperial Diet of 1521, that reformer Martin Luther refused to recant his theses. Three hundred years later, in Koblenz, the liberal paper "Rheinischer Merkur" inveighed against Napoleonic rule and

Pfalzgrafen-
stein castle
and moat and
Burg Guten-
fels, nr. Kaub
on the Middle
Rhine

censorship of the press. In 1832 Hambach Castle was the scene of the first democratic-republican assembly in Germany. The worldfamous Gutenberg Museum displays its treasures in Mainz, the birthplace of Johannes Gutenberg (1400-68), who invented the art of printing books with movable type and who was voted worldwide "Man of the Millennium" in 1999. The philosopher and father of scientific socialism, Karl Marx (1818-83), was born in Trier.

Viticulture and industry. Products from the state of Rhineland-Palatinate are in high demand. With an export rate of around 41.2 percent, it ranks first in this category among Germany's states. Its economy is remarkably diversified: Rhineland-Palatinate is a wine-growing center (two thirds of the country's wine comes from here) and an important wood producer as well as a major center of the chemical industry and a leading supplier of automobile components. Distinctive regional industries include the gemstone industry in Idar-Oberstein, ceramic and glass products from the Westerwald. Small and medium-sized businesses form the backbone of the Rhineland-Palatinate economy. The state's principal industrial employer is the chemical and plastics processing industry: BASF in Ludwigshafen is Europe's largest chemical factory complex and Rhineland-Palatinate's largest manufacturing firm. Also situated on the Rhine are the state's four next-largest companies: Boehringer (pharmaceuticals) in Ingelheim, Joh. A. Benckiser (chemicals, cosmetics) in Ludwigshafen, SGE Deutsche Holding (construction) in Ludwigshafen and the Schott Glassworks in Mainz. Europe's largest television network, ZDF (Channel Two), has its headquarters in Mainz, the state capital, as does the broadcasting company SAT.1.

Panorama view of BASF in Ludwigshafen

The confluence of the Mosel and Rhine is at Deutsches Eck in Koblenz

Picturesque landscapes. Rhineland-Palatinate lies in the center of the Rhenish Schist Massif. One of the most beautiful landscapes in the world is the stretch of the Rhine Valley between Bingen and Bonn. Dotted with castles, it is steeped in legend, and its praises have been sung by countless poets. Here and in the valley of the Mosel River grow wines which are prized by connoisseurs all over the world. At the foot of the Palatinate Forest runs the "German Wine Route".

The Rhine has been the region's economic artery since time immemorial. On it lie the cities of Ludwigshafen (165,000 inhabitants), Mainz (186,000 inhabitants), and Koblenz (109,000 inhabitants). Emperor Frederick I Barbarossa built a castle in Kaiserslautern (101,000 inhabitants) in the 12th century. The city of Trier (100,000 inhabitants) is 2,000 years old; its buildings dating from Roman times appear on the UNESCO World Heritage List, as do the cathedrals in Speyer, Worms and Mainz, the abbey church Maria Laach in the Eifel, Eltz Castle, the town of Oberwesel on the Rhine, St. Catherine's Church in Oppenheim, the Church of St. Paulinus in Trier and the Ehrenbreitstein Fortress at Koblenz.

Artists of yesterday and today. The unusual light above the lovely hilly countryside of the Palatinate was captured by painters Max Slevogt (1868-1932) and Hans Purrmann (1880-1966). Prominent contemporary artists from Rhineland-Palatinate include painters Heijo Hangen, Karl Otto Götz and Otto Greis as well as sculptors Franz Bernhard, Erwin Wortelkamp and Michael Croissant. Every year, between 1 May and 3 October, the "Rhineland-Palatinate Summer of Culture" features a wide variety of cultural events which are held all over the state.

Further information:
– Rheinland-Pfalz, Staatskanzlei (State Chancellery)
  Peter-Altmeier-Allee 1, 55116 Mainz
  Internet: http://www.stk.rlp.de
  E-mail: poststelle@stk.rlp.de

Saarland

Population	1.1 million
Area	2,570 sq km
Capital	Saarbrücken

State election 1999	
CDU	45.5%
SPD	44.4%

An eventful history. The political evolution of the smallest German state (apart from the city-states) mirrors the vicissitudes of German history in the 20th century. After World War I, after the Treaty of Versailles came into force in 1920, this coal and steel region was detached from the German Reich and placed under the administration of the League of Nations. In 1935 the people of the Saar voted by a majority of more than 90 percent in favor of its political reintegration into Germany.

The same thing happened after World War II. France, the occupying power, closed the border between the Saarland and the rest of Germany. In a referendum held in 1955, the Saarlanders again voted by a large majority in favor of the Saar once more being returned to the Federal Republic. France's consent to this wish was a milestone in the process of Franco-German reconciliation.

The reintegration of the Saarland on 1 January 1957 was effected in accordance with Article 23 of the Basic Law (the German

Festival in Saarlouis

Hans Peter Kuhn illuminated the Völklinger Hütte world cultural heritage in 1999

constitution) – setting a precedent for the process of German unification in 1990.

City, state and river. The Saarland takes its name from the Saar River, a tributary of the Mosel; the Saar also appears in the names of the state's largest cities. The Saar meanders charmingly through scenic countryside – a popular destination for tourists and hikers is the loop of the Saar near Orscholz. Grapes grown along the lower reaches of the Saar yield a wine prized by connoisseurs. Saarlanders have a partiality for more than the wine, however: Their local cuisine combines German tradition with French finesse – just one example of the symbiosis of the French and German way of life which is typical of the Saarland. The state capital Saarbrücken (185,000 inhabitants) is also an industrial hub and a convention center, the venue of the International Saar Fair. One fine Baroque building is the Ludwigskirche built in 1762-75 by Friedrich Joachim Stengel. The University of the Saarland in Saarbrücken, the colleges of art and music, and other higher education institutions and Fachhochschulen are attended by many students from neighboring countries as well. Saarbrücken offers a wealth of cultural attractions including film and theater festivals, museums, orchestras and choral groups. The director Max Ophüls (1902-57), who was born in Saarbrücken, made film history with his delightful comedies.

The name of the city of Saarlouis recalls the fact that here, about 300 years ago, the French king Louis XIV ordered his military engineer Sébastien le Prestre de Vauban to erect a fortress to defend his conquests in the western part of Germany. Today Saarlouis is an important industrial city (automobiles, steel, food and electronics).

Völklingen was shaped by the ironworks founded here in 1873, which by 1890 had already become one of the former German Empire's principal iron producers. This ironworks eventually became unable to compete on the world's markets and was shut down in 1986; substantial parts of it, however, were preserved. Today it is an industrial museum and is used for cultural purposes. In 1995, the Völklinger Hütte ironworks was placed on the UNESCO World Heritage List.

One of Europe's core regions. "The Saarlanders show us by their example how it is possible to be a good Saarlander, a good German, a good European and a good neighbor all at the same time." Thus the former Federal President Richard von Weizsäcker characterized the people of the Saar. The Saarland in Germany, Lorraine in France, and Luxembourg – often referred to by the abbreviation "Saar-Lor-Lux" – are developing ever closer ties, not least as a result of extensive new transportation projects. Traditional branches of industry of supraregional importance are glass and ceramics as well as mechanical engineering, metal processing and chemicals. The Saarland also furthers research projects of great significance. Future-oriented areas of emphasis include information and communications technologies, materials research, electronics, production technologies and medical technology. Numerous top-notch university and university-affiliated institutes form the interface between research and practical applications: the Max Planck Institute for Computers, for example, as well as the German Research Centre for Artificial Intelligence, the Fraunhofer Institute for Non-Destructive Testing, the Fraunhofer Institute for Medical Technology, the Institute for Information Systems and the world-famous Institute for New Materials.

Further information:
  — Saarland, Staatskanzlei (State Chancellery)
  Am Ludwigsplatz 14, 66117 Saarbrücken
  Internet: http://www.saarland.de/menue_regierung.html
  E-mail: presse@stk.saarland.de

The Free State of Saxony

Population	4.5 million
Area	18,413 sq km
Capital	Dresden

State election 1999	
CDU	56.9%
PDS	22.2%
SPD	10.7%

Industrial center of the east. With approximately 244 inhabitants per square kilometer, the Free State of Saxony is the most populous of the new states. It is a state with a long industrial tradition: Prior to the Second World War, the triangle formed by the cities of Dresden, Leipzig and Chemnitz was the industrial heart of Germany. Leipzig (437,000 inhabitants) was one of the main centers of peaceful resistance to the regime of the former GDR; the large Monday demonstrations culminated on 9 October 1989 in the chant: "We are the people!"

The fall of the Wall ushered in a massive restructuring of the Saxon economy. Today about 60 percent of the entire work force is employed in the service sector. A highly diversified and productive small and medium-sized business sector has emerged, comprised of more than 125,000 firms.

Industry nevertheless plays a more important role here than in the other new states: 7.6 percent of Saxony's inhabitants are employed in the industrial sector, accounting for roughly 33

Infineon AG in Dresden – one of the world's largest computer chip manufacturers

percent of the industrial production in eastern Germany. The bulk of Saxony's industrial output (manufacturing industry) is generated by the food industry (15 percent), the mechanical engineering industry (13 percent), metal production and processing (12 percent), and manufacturing of data processing equipment and installations (10 percent); automobile manufacturing especially is in the midst of very dynamic development, accounting for with 21 percent. At the same time, Dresden and the surrounding area continue to be a center for the microelectronics industry.

The Meissen porcelain factory has been producing exquisite merchandise continuously since 1710. Its trademark – crossed blue swords – are known the world over. Johann Friedrich Böttger (1682-1719) discovered the formula for this "white gold" in 1708 while working in his laboratory in Dresden.

The world's first SLR camera was constructed in Dresden, and such everyday articles as the toothpaste tube, filter cigarettes, mouthwash, beer bottle caps and coffee filters were developed here as well.

With four universities in Leipzig, Freiberg, Dresden and Chemnitz, twelve Fachhochschulen and five colleges of art, the International Graduate School of Zittau, as well as the Palucca School Dresden – Academy of Artistic Dance, Saxony has the most highly diversified network of higher education institutions in the new states. Small seminars, state-of-the-art research institutions and cooperation with business and industry ensure a high standard of education and training. This as well as the strong technical and scientific orientation of the state's higher education institutions make Saxony a particularly attractive location for firms engaged in the development and distribution of technological products and systems.

Evening sunlight falls on the Neue Messe Leipzig trade fair

The Leipzig Graduate School of Management is the only private university in eastern Germany.

"Florence on the Elbe" and "Paris in miniature". Not only is Dresden (453,000 inhabitants) reconstructing substantial parts of the historical city, which was almost completely destroyed at the end of World War II, but it is emerging as a European high-tech location. The baroque Church of Our Lady (built 1726-43 by George Bähr) will be reerected from the rubble of war in time to celebrate the 800th anniversary of the city's founding. For almost 50 years, the ruin has served as a cautionary reminder of the horrors of war. About one third of the original stones will be returned to their former positions.

Dresden is regaining its traditional center as old quarters and historical buildings are reconstructed. Avant-garde architecture like the St. Benno Gymnasium and the Ufa Kristallpalast will stand alongside magnificent old buildings like the Taschenberg and the Coselpalais. The city once referred to as "Florence on the Elbe" because of its architectural elegance places great value on the preservation of its baroque tradition; but that is not to say it has not recognized the signs of the 21st century in science and research and set its sights on future technology and high tech: firms such as Infineon, Motorola, AMD, Volkswagen, Gruner + Jahr and Daimler-Chrysler are investing in the state capital of Saxony so they can carry out research, manufacture and do business there.

Dresden has once again become a tourist magnet, attracting around seven million visitors per year. As early as 1985 the Italian renaissance-style Oper, built by Gottfried Semper 1870-78, was re-opened. Another of the city's landmarks is the Residenzschloss. It has been rebuilt with public funding – the

process now nearing completion. The castle will eventually house a museum of Saxony history and culture.

Leipzig, referred to in Johann Wolfgang von Goethe's "Faust" as "Paris in miniature", has been a trade fair venue for more than 800 years. At a cost of about DM 1.3 billion, the former Mockau Airport was transformed into a modern trade exhibition complex that opened in 1996. Since time immemorial, Leipzig has been a center of the publishing industry; the book fair held here each year has established itself, along with the book fair in Frankfurt/Main, as a key fair for contacts with Eastern Europe in particular. The university was founded as early as 1409. The city is becoming more and more of a media location and has been endowed with the first German chair for public relations.

The traditional and the modern. Saxony has helped to write many a chapter of German cultural history. The composers Heinrich Schütz, Johann Sebastian Bach, Carl Maria

The Chemnitz Congress Center

A pearl of Dresden Baroque – the Wall Pavilion at the Zwinger

von Weber, Felix Mendelssohn Bartholdy, Robert Schumann, Richard Wagner and Richard Strauss lived, worked and performed famous pieces for the first time here. The Saxony state opera, Semper Oper, with its Staatskapelle in the Dresden Kreuzchor, the St. Thomas Choir and Leipzig's Gewandhaus Orchestra are all internationally renowned.

The state boasts a wide variety of museums: In Dresden, the Green Vault displays the exquisitely crafted treasures accumulated by the Saxon electors, especially Augustus II the Strong (1670-1733); priceless art collections are to be found in the Old Masters Gallery, where Raphael's "Sistine Madonna" is on view, and in the New Masters Gallery, which features outstanding works from the Romantic period. Also worthy of special mention are the lace museum in Plauen, the automobile museum in Zwickau, the museum of industry in Chemnitz, the mineralogical collection in Freiberg, the Lessing Museum in Kamenz, and the Sorbian Museum in Bautzen, the center of the Lusatian Sorbs, a Slavic minority.

Saxony has a wealth of magnificent palaces and elaborately landscaped parks and gardens. Notable examples, in addition to the Dresden Zwinger, are Moritzburg Palace, Rammenau Palace, the moated Klaffenbach Palace, Pillnitz Palace and Pillnitz Park. Other tourist attractions include the "Silver Route" in the Erz Mountains and the "Saxon Wine Route" as well as festivals such as the Dresden Music Festival, the International Dixieland Festival and the Elbe Slope Festival in Dresden, the Karl May Festival in Radebeul, as well as the "Encounters" festival, in Chemnitz, the International Gottfried Silbermann Days in Freiberg and the euro-scene in Leipzig.

Further information:
— Freistaat Sachsen, Sächsische Staatskanzlei (Saxon State Chancellery)
Archivstrasse 1, 01097 Dresden
Internet: http://www.sachsen.de
E-mail: info@sk.sachsen.de

Saxony-Anhalt

Population	2.65 million
Area	20,455 sq km
Capital	Magdeburg

State election 1998	
SPD	35.9%
CDU	22.0%
PDS	19.6%
DVU	12.9%

State in the heart of Germany. Saxony-Anhalt stretches
from the Altmark heathland, which borders the state of Lower Saxony to the north, across the fertile lowlands of the
Magdeburger Börde and the industrial areas around Halle
and Bitterfeld to the vineyards along the Saale and Unstrut
rivers, the northernmost wine-growing region in the Federal
Republic of Germany. The Elbe River flows through the state
over a distance of about 300 kilometers. In the southwestern
portion of the Magdeburger Börde rise the Harz Mountains;
their highest peak is the Brocken (1,142 meters). Extensive
and extraordinarily scenic landscape reserves include the
Hochharz National Park and the Elbe Reserve, where beavers
can be found living in the wild. Saxony-Anhalt's history as a
state in its own right is brief: It existed only from 1947 to
1952 and was not reestablished until the unification of Germany on 3 October 1990. Some of its regions are among the
heartlands of German culture. The Altmark in the north was
long under the influence of Brandenburg; the south and the
east were dominated by Saxony. Anhalt was constituted in
1212 under the Ascanian princes and experienced its cultural
zenith in the 18th century under Prince Leopold III of
Anhalt-Dessau. The Russian empress Catherine the Great was
a descendant of the House of Anhalt-Zerbst.

Cities taken from a picture book. First mentioned in a
document dating from 805, the state capital Magdeburg
(239,000 inhabitants) is the second largest city in this rather
sparsely populated state. Here stands the first Gothic cathedral built on German soil: Dedicated in 1363, it contains the

grave of Emperor Otto I. Magdeburg's oldest structure is the Abbey of Our Lady, which was completed in 1160 and has survived the centuries virtually unchanged. The city of Halle (261,000 inhabitants), which prospered in the Middle Ages from salt extraction, is dominated by its cathedral, the Church of Our Lady and the Red Tower. In Dessau (86,700 inhabitants), Walter Gropius began setting global standards in architecture in 1925 with the "Bauhaus". Especially picturesque are the Harz towns of Halberstadt, Wernigerode and Quedlinburg with their half-timber houses dating from the 16th18th centuries. Quedlinburg's Old Town graced with more than 1,200 half-timber houses (which are now being renovated one by one) has been placed on the UNESCO World Heritage List. Of particular interest in the city of Naumburg is the St. Peter and Paul Cathedral with the donor figures Ekkehard and Uta dating from the 13th century. Spread out over an area of 112 hectares, Wörlitz Park near Dessau with the palace of Leopold III dedicated in 1773 is one of the most beautiful English-style gardens in Europe. A popular tourist attraction is the "Romanesque Route", which winds through Saxony-Anhalt for about 1,000 kilometers and passes by more than 70 notable architectural monuments.

Agriculture and large-scale industry. The soils of the Magdeburger Börde and the Harz foreland are some of the most fertile farmland in Germany – mainly grain, sugar beets, potatoes and vegetables. Ten years after German unification, Saxony-Anhalt has developed into an innovative location in economic terms. Numerous well-known firms from inside and outside Germany are now located here. Aspirin tablets, known the world over, are produced here in Bitterfeld. The glass for the Reichstag's new dome in Berlin came

Oil refinery in Leuna

from the US flat glass producer, Guardian Industries' factory in Wolfen.

Playing a dominant role in the economy of Saxony-Anhalt are the chemical industry with its long tradition, the food industry and increasingly the automobile industry. Their plants are among the most modern of their kind in the world. Along with Saxony-Anhalt, the Halle-Leipzig region is also becoming a center for bio- and gene technology. Modern information and communication technologies are also increasing their presence in Saxony-Anhalt. No state in the eastern part of Germany receives as much direct investment from overseas, and this attests to the good basic economic conditions here. Apart from its central European location, it boasts a modern infrastructure, a qualified work force and speedy approval processes.

Music, art and scholarship. The annual Handel Festival in Halle draws music aficionados from all over the world. One of the most famous of the state's 140 museums is the Moritzburg State Gallery, which features a large collection of paintings by the German-American painter Lyonel Feininger. The cathedral treasures of the Church of St. Servace in Quedlinburg are among the most valuable in Germany; stolen during World War II, they were returned to the church after a spectacular odyssey. Saxony-Anhalt was the heartland of the Reformation; to this very day visitors encounter many a testimony to the life and work of Martin Luther and Philipp Melanchthon, especially in the "Luther towns" of Wittenberg and Eisleben.

The Otto von Guericke University in Magdeburg is the newest higher education institution in Germany. It was created in October 1993 by the merger of the Technical University, the

Magdeburg cathedral was completed in 1520

St. Mary's Town Church in Wittenberg, birthplace of Martin Luther

College of Education, and the Medical Academy. More than 13,000 students are registered at the over 300-year-old Martin Luther University of Halle-Wittenberg. The College of Art and Design at Giebichenstein Castle in Halle is gaining increasing recognition.

Prominent individuals. Martin Luther (1483-1546) was born in Eisleben and died there as well. He was laid to rest in the castle church in Wittenberg, to the door of which he had nailed his Ninety-Five Theses in 1517. Working at Falkenstein Castle in the 13th century, Eike von Repgow wrote the "Sachsenspiegel" (Saxon Mirror), the most important compilation of medieval law. The "Merseburg Charms", two linguistic monuments written in Old High German, date from the 10th century.

George Frideric Handel was born in Halle, Georg Philipp Telemann was a native of Magdeburg, and Johann Sebastian Bach composed his "Brandenburg Concertos" at the royal court in Köthen. Kurt Weill, one of the most expressive composers of our century, came from Dessau.

The scientist Otto von Guericke discovered the principle underlying the air pump and demonstrated the effect of a vacuum using his "Magdeburg hemispheres" in 1663. Quedlinburg was the birthplace of the first German woman doctor, Dorothea Christiana Erxleben, who earned her doctorate in 1754 at the university in Halle. Otto von Bismarck, German Reich Chancellor from 1871 to 1890, was born in Schönhausen in 1815; a Bismarck Museum was opened there in 1998 on the occasion of the 100th anniversary of his death.

Further information:
  — Sachsen-Anhalt, Staatskanzlei (State Chancellery)
    Domplatz 4, 39104 Magdeburg
    Internet: http://www.sachsen-anhalt.de
    E-mail: staatskanzlei@stk.sachsen-anhalt.de

Schleswig-Holstein

Population	2.7 million
Area	15,729 sq km
Capital	Kiel

State election 2000	
SPD	43.1%
CDU	35.2%
FDP	7.6%
Alliance 90/The Greens	6.2%
SSW	4.1%

Hub of the Baltic region. Schleswig-Holstein is the only German state bordered by two seas: the North Sea and the Baltic. The sparsely populated state (2.7 million inhabitants) makes the most of its geographical location between Scandinavia and Eastern Europe: It aims to be the hub for countries encircling the Baltic Sea, which with a total population of more than 50 million constitute one of Europe's regions of the future. In order to preserve Schleswig-Holstein's natural beauty, great importance is attached to environmental protection measures. Efforts to keep the seas clean as well as nature and soil conservation measures are therefore key priorities of state policy. This conforms with a technological development which has transformed Schleswig Holstein into an attractive high tech location in the Baltic region.

Cities with long-standing traditions. Every summer during "Kiel Week", the state capital Kiel (237,000 inhabitants) is the meeting place for the international sailing elite and the venue of the popular cultural festival held in conjunction with the regatta. Shipbuilding and ferry traffic – especially to Scandinavia – are just as much a part of the city as the imposing sailing ship "Gorch Fock", a training ship which documents Kiel's close ties to the navy. Lübeck (214,000 inhabitants), the "Queen of the Hanseatic League" graced with many notable medieval buildings, has been placed on the UNESCO World Heritage List. The novels of Lübeck's famous sons Heinrich and Thomas Mann rank among the world's great literary works. Lübeck-Travemünde is one of Europe's most important ferry ports. Once a year, meticulously restored sailing ships and replicas converge in Flensburg (86,600 inhabitants) for the "Rum Regatta".

An economy in transition. In recent years Schleswig-Holstein has undergone a profound structural transformation from a region based on agriculture and fisheries to a modern location for business, industry and technology. The shipbuilding industry, which at one time dominated the economy of the state capital Kiel in particular, survived the structural crisis by focusing on construction of specialized ships amongst other things. Approximately one million hectares of the state's land are given over to farming; the future, however, belongs to marine and medical technologies, software production, and energy and environmental technologies. With more than 1,500 wind turbines, Schleswig-Holstein is Germany's number one supplier of wind power. It also ranks near the top in terms of technology centers and boasts well over 1,000 firms in the IT and communications sector alone. At the same time, the state has taken action to create the necessary infrastructure. Autobahns form not only the important north-south axis; links with the west coast are equally important for tourism, business and industry. Three universities as well as four public and two private Fachhochschulen furnish facilities for training young scholars. All of the above have helped to solidify Schleswig-Holstein's acknowledged strong position both nationally and internationally as an attractive site for business and industry.

"Gentle tourism". The North Sea island of Helgoland with its famous red cliffs was the backdrop for the poet August Heinrich Hoffmann von Fallersleben in 1841 when he wrote the German anthem. The North Frisian Islands of Sylt, Föhr and Amrum are a holidaymaker's paradise; the same is true of

The Holsten gate in Lübeck, seen from the city

A view out over the Flensburg Firth toward St. Jürgen

the resorts on the Baltic such as Hohwacht and Timmendorf. Nature lovers are drawn to the tidal mud flats of the Wattenmeer National Park on the North Sea. Farther inland lies the scenic area known as "Holstein Switzerland" with its many lakes. Well worth a visit are places such as Mölln, the town of the legendary jester Till Eulenspiegel, or the cathedral town of Schleswig with the Late Gothic Bordesholm Altarpiece, a masterpiece of woodcarving created in 1514-21 by Hans Brüggemann, and, of course, the city of Lübeck.

Museums and music. Every town of any size has its own museum of local history, but the regional museum in Gottorf Palace near Schleswig enjoys a particularly high reputation nationwide. Other notable attractions are the Molfsee Open-Air Museum near Kiel, which offers a glimpse of what country life was like years ago, and the museum on the site of the old Viking town Haithabu. The Buddenbrook House in Lübeck was completely remodelled in time for EXPO 2000: Rooms were restored to their original condition as one knows then from the world-famous novel "Buddenbrooks" by Thomas Mann. For eight weeks during the summer – 1999 marked the 14th year in succession – the entire state of Schleswig-Holstein is transformed into a concert hall. The Schleswig-Holstein Music Festival entices international stars and audiences to such unusual settings as barns and stalls – but also to estates, manor houses and palaces. Many prominent literary figures, too, have chosen to live in Schleswig-Holstein, among them Günter Grass, Günter Kunert, Siegfried Lenz and Sarah Kirsch.

Further information:
— Schleswig-Holstein, Staatskanzlei (State Chancellery)
  Landeshaus, Düsternbrooker Weg 70, 24105 Kiel
  Internet: http://www.schleswig-holstein.de/landsh.landesreg.html
  E-mail: Klaus.Gärtner@stk.landh.de

The Free State of Thuringia

Population	2.5 million
Area	16,171 sq km
Capital	Erfurt

State election 1999	
CDU	51.0%
PDS	21.3%
SPD	18.5%

Germany's center. Thuringia lies in the geographical center of Germany and encompasses as its heartland the bowl-shaped Thuringian Basin and the Thuringian Forest. It stretches westward to the Werra River and southeastward past the Saale River to the Weisse Elster River. To the southwest lies the Rhön, and in the south the state abuts the Franconian Forest. Thuringia neighbors five states; further improvement and enlargement of the transportation network is consequently one of the paramount objectives of infrastructure plans. The autobahns A 4 and A 9, which traverse Thuringia in a west-east and north-south direction respectively, are presently being widened to six lanes. With the construction of a new traffic axis through the Thuringian Forest (an autobahn and a stretch of track for high-speed trains), an urgently needed link is being created, one which will do justice to Thuringia's central location and which would have been completed much earlier had Germany not been divided. Erfurt (203,000 inhabitants), the state capital, is referred to as the "city of flowers". The old part of the city is graced with an unusually large number of patrician homes, churches and monasteries which virtually make it an architectural open-air museum.

Territorial fragmentation and culture. Thuringia was particularly affected by Germany's earlier territorial fragmentation. The region's rulers competed intensely with one another, especially in the cultural sphere, and took great pride in their role as patrons of the fine arts. By far the most prominent among them was Duke Carl August of Saxony-Weimar-Eisenach (1757-1828). He brought to his court the poet and translator of Shakespeare's works Christoph Martin Wieland (1733-1813), the poet and philologist Johann Gottfried von Herder (1744-1803), and above all Johann Wolfgang von Goethe (1749-1832). Thus at that time, around 1800, Weimar became a center of German and European intellectual life. In this city Goethe wrote some of his most famous works, including the final version of "Faust". Weimar was also home to Friedrich von Schiller from 1787 to 1789 and from 1799 to 1805. Here he wrote, among other works, his "William Tell".

In the second half of the 19th century, Franz Liszt (1811-86) composed and gave concerts in this city distinctive for its keen appreciation of the fine arts. Here, in 1919, Walter Gropius founded the Bauhaus, a school of architecture which sought to overcome the divisions between art, handicraft and technology. In 1925, the Bauhaus moved to Dessau, and a few years later to Berlin. There, in 1933, it fell victim to the barbarity that followed Hitler's seizure of power and sealed the fate of the first German republic, the Weimar Republic, whose constitution had been drafted and adopted in Weimar in 1919.

Weimar (62,000 inhabitants) was selected as the Cultural City of Europe for the year 1999, the 250th anniversary of Goethe's birth. Johann Sebastian Bach, the scion of a renowned family of musicians, was born in Eisenach in 1685. Ensconced in the nearby Wartburg in 1522, Martin Luther translated the New Testament into German – a key step in the emergence of modern German in written form. Thuringia marked the 450th anniversary of the reformer's death with a "Luther Year 1996". Meeting at the Wartburg in 1817, representatives of patriotic student groups known as "Burschenschaften" called for a united Germany.

Quality controls at a generator test track at the Siemens plant in Erfurt

Göltzschtal Bridge: 574 m long and 78 m high, completed in 1851

Industry and crafts. In Thuringia, where important roads intersected, commerce and the craft trades found favorable conditions for growth. Woad, a plant yielding blue coloring matter, brought the region early prosperity. A tradition of weapons craftsmanship led Suhl to become the "armorer's workshop" for hunting and sporting guns. The industrialization of Germany in the 19th century began in Saxony and Thuringia; important branches were mining (potash), porcelain, glass, toys, and above all machine tools and the optical industry associated with the names Zeiss and Schott in Jena.

Thuringia has once again picked up the thread of these old traditions. In the wake of the wrenching economic changes brought on by the fall of the Wall and the end of the GDR, new structures in line with market conditions have been developed which make it possible to attract future-oriented technologies to the Free State of Thuringia. Since the restructuring of JENOPTIK, for instance, the firm has grown to become a successful high-tech group with international operations. With four universities (in Jena, Weimar, Erfurt and Ilmenau), a number of Fachhochschulen, roughly 50 research institutions and 20 technology centers, Thuringia now has a strong academic and scientific base. Jena (99,000 inhabitants) continues to be the heart of the optical industry. Machinery is manufactured above all in Gera (116,000 inhabitants) and Erfurt. The state capital is also a center for microelectronics. In Eisenach the traditional automobile industry with its suppliers predominates; the new Opel plant there has the highest productivity of any automobile factory in Europe. Other industries in Thuringia are the electronics, glass, fine ceramics, wood processing, textile, clothing and chemical industries. The media sector in Thuringia is also becoming increasingly important.

Half of Thuringia's land area is given over to farming; some of its farmland has soil of the highest quality. Important crops are

Jenoptik – quality assurance for optical measuring devices

grain, rape, potatoes and sugar beets. Thuringia has also long enjoyed an excellent reputation for the processing of agricultural products into foods for human consumption.

Germany's "green heart". Extensive forests and broad expanses of fields as well as romantic valleys and gorges make the Thuringian Forest an attractive hiking and winter sports area. The Rennsteig, which runs along the crest of the ridge of the Thuringian Forest for a length of 168 kilometers, is – next to the Eselsweg in the Spessart region – Germany's oldest and most famous hiking path. The state's wealth of medicinal and mineral springs has fostered the growth of many health resorts. Approximately 170 artificial lakes afford optimal conditions for water sports enthusiasts. Of course visitors are also drawn to Thuringia by its rich cultural heritage. The 300-kilometer-long "Thuringian Classical Route", which was opened in 1992, takes people to the state's most beautiful spots, to castles and palaces, to museums and memorials – always calling to mind the time when Thuringia was the center of German intellectual life.

Meiningen is once again the home of a flourishing theater; in the 19th century, this city became famous throughout Europe for its court theater troupe "The Meiningen Company". Its spectacular success was attributable to the patronage of the local sovereign, Duke George II of Saxe-Meiningen, who also directed the company. Today this theater is one of the most popular in Germany.

Further information:
– Freistaat Thüringen, Thüringer Staatskanzlei (State Chancellery)
  Regierungsstrasse 73, 99084 Erfurt
  Internet: http://www.thueringen.de
  E-mail: GnauckJ@TSK.thueringen.de

History

German history up to 1945

Up to the last century, it was a widely held belief that German history began in the year A.D. 9. That was when Arminius, a prince of a Germanic tribe called the Cherusci, vanquished three Roman legions in the Teutoburg Forest (southeast of modern-day Bielefeld). Arminius, about whom not much else is known, was regarded as the first German national hero, and a huge memorial to him was built near Detmold in the years 1838-75.

Nowadays a less simplistic view is taken. The gradual emergence of a distinctly German nation was a process which took hundreds of years. The word "deutsch" (German) probably first became common currency in the 8th century and initially defined only the language spoken in the eastern part of the Franconian realm. This empire, which reached the zenith of its power under Charlemagne, incorporated peoples speaking both Germanic and Romance dialects. After Charlemagne's death (814), it was not long before it fell apart. In the course of various divisions prompted by the respective lines of noble inheritance, a western and an eastern realm developed, whose political boundary approximately coincided with the boundary between German and French speakers. Only gradually did a feeling of cohesion develop among the inhabitants of the eastern realm. It was not until then that the term "deutsch" was transferred from the language to its speakers and ultimately to the region they lived in, henceforth termed "Deutschland".

The German western frontier was fixed relatively early and remained fairly stable. But the eastern frontier moved to and fro for hundreds of years. Around 900 it ran approximately along the Elbe and Saale rivers. In subsequent centuries German settlement extended far to the east. This expansion stopped only in the middle of the 14th century. The ethnic boundary then made between Germans und Slavs remained until World War II.

High Middle Ages. The transition from the East Franconian to the German "Reich" is usually dated from 911, when, after the Carolingian dynasty had died out, the Franconian duke Conrad I was elected king. He is regarded as the first German king. (The official title was "Frankish King" and later "Roman King"; from the 11th century the name of the realm was "Ro-

Emperor Frederick I, Barbarossa, Romano-German emperor (1122-90); book miniature (c. 1180)

man Empire", from the 13th century "Holy Roman Empire", and in the 15th century the words "of the German Nation" were added.) It was an electoral monarchy; that is to say, the high nobility chose the king who then ruled over them. In addition, "dynastic right" applied: The new king had to be a blood relation of his predecessor. This principle was broken several times. There were also a number of double elections. The medieval empire had no capital city; the king ruled from a court which moved from place to place. There were no imperial taxes; the king drew his sustenance mainly from "imperial estates" he administered in trust. His authority was not always recognized by the powerful tribal dukes unless he was militarily powerful and a skillful forger of alliances. Conrad's successor, the Saxon duke Henry I (919-36), was the first to succeed in this complex tactical role, and to an even greater extent so did his son, Otto (936-73). Otto made himself the real ruler of the realm. His great power found obvious expression when he was crowned Emperor in 962 in Rome.

From then on, the German king could claim the title "Emperor". The emperorship was conceived as universal and theoretically gave its incumbent control over the entire Occident. However, this notion never became full political reality. In order to be crowned Emperor by the Pope, the king had to make his way to Rome and this inaugurated an ongoing orientation toward Italy by the German kings. For 300 years they were able to retain control of upper and central Italy, but because of this they were diverted from important tasks in Germany. And so Otto's successors inevitably suffered big setbacks. However, under the succeeding Salian dynasty a new upswing occurred. With Henry III (1039-56), the German kingship and emperorship reached the zenith of its power, maintaining above all a supremacy over the Papacy.

Henry IV (1056-1106) was not able to hold this position. In a quarrel with Pope Gregory VII over whether bishops and other influential church officials should be appointed by the Pope or by the temporal ruler, he was superficially successful. But Gregory retaliated by excommunicating Henry, who thereupon surrendered his authority over the church by doing penance to the Pope at Canossa (1077), an irretrievable loss of power by the emperorship. From that point onward, the Emperor and the Pope were equal-ranking powers.

In 1138 the century of rule by the Staufer, or Hohenstaufen, dynasty began. Frederick I Barbarossa (1152-90), in wars with the Pope, the northern Italian cities and his main German rival, the Saxon duke Henry the Lion, led the empire into a new golden age. But under him began a territorial fragmentation which ultimately weakened the central power. This decline continued under Barbarossa's successors, Henry VI (1190-7) and Frederick II (1212-50), despite the great power vested in the emperorship. The ecclesiastical and temporal princes became semi-sovereign territorial rulers. The end of Hohenstaufen rule (1268) also meant the end of the Emperor's universal rule in the Occident. Internal disintegrative forces prevented Germany from becoming a national state, a process just beginning then in other western European countries. Here lies one of the reasons why the Germans became a "belated nation".

Late Middle Ages to modern times. Rudolf I (1273-91) was the first Habsburg to take the throne. Now the material foundation of the emperorship was no longer the lost imperial estates but the "house estates" of the dynasties, and house power politics evidently became every emperor's main preoccupation.

The "Golden Bull" (imperial constitution) issued by Charles IV in 1356 regulated the election of the German king by seven electors privileged with special rights. These sovereign electors and the towns, because of their economic power, gradually gained influence while that of the small counts, lords and knights declined. The towns' power further increased when they linked up in leagues. The most important of these, the Hanseatic League, became the leading Baltic power in the 14th century.

From 1438 the crown – although the empire nominally was an electoral monarchy – practically became the property of the Habsburg dynasty, which had become the strongest territorial power. In the 15th century, demands for imperial reform increased. Maximilian I (1493-1519), the first to accept the imperial title without a papal coronation, tried to implement such a reform but without much success. The institutions newly created or reshaped by him – Reichstag (Imperial Diet), Reichskreise (Imperial Counties), Reichskammergericht (Imperial Court) – lasted until the end of the Reich (1806) but were not able to halt its continuing fragmentation. A dualism of "Emperor and Reich" developed: The head of the Reich was offset by the estates of the Reich – electors, princes and towns. The power of the emperors was curtailed and increasingly eroded by "capitulations", which they negotiated at their election with the respective electors. The princes, especially the powerful among them, greatly expanded their rights at the expense of imperial power. But the Reich continued to hold together, the glory of the imperial idea remained alive, and the small and medium-sized territories were protected in the Reich system from possible attack by powerful neighbors.

The towns became centers of economic power, profiting above all from growing trade. In the burgeoning textile and mining industries, forms of economic activity grew which went beyond the guilds system of the craftsmen and, like long-distance trading, were beginning to take on early capitalistic

The Luther Monument on the Eisleben market place and the spire of the Church of St. Andrew

traits. At the same time an intellectual change was taking place, marked by the Renaissance and Humanism. The newly risen critical spirit turned above all on church abuses.

Age of religious schism. The smoldering dissatisfaction with the church broke out – mainly through the actions of Martin Luther from 1517 – in the Reformation, which quickly spread. Its consequences went far beyond the religious sphere. Social unrest abounded. In 1522-3 the Reich knights rose up, and in 1525 the Peasants' Revolt broke out, the first larger revolutionary movement in German history to strive for both political and social change. Both uprisings failed or were bloodily quelled. The territorial princes profited most from the Reformation.

After the changing fortunes of war, they were given the right to dictate their subjects' religion by the 1555 Peace of Augsburg. This accorded the Protestants equal rights with those of the Catholics. The religious division of Germany was thus sealed. On the imperial throne at the time of the Reformation was Charles V (1519-56), heir to the biggest realm since the time of Charlemagne. His international political interests were too demanding for him to be able to assert himself within Germany. After his abdication, the empire was split up. The German territorial states and the western European national states together now formed the new European system of states.

At the time of the Peace of Augsburg, four fifths of Germany was Protestant, but the struggle between the faiths had not ended. In the following decades, the Catholic Church was able to recapture many areas (Counter-Reformation). The differences between the faiths sharpened; religious parties – the Protestant Union (1608) and the Catholic League (1609) – were formed. A local conflict in Bohemia then triggered the Thirty Years' War, which widened into a European conflict over religious and political differences. Between 1618 and 1648, much of Germany was devastated and depopulated. The 1648 Peace of Westphalia brought the cession of territories to France and Sweden and confirmed the withdrawal of Switzerland and the Netherlands from the Reich. The estates of the Reich were accorded all major sovereign rights in religious and temporal matters as well as the right to enter into alliances with foreign partners.

Age of absolutism. The almost sovereign principalities took over the absolutist form of government modeled on the French. Absolutism gave the ruler limitless power while at the same time allowing tight administrations to be built up, an organized fiscal policy to be introduced and new armies to be mobilized. Many princes aspired to making their residences cultural focal points. Some of them, representatives of "enlightened absolutism", encouraged learning and philosophy, albeit within the confines of their power interests. The policy of state control of all economic life also allowed the absolutistically ruled states to gain in economic strength. Thus lands such as Bavaria, Brandenburg (the later Prussia), Saxony and Hanover were able to develop into power centers in their own right. Austria, which repelled the attacking Turks and acquired Hungary as well as parts of the formerly Turkish Balkan countries, rose to a large power. A rival to it developed in the 18th century in the form of Prussia, which

Frederick II (the Great), King of Prussia (1712-86); painting by Johann Heinrich Christian Franke (1763)

**Roman-German Empire
(about 950)**

**Holy Roman Empire of the German Nation
after the Peace of Westphalia (1648)**

Swedish possession

Boundary of the
German Confederation
(1815–66)

**German Empire
1871–1918**

**Germany within the
borders of 1937**

1:15 000 000

under Frederick II the Great (1740-86) grew into a first-rank military power. Both states sought to assert their authority in Europe.

Age of the French Revolution. The nudge which brought the crumbling Reich crashing down came from the west. Revolution broke out in France in 1789. Under pressure from the middle classes, the feudal social order which had existed since the early Middle Ages was swept away; a separation of powers and human rights were to assure the liberty and equality of all. The attempt by Prussia and Austria to intervene by force in events in the neighboring country failed ignominiously and triggered a counter-thrust by the revolutionary armies. Under the stormy advances of the forces of Napoleon, who had assumed the revolutionary heritage in France, the Reich finally collapsed. France took the left bank of the Rhine.

To compensate the former owners of these areas for their losses, an enormous territorial reshuffling took place at the expense of the smaller and particularly the ecclesiastical principalities. Through the Final Recess (Reichsdeputationshauptschluss) of 1803, some four million subjects changed rulers. The medium-sized states were the beneficiaries. In 1806 most of them grouped together under French protection in the Confederation of the Rhine (Rheinbund). In the same year Emperor Franz II laid down the crown and the Holy Roman Empire of the German Nation ceased to exist.

The French Revolution did not spread into Germany. Although there, too, various individuals had over the years tried time and again to do away with the barriers between the aristocracy and the common people, and although leading thinkers welcomed the overthrow in the west as the start of a new era, one major reason why the spark could not catch easily was that, in contrast to centrally oriented France, the federalistic structure of the Reich hampered the spread of new ideas. Another big reason was that France, the motherland of the revolution, opposed the Germans as an enemy and an occupying power. Indeed, the struggle against Napoleon forged a new national movement which culminated in wars of liberation.

Germany did not remain unaffected by the forces of social change. First in the states of the Confederation of the Rhine and then in Prussia (in the latter connected with names such as Stein, Hardenberg, Scharnhorst and W. von Humboldt) reforms were begun which were aimed at breaking down feudal barriers and creating a society of free, responsible citizens. The objectives were the abolition of serfdom, freedom of trade, municipal self-administration, equality before the law and general conscription. But many reform moves were pulled up short. Participation by the populace in legislation was refused almost everywhere. Only hesitantly did some princes grant their states constitutions, especially in southern Germany.

The German Confederation. After the victory over Napoleon, the Congress of Vienna (September 1814 to June 1815) redrew the map of Europe. The hopes of many Germans for a free, unitary nation-state were not fulfilled. The German Confederation (Deutscher Bund) which replaced the old Reich was a loose association of the individual sovereign states. Its sole organ was the Federal Diet (Bundestag) in Frankfurt, which was not an elected but a delegated diet. It was able to act only if the two great powers, Prussia and Austria, agreed. It saw its main task in the ensuing decades in suppressing all aspirations and efforts aimed at unity and freedom. Press and publishing were subject to rigid censorship, the universities were under close supervision, and political activity was virtually impossible.

Nevertheless, a modern economic development which worked against these reactionary tendencies had begun. In the year 1834 the German Customs Union (Deutscher Zollverein) was founded, creating a single inland market. In 1835 the first German railway line went into operation. Industrialization began. With the factories there grew the new class of factory

Karl, Reichsfreiherr vom und zum Stein (1757-1831); drawing by Julius Schnorr von Carolsfeld (1794-1872)

workers. At first they found better incomes, but the rapid growth of the population soon led to a labor surplus. And since there were no social welfare provisions, the mass of factory workers lived in great misery. Tensions came to a violent head, for example, in the 1844 uprising of the Silesian weavers, which was harshly put down by the Prussian military. Very hesitantly at first, a workers' movement began to form.

The 1848 revolution. In contrast to the revolution of 1789, the French revolution of February 1848 triggered an immediate response in Germany. In March, there were uprisings in all states, and these forced many concessions from the stunned princes. In May, the National Assembly (Nationalversammlung) convened in St. Paul's Church in Frankfurt/Main. It elected Archduke John of Austria as Regent of the Empire (Reichsverweser) and set up a Reich Ministry which, however, had no powers or authority. The tune was called in the National Assembly by the Liberal center, which strove for a constitutional monarchy with limited suffrage. The splintering of the National Assembly from Conservatives to Radical Democrats, which already indicated the spectrum of parties to come, made it difficult to draw up a constitution.

However, not even the Liberal center could overcome the differences between the protagonists of the "greater Germany" and "smaller Germany" concepts, in other words, a German Reich with or without Austria. After hard bargaining, a democratic constitution was drawn up which attempted to combine old and new ideas and required a government responsible to parliament. But when Austria insisted on bringing into the future Reich its entire realm, encompassing more than a dozen different peoples, the "smaller Germany" concept won the day and the National Assembly proffered Frederick William IV of Prussia the hereditary German imperial crown. The king turned it down, not wanting to owe imperial majesty to a revolution. In May 1849 popular uprisings in Saxony, the Palatinate and Baden aimed at enforcing the constitution "from the bottom up" failed.

That was the seal on the failure of the whole revolution. Most of its achievements were rescinded, and the constitutions of the individual states were revised along reactionary lines. In 1850, the German Confederation was restored.

The rise of Prussia. The 1850s were years of great economic advances. Germany became an industrial country. Although its production output still lagged far behind England's, it was growing faster. Pacemakers were heavy industry and mechanical engineering. Prussia also became the predominant economic power of Germany. Industrial power strengthened the political self-confidence of the liberal middle class. The German Progress Party (Deutsche Fortschrittspartei), formed in 1861, became the strongest party in the Prussian Diet and denied the government approval of the funds when it wanted to make reactionary changes to the structure of the army. The newly appointed Prime Minister (Ministerpräsident), Otto von Bismarck (1862), took up the challenge and for some years governed without the parliamentary approval of the budget which was required by the constitution. The Progress Party dared offer no further resistance than parliamentary opposition, however.

Bismarck was able to offset his precarious position on the domestic front by foreign policy successes. In the German-Danish War (1864), Prussia and Austria forced the Danes to cede the duchies of Schleswig and Holstein, which they initially administered jointly. But Bismarck had from the outset pursued the annexation of the two duchies and steered for open conflict with Austria. In the Austro-Prussian War (1866), Austria was defeated and had to leave the German stage. The German Confederation was dissolved and replaced by the North German Confederation (Norddeutscher Bund) of states north of the Main River, with Bismarck as Federal Chancellor (prime minister).

The Bismarck Reich. From then on, Bismarck worked towards "smaller German" unity. He broke France's resistance in the Franco-German War of 1870-1, triggered by a diplomatic conflict over the succession to the Spanish throne. Defeated France had to cede Alsace-Lorraine and pay huge reparations. In the patriotic enthusiasm of the war, the southern German states joined up with the North German Confederation to form the German Empire (Deutsches Reich). At Versailles near Paris, King William I of Prussia was proclaimed German Emperor on 18 January 1871.

German unity had not come about by popular decision "from below" but by a treaty between princes "from above". Prussia's predominance was stifling. To many, the new Reich seemed like a "greater Prussia". The Reichstag (Imperial Diet) was elected by universal and equal suffrage. Although it had no say in the formation of the cabinet, it could influence government by its participation in lawmaking and its budgetary power. Although the Reich Chancellor was accountable only to the Emperor and not to parliament, he did have to try to get majorities for his policies in the Reichstag.

Suffrage in the individual Länder (states) still varied. In eleven it was still class suffrage, dependent on tax paid; in four there was still the old division into estates. The south German states, with their longer parliamentary tradition, reformed their electoral laws after the turn of the century, and Baden, Württemberg and Bavaria made theirs the same as the Reich laws. Although Germany's emergence as a modern industrial country strengthened the influence of the economically successful middle class, the people who still called the tune in society were the aristocrats, above all in the army officer corps where they predominated.

Bismarck ruled as Reich Chancellor for 19 years. Through a consistent peace and alliance policy, he tried to give the Reich a secure position in the new European balance of power. In contrast to this farsighted foreign policy was his home policy. He had no feeling for the democratic tendencies of his time. To him, political opposition was "hostility to the Reich". Bitterly, but ultimately vainly, he fought the left wing of the liberal middle class, political Catholicism and especially the organized labor movement, which for twelve years (1878-90) was practically banned by a "Socialists Act" (Sozialistengesetz). Hence the vastly growing working class, despite progressive social legislation, was alienated from the state. Bis-

Reich's Chancellor Otto von Bismarck (1815-98); photo dating from Dec. 27, 1886, colored

marck ultimately became a victim of his own system when he was dismissed in 1890 by the young Emperor William II.

William II wanted to rule himself, but he lacked the knowledge and staying power. More by speeches than by actions, he created the impression of a peacethreatening dictator. Under him there took place a transition to "Weltpolitik" (world policy), with Germany trying to shorten the lead of the great imperialist powers and thereby becoming more isolated. In his home policies, William soon took a reactionary course after his attempt to win the working class over to a "social emperorship" failed to bring the quick success he had hoped for. His chancellors had to rely on changing coalitions of Conservatives and National Liberals. The Social Democrats, although one of the strongest parties, obtaining millions of votes, continued to be excluded from participation in government.

World War I. The assassination of the heir to the Austrian throne on 28 June 1914 triggered the outbreak of World War I. The question as to who was to blame for this war remains a matter of dispute. Certainly Germany and Austria on the one side, and France, Russia and Britain on the other, did not consciously seek it but they were prepared to risk it. From the start, all had definite war aims for which military action was at the least not unwelcome. The Germans failed in their aim to quickly vanquish France. After the defeat of Germany in the Battle of the Marne, the fighting in the west soon froze into trench warfare, ultimately peaking in senseless material attrition with enormous losses on both sides. With the outbreak of war, the Emperor receded into the background. As it progressed, the weak Reich Chancellors had to submit more and more to the will of the army supreme command, whose nominal chief was Field Marshal Paul von Hindenburg but whose real head was General Erich Ludendorff.

The entry into the war of the United States of America in 1917 brought the decision which had long been developing and which could no longer be changed by the revolution in Russia and the peace in the east. Although the country had bled dry, General Ludendorff, completely misjudging the situation, continued until September 1918 to insist on "peace through victory", but then he surprisingly demanded an immediate armistice. Military defeat also meant political collapse. Unresisting, Emperor William II and the princes yielded their thrones in November 1918. Not a hand stirred to defend a monarchy which had lost all credibility. Germany became a republic.

The Weimar Republic. Power fell to the Social Democrats. Their majority had long since abandoned the revolutionary notions of earlier years and saw their mission in securing an orderly transition from the old to the new form of state. Private ownership of industry and agriculture remained untouched. The mostly antirepublican civil servants and judges were taken over without exception. The imperial officer corps retained command of the armed forces. Attempts by radical leftists to drive the revolution in a socialist direction were quelled by the army. In the National Assembly elected in January 1919, which convened at Weimar and drew up a new Reich constitution, three unconditionally republican parties – the Social Democrats, the German Democratic Party and the Catholic Centre – had the majority. But during the 1920s, the parliamentary parties and popular forces which were more or less hostile to a democratic state became ever stronger. The Weimar Republic was a "republic without republicans", rabidly fought by its opponents and only halfheartedly defended by its supporters. Especially the postwar economic misery and the oppressive terms of the Treaty of Versailles which Germany had to sign in 1919 made the people deeply skeptical of the republic. Growing domestic instability was the result.

In 1923, the confusion of the postwar era reached its peak (inflation, occupation of the Ruhr by France, Hitler's coup, communist attempts to seize government). This was followed by economic recovery and with it some political pacification. The foreign policy of Gustav Stresemann regained political equality for defeated Germany through the Locarno Pact (1925) and accession to the League of Nations (1926). The arts and sciences experienced a brief, intensive flowering in the "golden 20s". After the death of the first Reich President, Friedrich Ebert, former Field Marshal Paul von Hindenburg was elected head of state in 1925 as the candidate of the right. Although he abided strictly by the constitution, he never developed a personal commitment to the republican state.

The ultimate collapse of the Weimar Republic began with the world economic crisis in 1929. Left-wing and right-wing radicalism exploited unemployment and the general recession. No more majorities capable of government were to be found in the Reichstag, the cabinet being dependent on the support of the Reich President. From 1930, the up to then insignificant National Socialist movement of Adolf Hitler, which fused extreme anti-democratic tendencies and a raging anti-Semitism with pseudo-revolutionary propaganda, grew ever stronger and by 1932 had become the most powerful party. On 30 January 1933, Hitler became Reich Chancellor. Apart from members of his own party, his cabinet included politicians of the right and non-partisan specialist ministers, so it was hoped that sole rule by the National Socialists could be prevented.

The National Socialist dictatorship. Hitler soon rid himself of his allies. An "Enabling Act", approved by all the middle-class parties, gave him practically limitless power. He banned all parties but his own. The trade unions were smashed, basic rights virtually removed and press freedom abolished. The regime exercised ruthless terror and violence against anyone who stood in its way. Thousands disappeared without trial in hastily constructed concentration camps. Parliamentary institutions at all levels were abolished or made powerless. When Hindenburg died in 1934, Hitler assumed the roles of president and chancellor. By this he gained control as commander-in-chief of the armed forces, which up to then had still had a certain inner life of their own.

In the few years of the turbulent Weimar Republic, the majority of Germans had not acquired any deeprooted affinity to democracy. More than anything else, years of political turmoil, violence between the various camps – including bloody street battles – and the mass unemployment engendered by the world economic crisis had shattered confidence in government.

Hitler, on the other hand, succeeded with jobcreation and armament production programs in reinvigorating the economy and quickly reducing unemployment. He was helped by the fact that the world depression came to an end.

The fact that initially Hitler was also able to achieve his foreign policy aims virtually without resistance further strengthened his postion. In 1935, the Saar region, until then administered by the League of Nations, returned to Germany, and in the same year the Reich regained its defense sovereignty. In 1936 German troops moved into the Rhineland, which had been demilitarized since 1919. In 1938 Austria was joined to the Reich, and the Western powers allowed Hitler to annex the Sudetenland. All this made it easier for him to achieve his further aims, even though there were people from all walks of life who courageously resisted the dictator.

Immediately after taking power, the regime began to carry out its anti-Semitic program. Step by step, the Jews were stripped of all human and civic rights. Those who could tried to escape the persecution by fleeing abroad. The persecution of political opponents and the suppression of free speech also drove thousands out of the country. Many of the best German intellectuals, artists and scientists fled the country.

World War II and its consequences. But Hitler wanted more. From the outset he prepared for a war he was willing to wage to subjugate Europe. He demonstrated this as early as March 1939 when he had his troops march into Czechoslovakia. With his attack on Poland on 1 September 1939, he unleashed World War II, which lasted five and a half years, devastated much of Europe and killed some 55 million people.

The German armies first defeated Poland, Denmark, Norway, Holland, Belgium, Luxembourg, France, Yugoslavia and Greece. In the Soviet Union they advanced to a position just short of Moscow, and in North Africa they threatened the Suez Canal. Harsh occupation regimes were set up in the conquered countries. They were fought by resistance movements. In 1942 the regime began the "Final Solution of the Jewish Question": All the Jews the regime could lay its hands on were taken to concentration camps and murdered. The total number of victims is estimated at six million. The year in which this inconceivable crime began marked the turning point in the war. From then on, Germany and its allies suffered setbacks in all theaters.

The terror of the National Socialist regime and the military setbacks strengthened resistance against Hitler in all classes of society. A coup attempt on 20 July 1944, carried out mainly by officers, failed. Hitler survived a bomb planted in his headquarters and took terrible revenge. More than 4,000 people from all walks of life who had been involved in the resistance were executed in the following months. Outstanding figures of the resistance, whose names stand for all the victims, were General Ludwig Beck, Colonel Claus Graf Schenk von Stauffenberg, the former lord mayor of Leipzig Carl Goerdeler, and the Social Democrat Julius Leber.

The war continued. Hitler pursued it under enormous losses until the entire Reich area was occupied by the Allied forces. Then, on 30 April 1945, the dictator killed himself. Eight days later, the successor he had appointed in his will, Grand Admiral Karl Dönitz, signed the country's unconditional capitulation.

From 1945 to the present

Reorientation after 1945. Following the unconditional surrender of the German forces on 8-9 May 1945, the last government of the German Reich, headed by Admiral of the
Fleet Dönitz, remained in power for another two weeks. Its
members were then arrested and, together with other Nazi
leaders, brought before the International Military Tribunal in
Nuremberg and tried for crimes against peace and humanity.

On 5 June, the victorious powers – the United States, the United
Kingdom, the Soviet Union, and France – assumed supreme
authority in the territory of the Reich. Their main objective,
according to the London Protocol of 12 September 1944 and
subsequent agreements, was to exercise total control over
Germany. This policy rested on dividing the country into
three zones of occupation and Berlin, the capital, into three
sectors; there was to be an Allied Control Council composed
of the three commanders-in-chief.

At the conference held in Yalta (Crimea) in February 1945, the
Big Three decided that France should be involved as the
fourth controlling power and allocated its own occupation
zone. Territorial reparations were agreed for Poland to the
detriment of Germany; there was initially dissent as to the exact borders to be adopted. The three powers agreed on a "Declaration on liberated Europe" which foresaw establishing

From the l.:
Winston
Churchill
(Gt. Britain),
Franklin D.
Roosevelt
(USA), Joseph
Stalin (USSR)
at the Yalta
Conference

transitional governments in the countries in eastern Central Europe "on a broad democratic basis" and free elections soon thereafter; in the years that followed, the Soviet Union did not honour this declaration of intent, as it wished to create around it a cordon sanitaire of states friendly to the Soviet Union. The agenda of sub-dividing Germany into several states, initially voiced by Stalin in 1941, was again fundamentally confirmed, without a consensus being reached on how it should be implemented in practical terms. In the months that followed, first the Soviet Union distanced itself from this plan for political and economic reasons, and the Western Allies then followed suit, as they were interested in the medium term in having a stable Germany as the core of a Europe strongly in need of stability. U.S. President Roosevelt therefore quickly discarded the notorious Morgenthau Plan September 1944), which had initially been approved and would have reduced Germany to an agricultural country, divided into a north German and a south German state.

Differences between the victorious powers continued to grow, however. As a consequence, the original aim of the Potsdam Conference (17 July to 2 August 1945), namely the creation of a new postwar order in Europe, receded into the background. The four powers were only able to agree on the matters of denazification, demilitarization, economic decentralization and the re-education of the Germans along democratic lines, although the actual substance to the concept remained contentious. The Western powers also gave their fateful consent to the expulsion of Germans from the eastern German territories that had been placed under Polish administration as well as from northeastern Prussia, Hungary and Czechoslovakia.

The West had insisted that the transfer be carried out in a "humane" fashion, but in blatant contrast to this in the following years some 12 million Germans were brutally expelled. They were made to suffer both for Germany's war crimes and for the shift in Poland's western border as a result of the Soviet Union's occupation of Königsberg and eastern Poland. A minimum consensus was at least reached in the form of an agreement to treat Germany as an economic entity and in the medium term to establish central administrations for Germany as a whole. This resolution in fact had no effect, as the different developments in the zones occupied by the Soviet Union and the Western Allies respectively as well as the handling of the reparations issue to all intents and purposes excluded any uniform arrangement.

The question of reparations was of crucial importance specifically for the Soviet Union, which had suffered substantially from the German invasion. Moscow demanded that Germany be made to make overall reparations payments – above all by disassembling plant and by contributions from ongoing production – of USD 20 billion, of which USD 10 billion should go to the USSR. The solution that was finally devised entailed each of the victorious powers drawing the reparations due to it from the zone it respectively occupied and, in addition, the USSR was to receive 25 percent of the plant and equipment to be removed from the Western zones. This move contributed to the economic division of Germany. In actual fact, according to Western calculations, the SOZ/GDR made reparations and occupation payments to the Soviet Union of a total of US$ 14 billion, in other words far more than the USSR had originally demanded from Germany as a whole.

With the arrangement for reparations and by linking the four zones to different political and economic systems Germany became the country where the Cold War manifested itself most of all it came to be divided by the front line in that bellicose period. By this time, the task of establishing German political parties and administrative authorities had begun in the individual zones of occupation. This happened very quickly in the Soviet zone,where it was subject to rigid control, with the result that even before the end of 1945 parties and several central administrative bodies had been formed. At the same time, with the assistance of the German Commu-

Potsdam Conference: July 17 – Aug. 2, 1945; from the l.: Clement Attlee (Gt. Britain), Harry Truman (USA), Joseph Stalin (USSR)

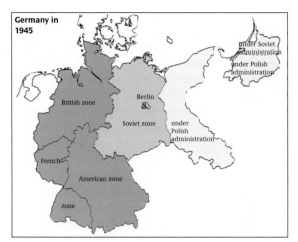

Germany in 1945

— Germany within the borders of 1937

Western zones and Western sectors of Berlin
(Federal Republic of Germany from 1949)

Soviet zone and Eastern sector of Berlin
(German Democratic Republic from 1949)

German eastern territories under Polish or Soviet administration

nist Party leadership, which had returned from exile in Moscow, the Soviet occupying power pushed ahead with political and social change. Termed an "anti-fascist democratic upheaval", this concentrated all key political and social functions in the hands of the German communists and persons they trusted (Ulbricht: "It must look democratic, but everything must be in our hands.")

In the three Western zones the development of a political system was a bottom-up process, that is to say, political parties were permitted only at the local level at first, then at the state level after the Länder had been created. Only later were they allowed to form associations at the zonal level. Zonal administrative structures were materializing very slowly, and as the destroyed country's material needs could only be overcome by means of generous planning across state and zonal borders, and as the Four Powers' administration was not functioning, the United States and the United Kingdom decided in 1947 to merge their zones economically into what was known as the bizone.

The divergence in the systems of government in East and West as well as the very different approaches to reparations in the individual zones of occupation were an obstacle to the introduction of uniform financial, fiscal, raw materials and production policy throughout Germany and led to the regions developing in very different ways. France was not interested in a common economic administration (bizone/trizone) at first. Stalin wanted to have a say in control of the Ruhr region but at the same time sealed off the Soviet-occupied zone. The Western powers were powerless to prevent the arbitrary Soviet measures in the eastern part of Four-Zonal Germany, such as the compulsory merger of the German Communist Party (KPD) and the Social Democratic Party (SPD) to form the Socialist Unity Party (SED) in April 1946. Another such measure was to eliminate the effective powers of all the other parties within the block of parties led by the communists.

In view of the intensifying conversion of the Soviet zone of occupation into a communist dictatorship, the British and Americans began to work harder to promote the development and merger of their own zones. The Western powers were intent on alleviating misery and need in the Western zones and on paving the way for the creation of a democratic state structure based on freedom.

An enemy becomes a partner. With his famous speech in Stuttgart on 6 September 1946, U.S. Secretary of State Byrnes had firmly presented the change in approach. Stalin's occupation of Poland and the redrawing of that country's borders were described as merely temporary measures. As Byrnes saw it, the military role of the Western Allies in western Germany had therefore changed from one of occupation and control to one of protection. Finally, at the initiative of the United Kingdom and the United States and after initial French resist-

1948-9: West Berlin received its supplies by air for 462 days (the "Berlin Air Lift")

ance, a trizone was established as a unified Western economic area. The threat of another Soviet advance westwards following the coup d'état in Prague on 25 February 1948 induced the French to fall into line. Byrnes' views were reflected first in the Brussels Pact of 17 March 1948 and ultimately in the North Atlantic Treaty of 4 April 1949.

For such an organization to work, western Germany had to have a coherent political and economic system. Thus, at the Six-Power Conference in London (23 February to 3 March and 20 April to 1 June 1948), which was attended for the first time by the Benelux countries, France, the United Kingdom and the United States agreed that the Western zones of occupation should have a common political structure.

At the 82nd meeting of the Allied Control Council on 20 March 1948, the Soviet representative, Marshal Sokolovski, asked for information on the London Conference. When his Western colleagues answered evasively, Sokolovski walked out, never to return.

While the Western powers were still finalizing their recommendations for a constituent assembly to be convened by the western German minister-presidents (the heads of government of the states), Stalin used the introduction of the Deutsche Mark (DM) in the west (currency reform of 20 June 1948) as a pretext for imposing a blockade on Berlin (West) with the aim of annexing it to the Soviet-occupied zone. During the night of 23 June 1948, all land routes between the Western zones and Berlin (West) were closed. Supplies of energy and food from the Eastern sector of Berlin and the Soviet-occupied zone were discontinued. Until 12 May 1949, Berlin (West) was kept supplied by an Allied airlift. This visible solidarity with Berlin (West) as a Western outpost, together with America's demonstration of strength, furthered a willingness in western Germany to cooperate with the occupying powers.

The founding of the Federal Republic of Germany. Western Germany had already begun receiving American foreign aid in 1946 (GARIOA Program), but it was the program to combat "hunger, poverty, despair and chaos" (the Marshall Plan) that provided the crucial stimulus for western Germany's economic recovery (USD 1.4 billion between 1948 and 1952). While in the Soviet-occupied zone the process of transferring industry to public ownership continued, the system Alfred Müller-Armack in 1947 termed the "social market economy" system continued to gain ground in the west with the currency reform. The new economic order was intended to prevent, on the one hand, what Walter Eucken termed the "stagnation of capitalism" and, on the other, a centrally planned economy which would be a hindrance to creativity and initiative. This economic goal was supplemented by the constitutional and welfare-state principles embodied in the Basic Law and by the federal structure of the Federal Republic of Germany. The newly drafted constitution was deliberately termed the "Basic Law" in order to emphasize its provisional character. The idea was that a definitive constitution should only be adopted after Germany's had been reunited (Art. 146 of the Basic Law). This was also outlined in the pledge to the goal of German Unity in the Preamble to the Basic Law (Art. 23, old version of the Basic Law). Upon its formal proclamation by the Parliamentary Council in Bonn, the Basic Law entered into force on 23 May 1949.

The Basic Law naturally included many of the intentions of the Western occupying powers, who, on 1 July 1948 (Frankfurt Documents) had instructed the western German minister-presidents to draw up a constitution. But the document also reflects past experience with the Weimar Republic and the unjust Nazi state. The constitutional convention at Herrenchiemsee (10-23 August 1948) and the Parliamentary Council which met in Bonn on 1 September 1948 (65 delegates of the state parliaments) incorporated into the Basic Law provisions requiring future governments, parties and other political groupings to uphold democratic-constitutional principles.

Ever since, all attempts to do away with the free, democratic constitutional order or to replace it with a rightwing or left-wing dictatorship can be treated as criminal offenses, and the organizations concerned can be banned. As a direct response to past experiences under the Nazi dictatorship, the Basic Law contained commitments to a basic order which rested on fundamental inviolable free, democratic, constitutional and welfare-state principles (Art. 1ff, 20, and 79 of the Basic Law) and to the goal of a united Europe (Preamble, Art. 24, Art. 23, new version).

Konrad Adenauer, President of the Parliamentary Council, approves the Basic Law on May 23, 1949

In the post-1945 period, most of the "politicians of the Federal Republic's first hour" had suffered at the hands of the Nazis. These men and women now set about rebuilding Germany on the democratic traditions of 1848-9 and 1919 and in the spirit of the "revolt of the conscience" of 20 July 1944. All of them personified in the eyes of the world the "other Germany" and won the respect of the occupying powers. They included the first Federal President Theodor Heuss (FDP), the first Federal Chancellor Konrad Adenauer (CDU) and Economics Minister Ludwig Erhard (CDU), the "father" of the "economic miracle", as well as the outstanding leaders of the SPD opposition such as Kurt Schumacher, Erich Ollenhauer, or Carlo Schmid. It was they who gave the new party system in western Germany its unmistakable shape. Gradually, German involvement and political influence increased (Occupation Statute, Petersberg Protocol, GATT membership, accession to the European Coal and Steel Community).

In July 1951, the United Kingdom, France and the United States declared that the state-of-war with Germany was terminated. The Soviet Union did the same in January 1955. In the Soviet Occupation Zone on 7 October 1949 a separate state had been declared, named the "German Democratic Republic". This was formally a reaction to the foundation of the Federal Republic, although in factual terms it had been long since prepared by the fundamental changes initiated in the Soviet Occupation Zone and the constitution devised there – initially with a thrust geared to Germany as a whole. This state followed the pattern of the "people's democracies" set up as Soviet protectorates in east central and southeast European states – with elections based on "Unity" lists of candidates and strict control and direction of government and society by the Socialist Unity Party. As of 1952, the foundation of socialism (officially) commenced, and the border to the Federal Republic was simultaneously closed.

Uprising in East Germany on June 17, 1953: workers demonstrate in front of the Brandenburg Gate

As a result of the East-West conflict, two states had arisen in Germany, each of which claimed to be the core and model for a single united Germany that was to be created in the future. The growing number of refugees fleeing the Soviet Occupation Zone/GDR and the June Uprising of 1953 showed, however, that the SED state did not rest on the support of the great majority of the population and its external stability depended above all on Soviet hegemony, which guaranteed its existence. This fact essentially remained unchanged until 1989.

Security through integration with the West and European reconciliation. In the eyes of Federal Chancellor Konrad Adenauer, who personally played a strong part in defining Germany's domestic and foreign policy until 1963, ("Chancellor's Democracy"), securing the Federal Republic against the extension of Soviet power, allying the country with the West's ethical and defence community, and reunification in peace and freedom were the foremost political objectives. Accordingly, the repeal of the Occupation Statute on 5 May 1955 coincided with the Federal Republic joining NATO. At the same time, efforts to further develop the European Communities were intensified (Treaties of Rome, 1957). On joining NATO, the Federal Republic and the three Western Occupying Powers concluded the "German Treaty"; according to Art. 7 thereof, the parties to the treaty commit themselves to jointly bringing peaceful means to bear to achieve the goal of a united free constitutional German state integrated into Europe.

Adenauer's distrust of Moscow was so deep-rooted that in 1952 he affirmed the Western powers in their rejection of Stalin's "March Note". In it, Stalin had offered to reunite Germany as a neutral country as far as the Oder-Neisse line as a "democratic and freedom-loving" country with neutral status. This offer was too unclear as to warrant placing the upcoming integration of the Federal Republic into the West at risk. The suspicion seemed only too justified when, on 17 June 1953, the people's uprising in the GDR in protest against their lack of freedom and against what Hans Mayer has termed the "unbearable output norms" imposed by the regime was put down by Soviet tanks. It was, however, also evident that without Moscow little progress could be made on the German question. Thus for sober raison d'etat it was expedient to establish diplomatic relations with the Soviet Union as the largest power in Europe.

The crushing of the popular revolt in Hungary by Soviet troops in November 1956, as well as the "Sputnik shock" (4 October 1957), signaled a considerable growth of Soviet power. This was also expressed in further compulsory measures carried out in the process of setting up a socialist system in the GDR but above all in the Berlin ultimatum issued by Stalin's successor, Nikita Khrushchev, who demanded that the Western Allies leave Berlin (West) within six months.

The Western powers admittedly rejected the ultimatum, but under President Eisenhower (Khrushchev visited the United States in 1959) and his successor John F. Kennedy they indicated a certain willingness to concede some of the Soviet Union's demands. However, the solution to the crisis served to further rigidify the status quo. The Soviet Union allowed the GDR government to erect barricades between the eastern section of Berlin and the western section and surrounding areas, and it was not long before these barriers were replaced by the Berlin Wall.

At the same time, the border between the two Germanies was increasingly sealed tight (13 August 1961). The Soviet leadership thus respected the "three essentials" Kennedy had specified (freedom of access, presence of the Western Allies and

The Treaty of Rome is signed on March 25, 1957

security of West Berlin), but the barriers, death strips and repression prevented the people from ever "voting with their feet" against the GDR regime. Prior to the building of the Wall, almost three million people had left the GDR. In July 1961 alone, more than 30,000 had fled.

Despite the building of the Wall and the tensions triggered by the Bay-of-Pigs Crisis of 1962, the two superpowers continued to seek a better understanding – they had to on account of the nuclear stalemate. Bonn therefore had no option but to look for other ways by which it could strengthen joint Western rejection of the Soviet pressure in Berlin, adapt to the trend toward detente in the East-West conflict, and yet prevent divided Germany becoming a permanent fixture created by the victorious powers in the Second World War. The signing of the Elysée Treaty in January 1963 marked the culmination of the process of Franco-German reconciliation. This treaty laid the foundations for better understanding between the people of both countries and for close cooperation in many areas.

As the Federal Republic became increasingly integrated into the Western community, the atmosphere also began to improve in the relationship with Eastern Europe. In December 1963, at a ministerial meeting in Athens, NATO had signaled this change with its new strategy of "flexible response" in place of that of massive retaliation.

In an attempt to soften the rigid East-West relationship, the Federal Republic tried to improve contacts at least with the Soviet Union's satellite countries. Without officially abandoning the Hallstein Doctrine as a brake against diplomatic recognition of the GDR – Bonn's policy of refusing to establish diplomatic relations with any country that maintained or estab-

President Kennedy, Willy Brandt, Lord Mayor of Berlin, and Chancellor Adenauer during Kennedy's visit to Berlin in March 1963

Israeli Prime Minister Ben Gurion and Chancellor Adenauer on March 14, 1960 in New York

lished diplomatic relations with the GDR – in order to prevent diplomatic recognition of the GDR and thus the permanence of Germany's division, during his final years as chancellor Adenauer and then his successors, Ludwig Erhard and Kurt Georg Kiesinger, tried to lock into efforts to forge East-West detente (in 1966 the Erhard Government offered to waive the resort to force in its "Peace Note", and took its cue from the "European Peace Order" devised by the Grand Coalition 1966-9). They were prompted to do so not least by the new approach adopted by the SPD opposition, which promoted Egon Bahr's formula of "change through rapprochement" (15 July 1963).

In the West, there were increasing efforts to merge the European Coal and Steel Community (ECSC), the European Atomic Energy Community (EURATOM) and the European Economic Community (EEC) into one European Community (EC; both based on the Treaty of Rome of 25 March 1957). The establishment of diplomatic relations with Israel despite pan-Arab protests was a major step in the Federal Republic's policy of rapprochement. At the beginning of 1967, Bonn established diplomatic relations with Romania, and in June 1967 the Federal Republic and Czechoslovakia opened trade missions in their respective capitals. The Harmel Report of December 1967 at least prepared the way for further steps towards détente by laying down the Western Alliance's twofold aim of maintaining its military strength while at the same time being ready to talk to the Eastern bloc. At the same time, the NATO partners specified that a European Peace Order presumed that the division of Germany would be revoked.

In addition to the policy of reconciliation with Germany's European neighbors and its integration into the Western community, Adenauer had attached special importance to restitution for the Jews. Six million Jews had been systematically exterminated by the National Socialists. It was not least the close personal relationship between the Federal Republic's first Chancellor and Israel's first Prime Minister David Ben-Gurion which fostered the process of reconciliation between the Jews and the West Germans. Addressing parliament in 1961, Adenauer stressed that the Federal Republic could only prove that the Germans had broken completely with their National Socialist past by making material restitution as well.

As early as 1952, the first agreement had been signed in Luxembourg. It provided for assistance for the integration of Jewish refugees in Israel. Of the total sum of about DM 90 billion provided for restitution purposes, roughly one third went to Israel and Jewish organizations, and especially to the Jewish Claims Conference, a hardship fund which helped Jews all over the world who had been persecuted by the National Socialists. However, diplomatic relations between Israel and the Federal Republic of Germany were not established until 1965.

German-German dialogue in spite of the GDR's demarcation of its borders. In spite of the GDR's continuing efforts to cut itself off completely from the West (e.g. by requiring passports and visas for persons in transit between the Federal Republic and Berlin (West)) and in spite of the Warsaw Pact's crushing of attempted reforms in Czechoslovakia (the so-called Prague Spring) in 1968, efforts to bring about detente also persisted in Germany. In April 1969, Bonn said it was ready to enter into agreements with the GDR below the level of international recognition.

On 21 October 1969, the new government of Social Democrats and Liberals went a decisive step further – namely as far as recognizing the GDR as a second German state, although not accepting its recognition under international law as a foreign country.

A few months previously (5 March 1969), Gustav Heinemann, who even in Adenauer's day had been a strong advocate of East-West rapprochement, had been elected Federal President. Willy Brandt, who had played an active part in the resistance against the Hitler dictatorship, was now head of a Federal Government which directed its energies to the construction of a peaceful order throughout Europe. The international constellation was favorable. Moscow and Washington were negotiating on the limitation of strategic arms (SALT), and NATO proposed negotiations on mutual and balanced force reductions (MBFR). On 28 November 1969, the Federal Republic became a party to the Treaty on the Non-proliferation of Nuclear Weapons (NPT). Following the turbulence experienced by its predecessor, the so-called grand coalition government (Vietnam conflict, Auschwitz trials, ExtraParliamentary Opposition and student revolts), the new cabinet, by embarking on its "Ostpolitik", placed itself under considerable pressure for their consensus policy to produce results, whereby the focus was initially necessarily on reaching agreement on the hegemony of the Eastern bloc.

While talks on a non-aggression agreement were being conducted in Moscow and Warsaw, Bonn and Berlin (East), too, explored the possibilities of improving relations. On 19 March 1970, the heads of government of the two German states, Willy Brandt and Willi Stoph, met for the first time in Erfurt. This was followed by another meeting on 21 May 1970 in Kassel.

On 12 August 1970, a treaty on the renunciation of force and recognition of the status quo was signed in Moscow. Both sides proclaimed that they had no territorial claims against "anyone". Part of the treaty was the "Letter on German unity", later appended to the Inner-German Basic Treaty, in which the Federal Government declared that the treaty did not contradict its political goal of endeavoring to bring about peace in Europe by the German people re-achieving its unity in a process of free self-determination.

On 7 December of that year the Treaty of Warsaw was signed, which reaffirmed the inviolability of the existing border (the Oder-Neisse line). Warsaw and Bonn, too, gave an assurance that they had no territorial claims against one another and declared their intention of improving mutual cooperation. In

A historical moment: Chancellor Brandt before the Monument to the Warsaw Ghetto (Dec. 1970)

an "information" document on humanitarian measures, Warsaw agreed to the transfer of ethnic Germans from Poland and the reunion of separated families by the Red Cross.

In exchange, the Soviet negotiators agreed in the treaty to the Four Powers Agreement on Berlin which essentially confirmed the existing state of the city. Accordingly, the Western sectors of Berlin were not a constituent part of the Federal Republic but Bonn was entitled to represent Berlin in international treaties. Likewise, the "ties" between Berlin (West) and the Federal Republic were to be improved and relations between Berlin (East)/GDR and Berlin (West) developed.

After a failed vote of no confidence against Brandt, the German Bundestag ratified the treaties with the Soviet Union and Poland on 17 May 1972. Most CDU/CSU members of parliament abstained. The Bundestag, in an "interpretative resolution", declared that the treaties did not conflict with the aim of restoring German unity by peaceful means.

The series of treaties with Eastern Europe was rounded out by a Treaty on the Basis of Relations (Basic Treaty) between the two German states which had been preceded by talks and negotiations since June 1972. After Willy Brandt's reelection as Chancellor on 14 December 1972, the way was clear for the signing of the Treaty in December. Both sides undertook not to threaten or use force against one another and to respect each other's independence. The inviolability of the border between the two German states was also endorsed.

Furthermore, the two sides expressed their willingness to resolve humanitarian problems in a practical manner. It was agreed that, owing to the special nature of their relationship, they would establish "missions" in their respective capitals instead of the usual embassies. The Federal Constitutional Court, to which the State Government of Bavaria had appealed, confirmed that the treaty was in conformity with the constitution when duly interpreted: the Federal Republic was legally identical but only in part territorially identical with the "German Reich", which had not ceased to exist in legal terms. The express commitment to reunification in the Basic Law and the rights of reservation the Four Powers held over Germany as a whole remained unaffected by the treaty. The GDR could not be considered a foreign country, but only part of the home country.

In 1973, the Treaty of Prague between Czechoslovakia and the Federal Republic was signed. It declared the Munich Agreement of 1938 to be null and void "in accordance with this Treaty". The two sides also agreed that their borders were inviolable and that they would therefore not use force against one another.

While negotiations were going on in Vienna on mutual and balanced force reductions (MBFR), the Soviet Union and the United States completed an agreement designed to limit strategic nuclear weapons, and 35 countries attended the Conference on Security and Cooperation in Europe (CSCE) in Helsinki, little change occurred in the relationship between the Federal Republic and the GDR. Nonetheless, Chancellor Helmut Schmidt, too, strived to continue the policy of developing a balanced relationship. On 16 May 1974, he had succeeded Willy Brandt, who had resigned when one of his aides, Günther Guillaume, was unmasked as a GDR spy.

The Final Act of the CSCE (Helsinki, 1975), which called for greater freedom of movement in transboundary traffic and more respect for human and civil rights, came to form one of the grounds for appeal by domestic resistance groups opposing the ossified regimes of Central and Eastern Europe. For the sake of the people in the GDR, the Federal Republic resolutely pursued its efforts to improve relations.

Thus in 1978 an agreement was reached to build an autobahn from Berlin to Hamburg and to repair the transit waterways to Berlin (West), the greater part of the cost being borne by the Federal Republic. The Federal Government also continued to buy the release of political prisoners from the GDR. Bonn ultimately paid some DM 3.4 billion to obtain the release of 33,755 people and to have 250,000 families reunited.

Missiles versus détente. Whereas the process of European integration continued steadily in the West, the transition from the 1970s, the decade of détente, to the 1980s was marked by fresh conflicts in Eastern Europe. The Soviet invasion of Afghanistan, the imposition of martial law in Poland and the emplacement of new intermediate-range missiles (SS-20) in the Soviet Union worsened the climate of East-West relations.

NATO reacted to this serious upset of the balance of security by deciding that it, too, would introduce new missiles as from

1983. But at the same time it proposed arms control negotiations to the Soviet Union. This was the "two-track" decision. In protest at the invasion of Afghanistan, the United States, the United Kingdom, Canada, Norway and the Federal Republic refused to take part in the Moscow Summer Olympics (1980).

The United States tried a new initiative, the "zero" solution, by which the Soviet Union would remove its intermediate-range missiles while NATO would promise not to deploy its Pershing II and the new cruise missiles.

While Chancellor Schmidt insisted on the missile modernization alternative so as not to leave any gaps in the Western security shield, he at the same time tried to minimize the damage to the German-German relationship. Despite GDR leader Erich Honecker's demand for recognition of a separate GDR citizenship and for the "Permanent Missions" to be upgraded to the status of full-fledged embassies (i.e. elimination of the symbols of the special German-German relationship), and despite the drastic increase by the GDR government in the minimum daily exchange requirement for visitors from the West, Schmidt visited the GDR – but without getting any substantial concessions from Honecker. The regime's hardening ideological stance was not least a reaction to the growing protest movements in neighboring Poland, where more and more people were demanding economic reform, freedom and disarmament.

But the missile question was not only problematical in the East. In Bonn the FDP decided to change its tack on economic policy and began to break away from the coalition. Grass-roots SPD followers, largely because of pressure from the peace movement and some union factions, withdrew their support from Schmidt for adhering to the NATO two-track decision. As a result, Helmut Kohl replaced him as Chancellor at the head of a CDU/CSU-FDP coalition after a constructive vote of no confidence on 1 October 1982. The new Chancellor continued the Federal Government's security policy and close co-operation with Paris and Washington with a view to uniting Europe within a stable and secure framework. In spite of massive peace demonstrations, Helmut Kohl's government stood firm: In November 1983 the German Bundestag agreed to the deployment of the new missiles. The credibility of the

Western Alliance was thus strengthened and a crisis within NATO averted.

A new dialogue on disarmament between the superpowers began as early as the mid-1980s. It was soon possible for the missiles which had just been deployed in the Federal Republic to be removed once again.

From the decline of the GDR to German unity. The German Democratic Republic, which had been founded on 7 October 1949, was a product of the Soviet Union. It was from the outset a communist dictatorship built on the foundations of the rule of the Socialist Unity Party (SED) and the presence of the Red Army. The command economy, the secret police, the all-powerful SED and strict censorship increasingly alienated the people and the regime. However, very inexpensive housing, health care and social services – made possible by government price-fixing and subsidies – gave this self-contained system that flexibility which enabled numerous lifestyles to be adopted in niche area. Major successes by the GDR on the international sports stage provided compensation as well as satisfaction for the "working people" who, despite the extremely high reparations payments to the Soviets had soon staked the GDR's claim within the Eastern bloc to being the country with the highest industrial output and the highest standard of living.

In spite of all the propaganda, it became increasingly clear to the people that GDR's original intention of overtaking the Federal Republic economically would remain a dream. Depleted resources and loss of productivity as a consequence of central planning forced the SED regime to water down its promises. It increasingly had to raise large loans in the West. Improvisation became the order of the day with regard to consumer goods. The quality of life and infrastructure (housing, transport, environment) thus deteriorated.

A comprehensive spy network kept close watch on everyone, and the system's incessant propaganda and mendacious appeals for solidarity made the claim about the leadership role of "the working class and their Marxist-Leninist party" (Article 1 of the GDR constitution) sound like hollow rhetoric, especially to the young generation. The people began to demand a say in running their own lives, more individual freedom, and more and better consumer goods.

As overall inner-German diplomatic relations deteriorated as a result of the quarrel over the deployment of intermediate-range missiles, the proposed Strategic Defense Initiative (SDI, a space-based defensive umbrella proposed by the Americans), and the GDR's continued aggravation of the West (by building a second wall at the Brandenburg Gate, and impeding traffic in the air corridors to Berlin), the people of the GDR themselves started to put pressure on their own leadership. For example, from the beginning of 1985 more and more GDR citizens who had entered the Federal Republic's mission in Berlin (East) refused to leave it until they had been given definitive permission to leave for the West. In order to make certain the situation for GDR citizens eased, the Federal Republic on several occasion helped secure large bank loans for the GDR.

Since early 1985, an ever greater number of people flocked to the Federal Republic's diplomatic mission in Berlin (East) and to the German embassies in Prague and Warsaw.

In 1986, the new General Secretary of the Soviet Communist Party, Mikhail Gorbachev, declared that his main political objective was to eliminate nuclear weapons by the end of the century. His meetings with U.S. President Reagan in Geneva and Reykjavik, the Conference on Confidence- and Security-Building Measures and Disarmament in Europe (CDE) held in Stockholm and the preparations for negotiations on the reduction of conventional forces in Europe indicated a new readiness for dialogue between East and West. This new approach was conducive to agreements between the two German states on cultural, educational and scientific cooperation.

But the SED regime did not want to be caught up in the zest of Gorbachev's "perestroika" and "glasnost". The extent to which the GDR leaders ignored the expectations of their own people was shown by the protest demonstrations in Berlin (East) on 13 August, the anniversary of the building of the Wall. Chancellor Helmut Kohl spoke out against the continuation of Germany's division when, during Honecker's working visit to Bonn in 1987, he said: "We respect the present borders but we want to overcome the country's division by peaceful means through a process of mutual understanding. We have a joint responsibility for preserving the vital foundations of our nation."

One step towards disarmament was the INF Treaty signed by Reagan and Gorbachev. Under the terms of that accord, all U.S. and Soviet missiles with a range of 500 to 5,000 kilometers deployed in Europe had to be withdrawn and destroyed. In this context, the Federal Republic pledged to decommission its 72 Pershing IA missiles.

The general climate of détente led to increasing demands for greater freedom and reform in the GDR. During demonstrations in Berlin (East) in early 1988, 120 supporters of the peace movement known as "the Church from Below" were arrested. Prayers were said for them in the Gethsemane Church. Over 2,000 people attended the service, and a fortnight later their number had swollen to 4,000. In Dresden, the police broke up a demonstration for human rights, free speech and freedom of the press.

In September 1989 – after preparatory steps initiated as early as May – Hungary opened its border, thus permitting thousands of people from the GDR to pass through to Austria and from there into the Federal Republic. This breach of Warsaw Pact discipline encouraged ever more people in the GDR to take to the streets in protest. They were able to take their cue from the spreading opposition movement, which, after very modest beginnings, had formed since the end of the 1970s primarily under the protection of churches and which had become ever more courageous as of the mid-1980s. When the GDR leaders celebrated the 40th anniversary of the founding of the GDR with great pomp and circumstance at the beginning of October 1989, mass demonstrations were held, primarily in Leipzig. ("We are the people!") It became clear that the GDR leadership under Honecker was not receiving any support from the Soviet Union.

Chancellor Kohl and Foreign Minister Genscher with General Secretary Gorbachov in the Caucasus (July 1990)

In a last-ditch effort to preserve the underlying pillars of the SED regime, Erich Honecker was forced to resign his offices as head of state and General Secretary of the SED on 18 October 1989. He was succeeded by Egon Krenz, but the latter's promise of "change" was drowned out by the protests of the people, who did not trust him. Under the pressure of events, the Council of Ministers and the SED Politburo resigned en bloc.

The peaceful revolution seemed to paralyze the authorities. As a result, a casual and awkwardly worded announcement that travel restrictions were to be eased prompted the opening of the border crossings in Berlin on the evening of 9 November 1989, ushering in a night of indescribable joy.

The upheaval in the GDR opened up the opportunity for Germany's reunification after a wait of decades. Helmut Kohl therefore published a ten-point program on 28 November 1989 which envisaged a path to a confederal reunified Germany entailing several stages – starting with current economic aid on the condition that there was a fundamental change in political and economic system, a contractual community, confederal structures.

On 15 January 1990, 150,000 people demonstrated in Leipzig, chanting "Germany – united Fatherland". The people in the GDR distrusted their new government, which was headed by Hans Modrow. They became increasingly drawn to the West, and the process of destabilization in the GDR accelerated rapidly. But still Gorbachev held back, particularly since Poland and Hungary were escaping Moscow's grasp, Romania's Nicolae Ceausescu had been overthrown in December 1989, and the GDR's departure from the Warsaw Pact would inevitably upset the balance of power. From Western quarters, too, came exhortations to the Germans to "take account of the legitimate concerns of neighboring countries" (U.S. Secretary of State James Baker, speaking in Berlin) as they pursued national unity. The U.S. government emphatically supported the policy of re-unification to the extent that Germany's national borders were not changed and that Germany remained a member of the Atlantic alliance and, in the case of the eastern part of the country, became part of NATO.

On 18 March 1990, the first free elections in 40 years were held in the GDR. Lothar de Maizière became Prime Minister, heading a grand coalition made up of the CDU, DSU, DA, SPD and FDP. The Bonn government agreed a timetable with this new government for monetary, economic and social union with effect from 1 July 1990, it having become palpably clear that the GDR had no economic basis on which to continue alone and that the majority of the people in the GDR wanted accession to the Federal Republic. In August 1990, the Volkskammer (the GDR parliament) voted in favor of accession as soon as possible, and on 31 August GDR State Secretary Günter Krause and Federal Minister of the Interior Wolfgang Schäuble finally signed the "Unification Treaty". Thus, on 3 October 1990, the German Democratic Republic officially acceded to the Federal Republic in accordance with Article 23 of the Basic Law. The – newly reestablished – GDR states of Brandenburg, Mecklenburg-Western Pomerania, Saxony, Saxony-Anhalt and Thuringia became states (Länder) of the Federal Republic of Germany. Berlin was made the capital and the Basic Law, after appropriate amendments, entered into force in the territory of the former GDR as well.

The road to unity had been opened by General Secretary Mikhail Gorbachev, who had given his approval after talks with Chancellor Helmut Kohl and Foreign Minister Hans-Dietrich Genscher in Moscow and in the Caucasus in July 1990. He did so on the condition that the Federal Republic would forgo the use of ABC weapons and reduce its standing armed forces to 370,000, and that NATO's military organization would not be extended to GDR territory as long as Soviet forces remained stationed there. It was also agreed that the Soviet troops would be withdrawn from eastern Germany by the end of 1994.

Federal Minister of the Interior Schäuble and East German Secretary of State Krause sign the Unification Treaty on Aug. 31, 1990

Gorbachev's agreement cleared the way for signature of the so-
called Two-plus-Four Treaty in September 1990. Within that
framework the Soviet Union, the United States, France and
the United Kingdom as well as the representatives of the two
German states confirmed the unification of Germany consisting of the territories of the former GDR, the Federal Republic
and Berlin. Germany's external borders were recognized as
definitive. Bonn and Warsaw concluded a separate treaty to
take account of Poland's special security needs in the light of
history. Both agreed to respect each other's territorial integri-
ty and sovereignty.

The ratification of the Unification Treaty and the Two-plus-Four
Treaty marked the termination of the rights and responsibilities of the four victorious powers "with respect to Berlin and
Germany as a whole". Germany thus regained the complete
sovereignty over its internal and external affairs which it had
lost after the fall of the National Socialist dictatorship.

In Dec. 1990,
thousands
of people
celebrated
German
Unification on
both sides of
the Branden-
burg Gate

Setting the stage for the future. Following the restoration of German unity and the massive political changes which occurred in the wake of the collapse of the communist states in Eastern Europe, Germany and its partners faced formidable challenges. Although considerable progress has been made, major tasks still lie ahead.

— The recovery process in eastern Germany needs to be accelerated and the internal unity of Germany completed.

— The European Union must be further developed, deepened and enlarged.

— A global structure promoting peace and security must be established and maintained.

National, European and global responsibilities are inseparably intertwined. Recovery and consolidation in eastern Germany cannot take place unless the states there are closely tied into the process of European integration. Europe cannot retain its new structure without opening itself up to the reformist states in Central and Eastern Europe. Economically as well as politically, the states of eastern Central Europe must be led step by step towards membership of the joint European and Atlantic organizations. In this spirit, a Partnership and Cooperation Agreement was signed between the European Union and Russia in Corfu on 24 June 1994. The extensive aid provided by the Federal Government to Russia is in keeping both with its vital interest in the success of the democratic transformation process and with the newly shared political values. Since 1989, Germany's financial contributions and existing obligations to the former Soviet Union and the present CIS states have totaled more than DM 90 billion. The greater part of the German support for the political and economic reform process in the CIS states has consisted of the credit guarantees and sureties of the Hermes-Export-Kreditversicherung (export credit insurance scheme) amounting to DM 47.1 billion.

Despite drastic cuts in public spending, the Federal Republic will continue to stand by its financial commitment to the developing countries as well in the coming years. It helps them to help themselves in order to improve the economic, social and political conditions experienced by the people living there. Respect for human rights, participation of the people in the political process, the guarantee of the rule of law, the intro-

duction of a socially oriented market economy, and the development orientation of government action in the recipient
countries are important criteria used by the Federal Government in the giving of development aid.

The fact that the Federal Republic of Germany ranks third
among contributors to the United Nations (9.857 percent of
the U.N. budget) and pays 21.2 percent of the NATO budget
and 16.75 percent of the WEU budget emphasizes the ongoing willingness of all the Federal Governments to date to contribute to stability and the maintenance of peace within a bilateral and multilateral framework.

At the request of the Secretary-General of the United Nations, a
transport unit of the Bundeswehr took part for the first time
in a United Nations blue helmet operation in the summer of
1993 in "pacified areas" of Somalia. This operation was the
subject of controversial political discussion in Germany. Then,
in July 1994, the Federal Constitutional Court ruled that German armed forces could participate in operations within the
framework of NATO or WEU activities in support of the implementation of resolutions of the United Nations Security
Council. According to the judgment of the Court, the same
applies to the participation of German armed forces in United Nations peacekeeping troops. On 6 December 1995, the
German Bundestag voted by a large majority to approve the
mission of 4,000 Bundeswehr soldiers within the framework
of the U.N. operations in Bosnia. At the beginning of 1997,
the German Minister of Defence, with the approval of the
German Bundestag, placed 3,000 Bundeswehr soldiers under
the command of the Stabilization Force (SFOR), NATO's international peacekeeping force for Bosnia and Herzegovina.
Germany has also supplied the second largest police contingent for the International Police Task Force (IPTF) stationed
in former Yugoslavia.

Defining the European Union. The joint single market of
what were initially twelve EU states was launched at the beginning of 1993. This market united 345 million Europeans
to form the economic area with the greatest purchasing power on earth. With the exception of Switzerland, the states of
the European Free Trade Association EFTA (Austria, Sweden,
Norway, Finland, Iceland and Liechtenstein) and the European Community together formed the European Economic

The EU Summit in Maastricht (Dec. 9-10, 1991) laid the basis for European political unity

Area. The first stage for achieving monetary union began in mid-1990. During this period capital transfers among EC states were liberalized, and coordination of economic policy between the partners as well as cooperation between their central banks were intensified. In the second stage, which began in 1994, the European Monetary Institute (EMI) made preparations for the establishment of a European Central Bank (ECB) with headquarters in Frankfurt/Main.

After the Heads of State or of Government resolved on 2-3 May 1998 to initially have eleven Member States enter the third stage of Economic and Monetary Union, the European Central Bank took up its work on 1 June 1998. Consistent adherence to the convergence criteria, above all maintenance of a high degree of monetary stability and budgetary discipline, is a precondition for the success of the third stage, which began on 1 January 1999 pursuant to the Treaty on European Union. The national currencies in Euroland cease to be legal tender at the latest on 1 March 2002.

The Federal Government attached particular significance to the fact that in 1991 in Maastricht the Heads of State or of Government not only negotiated the Treaty on Economic and Monetary Union but furthermore agreed on European Union, which provides a superstructure for the further deepening of the European Community. The Treaty came into force in November 1993. In the view of the Federal Government, the deepening of the European Union must go hand in hand with its enlargement – after the accession of the former EFTA states Finland, Austria and Sweden (on 1 January 1995) also by bringing the states of Central, Eastern and Southeastern Europe closer to the EU.

With this in mind, at the EU summit which took place in Essen in December 1994 and was attended by 21 Heads of State or of Government; a concept was adopted for smoothing the path towards the European Union for the emerging Central and Eastern European market economies linked to the EU by Europe Agreements.

In recent years, thanks to the Treaty of Amsterdam and the European Councils of Cologne, Berlin, Tampere, Helsinki and Lisbon, considerable progress has been made in almost all areas (justice and domestic policy, employment policy, security and defense policy). In 1997, the European Council in Luxembourg resolved to expand the EU to include the central and eastern European countries as well as Cyprus and Malta. On March 30 1998, the expansion progress was inaugurated and covered 11 candidates: Bulgaria, Cyprus, the Czech Republic, Estonia, Hungary, Latvia, Lithuania, Poland, Romania, Slovakia, and Slovenia. In 1999, Malta was included as the 12th candidate for accession.

The Schengen Agreement has been in force since March 26, 1995. Personal identification papers are no longer checked at the borders between Austria, the Benelux countries, France, Germany, Italy, Portugal, and Spain, whereas passport and customs controls have been intensified on all remaining borders. The Treaty of Amsterdam foresees this cooperation being incorporated into the EU Treaty. The heads of state and government agreed on this treaty on June 16-7, 1997.

The EU Special Summit in Berlin in March 1999 approved "Agenda 2000", which entails a budget of DM 1.3 trillion with which the EU will prepare for the accession of new member states. At the Cologne Summit in June 1999, in line with the new concept for a joint external and security policy, the former NATO Secretary general Javier Solana was appointed EU "Foreign Minister". Plans are for the preparations for expanding the EU to be complete by 2003. At the December 1999 Helsinki Summit, Turkey was accorded the status of a candidate for membership. The Lisbon Summit (March 2000) addressed pan-European unemployment and modern communications technology. The conference of governments opened in February 2000 on institutional reform of the EU is scheduled to end in December 2000 at the European Council in Nice. This will lay the foundations for the EU to remain fully functional after its expansion.

Germany in a process of change: renewal and securing the future. Ongoing European integration, the ever closer links within the global economy, and the global need for sustainable development, such as is laid down in Agenda 21, today form the overall framework for German policymaking. Overcoming still existing economic and social differences in living conditions in eastern and western Germany remains a major challenge to the nation, and the top priority is to reduce unemployment.

"Renewing Germany" is thus the motto the Federal Government adopted when tackling the backlog of reforms which confronted it when it took office in October 1998. In less than a year it laid the foundations for innovations in government, the economy, and society as a whole in the form of a future agenda for work, growth, and social stability.

The policy turn toward securing the future generated a federal budget for 2000 which initiated the largest savings program in the history of the Federal Republic. It foresees savings of DM 30 billion, and the medium-term financial planning for the next four years envisages saving a total of more than DM 160 billion. With the tax reform enacted in July 2000 the next step has been taken in this agenda for the future. The tax reform package will ease the tax bill Germans face – in several stages, by the year 2005 tax payers will have to contribute DM 93 billion less than in 1998, without this endangering the consolidation of public-sector budgets.

On the basis of budget consolidation and the tax reform, the strategic goals of the sustained promotion of growth and employment look very realistic as early as the short- and medium-term:

– Economic growth is becoming ever stronger, a success that even independent experts attribute to the Federal Government's financial policy. The reform of corporation tax is expected to give investment activity a massive boost.

Panel discussion on "The Basic Law – The First 50 Years", in Berlin May, 1999

- Unemployment, which in 1997 averaged 4.4 million a year, has since steadily fallen. In 1998, it ran at 4.3 million, in 1999 at 4.1 million, and in 2000 it is estimated to reach only 3.5 million. A figure of three million is forecast for 2002. The Federal Government is especially intent on lowering youth unemployment and is bringing a package of qualification measures to bear in this context (see the section on "Bündnis für Arbeit/Alliance for Jobs" in the chapter on "Economic system").
- "Aufbau Ost", the agenda for economic recovery in eastern Germany. Here, the prime goal remains to bring living conditions in eastern Germany up to par with western Germany. In order to buttress this core policy requirement, the Federal Government is maintaining its transfers under the financial equalization program. The "Zukunftsprogramm 2000 ("Future Program 2000")" as well as the "Bündnis für Arbeit, Ausbildung und Wettbewerb/Alliance for Jobs, Training and Competition" are both designed to provide additional support for investment, innovation, and research. Owing to the high level of unemployment in eastern Germany, a far-reaching proactive labor-market policy is being conducted. The federal budget for 2002 contains an item of some DM 38 billion for the "Aufbau Ost" agenda.

In May 2000, Federal Chancellor Schröder and the minister presidents of the federal states in eastern Germany agreed to continuing the solidarity financial contributions for the "Aufbau Ost" agenda after the year 2004, as otherwise the financial support provided until that time would cease.

Alongside efforts to bring living conditions in eastern Germany up to the standard of western Germany, a major political step toward completing Germany unity has already been taken.

Federal Chancellor Schröder visiting the former Lichterfeld open-seam lignite mine while touring eastern Germany

With the enactment of the Act Rectifying Injustices Committed by the SED on January 1, 2000, the Federal Government has improved compensation for victims of such injustices and for ensuring the restoration of such persons' reputation.

Other pre-eminent modernization and reform projects that have already been completed either in full or in part include:

— reform of the social insurance sector: the goal is to ensure a balanced spread of burdens between the generations. The Federal Government therefore wishes to supplement the statutory pension insurance with capital-based pension plans; only in this way can the interests of future generations be duly considered. The solution of another key reform project, namely the ecological tax reform, is also geared to sourcing finance for the pension insurance scheme, by impacting twofold: taking the strain off the labor market and enhancing Germany's international competitiveness while also lowering social insurance contributions. These are part of the ancillary wage costs which render labor more expensive. With the introduction of the eco-tax, employers' contribution to pension insurance has been slimmed from 20.3 to 19.3 percent, social insurance contributions have been slashed from 42.3 to 41.5 percent, and the final goal is to lower them still further to under 40 percent.

— the Act on the Prioritization of Renewable Energy Sources is designed to bring about the ecological modernization of society – with the objective of ensuring the long-term preservation of the natural basis for life and work.

— opt-out from nuclear energy: In June 2000 the Federal Government and leading power utilities agreed on an orderly termination of nuclear power. The consensus reached is considered a historic solution to a social conflict that has simmered for long. The agreement covers provisions on terminating the use of nuclear power and current atomic waste disposal issues. It demonstrates that a non-damaging opt-out from this controversial technology is possible. On this basis, the Federal Government will be amending the Atomic Energy Act (see the chapter on Environmental Protection)

— new law on citizenship: as of Jan. 1, 2000 a new, modern law on citizenship was enacted in Germany which takes its cue from the European norm and abandons the principle of hereditary origin in favor of the principle of place of birth.

A law which by no means fits in with the above context nevertheless bears mention owing to its historical background and its forward-looking and humanitarian nature, namely the Act on the Creation of the Foundation "Memory, Responsibility, and Future", passed by parliament on July 6, 2000 – as a joint initiative by the Federal Government and the political parties represented in the Bundestag. Together with the two intergovernmental treaties signed by the heads of the US and German negotiating teams on July 17, 2000, this law regulates the modalities for payment of compensation for those forced to work as slave laborers during the Third Reich. Federal Chancellor Schröder, at whose behest the foundation was first set up, considers the agreements reached 55 years after the end of World War II to be a "long overdue humanitarian gesture". The estimated 1.5 million victims still alive today can expect to receive payments of between DM 5,000 and DM 15,000.

A part of the finances will be injected into a fund for "Memory and the Future". The ongoing task of the fund will be to provide financial assistance for projects that serve international understanding, the interests of survivors, youth exchanges, social justice, commemoration of the threat posed by totalitarian rule and the rule of force, as well as international cooperation in the humanitarian realm.

Federal Chancellor Schröder and leading German corporations agreed to establish such a foundation in their joint declaration of Feb. 19, 1999 – with the goal of providing an answer to the issue of moral responsibility of German companies for the exploitation of forced labor, aryanization, and other unjust acts during the Nazi regime, to promote humanitarian and future-oriented projects, and to reduce the damage to US-German business relations and bilateral relations in general as a result of complaints brought against German corporations in the United States.

On Dec. 15 1999, the representatives of the German business world, the Federal Government, and the US administration agreed on a figure of DM 10 billion as total compensation. This offer was accepted by Jewish organizations and the attorneys representing the victims. The Federal Government and the German Corporations' Foundation Initiative will each contribute DM 5 billion to this sum.

Government, constitution and legal system

The Basic Law

In 1999, the Germans were able to look back on a half century of experience with their constitution, the Basic Law. Already on the occasion of the Federal Republic's 20th anniversary in 1969, the Basic Law was acknowledged to be the best and most liberal constitution Germany had ever had. More than any previous German constitution, the Basic Law has been accepted by the people. It created a state and society which so far has been spared any serious constitutional crises.

The Basic Law for the Federal Republic of Germany was adopted in 1949. Its authors intended it as a "temporary" framework for a new democratic system, not as a definitive constitution. The Basic Law called upon the people "to achieve in free self-determination the unity and freedom of Germany".

The bodies promulgating the constitution in 1948 were the parliaments of the states that had been formed in the Western occupation zones and the Parliamentary Council elected by the state parliaments. This Council, which was chaired by Konrad Adenauer, adopted the Basic Law on 8 May 1949. After ratification by the state parliaments, the Basic Law was promulgated by the Parliamentary Council on 23 May 1949.

The Basic Law's content was greatly influenced by the personal experience of its authors under the National Socialist dictatorship. In many parts it clearly indicates that they were trying to avoid the mistakes that had been partly responsible for the demise of the Weimar democracy.

As time passed by, the Basic Law proved to be a solid foundation for democracy. Its requirement of national reunification was fulfilled in 1990. The preamble and concluding article of the Basic Law were amended in accordance with the Unification Treaty, which formed the basis for the accession of the German Democratic Republic (GDR) to the Federal Republic. They now state that, by virtue of the GDR's accession, the German people have completed their unity. Since 3 October 1990, the Basic Law has been valid for the whole nation.

The basic rights. Pride of place in the constitution is given to a charter of basic rights, the first of which obliges the state to respect and protect the dignity of man. This guarantee is supplemented by the right to self-fulfillment. It affords comprehensive protection against unlawful interference by the state. Both Germans and non-Germans can invoke these constitutional rights. The classical freedoms embodied in the Basic Law include freedom of religion and conscience, freedom of expression, freedom of the press, and the guarantee of property. There are also freedom of art and scholarship, freedom of association, the right to form coalitions, the right to privacy of correspondence, posts and telecommunications, freedom of movement, free choice of occupation or profession, protection from forced labor, privacy of the home, and the right of conscientious objection.

Civil rights which apply only to German nationals relate for the most part to the latter's involvement in the political process and free choice of occupation or profession. In essence they include freedom of assembly, the right to form associations, partnerships and corporations, freedom of movement

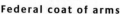

Federal coat of arms   **Federal flag**

throughout (including the right to enter) the federal territory, freedom of choice and practice of an occupation or profession, the ban on extradition, and the right to vote.

These freedoms are accompanied by rights which guarantee equality. The Basic Law expresses the general principle that all people are equal before the law by providing that no one shall be prejudiced or favored because of their sex, birth, race, language, national or social origin, faith, religion or political opinions, nor may anyone be discriminated against on account of their disability. It expressly states that men and women have equal rights and that all Germans are equally eligible for any public office. No one may be discriminated against owing to a handicap they have.

The basic rights also deal with the protection and guarantee of social institutions such as marriage, family, and the church. Some basic rights are expressly formulated as entitlements to services and benefits, for example that every mother is entitled to the protection and care of the community.

One basic right, which by its very nature can only apply to foreigners, is the right of political asylum. The Basic Law is the first German constitutional instrument to provide refuge in Germany for foreigners persecuted on political grounds. It was amended in 1993 and enshrined in the Basic Law as Art. 16a.

According to the Basic Law, to a certain extent most basic rights may be restricted directly by or indirectly pursuant to other laws. Never, however, may a law encroach upon the essence of a basic right. The basic rights are directly enforceable law. This was a crucial innovation compared with previous constitutions, whose basic rights were largely non-binding declarations of intent. Today all three branches of government – the legislative, the executive, and the administration of justice – are strictly bound by the basic rights. Every citizen has the right, having exhausted all other legal avenues, to lodge a constitutional complaint with the Federal Constitutional Court if he or she feels his or her basic rights have been violated by any decisions or actions by the state. With its accession to the European Convention for the Protection of Human Rights and Fundamental Freedoms in 1952, the Federal Republic of Germany subjected itself to international control (with effect from 1953). The 11th Protocol to the Convention of 11 November 1998 has established a standing European Court of Human Rights to which all complaints by individuals must be submitted as regards violations of human rights as guaranteed by the Convention. In 1973, the Federal Republic also ratified the United Nations' international covenants on human rights.

Fundamental characteristics of the state. The German constitutional state is based on the following principles: Germany is a republic and a democracy; it is a federal state based on the rule of constitutional law and social justice.

Its republican system is constitutionally manifest in the name "Federal Republic of Germany" and in the fact that the head of state is the elected Federal President. A democracy is based on the sovereignty of the people. The constitution says that all public authority emanates from the people. It thereby opted for indirect, representative democracy: In other words, the powers of the state must be democratically legitimated by the people, but they have no direct say in the exercise of such authority, except in elections. This responsibility is entrusted to the organs specially established by the constitution for this purpose: the legislature, the executive and the judiciary. The people mainly exercise their constitutional authority by periodically electing a new parliament. In contrast to some countries, provision for other forms of direct democracy, such as referendums, has been made only with regard to modifications of state boundaries.

The authors of the Basic Law opted for an "adversarial" form of democracy, having witnessed how the Weimar Republic was undermined by radical parties which were hostile to the constitution. In this context "adversarial" means that the free play of political forces must stop where any party or faction attempts to do away with democracy with democratic means. This explains why the Basic Law makes it possible for the Federal Constitutional Court to ban political parties that seek to damage or destroy Germany's democratic system.

The constitutional decision in favor of a federal state implies that not only the country as a whole but its 16 constituent parts, the Länder, have some of the features of a state. Each has its own powers, though they are restricted to certain spheres, which it exercises through its own legislature, executive and judiciary. Public responsibility has been apportioned in such

Ei - nig - keit und Recht und Frei - heit
Da - nach lasst uns al - le stre - ben

für das deut-sche Va - ter - land!
brü - der - lich mit Herz und Hand!

Ei - nig - keit und Recht und Frei - heit

sind des Glü - ckes Un - ter - pfand.

Blüh im Glan - ze die - ses Glü - ckes,

blü - he, deut - sches Va - ter - land!

The national anthem of the Federal Republic of Germany is the third verse of the "Lied der Deutschen".

The lyrics of the anthem were written by August Heinrich Hoffmann von Fallersleben (1798-1874), and the melody was composed by Joseph Haydn (1732-1809).

The national holiday is 3 October, the Day of German Unity.

a way that law-making is actually predominantly in the hands of the central state, the Federation, whereas the constituent states are primarily responsible for administration, in other words, implementation of the laws. This division of responsibilities is an essential element of the system of separation and balance of powers provided for in the Basic Law.

At the heart of the constitutional state established under the Basic Law is the concept of the rule of law. An essential element of its realization is the division of powers. The exercise of state power is entrusted to parliament, government and the judiciary, each of which is independent of the others. The significance of this separation of powers is that the power of the state is qualified by mutual checks and balances. It thus protects the individual's freedom.

A second key element of the rule-of-law principle is that all action by the state is strictly bound by the law. This fundamental concept of the lawfulness of administration stipulates that the executive may not contravene the law in force, especially the constitution and the laws of the land (primacy of the law). Furthermore, encroachments upon an individual's rights or personal liberty are only permissible on the basis of a law (proviso of the law). In principle, any action by the state may be examined by independent judges as to its consistency with the law if the person or persons affected should file for litigation.

The principle of the social state is a modern extension of the traditional rule-of-law concept. It obligates the state to protect the weaker members of society and to seek social justice. Numerous laws and court rulings in Germany over the years have ensured the application of this principle, which manifests itself in the provision of old-age, invalidity, health and unemployment insurance, social assistance for needy people, housing supplements, the child benefit, and laws on industrial safety and working hours, to name but a few examples.

Amendments to the Basic Law. The Basic Law may only be amended with a majority of two thirds of the members of the Bundestag (Federal Parliament) and two thirds of the votes cast in the Bundesrat (Federal Council). Since a single party or a coalition of parties only very rarely has such a majority in both the Bundestag and the Bundesrat, amendments to the Basic Law require a very broad consensus. This can only be achieved with the support of members of the opposition.

Some provisions of the Basic Law may not be changed at all. These are the provisions relating to democracy, the federal system, the separation of powers, the rule of law and the social state. Likewise untouchable are the basic rights and freedoms as well as the commitment to protect the dignity of man.

Amendments to the Basic Law with far-reaching practical implications in regard to the opening up of markets and European harmonization were adopted in connection with the privatization of the German Federal Railway (Article 87e, 20 December 1993) and the German Administration of Post Offices and Telecommunications (Article 87f, 30 August 1994).

On 15 November 1994, amendments to the Basic Law entered into force which commit the state to protect the environment, ensure equal treatment of men and women, and protect the disabled. They also provide for changes in the distribution of legislative jurisdiction between the Federation and the states.

Another constitutional amendment was made in the framework context of the Maastricht Treaty. The Basic Law's new Article 23 on the European Union makes it clear that the Federal Republic of Germany seeks the establishment of a united Europe which is based on democratic, rule-of-law, social and federal principles. The principle of subsidiarity plays a key role in this context. Article 23 also spells out how the Bundestag and the states are to be involved in the further development of European integration.

The constitutional bodies

The Federal President. The head of state of the Federal Republic of Germany is the Federal President. He is elected by the Federal Convention, a constitutional body which convenes only for this purpose. It consists of the members of the Bundestag and an equal number of members elected by the state parliaments. Sometimes eminent persons who are not members of a state parliament are nominated for the Federal Convention. The Federal President is elected for a term of five years with the majority of votes in the Federal Convention. He may only be reelected once.

The Federal President represents the Federation in its international relations and concludes treaties with other states on its behalf. He also accredits and receives envoys, although foreign policy as such is the responsibility of the Federal Government.

The Federal President appoints and dismisses federal judges, federal civil servants and commissioned and non-commissioned officers of the armed forces. The President can pardon convicted criminals. He checks whether laws have come about by the proper constitutional procedure befoofre they are subsequently announced in the Federal Law Gazette.

He proposes to the Bundestag a candidate for the office of Federal Chancellor (taking account of the majority situation in parliament) and, in response to suggestions from the Chancellor, appoints and dismisses the federal ministers. If the Chancellor seeks but fails to gain a vote of confidence, the Federal President may, on the Chancellor's proposal, dissolve the Bundestag. The Federal President personifies the country's political unity in a special way. He is the link between all elements in society regardless of party distinctions.

Although his tasks are mainly of a representational nature, he can exercise considerable personal authority through his neutral, mediating function over and above daily party politics. By commenting on fundamental aspects of current issues, he can rise above party-political controversy and set standards for the public's political and moral guidance.

The Bundestag. The German Bundestag is the parliamentary assembly representing the people of the Federal Republic of Germany. It is elected by the people every four years. It may only be dissolved prematurely under exceptional circumstances, the final decision lying with the Federal President. The Bundestag's main functions are to pass laws, to elect the Federal Chancellor and to keep check on the government.

The Bundestag is the scene of parliamentary battles, especially over crucial foreign and domestic policy issues. It is in the parliamentary committees, whose meetings are not usually open to the public, that the extensive preparatory work for legislation is done. Here it is a question of harmonizing political intentions with the detailed knowledge provided by the experts. It is likewise in the committees that parliament scrutinizes and controls government activity. Otherwise it would not be possible to cope with the multitude of technical questions. The Bundestag's committees correspond to the Federal Government's departments and range from the Committee on Foreign Affairs and the Committee on Labour and Social Affairs to the Budget Committee. The latter is particularly important because it represents parliament's control of the budget. Anyone may directly address requests and complaints to the Petitions Committee of the German Bundestag.

From 1949 until the end of the last legislative term in 1998, more than 8,400 bills were introduced in parliament and 5,150 of them enacted. Most of them entail amendments to existing acts. Most bills are initiated by the Federal Government, the others coming from members of the Bundestag or from the Bundesrat. They receive three readings in the Bundestag and are usually referred to the appropriate committee once. The final vote is taken after the third reading. A bill (unless it entails an amendment to the constitution) is passed if it receives a majority of the votes cast. Where To the extent that this is foreseen required by the Basic Law, the approval of the Bundesrat must, however, be obtained.

Members of the German Bundestag are elected in general, direct, free, equal and secret elections. They are representatives of the whole people; they are not bound by any instructions,

The German Federal Presidents

1: Theodor Heuss (FDP) 1949-59
2: Heinrich Lübke (CDU) 1959-69

3: Gustav Heinemann (SPD) 1969-74
4: Walter Scheel (FDP) 1974-9

5: Karl Carstens (CDU) 1979-84
6: Richard v. Weizsäcker (CDU) 1984-94

7: Roman Herzog (CDU) 1994-9
8: Johannes Rau (SPD) since 1999

The German Federal Chancellors

1: Konrad
Adenauer
(CDU)
1949-63
2: Ludwig
Erhard (CDU)
1963-6

3: Kurt Georg
Kiesinger
(CDU)
1966-9
4: Willy Brandt
(SPD)
1969-74

5: Helmut
Schmidt (SPD)
1974-82
6: Helmut Kohl
(CDU)
1982-98

7: Gerhard
Schröder (SPD)
since 1998

The Bundesrat
The 69 votes of the states in the Bundesrat

North Rhine-Westphalia	○○○○○○	Saxony-Anhalt	○○○○
Bavaria	○○○○○○	Thuringia	○○○○
Baden-Württemberg	○○○○○○	Brandenburg	○○○○
Lower Saxony	○○○○○○	Schleswig-Holstein	○○○○
Hesse	○○○○○	Mecklenburg-Western Pomerania	○○○
Saxony	○○○○	Hamburg	○○○
Rhineland-Palatinate	○○○○	Saarland	○○○
Berlin	○○○○	Bremen	○○○

only by their conscience. In line with their party allegiances they form parliamentary groups. Independence and the requirements of party solidarity sometimes collide, but even if in such a situation a member feels obliged to leave his party he keeps his seat in the Bundestag. This is the clearest indication that members of the Bundestag are independent.

The relative strengths of the parliamentary groups determine the composition of the committees. The President (Speaker) of the Bundestag is elected from the ranks of the strongest parliamentary group, in keeping with German constitutional tradition.

Members of the Bundestag are paid remuneration ensuring their independence and reflecting their status as MPs. Anyone who has been a member of the Bundestag for at least eight years receives a pension upon reaching retirement age.

The Bundesrat. The Bundesrat represents the sixteen states and participates in Federal legislative process and administration. Unlike the senatorial system of federal states in the United States or Switzerland, the Bundesrat does not consist of elected representatives of the people, but of members of the state governments or their representatives. Depending on the size of the population, the states have three, four, five or six votes which may only be cast as a block.

More than half of all bills require the formal approval of the Bundesrat, which means that they cannot pass into law against its will. This applies especially to bills that concern vital interests of the states, for instance their financial affairs or their administrative powers. No proposed amendments to the constitution can be adopted without the Bundesrat's consent (two-thirds majority). In all other cases the Bundesrat only has a right of objection, but this can be overruled by the Bundestag. If the two houses of parliament cannot reach agreement a mediation committee composed of members of both chambers must be convened, which in most cases is able to work out a compromise.

In the Bundesrat state interests often override party interests; voting thus may not reflect party strengths in the Bundesrat. This points to an active federalism. The Federal Government cannot always rely on a state government where the same party is in power to follow its lead in every respect, for each state has its own special interests and sometimes takes sides with other states who pursue the same aim, irrespective of the party they are governed by. This produces fluctuating majorities, and compromises have to be made when the parties forming the Federal Government do not have a majority in the Bundesrat.

The Bundesrat elects its president from among the minister-presidents of the sixteen states for a twelvemonth term according to a fixed rotation schedule. The President of the Bundesrat exercises the powers of the Federal President in the event of the latter's indisposition.

The Federal Government. The Federal Government, the Cabinet, consists of the Federal Chancellor, who is chairman of the Cabinet and head of government, and the federal ministers. The Chancellor alone chooses the ministers and proposes them to the Federal President for appointment or dismissal. He also determines the number of ministers and their responsibilities. Certain ministries are mentioned in the Basic Law: the Federal Foreign Office as well as the Federal Ministries of the Interior, Justice, Finance and Defence. Institution of the three latter ministries is a constitutional requirement. The Chancellor is in a strong position primarily due to the fact that it is he who lays down the guidelines of government policy. The federal ministers run their departments independently and on their own responsibility but within the framework of these guidelines. In a coalition government, the Chancellor must also take account of agreements reached with the other party in the coalition.

This explains why the German system of government is often referred to as a "Chancellor democracy". The Chancellor is the only member of the government elected by parliament, and he alone is accountable to it. This accountability may manifest itself in a "constructive vote of no confidence", which was introduced by the authors of the Basic Law in deliberate contrast to the Weimar constitution. Its purpose is to ensure that opposition groups who are in agreement only in their rejection of the government but not as regards an alternative program are not able to overthrow the government. A Bundestag vote of no confidence in the Chancellor must at the same time be a majority vote in favor of a successor. Of the two attempts to bring down a Chancellor with the help of a constructive vote of no confidence, only one has succeeded. That was in October 1982, when a no-confidence motion removed Helmut Schmidt from office and put Helmut Kohl in his place. The Basic Law makes no provision for motions of no confidence in individual federal ministers.

The Federal Constitutional Court. The Federal Constitutional Court in Karlsruhe is the guardian of the Basic Law. It takes action only when called upon. A catalog of types of proceedings stipulates when cases may be brought before the Court.

Every citizen has the right to file a constitutional complaint with the Federal Constitutional Court if he feels his basic rights have been violated by public authority. Beforehand, however, he must as a rule have exhausted all other legal channels.

The Court also rules on disputes between the Federation and the states or between individual federal institutions. Only this court has the power to declare that a party constitutes a threat to freedom and democracy and is therefore unconstitutional, in which case it orders that party's dissolution. It examines federal and state laws to assess whether they conform with the Basic Law. If it rules that a law is unconstitutional, that law becomes null and void. The Court can act in such cases among other things if appealed to by certain authorities, such as the Federal Government, the state governments, at least one third of the members of the Bundestag, or the lower courts.

So far the Court has passed judgment in more than 127,000 cases. Approximately 122,000 dealt with constitutional com-

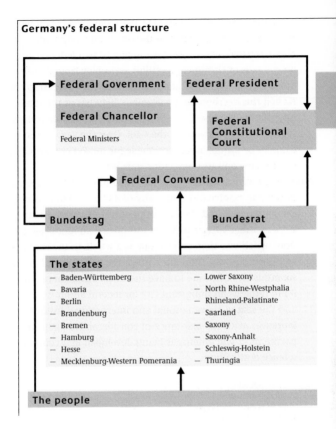

Germany's federal structure

Federal Government
Federal Chancellor
Federal Ministers

Federal President

Federal Constitutional Court

Federal Convention

Bundestag

Bundesrat

The states
— Baden-Württemberg
— Bavaria
— Berlin
— Brandenburg
— Bremen
— Hamburg
— Hesse
— Mecklenburg-Western Pomerania

— Lower Saxony
— North Rhine-Westphalia
— Rhineland-Palatinate
— Saarland
— Saxony
— Saxony-Anhalt
— Schleswig-Holstein
— Thuringia

The people

plaints, but only about 3,100 of these were successful (as at 31 December 1999). Often matters of great domestic or international significance are dealt with, for instance whether the involvement of German forces in missions of the United Nations is compatible with the Basic Law. Federal Governments of all political persuasions have had to submit to decisions of the judges in Karlsruhe. The Court has repeatedly stressed, however, that while its work indeed has a political impact, it is not a political institution. Its standard is the Basic Law alone, pursuant to which the constitutional scope for political decision-making has been established.

The Federal Constitutional Court consists of two panels, each with eight judges; half of them are elected by the Bundestag and half by the Bundesrat. The judges serve for twelve years and may not be reelected.

The federal capital. On 10 May 1949, the university town of Bonn on the Rhine, which at the time had a population of about 100,000, was chosen as the provisional federal capital (in the face of strong competition, especially from Frankfurt am Main) by the Parliamentary Council. The Bundestag confirmed this decision on 3 November 1949 but at the same time stated that the federal bodies would be moved to Berlin following free elections in the GDR. Over the years Bonn came to be synonymous worldwide for the Federal Republic of Germany and its democratic policies.

After the reunification of Germany, on 20 June 1991 the German Bundestag resolved by a majority of 337 to 320 to relocate the parliament and the government from Bonn to Berlin. On 27 September 1996, the Bundesrat passed an identical resolution, which was then carried out as a whole in the summer of 1999. Bonn was thereupon given the title "Federal city"; six ministries continue to have their first offices here. Thus, Bonn remains an important city for federal administration and the seat of supranational and international institutions. Moreover, with the assistance of considerable equalization payments, it will emerge is being developed as a center for science and culture.

Further information:
- Bundespräsidialamt
  (Federal President's Office)
  Spreeweg 1, 10577 Berlin
  Internet: http://www.bundespraesident.de
  E-mail: posteingang@bundespraesident.de
- Bundeskanzleramt
  (Federal Chancellor's Office)
  Schloßplatz 1, 11012 Berlin
  Internet: http://www.bundesregierung.de
  E-mail: bundeskanzler@bundeskanzler.de
- Deutscher Bundestag
  (German Bundestag)
  Platz der Republik 1, 11011 Berlin
  Internet: http://www.bundestag.de
  E-mail: mail@bundestag.de
- Deutscher Bundesrat
  (German Bundesrat)
  Leipziger Strasse 3-4, 10117 Berlin
  Internet: http://www.bundesrat.de
  E-mail: pressestelle@bundesrat.de

Federalism and self-government

The name "Federal Republic of Germany" itself denotes the country's federal structure. The Federal Republic consists of 16 Länder (states). The Länder are not mere provinces but states endowed with their own powers. Each has a constitution which must be consistent with the republican, democratic and social principles embodied in the Basic Law. Subject to these conditions they can shape their constitutions as they see fit.

Federalism is one of the constitutional principles that may not be changed. But this is not to say that the constituent states may not be altered. Provision for boundary adjustments has been made in the Basic Law.

The federal system has a long tradition in Germany and was interrupted only by the National Socialist unitary state of 1933-45. Germany is one of the classical federal states. Federalism has proved its worth: It is much easier for a country with a federal structure than a centralized state to take account of regional characteristics and problems.

Benefits of a federal system. German federalism, much as in the United States and Switzerland, binds the country's external unity with its internal diversity. Preserving that regional diversity is the traditional task of the federal system. This function today acquires new substance in the form of regional responsibilities such as the protection of monuments and historical sites, the preservation of architectural traditions, and the promotion of regional culture.

But the main purpose of federalism is to safeguard the nation's freedom. The distribution of responsibilities between the Federation and the states is an essential element of the power-sharing arrangement, the checks and balances, as provided for in the Basic Law. This also embraces the participation of the states in the legislative process at the federal level through the Bundesrat.

The federal structure also enhances the democratic principle. It enables the citizen to engage in the political process, i.e. in elections and referendums, in his own region. This gives democracy greater vitality. There are other benefits as well. The federal system leaves room for experiments on a smaller scale and for competition among the states. A single state may, for instance, try out innovative methods in education which may later serve as a model for nationwide reform.

Furthermore, a federal structure can best cope with different regional majorities. Opposition parties at the national level may hold a majority in some of the states and thus form the government there.

The powers of the states. The Basic Law determined the powers of the Federation in terms of whether laws should be the same for all the states or whether the states should be allowed to make their own laws. This is illustrated by the fact that the Federation's lawmaking powers fall into three different categories, namely exclusive, concurrent or framework legislation.

Areas of legislation which fall within the exclusive purview of the Federation are foreign affairs, defense, monetary matters, air transport and some elements of taxation.

In the case of concurrent legislation, the states may only pass laws on matters not covered by federal law. The Federation may only legislate in such cases where it is necessary to have a uniform law for the whole country. The areas which fall into this category are civil and criminal law, commercial law, nuclear energy, labor and land law, the law concerning aliens, housing, shipping, road transport, refuse disposal, air pollution and noise abatement. Since it has proved necessary to have standard laws for these matters, the states have more or less ceased to have any jurisdiction in these areas.

Where the Federation has the power to enact framework legislation, the states have a certain amount of legislative latitude. This applies, for instance, in the fields of higher education, nature conservation, landscape management, regional planning and water management.

There are also a number of other supraregional tasks which, though not mentioned in the Basic Law, are today jointly planned, regulated and financed by the Federation and the states. They were incorporated in the Basic Law in 1969 as "joint responsibilities" and cover the university system as well as the improvement of regional economic structures, agrarian structure and coastal protection.

Direct federal administration is more or less limited to the Foreign Service, labor placement, customs, the Federal Border Guard and the Federal Armed Forces. Most administrative responsibilities are carried out by the states independently.

The Federation's jurisdiction is confined to the Federal Constitutional Court and the supreme courts, which ensure the uniform interpretation of the law. All other courts fall within the ambit of state jurisdiction.

As mentioned above, the states can fill in any gaps left by federal legislation or in areas not specified in the Basic Law. Thus they are responsible for education and culture almost in their entirety as a manifestation of their "cultural sovereignty". They are also responsible for local government law and the police.

The Stadttor in Düsseldorf is the seat of the Minister President of North Rhine-Westphalia

The real strength of the states lies in their participation in the legislative process at the federal level through the Bundesrat. All internal administration lies in their hands, and their bureaucracy implements most federal laws and regulations. Thus state administration is threefold: It handles matters that fall exclusively within its jurisdiction (schools, police and regional planning, for example); it implements federal law in its own right and on its own responsibility (such as the law on planning of building projects, trade and industry, and environmental protection); and it implements federal law on behalf of the Federation (construction of national highways and promotion of training, for instance).

Thus in the course of its development the Federal Republic has become a country in which most laws are enacted centrally while the bulk of legislation is administered by the federal states.

Local self-government. Local self-government, as an expression of civic liberty, has a long tradition in Germany. It can be traced back to the privileges of the free towns in the Middle Ages, when civic rights freed people from the bonds of feudal serfdom. (As they said in those days, "town air makes people free".) In modern times, local self-government has primarily been linked to the great reforms of the Prussian minister Karl Reichsfreiherr vom und zum Stein, in particular the Local Government Code of 1808.

This tradition of civic liberty is manifest in the self-government of towns, municipalities and counties expressly guaranteed by the Basic Law. They accordingly have the right to regulate local affairs within the framework of the law. All towns, municipalities and counties must have a democratic structure. Municipal law falls within the ambit of the states. For historical reasons, the municipal constitutions differ from state to state, but in practice the administrative system is by and large the same.

Self-government embraces in particular local transport and road construction, electricity, water and gas supply, sewerage and town planning, as well as the building and maintenance of schools, theaters and museums, hospitals, sports facilities and public baths. Other local responsibilities are adult education and youth welfare. Duties are predominantly discharged independently and the municipalities are themselves responsible for their actions. The supervision of municipalities by the states is limited as a rule to assessing the legality of the formers' actions. Many such measures are beyond the means of smaller towns and municipalities; they can be taken over by the next higher level of local self-government, the county (Kreis). The county, too, is part of the system of local government through its own democratically elected bodies. The larger cities do not form part of a county.

Local self-government and independence are bound to suffer if the municipalities are unable to finance their programs. Their financial situation is frequently a subject of public debate. Local authorities raise their own taxes and levies, which include the real property tax and the trade tax. They are also entitled to raise local taxes on certain luxury goods. This revenue does not suffice to cover their financial needs, however. For example, for this reason they receive from the federal and state governments a share of the revenue from taxes on income and value-added tax . They also receive allocations under the financial equalization arrangement which applies in every state. The municipalities furthermore charge fees for services.

Local self-government gives all citizens an opportunity to play their part and have a controlling influence. They can discuss such matters as new building projects with elected councillors at town meetings and inspect budget estimates. The towns and municipalities are the smallest cells in the political system. They must always be able to thrive and develop as the basic source of freedom and democracy.

The legal system

The law of the Federal Republic of Germany is predominantly written law. It meanwhile applies to virtually all aspects of life; as a result, legislation today consists of adjustments and amendments to existing law. Germany's legal system has been shaped by constitutional law but is also influenced by the law of the European Communities and international law. The body of federal law encompasses approximately 1,900 acts and 3,000 statutory instruments. The states, too, pass laws, mainly on such matters as the police, local government, schools and universities as well as the press, radio and television.

A state based on the rule of law. German law goes back partly to Roman law and partly to numerous other legal sources in the German regions. In the 19th century, a uniform system of private law was created for the first time. It applied to the entire German Empire. The Civil Code and Commercial Code to this day preserve the liberal spirit of those times. Their underlying principle is freedom of contract.

The guarantees afforded by a democratic state are manifest above all in substantive and procedural law. Criminal law proceeds from the constitutional premise that no act is punishable unless declared so by law before it was committed. Thus judges may not make up for gaps in penal law by applying legal provisions which cover similar cases, nor may they apply laws retroactively. Another principle embedded in the constitution is that no one may be punished more than once for the same offense. Personal liberty may not be restricted except on the basis of a formal law. Only a judge may determine whether a person's imprisonment is justified, and only he can decide for how long. Whenever a person is detained without a judicial warrant, the matter must be brought before a judge for decision without delay.

Although the police may hold someone in temporary custody, they may not detain him any longer than the end of the day following the arrest. Everyone has a right to a court hearing – that, too, is guaranteed by the constitution and is a fundamental principle of the rule of law. The administration of justice is entrusted to independent judges who are answerable to the law only. They may not be dismissed from office nor transferred against their will. Special tribunals are banned.

Nearly all of these fundamental principles had already been established by the judiciary laws of the 19th century. They include the Courts Constitution Act, which governs the structure, organization and jurisdiction of the courts, the Code of Civil Procedure and the Code of Criminal Procedure.

The Civil Code, which came into force in 1900, and the Codes of Civil and Criminal Procedure were wrested by liberal and democratic forces from the Reich's government towards the end of the 19th century after protracted debates in parliament. German codified laws have found their way into foreign legal systems as well. The Civil Code, for instance, was the model for its Japanese and Greek counterparts.

The citizen and public administration. After an evolutionary period of more than 100 years, the Basic Law set the seal on a comprehensive system of legal protection against the actions of public authorities. It enabled the citizen to challenge any measure that affected him on the ground that it violated his rights. This applies to any administrative act, be it a tax assessment notice or a decision whether or not to promote a school pupil to the next grade, be it the withdrawal of a driving license or the refusal of a building permit.

Administrative courts were unknown in the GDR. Now administration in the new states, too, is subject to overall control by the courts.

The legal protection afforded by the courts with the relevant jurisdiction is complemented by a right of complaint to the Federal Constitutional Court. This "constitutional complaint" is open to every citizen and is an extra form of legal redress against any violations of basic rights by a public authority. The litigant must show that one of his basic rights has been infringed by a public act, for instance a court decision or an administrative measure but also a law. Normally, such complaints may only be lodged after all other remedies afforded

Simplified structure of the courts in Germany

	Federal Constitutional Court (2 panels)					Constitutional courts of the states
	Ordinary jurisdiction		Administrative jurisdiction	Fiscal jurisdiction	Labor jurisdiction	Social jurisdiction
	Civil jurisdiction	Criminal jurisdiction				
	Joint Panel of the Highest Federal Courts					
Federal Court of Justice	Grand Panel for Civil Matters / Civil panels	Grand Panel for Criminal Matters / Criminal panels	**Federal Administrative Court** — Grand Panel Panels	**Federal Finance Court** — Grand Panel Panels	**Federal Labor Court** — Grand Panel Panels	**Federal Social Court** — Grand Panel Panels
Higher Regional Court	Family panels / Civil panels	Criminal panels / Appellate court / Court of first instance for serious crimes against the fundamental order of the State	**Higher Administrative Court** — Panels	**Finance Court** — Panels	**Higher Labor Court** — Panels	**Higher Social Court** — Panels
Regional Court	Civil divisions / Commercial divisions	Small criminal divisions / Grand criminal divisions (courts of first and second instance) / Juvenile divisions (courts of first and second instance)	**Administrative Court** — Divisions		**Labor Court** — Divisions	**Social Court** — Divisions
Local Court	Civil court judge / Family Court	Criminal court judge / Criminal Court ("Schöffengericht") / Juvenile court judge / Juvenile Court ("Jugendschöffengericht")				

by law in the courts with subject matter jurisdiction have been exhausted.

Social justice. The Basic Law prescribes the development of the social-state order, hence much greater consideration is now given to the people's social needs than in former times. In the years since the creation of the Federal Republic, a whole range of special labor and social legislation has been enacted to provide the citizen with various financial benefits in the event of sickness, accident, invalidity and unemployment, as well as after retirement.

Labor law is a good example of how the principle of the social state has been put into effect. Originally, these matters were only briefly dealt with under the heading of "service contracts" in the Civil Code. Today, labor legislation embraces an abundance of laws and collective agreements but is also largely based on case law. It includes in particular the Collective Wage Agreements Act, the Protection against Dismissal Act, the Act on the Constitution of Business and Industrial Enterprises (Works Constitution Act), as well as the various laws on codetermination and the Labor Courts Act.

Administration of justice. The Federal Republic's courts are largely specialized and provide comprehensive legal protection. They fall into five categories:

– The "ordinary courts" are responsible for criminal matters, civil matters (disputes arising under private law such as sale or lease agreements, matrimonial or family proceedings) and non-contentious legal proceedings, which include conveyancing, probate and guardianship matters. There are four levels: the local court (Amtsgericht), the regional court (Landgericht), the higher regional court (Oberlandesgericht) and the Federal Court of Justice (Bundesgerichtshof). In criminal cases, depending on their nature, each of the first three courts can have jurisdiction, whereas in civil proceedings it will be either the local court or the regional court. Appeals may be lodged with up to two higher courts.

– The labor courts (three levels: local, higher – i.e. state – and federal) handle disputes arising from employment contracts and between management and labor, as well as matters covered by the Works Constitution Act. The labor courts decide, for instance, whether an employee has been fairly or unfairly dismissed.

— The administrative courts (local, higher and federal) handle all proceedings under administrative law that do not fall within the jurisdiction of the social and finance courts or, in exceptional cases, the ordinary courts (e.g. cases of official liability), or do not involve disputes which fall under constitutional law.

— The social courts (local, higher and federal) rule on all disputes concerned with social security.

— The finance courts (state and federal) deal with taxation and related matters.

Separate from the aforementioned five types of courts is the Federal Constitutional Court, which is not only the country's supreme court, but also an organ of the constitution. It rules on constitutional disputes.

There is a complex system of appeals which affords numerous possibilities for judicial review. The appeals procedure provides for a second level of jurisdiction in both legal and substantive terms. In other words, new evidence can also be introduced at this level. In the second stage (Revision), however, the court will only consider whether the law has been properly applied and the essential procedural formalities observed.

In the Federal Republic there are approximately 21,000 professional judges, more than three quarters of whom are assigned to the ordinary courts. Most judges are appointed for life and in exercising their profession are bound only by the spirit and letter of the law.

At the local court level, most non-contentious legal proceedings are handled by judicial officers, who are not judges but rather higher intermediate-level civil servants in the judicial service. In several types of courts, lay judges sit with the pro-

The Second Senate of the Federal Constitutional Court in Karlsruhe

fessional judges. Their experience and specialized knowledge in certain fields, such as labor and welfare matters, enable them to help the courts make realistic decisions. They are also a manifestation of the citizen's direct responsibility for the administration of justice.

The public prosecutors, who number about 5,000, are for the most part concerned with criminal proceedings and the execution of sentences. It is their responsibility to establish the facts where a person is suspected of a crime, to lead the investigations with the assistance of the police, who to this extent are subject to the supervision and factual instruction of the public prosecutor's office. Following completion of investigations, the public prosecutor's office decides whether the proceedings will be terminated or the person in question prosecuted. In court proceedings, they are the prosecuting counsel.

More than 100,000 lawyers are self-employed professionals and serve as independent counsel in all fields of law. Through representation of their clients in court they play a large part in the administration of justice. They must adhere to their professional code, and any violations are dealt with by disciplinary tribunals and the bar associations. All professional judges, public prosecutors, and attorneys at law must in principle have the qualifications of a judge; in other words, they must have successfully completed the course of study at a university law school and the compulsory course of practical training which follows, each of which ends with a state examination.

Data protection. The advance of IT in almost all areas of life in modern industrial society has created new problems for the judicial system and jurisprudence. Modern communications technologies have greatly eased the workload of many companies and public authorities and are in the process of transforming our society into a global information society. Modern IT also entails risks, however. Stored data can be put to improper use and fall into the hands of unauthorized persons. Anyone with sufficient quantities of data has access to information on a person's private life, which must remain inviolable. To pre-empt such an abuse of privacy, countless federal and state laws have been enacted in Germany to protect personal rights.

The staff of entities which process data are required to maintain confidentiality. People are legally entitled – with just a few exceptions – to find out what data concerning them is held by any body which processes data. They can demand correction of incorrect data and have any that are disputed blocked or any that have been improperly obtained erased.

On the recommendation of the Federal Government, the German Bundestag elects a Federal Commissioner for Data Protection with over half of the statutory number of its members. The person elected is then appointed by the Federal President. The Commissioner's task is to advise the Federal Government and the Bundestag on points of data protection law pertinent to the legislative procedure, monitor the handling of personal data by federal authorities and providers of telecommunications and postal services and make recommendations to these agencies for improving data protection. Any person who feels that his personal data has not been adequately protected by federal authorities or by companies, telecoms and postal service providers may lodge a complaint with the Federal Commissioner for Data Protection. Every two years the Commissioner submits an activity report to the Bundestag.

The Federal Republic of Germany has a pioneering role worldwide in the field of data protection legislation. It has helped increase public awareness of the need to protect the individual's right to privacy.

In 1995, an EU directive on data protection was issued which was decisively influenced by German law. The directive, which is to be translated into national law by the end of 2000, will specifically improve the legal position of the individual vis-à-vis private firms. The transformation in particular of the major industrial nations into information societies has necessitated granting citizens special protection for their personal rights. Since 1997, the Act on Information and Communications Service Providers has been in force and, at the state level, the State Media Service Provider Act. Thus, Germany is also playing a pioneering role world-wide as regards protecting personal rights on in the Internet.

Parties and elections

In a modern democracy, competing political parties are of fundamental importance. They are elected for a specific term during which they either assume the powers of government or
keep check on the activities of the current administration.
They therefore play a major role in shaping public policy.
These functions are taken into account in the Basic Law,
which devotes a separate article (Article 21) to the parties:
"The parties shall help form the political will of the people.
They may be freely established. Their internal organization
shall conform to democratic principles. They shall publicly
account for the sources and use of their funds and for their
assets."

Parties in the Bundestag. Since the first general election to
be held in the whole of Germany (1990) there have been six
parties in the Bundestag: the Christian Democratic Union of
Germany (CDU), the Social Democratic Party of Germany
(SPD), the Free Democratic Party (FDP), the Christian Social
Union (CSU), the Party of Democratic Socialism (PDS) and Alliance 90/ The Greens. The CDU has no party association in
the Free State of Bavaria, while the CSU puts up candidates
for election in Bavaria only. In the Bundestag, however, CDU
and CSU have a joint parliamentary party. The SPD, CDU,
CSU and FDP were formed in the western states between

**Gerhard
Schröder is
Chairman
of the SPD**

1945 and 1947. The SPD was a re-creation of the former mainly labor-oriented party of the same name which had been outlawed by the Hitler regime in 1933. The other parties were completely new. The Christian CDU and CSU parties, in contrast to the Catholic Centre Party of Weimar days, drew their support from both of Germany's two major Christian creeds, Roman Catholicism and Protestantism. The FDP adopted programs in the tradition of German liberalism (see chart, p. 500).

In the time that has elapsed since they were established over fifty years ago, these four parties have undergone significant changes. At the federal level they have all formed coalitions with one another once or been in opposition. Today they all

Angela Merkel, Chairperson of the CDU

see themselves as "popular" parties representing all sections of the community. They have different factions which reflect the various elements of a people's party.

From 1983 to 1990, the party "The Greens" was also represented in the Bundestag. It had been established at the national level in 1979 and was gradually voted into some of the state parliaments as well. Its roots lie in a radical ecologist movement which initially embraced factions opposed to nuclear energy as well as pacifist protest groups. In the 1990 general election, however, The Greens failed to clear the five percent hurdle, but they were nonetheless represented in the Bundestag, sharing a list with the party "Alliance 90", which put up candidates in the new states. In May 1993, the two parties merged into one under the name "Alliance 90/The Greens" and won seats in the Bundestag in the 1994 elections. In the 1998 election, "Alliance 90/The Greens" was the fourth

Edmund Stoiber, Chairman of the CSU in Bavaria

largest party and formed a coalition government with the SPD; the new Federal Minister for Foreign Affairs – who also serves as Deputy Federal Chancellor – is a member of this party.

The PDS is the successor to the former Socialist Unity Party of Germany (SED), the communist party which ruled in the former German Democratic Republic (GDR). It has not been able to establish itself as a major political force in united Germany. In 1990, the PDS – like the Alliance 90/The Greens group – was only represented in the Bundestag by virtue of an exception allowing the five percent clause to be applied separately in the new states and in the existing ones in the west for the benefit of the parties in the eastern part of the country. In the 1994 Bundestag election, the PDS achieved representation in the Bundestag on the basis of four constituency seats in Berlin. In the 1998 election, it not only won the same number of constituency seats but also cleared the five percent hurdle, thus acquiring the status of a parliamentary party.

The five percent clause. Of the 36 parties which sought election to the first Bundestag in 1949, only four remained in the parliament elected in 1990. This is the result of a "five percent debarring clause" which was introduced in 1953 and made stricter still in 1957. It stipulates that only parties gaining at least five percent of the valid second votes or at least

Renate Künast and Fritz Kuhn, federal chairpersons of Bündnis 90/ Die Grünen

Wolfgang
Gerhardt,
Chairman of
the FDP

three constituency seats can be represented in parliament.
This arrangement was explicitly accepted by the Federal Constitutional Court since its purpose was to prevent tiny splinter
parties from entering parliament (as had happened in the
days of the Weimar Republic) and thus more clearly enable
the larger parties to obtain majorities that would enable
them to govern.

In the case of national minorities, the five percent hurdle is
waived at state level. Thus the South-Schleswig Voters' Association, which represents the Danish minority, has three members in the state parliament of Schleswig-Holstein even
though it obtained fewer than five percent of the votes. Local
government elections sometimes produce results that differ
greatly from those of federal and state elections. Here the
"townhall parties", independent voters' associations, often
play an important role.

1998 Federal Elections to the Bundestag (German parliament)

Number of persons entitled to vote: 60,762,751

Political Party	Valid second votes	Percent	Number of members of parliament
SPD	20,181,269	40.9	298
CDU	14,004,908	28.4	198
CSU	3,324,480	6.7	47
Alliance 90/ The Greens	3,301,624	6.7	47
F.D.P.	3,080,955	6.2	43
PDS	2,515,454	5.1	36
Other	2,899,822	5.9	–
Total	49,308,512		669
Invalid second votes cast	638,575	(1.3%)	

The turnout was 82.2%.

The electoral system. Elections for all parliaments in Germany are general, direct, free, equal and secret. Any German who is 18 years of age or older, has been residing in Germany for at least three months and has not been disfranchised is entitled to vote. Upon fulfillment of certain conditions, Germans living abroad can also vote in elections. Anyone who has possessed German nationality for at least one year is eligible to stand for election if he or she has attained the age of 18 by the day on which the election is held and has neither been disfranchised nor lost his or her eligibility to stand for election or hold public office as a consequence of a judge's ruling. There are no primary elections. As a rule, the candidates are nominated by their parties; however, individuals with no party affiliation may also run for office. Elections for the German Bundestag are based on a system of "personalized" proportional representation. Voters have two votes, the first of which is given to a candidate in their constituency. The successful candidate is elected on a first-past-the-post basis. The second vote is given to a list of candidates put up by the parties.

The votes from the constituencies and those for the state lists are offset in such a way that the composition of the Bundestag almost identically reflects the distribution of votes among the parties. If a party has won more direct seats in the constituencies than its proportion of the votes would justify (these being known as "overhang" seats), it is allowed to keep them, whereby no compensation is provided for the other parties. Whenever this happens, the Bundestag has more than the 656 members prescribed by law, hence the present 669. The object of having the electorate vote for state lists is to ensure that the strengths of all parties in parliament re-

Gabi Zimmer, Chairperson of the PDS

Voters placing their votes

flect their shares of the votes obtained. The constituency vote, the first vote, gives people the chance to choose a particular candidate. Normally, the people take a keen interest in elections. The turnout for the Bundestag election of 1998 was 82.2 percent. It tends to fluctuate strongly at state and local elections.

Membership and finances. As of 31 December 1999, the memberships of the parties represented in the Bundestag were as follows: SPD 755,000; CDU 638,000; CSU 184,800; FDP 64,400; Alliance 90/The Greens 50,300; and PDS 94,000. All parties require their members to pay subscriptions, but these cover only part of their expenses. The donations received are also insufficient. Moreover, there is a danger of big donors influencing the parties for their own ends. Therefore, pursuant to the new provisions of the Law on Political Parties governing party financing which entered into force on 1 January 1994, the parties receive funds from the state each year of DM 1.30 per vote for up to five million valid votes which they poll in elections to the Bundestag, the European Parliament and the state parliaments. For each additional vote they receive DM 1.00. Moreover, 50 pfennigs are paid for each DM 1.00 which a party receives from members' subscriptions or from donations; in this context, only donations of up to DM 6,000 per year per individual are taken into account. These amounts may not exceed the funds raised by the party per year. The public grants for all parties together may not total more than DM 245 million (absolute limit) per year. The scale of part-financing of a party by the state must not exceed the sum of the revenue the party itself has procured elsewhere in the course of the year (relative upper ceiling).

The state and its citizens

Internal security

The maintenance of public security and order is one of the most important tasks of government. In Germany this task is carried out by both the states and the Federation. The police are for the most part under the jurisdiction of the states. Only in certain fields does the Basic Law assign responsibility to the Federation.

The police of the states. The jurisdiction of the states for the police encompasses all organizational and personnel matters pertaining to their state police forces. The branches of the police forces include the general police forces, the criminal police, the alert forces and the river police.

The general police forces are essentially responsible for ensuring public security and order. Their duties range from warding off dangers to prosecuting crime.

The criminal police are likewise responsible for the prevention and detection of crime. Whereas the general police forces are mainly concerned with cases of petty crime and minor offences, the criminal police deal with all instances of dangerous crimes and criminal offenses. These include in particular culpable homicide, serious property offenses and, increasingly, organized crime. In the prosecution of crime, the police assist the public prosecutor's office in charge of the given proceedings.

The criminal police have special units – in some cases jointly
with the general forces – to combat terrorism and hostage-
taking as well as for protective measures at special events and
for observation and searches.

The alert forces of the states, which are deployed as whole units,
were instituted pursuant to administrative agreements between the Federation and the states in order to be available in
case of internal emergencies, natural disasters and major accidents, in a state of tension or in a state of defense. In some
states the alert forces are responsible for the training of new
police recruits. They also provide support for individual police forces during demonstrations, sporting events and other
major events, traffic surveillance, police raids and large-scale
search operations and can be deployed to combat organized
crime. In accordance with the administrative agreements
concluded with the states, the Federation suitably equips the
some 16,500 law enforcement officers of the alert forces, in
particular for operations transcending state boundaries.

The Federal Border Guard. The Federal Border Guard (BGS)
is the police force at the federal level. It handles specific
policing tasks within the Federal Republic's security system
and answers to the Federal Ministry of the Interior. The Act
on the Federal Border Guard of 19 October 1994 as amended
in 1998, defines in detail the tasks of the BGS. Moreover, numerous other legal stipulations lay down its tasks, such as the
Aliens Act. The original tasks of the BGS include its activity
patroling the country's borders and, since 1992, policing the
railways as well as preventing attacks on the safety of air traffic at most of Germany's major airports. Its brief as the border patrol is becoming ever more important given the opening in particular of the eastern borders, which has triggered

Customs
checks at a
warehouse

not only greater freedom of movement for people in Europe with an ongoing increase in cross-border traffic, but has also opened up new fields of operation for cross-border criminality (examples are not just illegal immigration, but above all alien smuggling, car smuggling, and drug trafficking. Moreover, the Schengen implementation treaty enacted on 26 March 1995 calls for an effective border security system in the form of consistent patrols on all internal Schengen borders. Since 1 September 1998, the BGS has an extended brief. It can now also halt and check the papers of persons in certain places outside the 30-km border zone, railway stations, and passenger airports in order to prevent or stop illegal immigration.

Furthermore, the Federal Border Guard also has special-purpose departments (units) in the form of intervention forces who support specific BGS tasks and the police forces of the individual states in special operations, such as large-scale operations, disasters, and accidents. Moreover, the BGS is responsible for the protection of Germany's constitutional bodies and the federal ministries, exercise of police functions on the North Sea and the Baltic Sea, including environmental protection and policing inland waterways, as well as increasingly involvement in peacekeeping police activities abroad under the aegis of the United Nations, the Western European Union, and other international organizations.

On 1 January 1998, a comprehensive reorganization of the Federal Border Guard became effective which takes due account of both the changes in the basic police and security policy framework and the new fields of activity of the Federal Border Guard.

The Federal Border Guard presently has about 30,000 law enforcement officers (not including trainees), 1,800 police support staff for border-patrol tasks and air-passenger checks, and about 6,800 civilian staff for its wide-ranging service and admin. tasks.

The Federal Criminal Police Office (BKA), is based in Wiesbaden, Meckenheim (near Bonn), and Berlin. By providing central agencies, collections and services, it acts to support state police agencies in the prevention of and fight against crime in particular where criminals act across state or national borders or when crimes of considerable consequence have been committed. The Federal Criminal Police Office collects and evaluates information and other data to aid the police in combating crime and for strategic analyses of crime trends; it is an important institution in implementing information management methods in practical police work and for criminological research, developments, and tests.

As regards international police cooperation, the Federal Criminal Police Office has a pivotal function as the national central agency for Interpol, the international criminal police organization, and it is likewise the national center for the Schengen information system and for Europol.

The Federal Criminal Police Office is responsible for handling policing tasks and prosecution of certain, legally defined crimes. These include internationally organized drug trafficking and gun-running, certain serious crimes against members of Germany's constitutional bodies and their guests, and crimes committed by internationally organized terrorist organizations. The states and the Public Prosecutor General may also assign it responsibility for investigating specific individual cases. A further function of the Federal Criminal Police Office is the protection of federal witnesses. Its security unit in Berlin also protects the members of Germany's constitutional bodies and their foreign guests of state.

The Federal Criminal Police Office has a staff of about 4,600, of whom about one half are involved in executive criminal police work. The Federal Criminal Police Office comes under the authority of the Federal Ministry of the Interior.

Constitution-protection agencies. Safeguarding the free democratic basic order is defined in the Basic Law as "protection of the constitution". In order to be able to provide effective protection, the federal and state constitution-protection agencies collect information on extremist activities and on other developments which constitute a threat to national security and evaluate it for the federal and state governments, executive authorities and courts. Another important area of activity is counterespionage. The federal agency charged with these tasks is the Federal Office for the Protection of the Constitution (BfV) in Cologne, which is also responsible for central collection of documents pertinent to protection of the constitution. It is accountable to the Federal Ministry of the

Cologne
traffic control
center

Interior and cooperates with the state constitution-protection agencies. This agency has no executive police powers; in other words, it may not arrest or interrogate anyone. A law enacted in 1990 defined the legal basis for its activities more precisely and ensured greater protection for the citizens' rights of privacy.

The activities of the federal and state agencies for the protection of the constitution are closely supervised at a number of levels: by the competent ministers, by the parliaments and by the data protection commissioners. These controls are supplemented by the possibility of having an individual measure which incriminates a citizen reviewed by the courts. The mass media – the press, radio and television – also exercise a control function, although not in a legally institutionalized capacity.

Public finance

The core task of financial policy remains ensuring that central
government is able to rely on viable financing. Only by continuing the consistent Federal Government strategy of financial consolidation will it be possible to prevent state indebtedness burgeoning and scope for action be regained. At the
same time, it will be possible to reduce the tax bill and duties
levied on private individuals and corporations alike. In this
way, conditions will be created on the demand and supply
sides for dynamic economic growth and an enduring economic upturn.

Moreover, reducing unemployment is the Government's declared
top priority; all its measures in financial policy are oriented
towards achieving this aim. The tax reform will serve to create new jobs and to ease the burden on low- and middle-in-
come individuals.

The budget consolidation that is required is also an imperative
for international solidarity in the framework of EMU. The Euroland member states have pledged as part of the stability
and growth pact to more or less balance their budgets or
even, if possible, to score surpluses. By means of joint efforts
to secure long-term viable financial conditions in Euroland,
the basis will also be laid for enduringly stable monetary
value and favorable macro-economic conditions.

The Government's budget policy does not just entail cost-cutting.
Future-oriented tasks in particular in the fields of research,
education, and science are all being bolstered.

Distribution of responsibilities. The Federal Republic of
Germany has three levels of government: federal, state and
local. Their responsibilities in their respective areas are governed by the Basic Law. Generally speaking, they have to
meet the necessary expenditure themselves. Hence public
revenue does not flow into a joint account but is instead distributed among the federal, state and local governments. The

lowest level of public administration is that of the municipality. Allocation of responsibilities to the municipalities is reserved to the states. The municipality is concerned with all matters that directly concern the local community and individual citizens. It is thus responsible for water supply and disposal, waste disposal, maintenance of local roads, local welfare and health services as well as construction and maintenance of primary and secondary general schools.

The states have jurisdiction for all aspects of government, unless the Basic Law specifically provides otherwise or leaves open the possibility of a different arrangement. Their main responsibilities fall into the category of cultural affairs and primarily concern schools and education. The administration of justice, the police and public health services also fall within the states' purview.

Major tasks and thus a crucial financial burden is borne by the Federation. According to the Basic Law, its sphere of competence embraces all matters that directly secure the existence of the state as a whole, namely social security, defense, foreign affairs, national security, the construction of autobahns and federal highways, communications, major research and the promotion of science. The Federation also has authority in the areas of energy, promotion of industry, agriculture, housing and urban development, environmental protection and economic cooperation with developing countries.

There are various other tasks which the federal and the state governments plan, implement and finance jointly. These include university construction, the improvement of regional economic structures, agrarian structure and coastal preservation, as well as cooperation on educational planning and the promotion of science.

Many years of effort have gone into adapting the Frankfurt cloverleaf to modern traffic requirements

A fourth level of administration is also assuming increasing importance: the European Union.

Financial planning. A 1967 Law for the Promotion of Economic Stability and Growth requires the federal and state governments to draw up their budgets in the light of the principal economic policy objectives. These are price stability, a high level of employment, balanced foreign trade and steady economic growth ("the magic square"). The Federation and the states must draw up financial plans for their areas of responsibility in which incomes and expenditure are projected for a period of five years. The purpose of this multi-annual financial planning is to ensure that public revenue and expenditure are commensurate with national economic resources and requirements. The municipalities, too, must draw up medium-term financial plans.

The great importance of the public budgets requires close coordination through all levels of administration. The main body in this process of voluntary cooperation is the Financial Planning Council, which was set up in 1968 and consists of representatives of the Federation, the states, the municipalities and the Deutsche Bundesbank.

In view of the budgetary policy stipulations of the Treaty on European Union, which obligate the participating countries to limit their national debt and national deficit, the coordinating function of the Financial Planning Council is taking on additional importance. There is also a Business Cycle Council with coordinating and advisory functions.

Distribution of revenues. In order to meet their responsibilities, the federal, state and local governments must have the necessary funds. Wide-ranging as public responsibilities are, the sources of revenue are equally varied. The main source is

Federal Minister of Finance Hans Eichel and Federal Chancellor Gerhard Schröder

taxation. Total tax revenue in 1999 was DM 886.1 billion. The EU's share was 4.5 percent, that of the Federation 42.5 percent, that of the states 40.6 percent and that of the municipalities 12.4 percent.

Tax revenue has to be distributed according to the size of the responsibilities of the three levels of government. The income tax and the turnover tax are "joint taxes"; that is to say, revenues from them are distributed between the federal and state governments according to specific formulas (that of the turnover tax being renegotiated from time to time). Part of the revenue from the income tax also goes to the municipalities. In exchange they have to surrender to the federal and state governments part of the revenue they raise from the trade tax, which used to be a purely local government tax. Since 1 January 1998, the municipalities have been entitled to a share of revenue from the turnover tax as well.

Germany's payments to the budget of the European Union are financed from the tax revenues of the Federation. Customs duties and agricultural levies are remitted to Brussels according to their yield. In addition, the European Union receives own resources from value-added tax (VAT) revenues which are assessed according to a base uniformly defined for all the Member States.

The portion of EU expenditures not covered by these revenues is met by EU own resources in the form of contributions by the Member States which are assessed in accordance with their respective share of total EU GNP, calculated at current market prices.

Other taxes apply to only one level of government. The Federation obtains revenue from the insurance tax and all excise taxes except the beer duty (the mineral oil and tobacco duties, for instance). The states receive the revenue from the motor vehicle tax, inheritance tax, real property transfer tax, betting and lottery tax, fire protection tax and the beer duty. The municipalities obtain revenue from the trade tax (less the share taken by the federal and state governments), the real property tax and local excise taxes.

The largest slice of tax revenue is sourced by taxes on income (including the corporation tax), which account for almost 45 percent of the total. The wages tax is the one which affects the average person most of all. Employers deduct it from wages and salaries and remit it to the tax office. The rate of taxation rises with the individual's income. Pursuant to the 2000 income tax schedule, the rate is at least 22.9 percent and at most 51 percent of taxable income. Incomes of up to approximately DM 13,500 per year in the case of single persons and of up to approximately DM 27,000 per year in the case of married couples are exempt from taxation. The Federal Government's tax reform will lead to tangible relief for all employees through to the year 2005. The basic rate exempt from income tax will rise to some DM 15,000 for single persons and about DM 30,000 for married couples. The tax rate will fall to a minimum of 15 percent and a maximum of 45 percent.

The second largest source of revenue is the turnover tax (value-added tax and import turnover tax). It accounts for nearly one third of all tax revenue. The mineral oil duty and the trade tax generate about eight percent and six percent of tax revenue respectively.

Financial equalization. The financial situation of the individual states varies considerably because their natural resources and economic structures are also different. Thus financially powerful states such as Baden-Württemberg, Bavaria, Hamburg, Hesse or North Rhine-Westphalia have substantial financial resources, whereas the financially weak states, particularly in eastern Germany, do not. These financial disparities are mitigated by a nationwide financial equalization regime. This multilevel financial equalization is achieved by allocating the states' share of revenues from the turnover tax among the individual states according to a differentiated formula, by requiring financially strong states to make equalization payments to financially weak states, and, finally, by providing federal complemental grants to the latter.

A "vertical financial equalization" takes place between the states and the municipalities. The tax revenues and other revenues of the municipalities are inadequate for their tasks. They therefore depend on grants from the states. Some of these grants are tied to specific purposes, but others are freely disposable. The aim of this municipal financial equalization is to reduce the disparity in each state between municipalities with high and those with low tax revenues.

Public debt and auditing of public finances. Apart from levying taxes to finance public expenditure, the government can also borrow money. Especially in the 1970s and since reunification, the federal and state finance ministers – despite drastic economy measures – have been drawing increasingly on the capital markets. In 1999, the country's total public debt came to a record DM 2.291 billion, or almost DM 27,907 per inhabitant. In 1999, federal new indebtedness totaled DM 51.3 billion. The longer-term goal of Government financial policy is to achieve a balanced budget by the year 2006 and without any new borrowing requirement (see chart, p. 501). After 2006, Government indebtedness must be gradually reduced. This is the most important contribution financial policy can make to solidarity across the generations.

Auditing of federal and state administration of public finances in Germany has been assigned to the Federal Court of Audit and the 16 state courts of audit. This is in keeping with Germany's federal structure and the constitutional principle that the Federation and the states shall be autonomous and mutually independent in their budget management. As an independent body of government auditing, the Federal Court of Audit examines the accounts of the Federation and determines whether public finances have been properly and efficiently administered. It submits an annual report of its audit findings to the Federal Government as well as to the Bundestag and the Bundesrat. This report is also used by Parliament to approve the accounts for preceding years. The Federal Court of Audit has furthermore been given the task of making recommendations on the basis of its audit findings and of advising the bodies under audit and Parliament. Thus the Federal Court of Audit helps to enhance public sector management and performance.

The common good and individual interests

The public service in Germany encompasses all people employed by the Federation, the states and the municipalities as well as those employed by other corporations, agencies and foundations under public law. On 30 June 1999, a total of just under 5.0 million people were employed in the public service. Of this figure, 1.88 million (37.9 percent) were professional civil servants, judges and soldiers, 2.37 million (47.8 percent) were salaried employees, and 710,000 (14.3 percent) were wage earners. The Federation employed 10.3 percent of all public service employees, the states 46.5 percent, the municipalities 32.4 percent, the indirect public service 9.2 percent and the Federal Railway Property 1.6 percent. Of the total, 24.3 percent are part-timers (in public corporations in 1999), and the public service is a pioneer compared with the private sector in this area. As regards female employment, the public service, where the proportion is 52.3 percent, is also clearly ahead of the private sector.

As with the modernization of the administration, the modernization of the public service law has become a focus of domestic policy owing to the changed conditions over the decades:
- difficult conditions as regards public budgets
- expansion in the scope of government activities, in particular in the administration of services
- impact of changed demographic trends on areas to be covered exclusively by the state, such as professional civil servants, judges, and soldiers.

The savings that need to be made to consolidate state budgets, and in particular the jobs that must be cut, call for a public service that achieves more and costs less.

The main goal of modernizing public service law must focus on tapping the potential of each individual staff member.

With the enactment of the Service Law and Supply Reform Acts in 1997 and 1998 respectively, first steps were taken to press ahead as necessary with modernizing and advancing public service, and measures were initiated to reduce the future strain of providing such services. However, these steps are not in themselves sufficient. For this reason, currently reports are being compiled together with the states and municipalities and with the involvement of trade unions and professional associations in order to better gauge the efficiency of the new regulations passed and then to more precisely identify the further need for action by the legislative.

As regards service utilities, further developments depend on the measures envisaged in connection with the reform of the statutory pension insurance system, for the Government is endeavoring to reform the system of old-age provisions and bring them into line with each other.

Irrespective of the findings put forward in the reports, in order to implement the project to create the model of an "enabling state" and the agenda for a "modern state – modern administration" the public service pay law will be rendered more flexible for all public employers. A new Act on Public Service Pay Levels is expected to reduce the uniform nation-wide norms as regards pay for professional civil servants and give the public employers greater scope to take a more differentiated approach in their human resource policy. Moreover, staff will be offered new prospects and an achievement focus fostered.

Associations represent specific material interests of their members vis-à-vis the state and its institutions. These above all include the major labor and employers' associations, but there are numerous other organizations as well which represent certain professional, business or social interests. Homeowners, tenants, women's groups, war victims and motorists, for example, have formed associations, some with very large memberships. There are also organizations of minorities.

These common-interest associations engage in public relations to win sympathy for their causes. Their expertise can also be called upon in the preparation of legislation. Their influence is considerable, but it would be an exaggeration to say that Germany is ruled by associations.

Citizens' action groups. A fairly new type of association is the citizens' action group, many of which have been formed in the Federal Republic since the early 1970s. Citizens get to-

"Airplane noise is sickening": demonstration against the expansion to Frankfurt's Rhine-Main Airport

gether, usually spontaneously, to try to remedy a grievance when they feel a matter has been neglected by public authorities or parliaments. In most cases local issues are at stake, for example a children's playground, the preservation of old trees due to be felled to make way for a road, or efforts to prevent the extension of an airport. Sometimes action groups pursue contradictory aims: One may campaign for a bypass road to reduce traffic in a residential area, for instance, while another may oppose such a road for ecological reasons.

The Federal Government welcomes and supports groups that draw attention to social problems and play a constructive part in their solution. It is a basic right of all Germans to organize and take part in peaceful demonstrations. However, the final decision on controversial matters lies with the democratically elected governments and parliaments. They are bound to take the decisions that are best for the community as a whole. It is therefore important that individuals and citizens' action groups become involved as soon as possible in the preparation of government decisions, especially in the planning stage. Some legislation, for instance the Federal Building Act, already provides for such civic participation.

Germany and the world

Foreign policy

The basic framework of German foreign policy has changed fundamentally on the threshold of the 21st century. Germany is reunified and sovereign in its foreign policy. Its security situation has improved considerably. German foreign policy is and shall remain peace policy. It remains committed to safeguarding the future of the global community.

The end of the confrontation between East and West has created new freedom for all the states which were once caught in the maelstrom of ideological tensions. Previously inconceivable forms of cooperation are now possible in the whole of Europe and the world.

As an exporting nation which is integrated into the global economy, united Germany in the heart of Europe derives particular benefit from these new opportunities. In a world which is increasingly interdependent, national isolationism is no longer possible. The most important manifestation of this change is globalization, the internationalization of communication and economic activity which leaves national frontiers far behind.

In the whole of Europe, democracy, the rule of law and market economy principles have made crucial progress.

At the same time, however, Europe – along with other regions of the world – has also experienced an outbreak of open armed

conflict within its own borders. The creation of a stable and
enduring peaceful order in Europe, the further civilization of
international relations and the creation of a legal framework
for these relations, especially the development and elaboration of effective strategies for conflict prevention and peaceful resolution of conflicts, are therefore ongoing priorities of
German policy. Support for human rights, readiness to engage in dialogue, renunciation of force and confidence-building form the foundations of this policy.

By dint of its own history, Germany is particularly committed to
freedom, the rule of law and human rights. All over the
world, therefore, its policy is based on respect for human
rights and human dignity. Guided by these principles, it
strives to promote stability, peace and development.

Global problems such as sustainable development in its partner
countries in the south and east, overcoming underdevelop-
ment, preserving a habitable world worth living in, and con-
taining uncontrolled migration, cross-border crime and the
spread of weapons of mass destruction constitute the key
challenges of the 21st century, challenges which individual
states are no longer able to master alone.

The Federal Republic of Germany is prepared to assume greater
responsibility in this changing world. Its framework for action in the sphere of foreign policy will continue to be the
close relationships with its partners in the European Union
(EU) and the Atlantic Alliance (NATO) as well as its involvement in international organizations, especially the United
Nations and the Organization for Security and Cooperation in
Europe (OSCE).

German foreign policy is oriented towards the aims of maintaining peace and prosperity, promoting democracy and developing respect for human rights the world over. As a consequence, Germany's foreign policy endeavors are focused on
the following:

— the further development of the European Union; the EU
must become a full-fledged partner capable of action in all
areas of global policy;

— the safeguarding of peace, democracy and prosperity in the
whole of Europe; this is to be achieved inter alia through successful enlargement of the EU;

— the strengthening of cooperation within the OSCE;

French Prime Minster Lionel Jospin and Federal Chancellor Gerhard Schröder

— the further development of the Atlantic Alliance and transatlantic cooperation; in this context Europe must assume more responsibility of its own;

— the strengthening of international organizations, above all the United Nations, and the development of a more active role for Germany in these organizations;

— the promotion of respect for human rights all over the world;

— the further development of relations based on a spirit of equal partnership with the regions bordering the EU, in particular with those of the Mediterranean and the Middle East, in the interest of promoting development and stability; and

— more intensive cooperation with the states of Sub-Saharan Africa as a focal region of German development aid foreign policy.

The high productivity of the Federal Republic's economy remains the indispensable foundation for the nation's foreign policy influence and capacity to act.

Germany's role as one of the world's leading exporting nations and as the location of viable future-oriented industries must be safeguarded. As one of the largest industrial and trading nations, Germany is dependent upon a well-functioning world economic system which does not lose sight of the need for a reconciliation of ecological and social interests. Repeated crises on the international financial markets have made clear the degree to which national economies are interdependent and the considerable potential for social destabilization that this interdependence entails.

Strengthening the international institutions in the areas of trade and finance and creating a binding legal framework for the global economy which is oriented towards market economy principles is consequently in Germany's interest.

The Federal Republic of Germany intends to make its contribution towards peaceful progress in the world and an equitable reconciliation of the interests of the North and the South.

German foreign policy remains committed to the aim of achieving sustainable development throughout the world.

Germany maintains diplomatic relations with nearly all of the countries of the world and has more than 200 embassies and consular posts as well as including 12 missions attached to intergovernmental and international organizations.

The Atlantic Alliance. The North Atlantic Treaty Organization (NATO) remains the indispensable foundation of the security of its members in Europe and North America. The Federal Republic of Germany joined NATO in 1955. The defense capability of all NATO member states has, over the decades, safeguarded the existence of the free democracies, proceeding from the dual strategy of defense and dialogue in relation to the former Warsaw Pact countries as expressed in the Harmel Report of 1967. It was not least the Atlantic Alliance which paved the way for the transformation in Europe and in Germany.

As a result of the political transformation in Europe, the confrontation between East and West has meanwhile been overcome. The resulting fundamental change in the overall framework for security policy leaves NATO facing new challenges and new opportunities. In particular, pan-European cooperation on security is now a high priority for the Alliance. Since 1990, this European-wide cooperation has increasingly taken a differentiated and multi-faceted form.

The Euro-Atlantic Partnership Council (EAPC), which emerged from the North Atlantic Cooperation Council established at the initiative of Germany and the United States, is comprised of the NATO member states and 27 partner countries, including all the countries of the former Warsaw Pact and the newly independent states on the territory of the former Soviet

British Prime Minister Tony Blair and Federal Chancellor Gerhard Schröder

Union. This Council meets regularly and demonstrates the Alliance's readiness for a comprehensive security partnership in Europe. Within the context of the Partnership for Peace (PfP), which was founded in 1994, the Alliance cultivates close political and military cooperation with 27 partner countries in areas such as international peacekeeping operations. Among other things, the Partnership for Peace enables the partner countries to second personnel to NATO agencies and participate in a planning and review process which is similar to NATO force planning.

With the signing of the Founding Act on Mutual Relations, Cooperation and Security between the North Atlantic Treaty Organization and the Russian Federation in May 1997, the foundations were laid for a stronger security partnership between NATO and Russia. The NATO-Russia Permanent Joint Council was instituted, which, after its work was interrupted owing to differences of opinion during the Kosovo Crisis in 1999, in 2000 returned to its job as a platform for consultation and coordination.

The Alliance is also intensifying its cooperation with the Ukraine: In July 1997, the Charter on a NATO-Ukraine Distinctive Partnership was signed in Madrid. This Charter established a framework for the NATO-Ukraine Commission, which has meanwhile taken up its work.

The fact that the Alliance is now opening to new member states is part of this overall approach based on cooperation. For example, the Czech Republic, Hungary, and Poland all formally acceded as new members at the NATO Summit in Washington in April 1999. At the same time, the heads of state and government of the Alliance reiterated that NATO is open to new members ("the new members will not be the last") and resolved MAP, a membership action plan for countries which had expressly voiced an interest in accession (Romania, Bulgaria, Slovenia, the Slovak Republic, Estonia, Latvia, Lithuania, Albania, Macedonia).

At its April 1999 Washington Summit celebrating 50 years of NATO, the Alliance undertook a fundamental redefinition of its role, its tasks, and how it sees itself in the changed security scenario in Europe. The new Strategic Concept specifies that the fundamental security task is to strengthen security and stability for the entire Euro-Atlantic region by means of partnership and cooperation as well as conflict prevention and crisis management.

At the same time, the key significance for the Alliance was affirmed of collective defense and the maintenance of strong transatlantic ties. By stationing a peace-keeping force in Kosovo (KFOR), an act preceded by NATO air strikes, NATO is contributing decisively to the international community's objective of laying the foundations for enduring peace and stability in Kosovo. And in Bosnia-Hercegovina, too, NATO is pursuing its efforts to ensure implementation of the Dayton Peace Treaty by deploying a NATO-led international peace-keeping force SFOR (Stabilization Force).

Other core areas of German foreign and security policy are disarmament, arms control and non-proliferation. They serve to limit and, where possible, reduce weapon capabilities and, through cooperation and transparency, build confidence between states in matters of military and security policy.

The most important instruments of cooperative arms control in the area of conventional forces and weapons are:

— the Treaty on Conventional Forces in Europe (CFE), within the framework of which more than 50,000 heavy weapons in Europe have already been decommissioned and which has been adjusted to the new security policy scenario in Europe by an agreement signed by the heads of state and government of the 30 member states on 19 November 1999 in the framework of the OSCE Summit in Istanbul;

— the 1992 follow-up agreement on force limitations (CFE Ia);

— the Vienna Document on confidence- and security-building measures among the member states of the OSCE, which was further developed and improved in 1999;

— the OSCE Code of Conduct on Politico-Military Aspects of Security; and

— the 1992 Open Skies Treaty, which renders the airspace of contracting states accessible for aircraft surveillance.

Germany played an important role in bringing about the inclusion of arms control agreements in the Dayton accords, which are to safeguard peace and security in former Yugoslavia. Over 7,000 weapons systems have been dismantled since 1996, while confidence- and security-building measures have been established between the parties to the conflict. Germany has also provided active support for the process of regional stabilization in and around former Yugoslavia, which had likewise been agreed in Dayton and commenced at the beginning of 1998.

In mid-1998, Germany took the initiative for a joint EU campaign to limit and control small and light arms resolved by the EU Council on 17 December 1998. The goal of the Joint Action is to combat the excessive and uncontrolled accumulation and spread of small arms and to solve the problems in the context of existing excessive collections of such arms.

To promote the worldwide proscription of anti-personnel land mines, Germany completely renounced the use and export of these weapons as early as April 1996 and had destroyed the Bundeswehr's stockpiles by the end of 1997. Together with 120 other nations, it signed the "Convention on the Prohibition of the Use, Stockpiling, Production and Transfer of Anti-Personnel Mines and on their Destruction" in Ottawa at the beginning of December 1997. The strict verification provisions of the Ottawa Convention are largely the outgrowth of German proposals. After ratification by the requisite minimum number of nations (40; Germany ratified it on 23 July 1998), the Ottawa Convention entered into force on 1 March 1999.

In the area of disarmament, arms control and the non-proliferation of weapons of mass destruction, the 187 signatories of the Treaty on Nuclear Nonproliferation, unconditionally extended in 1995, agreed in May 2000 on practical steps to strengthen nuclear disarmament and non-proliferation. The five states possessing nuclear weapons at the same time affirmed their duty to completely abolish nuclear arsenals. The September 1996 Treaty on a Comprehensive Ban on Nuclear Tests has already been signed by over 150 states, including all five states possessing nuclear weapons. To date, it has been ratified by 56, which does not suffice to enable it to come into force. The ratification by certain states named specifically in the Treaty, and whose ratification is necessary for such enactment, has still to take place. Germany was also one of the main proponents of the Convention on the Prohibition of the Development, Production, Stockpiling and Use of Chemical Weapons and Their Destruction, which entered into force in April 1997. Experts are presently engaged in negotiations on the elaboration of an effective, legally binding verification

regime for the 1972 Convention on the Prohibition of Bacte-
riological and Toxin Weapons. A completely new departure
in the field of arms control is cooperation in the destruction
of nuclear and chemical weapons. The Federal Republic is also involved in this aspect of arms control through projects in
Russia and Ukraine.

Relations with Germany's western neighbors. The
transatlantic partnership is the main instrument of "Western" policy for Germany and the United States and is of central importance for German foreign policy.

The United States is Germany's closest ally and partner outside
the European Union. The NATO, EU-USA, G8, and OSCE summit meetings make 1999 the year of transatlantic relations.
Germany is working with the United States on a comprehensive concept for reorganizing and strengthening the Euro-Atlantic partnership for the 21st century in order to meet the
global political and economic challenges arising after the
turn of the millennium.

Germany's and Europe's ties with Canada and the United States
remain extremely close. The transatlantic partnership is
based on vital mutual interests and values. Europe, the United States and Canada have manifold historical, human, cultural and political ties. The United States' and Canada's involvement in Europe therefore continues to be of crucial importance to the Continent's, and hence Germany's, peace
and security. NATO remains an indispensable security bond
between Europe and North America.

G8. The G8 (foreign ministers) play an increasingly important
role in maintaining peace and stability, as a complement to
the UN and the UN General Secretary. In 1999, when Germany was President of the G8, it made a decisive contribu-

The G8 heads
of state and
government
at the June
2000 Okinawa
Summit

tion to solving the Kosovo Crisis and to the creation of a stability pact which completely integrated Russia as a partner in the circle of G8 foreign ministers. One of the key issues on the foreign and security policy agenda of the Eight at the beginning of the 21st century is how the various organisations (G8, UN, EU, OSCE, among others) can develop effective strategies to contain dangers to international peace in a timely and enduring manner. Under the Presidency of German Foreign Minister Fischer, at the Berlin Special Conference on Conflict Prevention in December 1999 the G8 foreign ministers resolved to jointly and practically promote a "culture of prevention" and announced an initial program of foreign and security policy measures for substantive and regional conflict prevention, and it will be further advanced under the Japanese G8 Presidency in 2000. Other key issues being addressed by the G8 Foreign Ministers are disarmament, non-proliferation and arms controls, as well as regional topics and conflicts.

Cooperation within the G8 is taking on great importance in the search for solutions to global issues of financial, monetary and foreign policy at the dawn of the millennium. Germany held the G8 presidency in 1999. Together with its partners it played an active role in the political structuring of globalization and in the reform of the global monetary and financial system to master acute economic crises. In the framework of the G8, Germany will also contribute to the political stabilization of regions fraught with crises, and search for solutions to the global challenges which arise from IT, in development, environmental, and climate policy, or as regards cross-border crime.

Biannual summit meetings and numerous bilateral consultations provide renewed stimulus for the special relationship between Germany and France established by Chancellor Konrad Adenauer and President Charles de Gaulle through the treaty signed in the Elysée Palace in Paris in 1963. In recent years attention has been focused on issues pertaining to the process of European unification, which has been decisively furthered by joint initiatives of the two governments.

Increasingly close relations between the parliamentarians of both nations likewise reflect the special quality of Franco-German cooperation in all areas. The stability of Franco-German friendship is guaranteed by the contacts between the citizens of both countries (more than 2,000 town twinnings and 3,000 school twinnings, as well as cooperation between the regions) and by the close economic relations between the two countries, who are each other's respective main trading partner.

Germany's cooperation with other Western countries has also been continuously intensified. Annual summit meetings are held with the United Kingdom, and a dense network of agreements, consultations and mutual visits makes for a similarly close standing relationship with Germany's other Western partners.

Even if there can be no talk of normalization of German-Israeli relations owing to the strain posed by the Holocaust, in recent years close and trusting relations have emerged between Germany and Israel. Bilateral contacts are intensive and good at all levels and in most spheres. Since ambassadors were first exchanged in 1965, they have in many respects developed into a genuine friendship. In keeping with its balanced Mideast policy, the Federal Government is concurrently further developing its friendly relations with the Arab countries and is making every effort to support the Mideast peace process.

Relations with Germany's eastern neighbors. Cooperation and partnership between Germany and its eastern neighbors have obtained a new quality since the end of Communist rule in Central and Eastern Europe. Following the accession of the Czech Republic, Hungary, and Poland to NATO on 12 March 1999, the security-policy links between these three countries and the Western Alliance have become even closer. The entire spectrum of cooperation between states in southeastern and east central Europe as well as the Baltic states has been expanded. Germany maintains close relations with the democratic countries in these regions. They are conducting accession negotiations with the EU, which will open up new prospects for growth, employment, constitutionalism and greater stability throughout Europe.

Germany has trusting and closely-knit economic, cultural, and political links with Poland, its largest immediate neighbor in eastern Central Europe – and the various joint projects attest to the special importance of the spirit of the German-Polish partnership for the interests of Europe.

Commitment to Southeastern Europe. Together with its
EU and NATO partner states, the German Government is
committed to the enduring stabilization of southeastern Europe. This includes, in particular, establishing a peaceful,
democratic, and multi-ethnic Kosovo on the basis of UN Security Council Resolution No. 1244 of 10 June 1999, which envisages an international administration and the creation of
wide-ranging autonomous structures. The Federal Government is providing financial and human resources for the
UN's UNMIK administration in Kosovo as well as for the military peacekeeping force (KFOR). The goal is to make it possible for refugees and displaced persons to return to their
homes. International efforts to rebuild the country are
geared to creating future economic prospects for the population. The goal of strengthening the process of democratization is fostered by holding elections, promoting the media, as
well as founding democratic institutions and other measures.

In Bosnia and Hercegovina, even in Year 5 after signature of the
Dayton-Paris Peace Agreement, not all the war wounds have
healed. However, the situation has normalized appreciably.
The international community has been strongly committed
to supporting the reconstruction of Bosnia and Hercegovina,
the return of refugees, and the creation of democratic and
constitutional structures. As a member of the Peace Implementation Council's steering committee, Germany has been
playing an active role in this process. German experts hold
leading positions as active members of the staff of the Higher
Representatives of the International Community as well as in
all the missions of the large international organizations such
as the OSCE and EU. The Bundeswehr has provided a large
contingent of soldiers for the SFOR peacekeeping force and is
making a strong contribution to security there. Moreover,
Germany is one of those countries which plays a large part in
the UN's International Police Mission.

Permanent stability in the region can only be achieved if the
Federal Republic of Yugoslavia also joins the switchover to
democratic means. The reform strategy pursued now by President Dyukanovic in Montenegro, and which the German
Government supports, shows the way forward. It is now decisive that Serbia also initiates democratic change. Together
with its partners, the German Government therefore fully

Chancellor Schröder and Prime Minister Zhu Rongyi of the People's Republic of China

supports the democratic forces at work in politics and society there. A key element of such support is promoting help campaigns German cities have helped organize for democratically led Serbian cities in the framework of the Szeged process.

Further development of constructive relations between Germany and the Russian Federation, Ukraine and the other newly independent states on the territory of the former Soviet Union remains a key priority of German foreign policy. Germany will continue to pursue a course of constructive cooperation with these states. The policy of the Federal Republic of Germany is geared to supporting the transformation process in these countries, creating the preconditions for European unity and to strengthen the fundamental values of democracy and the rule of law.

The states of Central and Eastern Europe. The states of Central and Eastern Europe, including Russia and the newly independent states on the territory of the former Soviet Union, are playing an increasingly important role as economic partners of the Federal Republic. The volume of trade with this region as a whole has risen – aside from certain special developments and setbacks (Russia Crisis, 1998) – at a disproportionately higher rate than Germany's overall external trade. The more advanced emerging market economies in Central and Eastern Europe have become increasingly attractive locations for German investment abroad. All in all, integration of these economic regions is moving forwards. The future development of these economic relations will largely hinge on continued resolute implementation in the individual countries of a policy of reform which will create efficient market economy structures and hence lay the foundations for a stable and internationally competitive economy.

Together with international economic and financial institutions as well as other bilateral donors, Germany has from the very beginning supported the reformist states in their efforts to rebuild democracy and a market economy. Between the end of 1989 and the end of 1999, German assistance totaled some DM 77 billion for eastern Central Europe and DM 150 billion for Russia and the newly independent states on the territory of the former Soviet Union. Germany thus furnished about one third of the total assistance.

The Federal Republic of Germany is continuing to strongly encourage and support the reform process in the countries in transition with consulting services and initial and further training measures, especially within the framework of the TRANSFORM Programme. The German concept for helping these states to help themselves, for which the Federal Government allocated DM 1.3 billion between 1994 and 1999, is particularly valued for its flexibility, effectiveness and orientation towards demand in the partner countries. DM 130 million were earmarked for this in 1999.

In addition, the Federal Government is providing approx. DM 1.2 billion over the coming years for Albania, Macedonia, Bulgaria, Romania, Bosnia and Hercegovina, Croatia, and the Yugoslav sub-republic of Montenegro under the terms of the "Stability Pact for Southeastern Europe". Of the figure of DM 300 million set aside for 2000, some DM 184 million are targeted for the measures initiated by the Federal Ministry for Economic Cooperation and Development, and are mainly to be deployed in Kosovo.

Germany and the developing countries. Relations with the developing countries are an important element of German foreign relations. Reducing the prosperity gap between the industrial and developing countries, protecting the natural sources of life, averting global threats and preventing armed conflicts are increasingly becoming the crucial tasks

Russia's President Putin and Chancellor Schröder (June 2000 in Berlin)

of the coming years. These can only be mastered through joint efforts. The end of the conflict between East and West has freed Germany's relations with the developing countries of ideological ballast. The realization that democracy, respect for human rights and an economic order based on market principles promote sustainable development has become widespread and forms the basis for Germany's relations with the developing countries.

The developing nations expect united Germany to assume a larger role on the world stage. At the same time, however, they are afraid it might neglect "the South" in favor of "the East" on account of the economic burden of the unification process and the aid provided for the reformist countries of Central and Eastern Europe. Since 1990, the year of unification, the Federal Government has therefore repeatedly reaffirmed its commitments to the developing countries and its intention to further develop and strengthen the existing bonds of friendship.

The industrial countries must meet their responsibility to create global economic conditions. This assumes that they pay stronger heed to the impact their national policy has on the developing countries and at the same time coordinate their respective individual policy areas such as to guarantee a coherent policy toward the developing countries. Priority must be attached to giving the developing countries a fair chance. They must in particular open their markets and promote the integration of the developing countries into the global economy.

Both internationally and especially within the European Union, the Federal Republic has therefore always urged the industrial countries to open their markets wider to the countries of Africa, Asia and Latin America. Germany supports the process of economic growth and development in the developing countries through its imports – the volume of which is already high by international standards (US$ 95 billion in 1996, a per-capita figure of US$ 1,153) as well as through substantial development assistance and private capital transfers (US$ 21 billion in 1996 – a per-capita figure of US$ 258). Germany is in agreement with other industrialized nations that support in solidarity for the poorer developing countries must be strengthened in quantitative and qualitative terms.

Participants at the conference on "Modern 21st Century Government" in Berlin

Relations with the developing countries are thus playing an important role in Germany's foreign and security policy and in the foreign relations of the EU.

German humanitarian aid is an expression of the country's solidarity with others in times of acute need and is thus also an important aspect of its cultivation of friendly relations with other nations and peoples. This aid focuses on human beings in need: saving their lives and alleviating their suffering regardless of their race, sex, religion, nationality or political convictions. In recent years the Federal Government has provided even more substantial humanitarian aid than in the past. Between 1991 and 1999, a total of DM 1,239 million was made available from the budget of the Federal Foreign Office alone for humanitarian aid furnished through German and international relief organizations.

Germany's overall expenditure for humanitarian aid, including food aid, emergency relief and aid for refugees provided by the Federal Ministry for Economic Cooperation and Development as well as Bundeswehr relief operations, contributions to European Union and United Nations relief measures, and measures undertaken by private German relief organizations, was several times the aforementioned amount. The focus was on assistance for the Kurds in Iraq, support for the victims of the armed conflict in former Yugoslavia and Chechnya, as well as assistance for refugees world-wide.

Humanitarian aid is also needed after such major natural disasters as endanger human life and destroy the basis on which many people make a living. One needs only think of Hurricane "Mitch" in Central America, the recent earthquake in Turkey, floods in Venezuela and Mosambique, or drought and starvation in Africa.

Membership of the United Nations. A major aim of German foreign policy is to strengthen the role of the United Nations as the principal institution of the community of na-

Federal
Chancellor
Schröder as a
speaker at the
Millennium
Summit in
New York
(Sept. 6, 2000)

tions. Only this will enable the world organization to respond
adequately to such global challenges as conflict prevention,
the population explosion and environmental protection. This
applies especially to the Secretary-General of the United Nations, who should be placed in a stronger position to mediate
in preventing conflicts.

The multilateral orientation of the Federal Republic of Germany
has been a consistent feature of its foreign policy since 1945.
Already in the early 1950s Germany joined subsidiary organizations of the United Nations; in 1973 it became a full member. For decades this membership was a cornerstone of the
Federal Republic's peace, security and human rights policies.
Not least because of the paramount importance of human
rights for the respect for human dignity, for the preservation
of peace and for endeavors to combat despotism and need,
human rights policy is a strong focus of Germany's work
within the United Nations (among other things, the Federal
Republic played a key role in the institution of the office of a
United Nations High Commissioner for Human Rights in
1993 and in the initiative leading to the adoption in 1989 of
the Second Optional Protocol to the International Covenant
on Civil and Political Rights Aiming at the Abolition of the
Death Penalty; since 1973, moreover, it has almost continuously been a member of the United Nations Human Rights
Commission). Another focus is in the area of disarmament
and arms control, where German efforts led to the creation
of the United Nations Register of Conventional Arms, which
furnishes information on movements of conventional
weapons.

The high esteem in which the Federal Republic of Germany is
held by the UN membership at large as a result of its strong
commitment and active role was reflected among other
things in its three-time membership of the Security Council
(1977-8, 1987-8 and 1995-6). Germany has declared its willing-

ness – once the reform of the Security Council called for by a large majority of the United Nations membership has been carried out – to assume greater political responsibilities as a permanent member of the Security Council as well, especially in regard to the peacekeeping mission of the UN. It will pursue the opportunity of becoming a permanent member of the Security Council if a joint European seat cannot be achieved. Germany has demonstrated its willingness to play an active role in a global policy for peace through its many different forms of participation in peacekeeping operations of the U.N. in recent years (in Cambodia, Somalia, Georgia, former Yugoslavia and Guatemala, for instance). Under the terms of an official agreement, it has made civilian components available to support the swift start-up of peacekeeping missions. Germany will offer separate units to the United Nations for peacekeeping measures.

Germany is the third largest contributor to the UN. Since 1 July 1996, it has also been a seat of the UN: Both the United Nations Volunteers and the Secretariat of the United Nations Convention to Combat Desertification (UNCCD) are based in Bonn. Hamburg is the home of the International Maritime Court.

Cultural relations. Cultural policy is one of the main elements of German foreign policy. Its tasks include

— presenting culture in Germany to the outside world as part of European culture;

— promoting a knowledge and the spread of the German language all over the world as the key to German culture;

— fostering cooperation in education and science in particular in the form of cultural and scientific exchanges;

— conveying to other countries a comprehensive and self-critical image of the Federal Republic which reflects the diversity of democratic opinion in the country;

— nurturing international cultural dialogue and art, cultural, and personal exchanges;

— promoting international encounters through youth and sports exchange schemes;

— making use of and developing the media on the basis of international cooperation.

The aim of this foreign cultural policy is not just to provide information on our culture and country, but to kindle dialogue, exchange, and cooperation between people and between cultures. It is also intended to foster understanding between both countries and individuals, to promote a cosmopolitan outlook and a worldly view of things, and, in the long term, to spawn credibility, reliability and an indispensable network for political and economic cooperation.

The promotion of cultural dialogue within the country is on an equal footing with Germany's participation in cultural dialogue. Foreign cultural policy turns up partners and friends for Germany and is thus a direct means of furthering our vital interests.

Germany has concluded cultural agreements with over 100 countries and also has intensive cultural exchanges with most other countries. Translating cultural policy into practice is largely the responsibility of organizations acting on behalf of the Federal Government. The most important of these are:

— the Goethe Institute, which as of June 2000 had 128 cultural institutes in 76 countries and the Palestinian-administered territories as well as 15 branches in Germany and whose main tasks are to cultivate the German language abroad and promote international cultural cooperation;

— the German Academic Exchange Service (DAAD), which promotes exchanges of students, post-graduates, and academic staff and maintains 13 branches outside Germany;

— the Alexander von Humboldt Foundation, which promotes highly qualified foreign academics by awarding fellowships for their research and stay in Germany;

— INTER NATIONES, which hosts foreign guests of the government and provides a wide range of information on the Federal Republic of Germany through audiovisual media;

President Rau greets Iran's President Chatami during the latter's state visit in July 2000 in Berlin

— the Institute for Foreign Relations, which among other things organizes German exhibitions abroad and foreign exhibitions in Germany; and

— the German-American Fulbright Commission, which promotes the mutual exchange of particularly qualified academics, students, teachers and multipliers between Germany and the United States of America.

The German Foreign Ministry controls and coordinates German schools abroad. The Federal Office of Administration – Central Agency for Schools Abroad, and the State Culture Ministers Standing Conference assist it in this task. At present 119 schools receive support in this way. These are open to German children and, as a rule, to local children, and are committed to fostering an encounter with the culture and society of the host country. Depending on local requirements, not only German school-leaving certificates but also local diplomas may be earned.

Further information:
  — Bundesministerium des Auswärtigen
    (Federal German Foreign Ministry)
    Werderscher Markt 1, 10117 Berlin
    Internet: http://www.auswaertiges-amt.de
    E-mail: poststelle@auswaertiges-amt

Germany and Europe

European unification. Ever since its founding in 1949, the Federal Republic of Germany has been one of the main advocates of European unification. Its founders clearly recognized the following: European unification strengthens Europe's position in the world and serves to promote peace, freedom and prosperity on the Continent. Through the process of European integration, a transparent system of close mutual consultation and cooperation has been created which aims to peacefully reconcile the interests of all.

This highly successful system did not appear overnight. Together with Belgium, France, Italy, Luxembourg and the Netherlands, the Federal Republic of Germany formed the European Coal and Steel Community (ECSC) in 1952 and then established the European Economic Community (EEC) and the European Atomic Energy Community (EURATOM) in 1957. Through the Treaty establishing a Single Council and a Single Commission of the European Communities (Merger Treaty) of 1965, the institutions of the ECSC, the EEC and EURATOM were merged with the aim of strengthening the political influence of the Council and the Commission and streamlining the work of the Community institutions.

With the Single European Act of 1986, the Treaty on European Union signed in Maastricht on 7 February 1992 and the new Treaty of Amsterdam of 2 October 1997, further steps have been taken towards the unification of Europe.

The Maastricht Treaty laid the foundations for economic and monetary union, the third and final stage of which began upon the introduction of a common currency, the euro, on 1 January 1999. Europe has thus become the world's second largest single-currency area. Since the Maastricht Treaty came into force, moreover, the European Union (EU) has had a Common Foreign and Security Policy (CFSP) and a common policy in the fields of justice and home affairs. Thus the preconditions have been created for the development of the EU into a truly comprehensive political union.

The new EU treaty. At the same time, the Treaty of Amsterdam laid the foundations for future enlargements of the European Union. The Federal Republic of Germany was the first Member State to ratify the Treaty. The Treaty went into force on 1 May 1999 and specifically contains the following new items:

— Overall, the European Union is to be put in closer touch with its citizens. This is to be facilitated by the strengthening of the principle of subsidiarity, better foundations for environmental protection, and improved protection of basic rights (equality between men and women, for instance, and a general prohibition of discrimination). Issues such as public broadcasting, public credit institutions, churches and sports are addressed in the new treaty.

— The efficiency and visibility of the Common Foreign and Security Policy (CFSP) is to be enhanced. This will be accomplished by delegating to the Secretary-General of the Council the additional function of High Representative for the CFSP. He is assisted by the policy planning and early warning unit which has been newly instituted within the Council. In the form of the "common strategy", a new instrument has been created for implementing the common foreign policy and for the first time enables CFSP decisions to be taken by qualified majority.

— Of significance in the area of security policy is the prospect the Treaty offers of integrating the Western European Union (WEU) into the EU. The so-called "Petersberg tasks" (peacemaking, peacekeeping and humanitarian tasks) have likewise been included in the Treaty on European Union.

The EU
heads of
government
approve the
Maastricht II
Treaty in June
1997 at their
Amsterdam
Summit

— Important aspects of policy in the fields of justice and home affairs will be transferred to the more effective Community procedure (overall visa policy, regulations pertaining to external borders, policy on asylum/refugees, immigration and residency requirements for citizens of third countries, cooperation between judicial authorities in civil matters, some aspects of customs cooperation, endeavors to combat fraud affecting the financial interests of the Community).

— In the case of those aspects of policy in the fields of justice and home affairs which will continue to be handled by intergovernmental cooperation, the new instrument of framework decisions will simplify the procedure. The role of the European Court of Justice has been significantly expanded. New as well are the vesting of the European Police Office (Europol) with operational powers and the incorporation of the successful Schengen cooperation into the framework of the EU.

— Flexibility clauses open up the possibility of closer cooperation in the fields of justice and home affairs between states which are willing and able to do so.

— The European Parliament will be markedly strengthened. The scope of its powers of codecision will be broadened and the number of procedures reduced.

— The Council will more often take its decisions by a qualified majority. Within the Commission, the position of the President will be significantly strengthened. In respect of the future size of the Commission and the weighting of votes in the Council, a multi-stage plan has been agreed which will provide for the necessary institutional reforms prior to the entry into force of the next enlargement.

— A separate chapter on employment policy forms the basis for the future development of a coordinated employment strate-

In June 1999 the European Council convened in Cologne

gy in Europe. In addition, the Agreement on Social Policy has been inserted into the EU Treaty.

Progress since Amsterdam. The European Council of Berlin (March 1999) reached agreement on Agenda 2000, which sets the budget framework for the period 2000-6. For Germany, the new financial framework entails contributions relief of EUR 500 million as of 2002, rising to EUR 700 million as of 2004. Thus, a significant turnaround has been achieved as regards Germany's financing of the EU.

At the European Council in Cologne (June 1999), a European Employment Pact was resolved which brings together all EU employment policy measures in one overarching concept and lays down a dialogue between the Council, the Commission, the European Central Bank (ECB) and employer and employee federations. Thus, the Union has rounded out its range of tools for combating unemployment.

At the Tampere (October 1999) Special European Council Conference on Legal and Domestic Policy an integration project was continued which is intended to forge a Single European Legal Region. Among other things, the creation of a common system of political asylum was agreed.

With its resolutions on principle on European Security and Defense Policy (ESDP), the European Council in Cologne (June 1999) opened up a completely new terrain for the EU. The European Council of Helsinki fleshed this project out in the form of far-reaching and ambitious resolutions to give shape to ESDP: a Political and Security Policy Committee, a Military Committee and a Military Staff attached to the Council Secretariat were all set up. Civilian crisis management was upgraded in the form of a separate committee and lent systematic form.

By 2003, the EU intends to have its own rapid response forces (50-60,000 strong, to be mobilized within 60 days for operations of up to one year).

The European Council of Lisbon (March 2000) agreed on a package of measures to modernize the EU economy and society, strengthening and advancing the European social model. In particular, concrete measures are envisaged for preparing Europe's transition to a new economy based on knowledge and innovation – by making use of new IT and communications technologies.

The European
Union (EU)

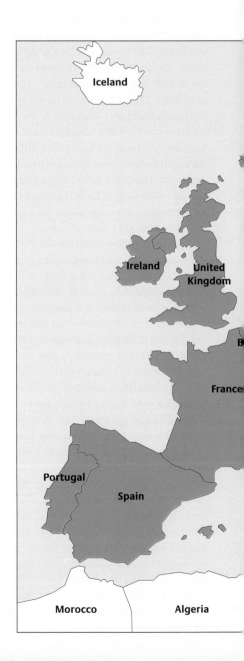

In order to guarantee functional viability even once the EU is expanded, comprehensive adjustments and changes to the EU's institutional framework are necessary. A continuation of the institutional structures established for the EEC with its six members will no longer be necessary once the next set of new members accedes. In February 2000, the EU accordingly convened a government conference to prepare its institutions for the forthcoming expansion at the latest for early 2003 (see chart, p. 508).

Europe in the 21st century. Since their founding, the EC and the EU have acquired considerable influence not only as an economic community and as a community of affluence but also as a political force and as a champion of democratic values. In 1997, the EU marked the 40th anniversary of the adoption of the Treaty establishing the European Economic Community. Over the years, the six signatory states of 1957 have been joined by the United Kingdom, Denmark, Ireland, Greece, Portugal, Spain, Austria, Sweden and Finland, so that the European Union now has 15 Member States.

The successful negotiations on the new Treaty of Amsterdam have clearly shown that the Europeans are in the process of writing a new chapter in their common history. The success of these endeavors will determine which role Europe and each European country will play in the next century.

Europe faces two major challenges which dwarf all others: All of Europe must enjoy the freedom, peace and prosperity which the EU has already attained for its part of the continent. The task of the EU is to overcome the legacy of the decades of division resulting from the conflict between East and West and to create ties that bind. Germany will do its part to help accomplish this. Europe must also hold its own in the process of globalization. It must be able to be a successful contender in the increasingly stiff global competition of products, labor costs and business locations brought on by the transition from the industrial to the information age. This is no longer possible at the national level alone.

The expansion of the EU as resolved at the European Council in Copenhagen in 1993 will overcome the decades-long artificial division of Europe. The EU has concluded the so-called Europe Treaty with governments in Central and Eastern Europe (CEE), intended to help them on their way to EU acces-

sion, and in 1998 it initiated the accession process. Alongside
the 10 CEE states (Poland, Czech Republic, Slovakia, Hungary,
Slovenia, Romania, Bulgaria, Estonia, Latvia, and Lithuania),
Cyprus, Malta and Turkey have also filed admission applica-
tions. In the form of its so-called "Copenhagen Criteria", the
EU has laid out the conditions for accession:

— institutional stability, democratic and constitutional rule;
  preservation of human rights, protection and respect for minorities (so-called political criteria);
— a functioning market economy and the ability to withstand
  competition within the EU;
— the ability to integrate the duties and goals arising from EU
  membership. While the economic and administrative preconditions can be fulfilled in the course of the EU accession
  process, the political "Copenhagen Criteria" constitute a precondition for the initiation of negotiations. Accession negotiations are individual and can be started and concluded with
  each candidate at different points in time. Candidates which
  embark on negotiations at a later date can in certain circumstances conclude the process earlier. The status of seisin ("ac-
  quis") which has arisen over the decades – i.e. EU law, as en-
  coded in some 80,000 pages of legal stipulations, must be
  taken on by countries acceding to it.
— Negotiations were initiated in 1998 with a group of the six
  countries which had made more progress (Poland, the
  Czech Republic, Hungary, Slovenia, Estonia, and Cyprus –
  the so-called Luxembourg Group). Now, the EU is negotiating with a further six states (Slovakia, Latvia, Lithuania, Romania, Bulgaria, and Malta – the so-called Helsinki Group).
  In 1999, the European Council in Helsinki gave Turkey the
  status of a candidate; however, negotiations have not yet
  started as Turkey still does not fulfil the political Copenhagen Criteria.

The negotiation materials, namely the EU seisin, are sub-divided
  into 31 chapters (e.g. agriculture, customs union, taxes, etc.).
  Negotiations presently cover all chapters for the Luxembourg
  Group (except institutions and miscellaneous), and this is targeted for the Helsinki Group for 2001. At present, for each
  country between four (Bulgaria) and 16 chapters (Cyprus)
  have been preliminarily concluded (status: July, 2000). No resolutions have yet been taken on the date of accession. Howev-

President of the Czech Republic Václav Havel and President Rau with their wives during a state visit

er, the EU has resolved to be in a position by the end of 2002 to incorporate new members.

The European Council of Luxembourg in 1997 established the "Europe Conference", a multilateral forum for EU member states, countries seeking accession, as well as other European countries which come into question for accession. The Conference discusses issues of joint political interest and has convened three times to date. The next conference will take place in the second half of 2000 under the French EU Presidency and will focus, among other things, on institutional reforms within the EU.

On 2 May 1998, the European Council decided which member states could introduce the euro as a single currency on 1 January 1999: Austria, Belgium, Finland, France, Germany, Italy, Luxembourg, the Netherlands, Portugal and Spain. Introduction proceeds as follows:

– From 1999 to 2001, cashless financial transactions may be denominated in euro as well as in the national currencies. Moreover, the euro can be used in business transactions, e.g. in contracts, to the extent that the business partners so wish.

– On 1 January 2002, the new euro banknotes and coins will be issued as legal tender.

– On 1 March 2002, at the latest the old currencies will cease to be legal tender; in Germany this will occur on 1 January 2002. Deutschmark notes and coins can then be exchanged for euros at any time.

Those Member States which initially cannot or do not wish to participate can be tied to the single European currency by a new Exchange Rate Mechanism ERM II. Since 1999, the Danish krona and the Greek drachma have participated in this. Greece will be introducing the euro on 1 January 2001.

The decision on the Economic and Monetary Union (EMU) of 2 May 1998 will go down in history. Economic and monetary union lends a new quality to the European unification process. With the introduction of the euro, the member states participating in EMU have rescinded their responsibility for monetary and exchange-rate policy. Their central banks have become part of the European System of Central Banks, led by the European Central Bank (ECM) in Frankfurt/Main. This is referred to as the "Euro system". The ECB Council as the key deciding body in the Euro system decides a single monetary policy for Euroland. The primary goal is to ensure price stability and – to the extent that this does not impair this goal – to support the general economic policy within the EU.

Economic relations between the states participating in the EMU have become more intensive thanks to EMU and the mutual interdependence of their national economic policies and trends will rise. The euro has the potential to emerge as the world's most important trading, investment and reserve currency alongside the US dollar. The euro capital market is the second largest in the world and it is backed up by a major economic power.

Euroland with a population of more than 300 million accounts for 19.4 percent of the world GDP and 18.6 percent of world trade. The United States of America, by comparison, accounts for 19.6 percent of world GDP and 16.6 percent of world trade; Japan accounts for 7.7 percent and 8.2 percent respectively.

In order to fulfill its functions, the European Union has a number of institutions, some of whose decisions become directly applicable law in the Member States. The most important institutions are:

– the European Parliament (EP), which since 1979 has been elected directly by the people; upon the entry into force of the Treaty of Amsterdam, the EP will acquire many new codecision powers and will thus become an equal partner of the Council of Ministers;

– the European Council, the meeting of the heads of state or of government, the ministers for foreign affairs and the President of the European Commission, in which basic issues of European policy are decided;

– the Council of Ministers of the European Union, which decides Union policy. It meets in various compositions of specialized ministers (such as the Transport Council and the Environment Council). The General Affairs Council (composed of the foreign ministers) is responsible for foreign policy and is also the Council's central control and coordination instrument;

— the European Commission, a supranational institution which is independent of the national governments; it ensures that the treaties are applied and drafts proposals for the further development of common policy;

— the European Court of Justice, which ensures that the law is observed in the interpretation and application of EU law. Its decisions play a large part in further developing European law and ensure that the legal instruments of the EU do not infringe basic rights;

— the Committee of the Regions, to which 24 representatives of the German states and municipalities belong, which advises the Council and the Commission in areas of policy affecting regional and municipal jurisdiction;

— the Economic and Social Committee, which advises the Council and the Commission on matters pertaining to employers and unions; and

— the European Court of Auditors, which examines the accounts of all revenue and expenditure of the Community and of all bodies set up by the Community.

The European Union is increasingly developing into a political union. Every citizen of an EU Member State is at the same time a citizen of the European Union. This citizenship of the Union above all gives him or her the right to move and reside freely within the territory of the Member States of the Union, subject to certain limitations and conditions. It also gives him or her the right to vote and stand as a candidate in both municipal elections and elections to the European Parliament even if he or she resides in a Member State other than that of which he or she is a national. A citizen of the Union enjoys the right to consular protection by the embassies or consulates of other EU Member States in a third country in which the Member State of which he or she is a national is not represented. Citizens of the Union also have the right to address a petition to the European Parliament and may, through an ombudsman designated by the EP, file complaints concerning the work of EU institutions.

In the fields of justice and domestic policy, the Member States above all work together to combat organized crime, which operates across frontiers on a massive scale and poses an increasingly serious threat to Europe's internal security. Drug dealers and traffickers in persons cannot be permitted to become the winners in a united Europe. Another important area is harmonization of asylum and refugee policy within the EU.

In accordance with the principle of subsidiarity, the Community only then takes action in areas not falling within its exclusive competence if the goals of necessary measures cannot be sufficiently achieved by action taken at the level of the Member States and therefore due to their scope or their effect can be better achieved by action taken at the Community level. There is thus a sensible balance between the European and national levels of action.

One of the Union's core elements is the Common Foreign and Security Policy (CFSP). It constitutes, as it were, the successor outlined in the EU Treaty to the European Political Cooperation (EPC), which was initially located outside the terms of the Treaty and after a modest start 20 years ago has become a major instrument of European foreign policy and a key aspect of the unification process. CFSP is the "second pillar of the EU" since the Maastricht Treaty on the foundation of the EU came into force (1992).

The Treaty of Amsterdam moved the CFSP forward in several regards (see page 211).

Since first coming into effect in May 1999, there have been decisive changes to the CFSP, which, following the completion of EMU, is now the next large EU integration project. In October 1999, the "High representative for Common Foreign and Security Policy", Javier Solana, took office, a move designed to strengthen the coherence and visibility of CFSP to the outside

Chancellor Schröder visiting French President Chirac in the Elysée Palace

world. He is supported by the newly-created Strategic Planning and Early Warning Unit attached to the Council Secretariat. The new instrument of CFSP has already been brought to bear in three instances: Common Strategies were resolved for Russia, the Ukraine, and the Mediterranean; in individual cases, measures have already been passed by qualified majority to implement these resolutions.

Finally, the resolutions of the European Council in Cologne of June 1999 heralded a new era in European security and defense policy. The EU intends to draw up the relevant resolutions by the end of 2000 to enable it to carry out future autonomous operations in the entire area covered by the so-called Petersberg operations (humanitarian, peacekeeping, and peace-founding steps). The functions the WEU has in this regard will then be incorporated into the EU. The goal: a comprehensive ability by the EU to act in the entire field of civilian and military crisis management. Accordingly, at the European Council in Helsinki in December 1999 establishment of a military planning target by the end of 2003 and establishment of an action plan to strengthen civilian crisis management were both passed. It bears mentioning here that the Cologne resolutions expressly do not cover the issue of common defense by the EU member states.

Economically, the European Union has become the most important internal market in the world. All customs and trade barriers between the 15 EU Member States have disappeared. The four fundamental freedoms of the European internal market are the free movement of goods, persons, services and capital.

The European Union pursues an outward-looking trade policy. It advocates a market-oriented world economic order and pursues these trade policy objectives within the framework of the World Trade Organization (WTO). Together with the United States, the European Union plays a leading role in the WTO. The EU also develops its economic and trade relations with third countries on the basis of a dense network of trade, cooperation and association agreements which it has concluded with numerous states and groups of states (for example in the Mediterranean basin, in Southeast Asia, in Central and South America, and in the territory of the former Soviet Union).

Polish Foreign Minister Bronislaw Geremak and German Foreign Minister Joschka Fischer

The central element of EU relations with developing countries is the cooperation with the countries of Africa, the Caribbean and the Pacific in existence since 1975. On 23 June 2000, a new partnership agreement with the now 77 ACP states was signed in Cotonou, Benin. It covers a period of 20 years and must still be ratified by all the EU member states. This cooperation will be financed by allocating EUR 13.5 billion to the 9th European Development Fund for the first five-year period. An additional EUR 1.5 billion loan will be provided by the European Investment Bank.

As the economically strongest Member State, Germany renders substantial net payments to the European Union. It will continue to support the further integration of the Union to the best of its ability. An equitable distribution of the financial burden remains a goal of Germany's European policy.

On the basis of the "New Transatlantic Agenda", Germany is working within the EU to further develop the Euro-Atlantic partnership for the 21st century. Central fields of activity in this process are industry and trade, especially the dismantling of transatlantic barriers to trade, cooperation in foreign policy, above all in regard to joint action in regions fraught with crises, the mastering of global issues such as the environment, migration and the war against organized crime, and intensification of cooperation between groups in society in the context of "people-to-people dialogue".

The Council of Europe. At its founding in 1949, the Council of Europe stood at the very beginning of European integration and cooperation.

From its inception, the Council of Europe has staunchly advocated the basic principles of pluralist democracy, protection of human rights and promotion of the rule of law and has thus created the guidelines for democratic Europe.

The Council of Europe now has 41 member states. Since 1990, it has welcomed 17 states in Central and Eastern Europe as well

The EU Summit in Vienna on Dec. 12, 1998 – the scene of talks with 11 applicants for membership

as the Caucasus. Azerbaijan, Armenia, Bosnia and Hercegovina, the Federal Republic of Yugoslavia, Monaco, and Bielorussia have all filed membership applications. The organization's reach extends in fact beyond the geographical borders of Europe. Observer status has been accorded to the United States, Canada, Japan, and Mexico. States from outside Europe have acceded to the CoE's conventions and sub-treaties or take part in them.

The institutions of the Council of Europe are the Committee of Ministers, the Parliamentary Assembly and the Congress of Local and Regional Authorities of Europe.

In addition to striving for improved protection of human rights, the Council of Europe is presently focusing its endeavors on facilitating the integration of the new member states from Central and Eastern Europe into European structures. Through a comprehensive consulting and assistance program, parts of which it implements jointly with the European Union and the OSCE, the Council of Europe is expediting the democratic reform process and the adjustment of legal standards in the Central and Eastern European states to meet those in West.

Among the 174 conventions which have meanwhile been adopted by the Council of Europe are the European Convention for the Protection of Human Rights and Fundamental Freedoms, the European Convention for the Prevention of Torture and Inhuman or Degrading Treatment or Punishment, the European Social Charter, the European Cultural Convention, the Framework Convention for the Protection of National Minorities, and the Convention for the Protection of Human Rights and Dignity of the Human Being with Regard to the Application of Biology and Medicine.

Violations of human rights can be brought before the now standing European Court of Human Rights which started work on 3 November 1998.

On 1 January 2000, the Spaniard Gil-Robles was appointed to the newly-created office of CoE Commissioner on Human Rights.

Effective monitoring of the obligations undertaken by the member states at the time of their accession has likewise been further developed. Ongoing, major violations of the CoE's principles can lead to sanctions against the respective country or even its expulsion.

Germany has been a member of the Council of Europe since 1950 and takes an intensive active part in its programs at all levels. As one of the five main financial backers alongside France, Great Britain, Italy, and Russia, Germany makes a contribution to the Council of Europe budget of 12.8 percent or some DM 45 million in 2000. Alongside this material contribution, its substantive contribution is also significant.

Each of the chief goals of the Council of Europe – the promotion of human rights, democracy and the constitutional rule of law – are equally important. Moreover, Germany has a special interest in promoting the transformation process in the new member states. It is only logical that Germany is Standing Representative attached to the CoE Chairman on "Reporting Group on Democratic Stability", which concerns itself with the specific problems of the new democracies and, among others, decisions of the Council of Ministers on support in the form of a wide variety of programs. However, in view of stagnating financial resources, an intense cost/benefit analysis is in order here.

Germany used its period as Chair of the Committee of Ministers (beginning of November 1997 to beginning of May 1998) in order to bring its own priorities to bear, for example in the form of a follow-up meeting to the 1996 Stockholm World Congress against Commercial Sexual Exploitation of Children which took place in Strasbourg.

Milestones in the field of protection of minorities are the Framework Agreement for the Protection of National Minorities as well as the European Charter on Regional and Minority languages, both initiatives which Germany played a considerable part in establishing. The two initiatives came into force in 1998. The Federal Government remains committed to more strongly emphasizing the role of German in the day-to-day work of the Council of Europe – alongside the official Council of Europe languages English and French. Today, Ger-

Wim Duisenberg and Petra Roth, Lady Mayoress of Frankfurt/Main, at the opening of the ECB

man translations are provided actively if required and otherwise passively not just at the meetings of the Committee of Ministers and the specialist ministerial conferences, but also the conventions of the steering committees. In 1998, with the financial support of the German Foreign Ministry the Council of Europe published a trilingual edition (German, English, and French) of all its conventions. The long-term goal remains to give German strong roots as the third official CoE language, yet this would require a two-thirds majority of the member states to change the CoE Statutes.

The Organization for Security and Cooperation in Europe (OSCE; until 31 December 1994 CSCE). With 54 participating states (all the European countries, the United States, Canada and the successor states of the former Soviet Union; the Federal Republic of Yugoslavia has been suspended from participation for the time being) the OSCE is the only forum for pan-European cooperation. The core documents of the OSCE are the Helsinki Final Act (1975) and the Charter of Paris (1990), as well as the "Charter on European Security" resolved at the OSCE summit in Istanbul in 1999. The participating states are committed to human rights, democracy, the rule of law, economic freedom, social justice and European unity. They have thus obligated themselves to observing high common values in their dealings with one another and in their treatment of their citizens.

The OSCE is the roof under which the 54 participating states seek to agree on mechanisms for peaceful resolution of conflicts, on norms for safeguarding human rights and the rights of minorities, and on rules governing cooperation between equal partner states. In carrying out its tasks, the OSCE works closely with NATO, the WEU, the EU, the Council of Europe and the United Nations. The Charter on European Security lays down the principles for such cooperation: avoid duplicate work, utilize comparative advantages, create synergies and rule out any hierarchy or competition between the various organizations.

As an organization, the OSCE – in contrast to the CSCE, which was largely a conference process – has permanent bodies and institutions. The Permanent Committee of the OSCE regularly meets at the headquarters of the Secretariat in Vienna. The OSCE Representative on the Freedom of the Media is also headquartered in Vienna; the Office for Democratic Institutions and Human Rights is in Warsaw, and the High Commissioner on National Minorities is in The Hague.

The OSCE now fulfills a number of operational functions, especially in the areas of early warning, conflict prevention and crisis management. Among the OSCE's most important instruments are its missions.

One of the major, and most difficult missions is that which the OCSE has taken on in the framework of the UN mission in Kosovo, where it is in charge of reconstruction in the areas among other things of democratization, constitutional rule by law, and human rights, as well as the implementation of elections. The lessons learned from the Kosovo mission have also led to the OSCE carefully expanding its range of instruments for responding swiftly to crisis situations. By devising its REACT program of Rapid Expert Assistance and Co-Operation Teams and setting up a planning unit in the OSCE in this regard the key preconditions have been established to facilitate rapid deployment of crisis response forces.

More than 200 international staff members work in each of the two long-term OSCE missions and other activities in the field (in Bosnia and Herzegovina and in Croatia). The OSCE has organized and supervised the elections which have been taking place in Bosnia and Herzegovina since 1996. Among its other tasks, pursuant to the Dayton Agreement on implementing the Federation of Bosnia and Herzegovina, are to help enforce respect for human rights and, by supporting arms control and confidence-building measures, to help prevent a new outbreak of hostilities. In Croatia, the OSCE is continuing the work of the UNTAES mission of the United Nations, contributing among other things to the reintegration and return of refugees to East Slavonia.

The OSCE now has the ability to arbitrate disputes peacefully within the framework of its Convention on Conciliation and

Arbitration, which was prompted by a Franco-German initiative. This Convention was ready for signing at the end of 1992, entered into force on 5 December 1994 and has meanwhile been ratified by 25 states. The Court of Conciliation and Arbitration created by the OSCE on the basis of this Convention is headquartered in Geneva.

It is in the Federal Republic's interest that the OSCE has created wide-ranging obligations in the field of human rights. Although not legally binding, they are of a very mandatory nature politically owing to the fact that they have been adopted by all participating states by consensus. To ensure continuous monitoring of OSCE standards, regular meetings are held at which the human rights situation in member countries is critically examined and publicly discussed.

The High Commissioner for National Minorities, an office created with strong German support at the 1992 Helsinki summit, identifies potential ethnic tensions at the earliest possible

The European Patents Office in Munich

time and helps to contain and reduce them through direct consultations with the affected parties.

The office of the OSCE Representative on the Freedom of the Media was established as of 1 January 1998 at Germany's initiative. The Representative functions as an appeal instance for journalists and works to ensure better adherence by the OSCE participating states to OSCE commitments in the area of freedom of the press and media.

The OSCE will continue to serve as a forum for dialogue, negotiation and cooperation in order to give fresh stimulus to the process of arms control, disarmament and confidence- and security-building, as well as to improved consultation and cooperation in security matters and to the reduction of the risk of conflict. The 1992 Helsinki summit established the CSCE Forum for Security Cooperation for this purpose. At the summit in Budapest (December 1994) it was already possible to adopt a code of conduct that elaborates the prohibition of the use of force presently in effect by establishing norms governing the democratic control of armed forces and their deployment both inside and outside frontiers. A declaration on the principles of nonproliferation of weapons of mass destruction was likewise adopted.

Further information:
  – Europäische Kommission, Vertretung der Bundesrepublik Deutschland
    (European Commission, Representative Office in Germany)
    Unter den Linden 78, 10117 Berlin
    Internet: http://www.eu-kommission.de
    E-mail: eu-kommission-de@cec.eu.int
  – Ständige Vertretung der BRD beim Rat der Europäischen Union
    (Standing Representation of the Federal Republic of Germany to the Council of the European Union)
    Rue Jacques de Lalaing 19-21, 1040 Brüssel, Belgien
    Internet: http://www.ue.eu.int
    E-mail: public.info@consilium.eu.int
    Homepage der EU: Internet: http://europa.eu.int

External security

The framework. The Basic Law obliges Germany to serve
peace in the world as an equal member of a united Europe.
Article 24 of the Basic Law stipulates that Germany shall take a
position within a system of mutual collective security and can
in this context approve to limit its sovereign rights in order
thus to achieve and secure a peaceful and durable order in
Europe and between the peoples of the world. As a member
of the North Atlantic Treaty Organization (NATO), Western
European Union (WEU), and the European Union, Germany
makes a contribution on the basis of a secured ability to defend itself to security provisions in the Euro-Atltanic region
commensurate with its economic and political power. This includes the oblgiation to participate in measures to prevent
conflicts and manage crises in the framework of alliances
and the United Nations, as well as to stand up for international law and human rights.

The fundamental definition of the mission of the German Armed
Forces is laid down in Article 87a of the Basic Law as being to
defend the country. In addition, Germany has pursuant to
section 5 of the NATO Treaty and Article V of the Brussels
Treaty on Support committed itself to participating in collective defense.

The situation for security policy. Following the end of the
East-West conflict, Germany's geostrategic situation has improved immensely. A massive attack on NATO as a whole is
improbable for the foreseeable future. That said, the situation
as regards security entails any number of trends that are
hard to forecast given a broad range of military and non-mili-
tary risks.

Securing peace is the prime aim of German foreign and security
policy. Security in Europe is indivisible from security for Europe and calls for comprehensive, multinational provisions.
Germany contributes to joint security as an active member of

the United Nations, the Organization for Security and Cooperation in Europe, the North Atlantic Alliance and the European Union and consistently pursues the path of expanding and strengthening European integration and cooperation in the Euro-Atlantic security organizations.

This goes hand in hand with the obligation to make a due military contribution to preserving stability and security in Europe and promoting world peace.

NATO will in the future remain the backbone of the European peace order on the basis of joint democratic values.

The German Armed Forces plays a key part in stabilizing the security policy situation by means of its confidence-building efforts and cooperation. As the preferred partner of numerous Eastern European countries, Germany is thus also an engine driving overall European cooperation forwards.

The Bundeswehr and its mission. The Bundeswehr

— defends Germany and its citizens from political blackmail and external danger;

— defends Germany and its allies;

— contributes to securing peace and stability in the Euro-Atlantic region;

— serves the cause of world peace and international security in accordance with the UN Charter; and

— provides support in the event of disasters and other emergencies, including humanitarian aid programs.

The tasks and abilities of the German Armed Forces are defined in the Constitution and in the commitments and international treaties signed jointly with our allies. Primarily, the scope and structure of the Bundeswehr is defined by the desire to defend the country and provide collective defense. Currently, the shape this shall take is being debated.

Soldiers from various countries discussing the situation

Citizens in uniform. The guideline for the future will continue to be the effort to integrate soldiers as citizens into society, to ensure they align themselves to the basic rights and the application of constitutional legal principles, as well as to the notion of humanity and the values enshrined in our Constitution.

Liberty and responsibility have been and remain the political-moral points of reference for the concept of inner leadership adopted and the role model of citizen in uniform. They are the core of our own tradition and the source of the roots the Bundeswehr has in society. At the beginning of the 21st century the soldier continues to require convincing values which give him a sense of place and orientation. He must know what he is being deployed to uphold and defend – human dignity, justice and liberty.

The Bundeswehr is bound to the constitutional rights and laws and serves to protect the rights and liberty of our people and our state. It is an army in a democracy and championing a democracy. The Bundeswehr is subject to the primacy of politics.

An important parliamentary control function is played by the Defence Commissioner of the German Bundestag. His task is to protect the constitutional rights of servicemen. Every member of the armed services has the right to complain to him direct without going through his superiors. The Commissioner may demand information and access to files from military units and visit any Bundeswehr facility unannounced. He submits an annual report to the Bundestag on the complaints he has received.

General conscription. The core mission of the German Armed Forces is to defend the country. In the future, too, this can only be guaranteed by general conscription. This remains an indispensable part of the provisions for security policy. General conscription involves a severe intervention in the rights of young male citizens. The time required for conscription must not last longer than is necessary to ensure the external security of our country and the readiness of our armed forces.

The shape given general conscription must on principle also take into account the career and personal plans of those eligible for military service.

Development policy

Development policy is an element of the Federal Government's policy of furthering international cooperation in order to secure the world's future. It is, to quote the words of former Federal Chancellor Willy Brandt, "the peace policy of the 21st century". As part of a global structural policy, its task is to help improve the economic, social, ecological and political conditions in our partner countries in the south and the east and to balance interests, on the one hand, between the regions of the world and within them and, on the other, between today's generation and future generations. It is based on a sense of ethical, humanitarian, global and ecological responsibility, on our interest in ensuring regional and global political stability and a process of global economic structural change which is beneficial to all. The aims of the development policy of the Federal Government are to

— promote social justice all over the world, alleviate poverty,
— support respect for human rights and democratic principles;
— move equal opportunities for men and women forwards;
— contribute to the peaceful resolution and management of conflicts;
— protect the environment and ensure sustainable use of natural resources;
— promote economic development in our partner countries.

Germany is one of the biggest donors of assistance provided within the framework of development cooperation. In a spirit of equal partnership, the Federal Government focuses on cooperation with 70 countries and within these on focal areas.

As early as 1961, a special Federal Ministry for Economic Cooperation was created (in 1993 the words "and Development" were added to the title) – the first time any country had appointed a cabinet minister with sole responsibility for development cooperation. This showed the determination of the German parliament, government and people to help other nations in need in light of their own country's experience after World War II, when only help from abroad made it possible to rebuild the economy so swiftly.

Following the collapse of the former East bloc, the scope of cooperation has been enlarged to include not only the traditional developing countries but also new partners: the transition countries of Central, Eastern and Southeastern Europe and the former Soviet Union.

In the course of more than 40 years of development cooperation, the Federal Government, together with non-governmental organizations (NGOs) and private institutions, has accumulated valuable experience and created a broad range of instruments for assisting our partner countries in the South and the East. Through close cooperation with our partner countries, assistance measures have been adapted to the differing political, economic and social conditions in Africa, Asia, Latin America, the Middle East, and Central and Eastern Europe.

Development cooperation cannot and must not relieve our partner countries of their responsibility for their own development and for making their own contributions to safeguarding the world's future. Inputs from outside are intended to provide impetus and start-up assistance but not to replace the efforts of our partners themselves. Development cooperation can thus make an important contribution to sustainable development in our partner countries and to the solution of global problems. Development policy also helps to create the global framework conditions conducive to economically, socially and ecologically sustainable development in all parts of the world.

Helping to alleviate mass poverty and remove its structural causes is a central aim of German development policy. The world

Training for modern communal administration in Nepal

of tomorrow will only be able to live in peace if it proves possible to alleviate hunger and need, reduce the prosperity gap between North and South, protect and preserve the natural sources of life, and ensure respect for human rights.

It is now common knowledge that people in rich and poor regions of the world are interdependent. This is clearly illustrated by the alarming extent of environmental destruction and its repercussions on industrial countries, developing countries and the countries in transition. The Federal Government therefore not only pursues a progressive environmental policy at home but also supports our partner countries in implementing ecologically sustainable development programs.

As a leading export nation, Germany is committed to free, liberal, and socially and ecologically responsible world trade. Healthy economic progress in our partner countries is thus not least in our own interest. The more efficient a country's economy becomes, the more attractive that country becomes as a partner for trade and investment.

But there is another motive for development cooperation as well. Improved living conditions in the countries of the South and the East open up better economic, political, ecological and social prospects for many people who otherwise might be forced to leave their native countries in quest of a new life elsewhere. Development policy thus also serves to combat the causes of refugee flight and crises; it is a pre-emptive peace policy.

Aims of development policy. It is our partner countries themselves who must decide – within the framework of the guidelines formulated by the world community inter alia at the major international conferences of the 1990s – what they want from development cooperation. Experience in recent decades has shown that the success or failure of development measures is determined by the internal political and economic conditions in our partner countries.

Development cooperation can only be effective if national framework conditions exist which enable the people to employ their skills in a meaningful and worthwhile manner. Experience has shown that such conditions are most likely to be found in countries which have a system that is based on the rule of law and has elements of a social and ecological market economy offering especial achievement incentives.

The Federal Government has therefore designated the five internal conditions most conducive to development as criteria for the deployment of instruments and resources. These five criteria, which influence both the type and scope of development cooperation, are:
- respect for human rights;
- popular participation in political decisions;
- the constitutional rule of law and the certainty of the law;
- the creation of a socially-oriented, ecologically-sustainable economic order based on the market economy (taking into consideration the core ILO labor norms: prohibition of compulsory and child labor; freedom of association for all employees; right to collective wage bargaining; no discrimination at the place of work; equal pay for men and women) and
- a development orientation to government actions (including a reduction of exaggerated outlays for arms).

Development cooperation not only entails changes in the partner countries. Instead, structures must also be created at the other two levels, namely in Germany and in other donor countries, as well as on the international stage. These requirements are summarized in the concept of global structural policy.

Development cooperation therefore supports specific measures undertaken by our partner governments and groups within society with the aim of improving the internal conditions for development.

It also logically supports the creation of international conditions conducive to development. Important aspects of a global structural policy are thus the reform and strengthening of the United Nations and its development programs as well as the establishment of international structures for "global governance".

Development policy starts in Germany itself. In the interest of coherence, changes are necessary here at home in areas affecting global sustainable development, such as protection of the climate. Measures to promote foreign trade are according greater attention to ecological, social and development policy concerns. Educating the German public in matters pertaining to development policy is a priority as well.

Development cooperation is carried out through
- direct bilateral assistance from government to government;

Federal Minister for Economic Cooperation Heidemarie Wieczorek-Zeul in Uganda

— multilateral assistance through international organizations, for example the United Nations, its specialized agencies, and the World Bank;

— the European Union, whose development cooperation has been a treaty-based commitment since the entry into force of the Maastricht Treaty;

— support for the activities of non-governmental organizations, who have many years of experience in cooperation with their partners abroad; and

— promotion of private-sector cooperation.

In 1999 the Federal Republic of Germany spent a net total (i.e. after deduction of repayments on loan principal) of DM 10.1 billion on official development cooperation. This amount, which included assistance provided by the Federal Government as well as assis-tance furnished by the states, was equivalent to 0.26% of the gross domestic product and was thus above the average for all industrial countries.

Financial, technical and personnel cooperation. With its development policy, the Federal Government sets out to promote economic, social, ecological and political development in our partner countries and thus contribute to improving living conditions there.

"Luxury goods and military goods and installations or contributions destined for such use are excluded from economic cooperation," state the Federal Government's guidelines on bilateral financial and technical cooperation. As a rule, the principle of least intervention applies. This means that projects should be planned and implemented as far as possible by our partner countries. The Federal Government determines the framework for cooperation, bears the political responsibility and takes control of development policy.

Competence within the Federal Government lies with the Federal Ministry for Economic Cooperation and Development. Ongoing contact with the governments of the developing countries is the responsibility of Germany's representations abroad. In cases involving financial cooperation, which usually takes the shape of granting concessionary loans, the Federal Government charges the Development Loan Corporation with the appraisal and implementation of its contributions. Technical cooperation is made available to our partner countries free of charge, usually by means of direct contributions. In most cases involving technical cooperation, the Deutsche Gesellschaft für Technische Zusammenarbeit GmbH (GTZ) is charged with implementation, but occasionally the Federal Institute for Geosciences and Natural Resources or the Federal Institute of Physics and Metrology. German business and industry are informed of opportunities to provide supplies and services within the framework of financial and technical cooperation projects, and especially of upcoming invitations to tender and prequalification procedures.

Personnel cooperation is the third level of bilateral cooperation with developing countries. On the basis of subsidies, a whole series of government and non-government organiziations are active in development cooperation.

Under the 1999 federal budget, the Federal Ministry for Economic Cooperation and Development was allocated DM 2.3 billion for financial cooperation and DM 1.2 billion for technical cooperation. Of significance are the budget's appropriations for commitments; within the framework of these the Ministry can make commitments which are binding under international law and which will for the most part be fulfilled from cash appropriations of the following years. The 1999 appropriations for commitments totaled DM 2.3 billion for financial cooperation and DM 1.15 billion for technical cooperation.

Within the framework of financial cooperation, financing is provided for materials and installations. This financing takes the form of low-interest loans for specific projects and, generally for the world's poorest countries, interest-free and non-repayable grants.

Technical cooperation sets out to improve the capacity of persons and organizations, particularly those of poorer population groups, in our partner countries by transferring or mobilizing know-how and skills or by improving the conditions for their application. "The spectrum ranges from counselling government through to supporting self-help groups and co-operatives." Experts, appraisers, advisers and instructors are seconded to our partner countries and paid by the German government; equipment and material for the promoted institutions are either supplied or financed; and training is provided for local experts and managerial personnel who are to later carry on the tasks of the German experts.

Personnel cooperation is intended to give people in the partner countries the opportunity to develop their existing abilities and knowledge. This includes providing training and advanced training for local experts in developing countries. In this context, among other organizations, in particular the Carl Duisburg Society and the German Foundation for International Development bear mentioning. Promoting the establishment of small businesses in developing countries and careers for specialists who have received training or further training in Germany is another focus of such work. The third aspect is to find, post, and deploy specialists from Germany. In this field, alongside GTZ and the Center for International Migration (CIM), six organizations are active which have joined forces to form the "Working Party for Development Services". The term "development worker" describes the German specialists who emigrate through these six organizations. The German Development Service (DED) provides the largest number of development workers (1998: 894), more than the other five, generally Church organizations, together.

At the end of 1996, about 7,900 local experts (including local staff) were already working alongside about 1,400 German experts on technical cooperation projects financed with German funds. These figures were for technical cooperation as a whole, i.e. not just projects involving the GTZ but also those

Agricultural quality controls in Pakistan

Setting up a drinking water supply plant in Tunisia

involving other organizations engaged in development cooperation, such as the German Development Service and political foundations. Of the 1,800 or so working on financial cooperation projects, approximately 900 were experts from our
partner countries.

Focal areas of development cooperation. Global structural policy is geared toward improving economic, social,
ecological and political structures. None of these objectives
can be enduringly achieved without the others also being attained. They mutually encourage and constrain one another.
The area of crisis prevention is of over-arching importance.
Approaches here, especially by reducing the causes of crises
and promoting peaceful mechanisms for conflict management, are encountered at all four levels. An expression of this
expanded notion of security policy is the fact that the Federal
Ministry for Economic Cooperation and Development is a
member of the Federal Security Council.

Even if the understanding of development has long ceased to focus solely on economic progress, economic growth and institutional stability, for example of the financial sector, still play
a major role. This is evidenced by the impact of world economic crises (for example, the Asian crisis in 1997) and by
the stagnation of many countries in which existing structures
make investments and trade difficult. The foreign debt of the
poorest countries is of overarching macroeconomic importance – it was reduced in the framework of the HIPC international debt reduction initiative following the G7/G8 Summit
in Cologne.

A new international financial and trade architecture is just as
necessary as are macroeconomic reforms in the framework of
socially and ecologically oriented structural adjustment programs, improving national and local institutional structures,
facilitating access to consultancy and loan providers, or
brokering specialist economic knowledge. Strengthening

SMEs plays a special role above all in economically weaker partner countries as regards creating jobs and income. The bilateral German promotion of the private sector therefore extends from consultancy on reforms to boost the market economy through loan programs to consultancy in the informal sector. Promotion for individual corporations is as a rule granted in the framework of development public-private partnerships. These bring public funding together with the capital of German and local corporations in the developing countries to run a joint project.

The point of departure when enhancing economic structures is a qualitative and as broad as possible growth concept which factors environmental strains, and ecological consumption, as well as social costs into the economic calculation. Topics such as working standards or land reform point up the close linkage between the economic, social and political dimension. When improving social structures, the goal must be to directly reduce poverty, create humane living conditions that are more dignified and social justice. To this end, investments in basic social services and systems securing nutrition, in education and health are necessary. Here, at the Copenhagen World Summit in 1995 the so-called 20-20 Initiative was founded. On a voluntary basis, donor and developing countries undertake to invest 20 percent each – the donor country commits 20 percent to development aid and the partner 20 percent of the national budget to the afore-mentioned sectors in the developing countries.

Many social and societal issues are of major political significance, for example where labor rights are concerned. Here, the International Labor Organization is providing sterling work, by acting as a central international forum together with govern-

Family planning and health education in Nepal

ments, employer associations and trade unions, to draw up rules for improving conditions in the world of work, e.g. minimum requirements for protection at the place of work, or the prohibition of exploitative child labor. Poverty and violations of human rights affect women and girls to a disproportionately high extent. It is therefore a key task to help them. For this reason, all development projects are assessed to establish their impact on women and equal opportunities issues. Participation and self-help are key principles when it comes to combating poverty. Impoverished sections of the population have a direct part in planning and shaping projects.

Poverty is one of the greatest challenges as regards maintaining the natural environment; at the same time, industrial development and the economic exploitation of natural resources such as the tropical rainforest in many partner countries is spawning new problems. The collapse of the East European economies has brought to light additional gigantic ecological problems which can only be overcome if nations work together. By promoting a global ecological balance, climate protection, and combating desertification, development policy plays a key role in securing the common global basis for sustained life and helps secure a place for human life and health in our partner countries in the future, too. This is achieved by promoting national ecological policies, programs and projects in the partner countries that are dedicated to environmental protection, as well as taking part in international initiatives to protect especially endangered eco-system and by the ecological design of all plans for development cooperation.

The political dimension receives greater weight in the new understanding of development policy and is no longer per-

Locksmiths during training in Zimbabwe

ceived as merely the underlying condition for development. Good governance, human rights, democracy, and development-oriented administrative and management structures are also a topic for projects, political dialogue, and international conventions. Additional importance is also granted to supporting peaceful conflict management: special mechanisms to allay conflicts, to monitor crises, or to support police and military reforms are all to be classified as part of this political dimension as they assist in strengthening human rights and democracy.

Given the highly differing state of development in the world's regions and individual countries, the German Federal Government is aspiring to differentiate within its development cooperation, a task long since necessary. Core problems and development potential, the priorities of partner countries, and Germany's comparative advantages, as well as the involvement of other donors are all factors determining cooperation with the partner country. Fostering projects and programs in the context of bilateral, European, and multilateral development cooperation is just one of the fields requiring a focus on the political level. Indeed, action in this area must be accompanied by progress in the two other dimensions, namely a commitment to shaping international regulations and concepts as well as information and coherence work inside Germany.

The "Center for International Cooperation" emerging in the federal city of Bonn offers those in Germany who are involved in international and development cooperation a new platform for increasing their effectiveness through cooperation with one another and with international partners. They can thus heighten the German public's awareness and recognition of their work and improve their opportunities for influencing decision-makers in the formulation of pertinent national and international policies.

Given the important ministries remaining in Bonn, the many institutions involved in development policy which are situated there and the city's infrastructure and international experience, the federal city of Bonn and the surrounding region are an ideal location for additional organizations and institutions as well. Hardly surprisingly, important UN organizations, for example, have already relocated to Bonn. As the venue for politically important national and international conferences, as a forum for dialogue and as a hub of development policy and international cooperation, the Center will soon become renowned far beyond Germany's borders.

Further information:
- Bundesministerium für wirtschaftliche Zusammenarbeit und Entwicklung (German Federal Ministry for Economic Cooperation and Development) Friedrich-Ebert-Allee 40, 53113 Bonn
  Internet: http://www.bmz.de
  E-mail: poststelle@bmz.bund.de
- Deutsche Gesellschaft für Technische Zusammenarbeit GmbH (German Society for Technical Cooperation) Dag-Hammarskjöld-Weg 1-5, 65760 Eschborn
  Internet: http://www.gtz.de

The economy

Economic system and policy

The Federal Republic of Germany is one of the major industrial
countries. In terms of overall economic performance it is the
third largest, and with regard to world trade it holds second
place. It is one of the seven leading western industrial countries (the Group of Seven, or "G7") who hold a summit meeting every year at which they coordinate their economic and
financial policies at the level of the heads of state or of government. In 1999, the gross domestic product (GDP), that is to
say, the value of all finished goods produced and services in
the course of a year, came to a record DM 3,8771.1 billion in
Germany. Statistically speaking, this amounts to DM 107,400
per gainfully employed person. Expressed in 1995 prices, that
is a growth from DM 3,346.0 billion in 1991 to DM 3,732.3
billion in 1999 (see charts, pp. 502-3).

After the Second World War, people often spoke of the German
"economic miracle". Ludwig Erhard, the Federal Republic's
Minister of Economics from 1949 to 1963, disliked this term.
He said it was no miracle, "merely the result of honest endeavor on the part of a whole nation who were given the opportunity and freedom to make the best of human initiative,
freedom and energy".

The social market economy. Since the war, the Federal Republic has developed a socially responsible market economy.

This system rejects both the laissez-faire doctrine of the Manchester school and government intervention in business and investment decisions. The state plays a mainly regulatory role in the market economy. It creates the general conditions for market processes. Within this framework, the millions of households and companies decide freely what they want to consume and produce. The question as to which and how many goods are produced and who gets how much of what is decided above all in the marketplace. The government largely forgoes any direct intervention in price and wage fixing.

The prerequisite for a well-functioning market system is competition. Without it there can be no market economy. Competition ensures that the individual pursuit of profit translates into a maximum supply of goods for the community as a whole. It encourages initiative and forces companies to improve their market position by lowering prices, improving the quality of their products, and offering better payment and delivery terms as well as additional services. It is also conducive to innovation and rationalization.

Open competition is undoubtedly hard for all concerned. Entrepreneurs time and time again try to neutralize competition, whether through agreements with rivals or mergers. However, mergers between companies must not create or strengthen a dominant market position. Preventing this is the purpose of the 1957 Law against Restraints of Competition (Cartel Act). It forbids concerted practices and agreements which influence market conditions by restricting competition and has been amended many times in order to ensure its effectiveness. Compliance with the law is monitored by the Federal Cartel Office in Berlin and the antitrust authorities of the states. In the course of European integration and the globalization of the economy, responsibility for competition policy is in-creasingly being shifted to the European Commission in Brussels. At the beginning of 2001, a law will come into force governing mergers between companies. Based on the European Parliament and Council's guideline for mergers (June 2000) the law provides regulation for the takeover of German firms whose shares are quoted on a stock exchange within the European Union. To date, there has been was no binding legal framework for company takeovers in Germany, though a voluntary takeover codex does exist. The new law seeks to ensure an orderly procedure which will also provide a sound basis for co-determination in mergers. As such it represents an appreciable contribution to the sustained modernization of Germany as an economic location; it strengthens competition and helps to improve the investment climate.

The aim of the Federal Government has been and continues to be to strengthen competition and provide more efficient services for the people. Intense competition can only develop if a healthy, broad-based small and medium-sized business sector plays an active role in the market economy. New innovative firms in particular must be given a good chance to compete.

To accomplish this, the Federal Government will improve the general conditions for small and mid-sized businesses, the crafts and trades, the independent professions and business start-ups. The promotion programs for small and medium-sized firms are to be simplified and concentrated. Access to venture capital is to be eased so that firms can expand their equity capital base. The innovativeness of business and industry is to be further enhanced by enabling firms to more swiftly convert the results of research conducted at higher education institutions and research institutes into marketable products.

The productivity of firms hinges on a well-trained work force. For this reason, Germany's dual system of vocational training, which splits responsibility for training between educational institutions and firms, will be further developed in order to increase its efficiency and practical orientation. Access to self-employment in the crafts and trades is also to be accelerated by enabling journeymen to acquire master craftsman certification while working in their respective occupation. And, last

The main hall at the Leipzig Trade Fair

but not least, the regulatory forest will be pruned in order to eliminate superfluous bureaucracy.

A social market economy which is heedful of environmental concerns will open up new fields of activity for many innovative firms and create new jobs. By promoting ecological innovations on the one hand and taxing energy consumption on the other, demand will be generated for new products and new production processes which will have good sales potential not only in Germany but in the rest of the world as well.

Industrial relations. Agreements on pay, working hours, holidays and general working conditions, for example, are negotiated between labor and management, who are often called "social partners" in Germany. Their central organizations – the trade unions and the employers' associations – thus play an important role. Although their main task is to represent their members' interests with both determination and a sense of proportion, they also bear considerable responsibili-

Federal Economics Minister Werner Müller presenting the 1999 Annual Economic Report

ty for the economy as a whole. Their disputes can profoundly affect the functioning of the economic system. Labor and employers in the Federal Republic have always been aware of this responsibility. The system's stability is due largely to them.

The social component of the economic system. One major reason why it has been easier to maintain social harmony in Germany than in other countries is that there is a dense social security network. Social protection is considerable, especially for the working community. Whether an employee is old or sick, injured by accident or jobless, affected by the bankruptcy of his or her employer or undergoing retraining for a more promising occupation – most of the financial hardships are cushioned by the welfare system. It is based on solidarity: Those in employment pay contributions to the various branches of the social insurance system. It not only covers the individual employee, but also encompasses housing supplements, social assistance for the needy and indemnification for war victims. Expenditure on social security is high. In 1999, it stood at 33.5 percent of GDP, largely due to the inclusion of the new states. It is becoming increasingly clear that this high share of GDP consumed by the social security system and the burden of the contributions required to finance it pose a threat to Germany's competitiveness and employment outlook. This burden must be alleviated without impairing social security. The Federal Government will therefore elaborate possibilities for modernizing the social security system. Private provision by citizens themselves will take on ever greater importance in this context in order to ensure that social security remains affordable in the future as well. The core elements of the social security system will remain, however.

Macroeconomic development. A market economy, too, can experience undesirable developments. The aims are stable prices, a high level of employment and a balance of foreign trade under conditions of steady, adequate growth.

Reducing unemployment is the central task of government economic policy. The key to higher employment lies in more investment and innovations which create jobs with a secure future. Accomplishing this will require the efforts not only of government but of the business community and the unions as well.

In order to mount a sustained, broad-based offensive against unemployment, the Federal Government has joined forces with the unions and business community to forge an "Alliance for Jobs, Training and Competitiveness and Training". The aim remains to create a significantly larger number of jobs and above all to afford young people and older members of the work force better employment prospects. Considerable progress has been made to date. It is up to the business community and unions to reorganize work in a manner conducive to higher employment and allow greater flexibility in regard to wages and working hours. The business community is called upon to intensify its efforts to boost investment and innovation, and above all to make still more training places available. To this end the Federal Government has already improved the general framework conditions, especially through a tax policy which alleviates the burden of tax and social insurance contributions for firms and citizens alike. In a second step, it will modernize public administration, and an "innovation offensive" is to be mounted in the areas of education, science and research.

The following bodies are involved in coordination of economic and fiscal policy in Germany:

— The Business Cycle Council, consisting of the federal ministers of economics and finance, one member from each state government, and representatives of the municipalities and associations of municipalities. The Deutsche Bundesbank may also take part in the consultations, which take place at least twice a year.

— The similarly composed Financial Planning Council, which has the task of coordinating financial planning at all levels of government. The federal and state governments have to draw up multi-annual plans so that public revenue and expenditure can be geared to the demands and capacities of the national economy.

Government decision-makers have come to rely on the advice of independent economic experts when formulating economic policy. In addition to the Council of Economic Advisers for the Federal Ministry of Economics and Technology established in 1948 and various research institutes, a key institution providing such advice is the Council of Experts on the Assessment of Economic Trends, which was set up in 1963.

Comprised of five independent economic experts, this body evaluates overall economic trends and presents a report every autumn as a basis for government decision-making and public judgment.

Every January, the Federal Government presents to the Bundestag and the Bundesrat an annual economic report which contains a response to the assessment of the Council of Experts for the previous year as well as an outline of economic and financial policy objectives for the current and subsequent years.

International trade. The Federal Republic of Germany is an advocate of free world trade and rejects all forms of protectionism. Because it exports a third of its gross domestic product, it depends on open markets. The economy therefore needs a growing European internal market. But outside the European Union as well, Germany must maintain traditional markets and develop new ones. This persistent pursuit of open markets and free world trade is in keeping with the country's internal market economy.

Germany: an economic hub

In the midst of globalization. The Federal Republic of Germany is a country with a high level of productivity, high incomes, extensive social benefits and widespread affluence. In order to maintain this high standard, it is essential to adapt to new developments in the field of science and technology and in world markets. An expensive industrial location can hold its own only as long as it is a good location – an exigency reflecting the fierce competition stemming from increasing world economic integration. At the same time, this integration offers new opportunities for satisfying people's needs for goods and services economically, opens up new prospects in the world's markets and affords new opportunities for employment.

The great opportunities presented by globalization are accompanied by profound challenges as well, however. Throughout the world, the barriers for goods and services are becoming more permeable, communication and transport costs are being reduced, and production technology is becoming increasingly mobile. Thus in other parts of the world a high level of productivity can be achieved with the same technology as in Germany. As a result, wage differentials and load ratios for manufacturers have a greater impact than ever before. Investment follows the best yield. The parameters of international competition dictate the direction efforts must take: More flexibility, greater readiness to work, more play for market forces and less state involvement are necessary in order to strengthen Germany's position as an internationally competitive location for business and industry.

Prerequisites. Germany has a number of advantages over its international rivals: a high level of productivity, a very skilled and motivated work force, high technical standards, creative scientists, a well-functioning infrastructure, social harmony, a stable currency and a reliable political environment. These assets alone, however, cannot ensure Germany's success in the future. In such matters as wage costs and costs additional to wages, operating times, company taxes, environmental protection regulations and social security contributions, German firms are at a distinct disadvantage.

All these factors must be counterbalanced by high increases in productivity. Germany must see to it that it remains internationally competitive in the area of research and development, in the development of new key technologies, and in the translation of innovative ideas into marketable finished products.

Free market competition is the best course of action. It makes possible the emergence of efficient production structures and ensures a supply of goods that is oriented toward the wishes of the ultimate consumers.

Investment promotion. The answer to this challenge can be neither protectionism nor a state-planned industrial policy, for trade restrictions and subsidies do more harm than good. The Federal Government supports free international trade and opposes any form of protectionism. Since Germany exports almost one third of its gross domestic product, it relies heavily on open markets. It is vital to the German business community that it employ an open-market strategy in order to utilize the advantages of the international division of labor, prepare for the European Economic and Monetary Union, and develop new markets both inside and outside the European Union.

The Federal Government therefore aims to improve the general conditions for private enterprise in Germany. By means of a tax reform, an innovation offensive, and efficient promotion of the small and medium-sized business sector, the competitiveness of German firms in the globalized markets is to be enhanced.

The tax reduction law will lower tax rates in a series of steps. In the framework of the government's reform of corporate tax, a flat maximum rate of 25 percent will be introduced both for profit earned and profit distributed. Moreover, social security costs will also be reduced. The present social security contribution of 42 percent is to be lowered to below 40 percent. These measures will ease the burden on both corporations and individuals.

The innovative capability of small and medium-sized businesses
in particular is to be enhanced, above all through by affording firms swifter and easier access to the results of research
conducted at universities and research institutes.

Small and medium-sized businesses are the most important pillar
of Germany's economic system. Creating the best possible
framework conditions for small and medium-sized businesses
is therefore a high priority of the Federal Government. In addition to the tax relief mentioned earlier, a number of further measures are planned specifically for smaller firms. Assistance for firms is to be streamlined and simplified.

Business start-ups benefit from particularly generous assistance.
Many firms lack a sufficient equity capital base to weather
difficult periods in a highly competitive environment. The
Federal Government will therefore create better institutional
conditions for the provision of venture capital. Together with
banks, capital investment firms and insurance companies,
moreover, it will explore the various options for establishing
venture capital funds. As a location for business and industry,
Germany is now challenged in the area of employment as
well. Unemployment has meanwhile topped ten percent, a
figure which imposes an intolerable burden on society as a
whole. The task of reducing unemployment cannot be mastered by the political sector alone, however. The business
community and the unions, too, are called upon to do their
part to reduce unemployment.

**Economic reconstruction in the east – a task for all
Germans.** The economic situation in eastern Germany was
desolate in October 1990. A very productive, internationally
competitive economy in the west faced an economy in the
east that was woefully ill-equipped and ill-prepared for the
upcoming process of integration.

The restructuring of a highly unprofitable economy into one
with competitive operational structures required immense
concerted efforts on the part of all involved – the business
community, the government, and especially the people of
eastern Germany, who to this very day have played a crucial
role in propelling the renewal process. Progress of this magnitude could only be achieved because the people in the new
states demonstrated exemplary initiative and willingness to
adjust to changed circumstances. Often they had to learn

new skills, move to another area or even come to terms with unemployment. Since reunification, considerable progress has been made in putting living conditions in East and West on a more equal footing. And though disparities remain in some economic sectors, taken overall, wages in the old states are now 91 percent of those in the old ones. Progress has also been made in per capita GDP which has risen from only 40 percent of the level in the west in 1991 to a current level of over 60 percent.

After the fall of the Wall, a key role in the first phase of the economic restructuring process in the new states was played by the Treuhandanstalt (Trust Agency), a public privatization agency founded in 1990. Its task was to privatize, reorganize or – if necessary – wind up the firms in eastern Germany. Within a relatively brief period of time (by the end of 1994), the Trust Agency succeeded in privatizing nearly all the state-owned industrial firms or returning them to their original owners. There is still an extensive portfolio of publicly owned real estate, however, which will gradually be sold.

In addition to the privatization of state-owned companies, efforts were focused from the very beginning on the revival of a healthy small and medium-sized business sector. With the aid of substantial funds from the Federal Government, the states and the European Union, a multitude of new businesses were established which were able to replace most of the jobs that had been eliminated during the restructuring of the state-owned combines. There are meanwhile more than 550,000 small and medium-sized businesses employing a total of about 3.2 million people.

Particularly visible is the progress which has been made in the creation of an efficient infrastructure. Never before in the his-

High-performance diode laser at Jenoptik in Jena

tory of Europe has an infrastructure been so extensively modernized in such a short time:

— By the end of 1999, 11,700 kilometers of federal highways and federal trunk roads and 5,400 kilometers of railway track had been newly constructed or thoroughly modernized.

— Deutsche Telekom AG has installed about 5.7 million new telephone accesses.

— In the area of housing construction, more than 4.3 million housing units – over half of the number of units that existed in 1990 – have been renovated or newly built with the aid of public funds.

— Considerable progress has been made in the restructuring of farm enterprises as well. Especially in the area of crop cultivation, structures have emerged which are particularly competitive by European standards.

The current situation. By international standards, the new states certainly qualify as an attractive industrial location. This can be seen from the investments of some 1,700 foreign firms from about 50 different countries. Among them are world-famous international corporations such as General Motors (U.S.A.; automobile industry), Elf Aquitaine (France; energy industry), Dow Chemical (U.S.A.; chemical industry), Advanced Micro Devices (U.S.A.; computer industry), Samsung (South Korea; electronics industry) and Kvaerner (Norway; shipyards). Foreign investors find a modern infrastructure in the new states. The level of education, motivation and flexibility of the work force is acknowledged to be exemplary. Moreover, foreign investors receive financial incentives which are particularly high by European standards.

Progress in the economic recovery process is reflected in dynamic rates of growth. Until 1995, the economy in eastern Ger-

Sulfur reclamation unit at the Leuna 2000 oil refinery in Saxony-Anhalt

many grew very rapidly, posting real growth rates of up to ten percent. These high growth rates were primarily attributable to the construction boom of the first few years following reunification. In the meantime, the situation has begun to normalize, and growth rates in the construction sector have declined. Although the industrial sector has continued to grow at a brisk pace, it has not been able to completely offset the decline in building activity. As a result, economic output in eastern Germany increased at a rate of only two percent in 1998. This was the first time since reunification that the growth rate in the east had been lower than that in the west (2.8 percent).

Strategy for industry in eastern Germany. The Federal Government is pursuing a development program – known as "Future of the East 2000" – to secure the necessary promotion framework for eastern Germany in the mid-term. Even though the necessary adjustments have been made to the budget, the funds earmarked in the federal budget for the recovery of eastern Germany surpass by far the 1998 level. The Federal Government has set aside some DM 38 billion of the budget for economic recovery in the east in 2000:

— DM 3.1 billion for the promotion of innovation and R&D
— DM 2.3 billion for regional economic development
— DM 19.1 billion for development of the infrastructure
— DM 11.9 billion for the promotion of jobs
— DM 1.7 billion for the successor to the Trust Agency and for handling residual pollution in the east

Moreover, as part of the solidarity pact eastern Germany will receive a further DM 14 billion in special supplementary appropriations from federal funds. This money is reserved for paying off special burdens incurred through partition, as well as compensating for the lower financial clout of municipal authorities. It remains the goal of the Federal Government to create in eastern Germany an effective economy capable of asserting itself on the market without outside support, and which offers its inhabitants sufficient work and earning opportunities. Though positive economic signs are evident and the jobless rate has dropped from 18.2 percent (1998) to 17.6 percent (1999), unemployment remains twice as high as in western Germany. Accordingly, the Federal Government will intensify its active labor market policy with a view to facilitating the transition of unemployed persons to the first labor market. In addition, in 2000 the "Work and Training" cash program will be continued for 100,000 young people in eastern Germany. Some 40 percent of the DM 2 billion total available has been earmarked for the program. Further support from the federal and state governments will be necessary until sufficient self-sustaining growth has been achieved. For this reason, preparations have already begun for a follow-on regulation to the solidarity pact which expires in 2004. Another important factor in the east's successful economic recovery is the nurturing of promising fields especially:

— The promotion of innovative talent and research skills. In this context, one should mention the "InnoRegio" program created specially for eastern Germany which aims at fostering innovation through regional cooperation between research institutes, corporations and administrations. Some DM 500 million will be available for this purpose up until 2005.

— Increasing the efficiency and effective targeting of development policy with a view to strengthening the industrial base and supporting small to medium-sized businesses (mittelstand). By virtue of the investment assistance law, around DM 6.6 billion is available every year for regional economic development. Support for the mittelstand and young start-ups will be available in the form of the ERP equity capital assistance program, the start-up money program operated by the Deutsche Ausgleichsbank and the consolidation and growth funds.

— Development of the transport infrastructure and housing. The transport investment program for 1999-2002 continues to attach high priority to expanding transport networks. Special precedence is still given to the "Germany unity" transport projects. High priority also continues to be given to the modernization of apartments. Measures include the Reconstruction Loan Corporation's modernization program which furnishes credit totaling some DM 10 billion.

The labor market

The German labor market has had to cope with profound
changes in the course of the past decades. In the early postwar years, the Federal Republic was preoccupied with finding jobs for millions of expellees from Germany's former eastern territories and for refugees from the GDR. But they in
particular made a large contribution to the country's economic upswing. From the end of the 1950s to the beginning
of the 1970s, hardly anyone was out of work, but as a result
of the crises during the 1970s and the early 1980s unemployment became an increasingly serious problem. When Germany regained its unity in 1990, there suddenly arose the
problem of a divided labor market. In the old states, the extraordinary burst of economic activity sparked by unification
had a very salutary effect on the labor market situation. After
this boom subsided, the west slipped into a severe recession
which had repercussions on the labor market until 1997.

In the states of eastern Germany, a great many jobs were initially
lost in the transition from socialist central planning to a social market economy, and unemployment soared. Then there
began to be indications that recovery was under way. This
was due among other things to increasing economic integration in the eastern and western parts of the Federal Republic
and to the massive transfer payments from the old states to
the new states. In 1998 and 1999, there was a slight improvement on the labor market in the old states, while it remained
unaltered in the new federal states.

Employment. Between 1950 and 1992, the number of gainfully
employed persons in the old states increased from 19.6 million to an estimated 29.5 million (average figure for the
year). It thereafter declined, reaching 27.9 million in 1997. In
1998, it rose again slightly. In the states of eastern Germany
new states, employment declined by about 3.6 million to 6.2
million between 1989 and 1993 as a result of the crisis pre-

cipitated by the transition to the social market economy. By 1997, the figure had dropped again to just under 6.1 million. This figure represents the current situation. In 1999, the total number of gainfully employed persons in Germany stood at 36.1 million (average figure for the year) – in other words, 110,000 or 0.3 percent more than in 1998.

Full employment in the old states reached its peak in 1970, when only 150,000 were out of work. At the same time almost 800,000 job vacancies were reported. During the recession in the 1970s, the labor force diminished and the number of unemployed increased. It rose above one million in 1975, and reached the record level of 2.3 million in 1985. Due to the recession and the ensuing sluggish growth during the 1990s, but also the drag on the labor market in eastern Germany as a result of privatization, unemployment reached a record level of 4.4 million in 1997. This trend saw a reversal in 1999 when the jobless rate in western Germany fell by some 150,000 on the previous year to the current figure of just under 2.8 million. Given the onset of economic recovery and the falling supply of workers for reasons related to demographic development, this trend is expected to continue. In eastern Germany, though, the level of unemployment declined only slightly in 1999, slipping from 18.2 percent (1998) to 17.6 percent (1999).

The annual average unemployment figure for 1999 was 4.1 million (equivalent to an unemployment rate of 10.5 percent); in the west 2.76 million people (8.8 percent) were out of work compared to 1.34 million (17.6 percent) in the former GDR. In 1999, federal subsidies for the (Bundesanstalt für Arbeit) stood at some DM 7.3 billion. In both east and west one group especially hard hit by unemployment are the long-

"Alliance for Work": DGB Chairman Schulte, Chancellor Schröder, and President of the Employers' Association Hundt

term unemployed. This group is typically made up of people with inadequate vocational qualifications, older people, workers who have health limitations, and, in the new states, women. Government and industry are making great efforts to help the long-term unemployed. Because of the increasing use of modern technology in the workplace, greater importance attaches to vocational skills. It is also, however, important that those affected by unemployment receive adequate social security.

Unemployment insurance. Germany's statutory unemployment insurance scheme was introduced in 1927. Since the beginning of 1998, a new revamped labor promotion law has been in force.

The authority administering the statutory unemployment scheme is the Bundesanstalt für Arbeit (Federal Institute for Employment) in Nuremberg. Unemployment insurance is obligatory for all employees as a matter of principle. Contributions are paid half by the employee and half by the employer. Any person who is unemployed, has registered with the employment exchange and has fulfilled the eligibility requirement (i.e. was employed for twelve months within a period of as a rule three years in work subject to compulsory insurance) may claim an unemployment benefit.

Unemployed persons must avail themselves of all opportunities to end their unemployment and must be available for referrals by the employment exchange. The benefit for unemployed persons with at least one child is 67 percent of their standardized net wages, and 60 per cent for other unemployed persons. As a rule, younger unemployed persons may draw the benefit for a maximum of one year, and older unemployed persons (age 57 and up) for a maximum of 32 months.

Those who are still unemployed after exhausting their entitlement to the unemployment benefit may apply for unemployment assistance. In the case of a person with at least one child or a person whose spouse has at least one child, this assistance can amount to as much as 57 percent of the individual's standardized net wages, and 53 per cent for other unemployed persons, though assets and other sources of income of the unemployed person, his or her spouse or the person with whom he or she lives are taken into account if they exceed a specific minimum amount.

The Bundesanstalt für Arbeit pays other benefits as well, such as short-time benefits, winter allowances for construction workers, partial unemployment benefits, integration subsidies, recruitment subsidies for newly-founded firms and tideover allowances. Assistance may also take the form of training measures, mobility assistance and other assistance related to job advice and placement.

Labor promotion is furthermore responsible for training place referral, job placement, labor market consulting for employers and vocational guidance. Another particularly important function is the promotion of vocational training. The Institute grants young people and adults subsidies for vocational training if they are unable to raise the funds themselves. It can also support vocational further training by paying a maintenance benefit, or by assuming the costs of training measures. The Institute likewise promotes the integration of disabled persons into the labour force.

For the active labor market policy, DM 45.3 billion was available in 1999. This is some DM 6.3 billion more than in 1998. The number of persons participating in labor market policy measures stood at an annual average of 1.5 million in 1999 – an appreciable increase (of 240,000) on the figure for 1998.

Job creation measures. Germany faces one of its greatest challenges in its post-war history. Policies to reduce unemployment are aimed at strengthening both the supply and demand side of the economy. To this end, the Federal Government consistently implements job creation measures and works to create general favorable economic conditions over the long term. Active labor market policy (e.g. premiums for employers who hire unemployed persons, financing vocational further training and financing workplaces on the second labor market) completes the array of measures. Given the complexity of these challenges, the political decision-makers realize that they rely on the support of all social groups in overcoming existing problems.

As early as December 1998, the Federal Government teamed up with representatives of the industrial associations and trade unions to create an "Alliance for Jobs, Training and Competitiveness". The alliance is intended as a permanent partnership based on understanding and cooperation aimed at creating mutual trust, but also as a platform for settling divergent interests and harmonizing conflicting opinions.

The Alliance has already scored several successes. For the "Pay Round 2000", participants had agreed to work for a longer-term pay rate policy geared towards the creation of employment. Further, the scope for income distribution aimed at increasing productivity, was to be used primarily to forge agreements which would impact favorably on the labor market. And they have already begun to put this pledge into practice. Pay settlements in important pay areas allow leeway for more investments, more growth and thus more job creation. Both the business community and the trade unions support the program of immediate assistance for the reduction of youth unemployment initiated by the Federal Government. In 1999, the program provided more than 200,000 young people with a new chance of work. Owing to the program's success there are plans to extend it beyond the year 2000.

In the early summer of 1999, participants in the Alliance reached an agreement on youth training measures which will increase the number of training places available and attaches higher priority to training in promising, forward-looking sectors. In 1999, some 63,660 young people concluded new training contracts in the framework of the dual system. This represents 24,800 or four percent more young people than in the previous year. The Alliance partners have also agreed to a joint offensive spanning several years for greater training in the new sectors of information and communications technology.

By the year 2003, companies will create at least an additional 20,000 training places in IT professions, bringing the total

IT – jobs in the future are inconceivable without it

number of training places in the new IT professions to 60,000.

At present, there is a high demand for IT specialists in Germany which the labor market cannot meet. An unbureaucratic, practical solution jointly crafted by the Federal Government and the business community seeks to counter the problem. Known as the "Green Card Program" it allows up to 20,000 foreign IT specialists to work temporarily in Germany. The accord became effective at the beginning of August.

Disproportionately large numbers of older people are affected by unemployment. On an annual average, 1.36 million people over the age of 50 were registered unemployed in 1999 (west: 94,000; east: 42,000). To make it easier for such persons to re-enter the work force, a modification was made to the Labor Promotion Law. The alteration, which became effective on August 1, lowers the age limit for the granting of integration premiums from 55 to 50 and has enhanced the chances of older people of re-entering the labor market. Further, on January 1, 2000 the "Altersteilzeitgesetz" came into force, a law allowing more older people to avail themselves of part-time work.

In July 2000, the Federal Government passed a law for the reduction of unemployment amongst severely handicapped persons intended to provide them with more equal opportunities. This move was prompted by the falling proportion of severely handicapped persons in gainful employment. For between 1982 and 1998 numbers dropped by 211,710 or 22.3 percent while the number of severely disabled persons out of work rose from 93,809 in 1981 to 188,449 in 1998. Efforts to reduce unemployment are also pursued in collaboration with the EU. Under the provisions of the Amsterdam Agreement,

Self-information system for job hunters at a Labor Office

EU member states present the EU commission every year with a joint annual report outlining the employment situation and implementation of labor policy guidelines. The report is based on the members' national action plans. The German "Labor Policy Action Plan 2000" sets out the aforementioned complex policy approach adopted in Germany for the promotion of growth and employment. The labor policy strategy pursued by the Federal Government underscores the peaceful interplay of an array of measures serving the following aims: spawning opportunities for the creation of work and training places, strengthening corporate dynamism and competitiveness, as well as stepping up the modernization of antiquated structures on the goods, services and capital markets. An important aspect of all the measures treated in the job creation action plan is the creation of equal opportunities for women.

Further information:
- Bundesanstalt für Arbeit
  (Federal Institute for Employment)
  Postfach, 90327 Nuremberg
  Internet: http://www.arbeitsamt.de
- Bundesministerium für Arbeit und Sozialordnung
  (German Federal Ministry of Labor and Social Affairs)
  Jägerstrasse 9, 10117 Berlin
  Internet: http://www.bma.bund.de
  E-Mail: bmail@bma.bund.de

Incomes and prices

Incomes. In recent decades, incomes have increased constantly in Germany. Between 1960 and 1991, the disposable income of private households in the western part of the country surged from DM 188 billion to DM 1,669 billion; in 1999 the disposable income of private households in the whole of Germany was about DM 2,448 billion. The family budget has grown considerably in real terms, too, that is to say, allowing for inflation.

Income derives from many different sources. The main source of gross income is employment, i.e. wages and salaries including social insurance contributions. In addition there are dividends from shares, income from property and other assets, as well as public support in the form of child and unemployment benefits, pensions and other remittances.

Disposable income is what is left over after deduction of taxes and social insurance contributions as well as specific remittances (e.g. by foreign workers to their native countries). A good two fifths of the disposable income is accounted for by net wages and salaries, more than one third by profit-drawing and net income from assets, and well over one fifth by social security benefits.

Standard of living. In 1964, the disposable monthly income of a four-person household headed by an employee with a medium income was DM 904 in the old states. DM 823 was spent on private consumption – nearly two thirds of this on food, clothing and housing. In 1998 the same type of household in the western part of Germany disposed of about DM 5,862 per month, of which DM 4,393 was spent on private consumption. Only about 57 percent of this amount had to be spent on food, clothing and housing. Spending on leisure, automobiles, education and telecommunications, by contrast, rose markedly. In comparable households in the east German states, the disposable monthly income in 1998 was DM 4,954. Of the DM 3,632 spent on private consumption, 53 percent was spent on food, clothing and housing.

Assets and disposable income are distributed unevenly, however. At the top of the income pyramid are the self-employed, followed by civil servants, salaried employees and retirees. Whereas the social structure in the new states is still being shaped, a process has taken place within the old states which has led to an approximation of the standard of living of most social groups. A very broad middle class has emerged. In many cases this high standard of living is attained and maintained because both husband and wife have a job. The vast majority of the working population live entirely or predominantly from the fruits of their labor; only a small minority can live on their assets.

Assets. The total value of the financial assets of private households – including cash, savings, securities and life insurance policies, for example – has tripled since 1980. At the end of 1998, gross private financial assets in the whole of Germany totaled approximately DM 5.7 trillion, compared to DM 1.5 trillion in western Germany at the end of 1980. The value of privately owned real estate must be added in as well. In 1998, 48 percent of the private households in the west and 33 percent of those in the east owned real estate. In the course of decades of widespread capital formation activity, private assets have become more evenly distributed. As a consequence of this development, private tangible and financial assets valued at between DM 100 billion and DM 200 billion are bequeathed to heirs each year, more than at any other time in Germany's history.

Since the 1950s, the government has promoted private capital formation by means of bonuses, allowances and tax concessions. Tax incentives encourage people to save through life insurance policies, the owner-occupied homes premium promotes acquisition of residential property, and the house-building bonus is paid to people contributing to home ownership savings plans. There are certain yearly limits on the amount of savings qualifying for state support, and the house-building bonus and owner-occupied homes premium are also tied to incomes.

In addition to the general incentives for capital formation available to all citizens, since the beginning of the 1960s special

Weekly market in the Stuttgart Market Halls

incentives have been available to employees. Under the Act Promoting Capital Formation by Employees, they are eligible for a special government savings premium for savings of up to DM 936 per year (provided their taxable income does not exceed a certain limit) if they have these savings transferred directly by the employer for a home ownership savings plan or for acquisition of holdings (including shares and investment funds for shares) or for the employer's equity participation scheme. As of 1990, people are eligible to a government savings premium of 20 percent (25 percent in the east) for annual savings up to DM 800 and ten percent on amounts up to DM 936 for home ownership savings plans and house-construction schemes. This premium is also tied to incomes. Up to a certain limit, amounts which employees invest in their company are also exempt from taxes and social security contributions.

In the western part of the Federal Republic of Germany, capital formation savings arrangements are made for most employees – primarily within the scope of collective wage agreements – in addition to their wages. Employees can also obtain bonuses for parts of their wages which they save. In 1998, about 23 million employees invested a total of about DM 16 billion. Roughly DM 9 billion of this amount was paid in by employers. About ten million employees received about DM 700 million in savings premiums for roughly DM 7 billion in capital formation savings for the year 1998. As from 1999, savings promotion through the granting of savings premiums will be significantly improved, especially for the acquisition of equity holdings; in the medium term, the total volume of these premiums will thus increase to DM 1.85 billion per year.

Prices. The standard of living depends not only on incomes but also on prices. The development of consumer prices is therefore a major domestic economic and political issue.

The Federal Republic of Germany has not been able to evade worldwide inflation entirely in recent years. Especially in the 1970s the cost of living in the old Federal Republic rose far too swiftly – at times by more than six percent annually. It then fell considerably, so that in April 1986, for the first time in almost 30 years, the cost of living was lower than it had been in the same month of the previous year. In the following years, prices rose once again, but not to the extent that they did in the 1970s. In the 1970s and 1980s prices fluctuated strongly, reflecting the sharp movements in the price of oil. Compared with other countries around the world, the price climate in Germany was characterized on the whole by above-average stability. However, the sharp fall in the rate of price increases experienced by other industrial nations at the start of the 1990s was not echoed in the Federal Republic. The high demand in connection with reunification, as well as steep increases in wages and tax to finance the recovery of the eastern Germany economy, badly battered in the course of 40 years, led to a steep increase in prices. The Federal Government, the Deutsche Bundesbank and the European Central Bank give high priority to monetary stability. This policy has proved successful: In recent years the inflation rate has dropped considerably and, in 1999, stood at an annual average of 0.6 percent. This marks the lowest rise in prices since the price index was first calculated for the whole of Germany.

Housing and urban development

Housing. At the end of 1998, there were about 37 million dwellings in Germany, some 30 million of them in the old states. Roughly 43 percent of the dwellings in the west are occupied by the owners themselves; 57 percent are rented. In the new states the figures are about 31.2 percent and 68.8 percent, respectively. The overwhelming majority of flats in multiple dwellings are rented.

Since the end of the 1970s, condominiums have become increasingly popular and meanwhile account for 13 percent of all inhabited dwellings. The majority of condominiums (52.4 percent), however, serve as investments and are consequently rented out.

In 1998, 14 percent of rented flats in the western states were subsidized by the government. This "social housing" is intended for large families, the disabled, the elderly and people with low incomes. Between 1991 and 2000, some DM 16 billion was made available for "social housing" in the form of federal financial assistance. Important reform proposals such as the "Law on Public Subsidies for Apartment Construction" are scheduled for the future, with a view to securing and enhancing the general conditions for an operable housing market.

In the mid-1980s, the housing market was slack. Thereafter, however, hefty increases in income, demographic shifts and high immigration generated a strong rise in demand that could not be matched by supply. Between the beginning of 1989 and the end of 1998, immigration alone led to a population increase of about 4.3 million. The consequence of this explosive increase in demand for housing was an acute shortfall in supply, especially in the conurbations of the west. This problem was met by the market making more housing available. In addition, Federal subsidies for housing were appreciably raised.

Between 1989 and 1995, new housing construction in Germany as a whole increased steadily. In 1995 a record 602,757 new units were completed; in 1996 and 1997 the figures were 559,488 and 578,179 respectively; in 1998 and 1999 another 500,690 and 472,805 units were constructed. In the territory of the old Federal Republic, the number of completed new units rose steadily from 1992 to 1994 (1992: 374,575; 1993: 431,853; 1994: 505,179). 498,543 units were completed in 1995, 416,122 in 1996 and 400,350 in 1997. Housing construction declined slightly in 1998 and 1999 (372,246 and 369,907 units respectively) since the housing markets have eased noticeably.

In eastern Germany, the number of completed new units rose from a low of 11,477 in 1992 to 143,366 in 1996 and 177,829 in 1997. In 1998 and 1999 numbers fell to 128,447 and 102,898 as there was meanwhile excess supply. Repair and modernization of existing housing is the main objective of government policy in the east, where much of the housing stock is still in markedly poorer condition than housing in the west due to the failings of the former GDR regime. Since 1990, moreover, about half of the apartments in the new states have been modernized and renovated with federal financial assistance. This was achieved in particular through tax benefits, the Federal Government stepping in to discharge DM 28 billion of the housing industry's existing debts, the furnishing of cheaper credits from the Reconstruction Loan Corporation (KfW Program I) totaling DM 79 billion between 1990 and 2000, and funds budgeted for social housing which were used both for modernization and renovation measures, but also for new construction. Since the fall of the Wall, the Federal Government has furnished DM 8 billion in financial assistance.

Renovating old buildings in Cottbus, Brandenburg

On February 8 2000, the Reconstruction Loan Corporation launched KfW Program II, with a credit volume of some DM 10 billion which is to focus on supporting specific, especially expensive projects receiving 50 percent of their funding from the states; it is in this last point that it differs from Program I.

Investment in new construction and housing stock has led to drastic improvements in both quality and quantity: average living space per person rose from 20.5 sq. m in 1993 to 32.8 sq. m in 1998. And though in 1993 only 57 percent of apartments had central heating, in 1998 the figure stood at just under 83 percent. In the meantime, more than 95 percent of all apartments have a bathroom and toilet.

A further priority in Germany's new states is the promotion of owner-occupied housing, which was systematically repressed in the former GDR for ideological reasons. Remarkable progress has been made in this area: between 1993 and 1998 the proportion of owner-occupied housing rose from 26 percent a year to 31 percent a year.

Housing supplement and tenants' rights. Dwelling space is a basic human need, which is why in Germany everyone whose income is insufficient to meet the cost of adequate accommodation has a statutory right to a housing supplement. It is paid as a grant towards the rent or as a subsidy towards the cost of home ownership, though subject to income limits. Special provisions apply to particularly low-income households which are also receiving social assistance. At the end of 1998, about 2.95 million households in Germany were receiving housing supplements. The cost to the federal and state governments, which each bear half of the burden, totaled about DM 7 billion in 1999. Since January 1991, housing supplements have also been paid in the new states under legisla-

Düsseldorf's
Neuer Zollhof
estate

tion which allows for the special situation there and is considerably more generous than in the west. On the whole, the housing supplement has proved to be an effective social measure.

The amending statute to the first all-German housing assistance law with improved benefits totaling DM 1.4 billion will considerably enhance housing assistance, by taking into account the development of rents and incomes since the last amendment in 1990.

Tenancy law, which is based on freedom of contract, is aimed at establishing a fair balance of interests between landlords and tenants. No tenant need fear unjust and arbitrary eviction or excessive rent increases. A landlord can only give notice to a tenant who has met the requirements of his contract if he can prove "justified interest" (for example if he can show that he needs the accommodation for his own purposes). He may put up the rent provided he does not go beyond what is charged for comparable accommodation in the same area.

Home ownership. 90 percent of all German families dream of owning a house or condominium. This coincides with the Federal Government's aim of spreading assets as far as possible. People deciding to build or buy their own home receive an owner-occupied homes premium, which is paid out directly by the tax office, and – depending on their income – may be eligible for other forms of state assistance such as grants or favorable loan conditions. The owner-occupied homes premium is paid for eight years, irrespective of the individual's income, and amounts to DM 5,000 per year for new buildings (DM 2,500 per year for existing buildings).

In addition, a child allowance of DM 1,500 per year is paid for each child. Together with the (likewise improved) measures to promote home ownership savings plans, this new arrangement will help to stimulate home acquisition, especially in the new states.

Urban development. New functions and challenges confront urban development in Germany on the threshold of the 21st century such as mastering the new urban development tasks associated with German unification. Other important goals include addressing the consequences of changes wrought by economic structural changes, protecting natural resources

In an architectural firm: explaining a building project with the aid of a model

and avoiding the production of environmental hazards. About 11.3 percent of Germany's total land area consists of settled areas and traffic routes. No single major metropolis dominates the settlement pattern in Germany; instead there is a relatively even distribution of larger cities and conurbations throughout the federal territory.

Assistance for urban development and village renewal, which began in 1971, is a joint undertaking by the federal, state and local governments to preserve, renew and develop Germany's cities, towns and villages. Almost 30 years of federal assistance for urban development in the old states and some ten years in the new states – supplemented by programs of the individual states – above all means:

— systematic, legally and financially sound, and municipally and socially responsible renewal and development of Germany's cities, towns and villages;

— improvements in both the quality of life and environmental quality;

— measures to support changes in economic structures; and

— maintenance and preservation of the cultural heritage of Germany's cities, towns and villages.

With its various forms of financial assistance, the Federal Government participates in the financing of urban development measures of the municipalities in order to compensate the latter's different economic strengths and promote economic growth. These measures are bundled together in the existing tried-and-tested urban development program and in particular the new "Social City" program. The latter, a joint undertaking of federal and state governments, marks a new approach to urban development: it involves greater meshing of urban development measures with other pertinent projects in urban problem areas. Such integrated programs operating for several years will unite urban development, housing policy measures, economic and transport policy measures, labor market policies as well as public safety. Resources from EU structural funds can be tapped to heighten the efficiency of such programs.

Notwithstanding the strapped state of public finances, it was again possible in 2000 to budget a total of DM 700 million in federal financial assistance for urban renewal and development (DM 600 million for urban development; DM 100 million for the "Social City" program).

Despite the visible successes already achieved, there is nonetheless an enormous need for eastern Germany to make up ground. Accordingly, the bulk of available funds will go to the east German states – some DM 520 million.

The most important areas of urban development are:

— urban development of towns and villages to remedy socially undesirable conditions (west and east)

— protection of historic sites and monuments to preserve and enhance our historical city centers (only in the east)

— further development of conurbations (only in the east)

The financial assistance provided thus far for urban renewal in the new states has signaled the resolve to save city centers from dilapidation and helped pave the way for economic development. It has also provided key impetus for the restructuring of the construction sector and the emergence of small and medium-sized businesses.

The investments in urban renewal and development areas supported with federal funds have generated a high volume of subsequent public and private investment and boosted demand for goods and services. This strong impetus is universally acknowledged and has been substantiated by surveys of various research institutes. Promotion of urban development has also had a particularly salutary effect on employment.

Planning a new residential area in the city planning office

Further information:
- Bundesministerium für Verkehr, Bau- und Wohnungswesen
(German Federal Ministry for Transport, Construction and Residential
Property)
Krausenstrasse 17-20, 10117 Berlin
Internet: http://www.bmvbw.de
E-mail: poststelle@bmv.bund. de

Environmental protection

Environmental policy. Germany has achieved a high level of environmental protection compared with other countries: in all processes where pollution is produced, strict limits have been set for pollutants entering the atmosphere or water. These measures have made it possible to appreciably enhance the quality of the environment in the east German states. Based on the principles of sustainable development, the focus of environmental policy is on reducing pollutants entering the environment, promoting the more efficient use of energy, closing substance cycles and the reversal of land depletion trends.

In Germany, the protection of the natural resources essential for life is anchored in the Basic Law as a government aim. It is the task of the Federal Government "to protect our vital natural resources on behalf of future generations," (section 20a). In other words, environmental protection goes far beyond preventing health hazards, encompassing an active policy of securing a healthy future. Industry and agriculture, urban planning and transport must handle limited natural resources like energy, raw materials, land and water with such care that future generations will also be able to enjoy a stable climate, rich flora and fauna, as well as fertile soil and adequate fresh water supplies

To achieve sustainable ways of living and doing business which are both enduring and environmentally sound, government action is as vital as is individual responsibility on the part of industry and consumers. In introducing ecological taxes, in abandoning the use of nuclear energy, pushing through an impressive CO_2 reduction program and establishing an effective recycling industry, Germany has pointed the way to the future and earned international recognition.

Responsibility for environmental matters at the federal level lies with the Federal Ministry for the Environment, Nature Conservation and Nuclear Safety. Falling within its purview are the Federal Environmental Agency in Berlin, the Federal Office for Nature Conservation in Bonn and the Federal Office for Radiation Protection in Salzgitter. Several of the states, too, have their own ministries for the environment. Cities, towns and municipalities have important environmental responsibilities as well.

As a modern, industrial nation, Germany is aware of the responsibility it carries in helping to solve global environmental problems. Within the framework of its cooperation with developing countries and technological transfer, Germany seeks world-wide to foster strategies for solving environmental problems. The central offices of the Global Climate Convention, Deserts Convention and the Convention for the Protection of Migratory Wild Species are all located in Bonn.

Protection of the atmosphere. A main thrust of environmental policy today is the protection of the atmosphere. Germany, which contributes roughly four percent to global warming, is engaged in concerted efforts to reduce CO_2 emissions. Between 1990 and 2005, it aims to lower emissions by 25 percent. By the end of 1999, it had already reduced emissions by 15.5 percent. Achieving this aim involved considerable modernization efforts with the main endeavors focusing on the east German states. Further reductions require greater development and use of energy-saving technology, as well as a substantial expansion of the production of renewable energy sources.

To provide an incentive for energy saving and the improvement of corresponding technologies, a gradually progressive energy tax has been charged on energy consumption since 1999. Investments in CO_2-free technologies such as solar and wind

Photovoltaic plant on the sea bridge at Graal, Müritz

energy are promoted through low-interest loans, while power supply companies buy renewable energy at statutory legally-fixed prices. This policy has paid off: since the mid-1990s Germany has been the leading producer of wind energy in the world.

Abandoning the use of nuclear energy. It is the Federal Government's declared aim to pursue the abandonment of the fossil fuel/nuclear age and usher in an era of efficient solar and alternative energy. Aside from the efficient use of energy and greater use of renewable energy sources, abandoning the commercial use of nuclear energy is central to this project. Reasons for the decision to discontinue using nuclear energy include possible consequences of accidents such as reactor meltdowns, the possibility of which cannot be excluded, the hazards posed by radiation and the still-unsolved issues surrounding disposal of nuclear waste. For these reasons, nuclear power cannot be seen as sustainable, especially since alternative energy sources are available which spare resources and are environmentally sound.

In reaching a consensus on opting to abandon nuclear energy, the Federal Government has paved the way for a new, sustainable energy mix which does not include atomic power. Operating licenses for nuclear generators are granted for a limited time only; on their expiry companies must have an alternative. They do not receive compensation.

At present, 19 nuclear power station blocks at 14 locations are in operation in Germany, producing a total output of 22,194 megawatts.

Keeping the air clean. The atmosphere in Germany, as in other industrial countries, is polluted above all by emissions from factories, road traffic, heating systems and power stations. This is particularly evident from the damage caused to forests. In 1999, 22 percent of tree stocks still showed signs of substantial damage. Human health, the soil, lakes, rivers, buildings and art monuments must therefore be protected from further air pollution.

A comprehensive clean-air program has been introduced to get to grips with pollution at its source and reduce it drastically. Pollutants emitted from power stations and district heating plants, for instance, as well as car exhaust fumes are largely reduced by filters and catalytic converters. Measures such as the Ordinance on Large Firing Installations and the Technical Instructions on Air Quality Control compelled power station operators and industry to swiftly refit their installations with modern technology. As a result, sulfur dioxide emissions from industrial firing installations and power stations in the old states decreased by more than 60 percent between 1990 and 1996, and nitrogen oxide emissions decreased by over 40 percent. Sulfur dioxide emissions from power stations in the new states decreased by some 90 percent between 1983 and 1996, while nitrogen oxide emissions fell by over 70 percent in the same period.

As far as traffic is concerned, air pollution has been reduced through constant tightening of emission levels, especially for automobiles, trucks and buses, and the use of unleaded gasoline. Indeed, leaded gasoline has been banned since the start of 2000. Ever more progress has been made in lowering concentrations of nitrogen oxide, hydrocarbons and carbon monoxide in the air, above all by the introduction and improvement of the three-way catalytic converter, which limits emissions of these pollutants. Today all new automobiles with gasoline engines throughout the European Union must meet emissions standards that presently can only be attained with such an exhaust treatment system. Germany has also succeeded in bringing about the adoption of uniform and cleaner fuel formulas in the whole of the EU. At present, Germany is seeking to establish the use of sulfur-free gasoline in Europe.

Noise abatement. Noise, especially from traffic, has become a serious threat to health in densely populated areas. Noise abatement measures are therefore urgently needed. In the Federal Republic, the planning and construction of residen-

Noise protection wall on a ring road

tial areas, traffic networks and industrial installations are subject to legal provisions mandating measures to protect the public from unreasonably loud noise. Residential streets are also being redesigned as reduced-traffic zones, noise levels for cars are being lowered, and incentives are being created for the operation of quieter aircraft. More and more streets are being surfaced with noise-absorbing paving materials. Efforts are also being made in industry and in the building trade to reduce noise levels. The "Blue Angel" environmental label draws consumers' attention to low-noise products, machines and appliances.

Protection of rivers, lakes and seas. Major improvements have been achieved in improving the water quality of rivers, lakes and seas through the introduction of tougher legislation on the discharge of waste water. Some 50 different sectors of industry must comply with limits on pollutants and nutrients levels. Moreover, under the provisions of the Waste Water Charges Act, the charges levied for such waste discharge are used for water protection. These regulations have led to the construction of new sewage treatment facilities and the introduction of industrial procedures involving low or zero-level waste water discharge. As a result, the pollution of many rivers like the Rhine, the Main and the Elbe has fallen drastically and the diversity of species they contain has improved.

In order to better evaluate the condition of rivers and lakes, quality levels have been established for the most important industrial chemicals and plant protection agents; these pollutant concentrations are so low that one can assume they do no damage to the eco-system. Industry has not yet been able to meet the quality goals of some heavy metals and chlorinated organic substances. Since the inputs industry and municipalities make to river and lake pollution have declined considerably, pollutants stemming from other areas such as agriculture have assumed greater importance. In this context, mention should be made in particular of nitrate from the spreading of fertilizer, but also the use of plant protection agents which lead to high concentrations in rivers and lakes. If these concentrations are to be reduced, it will be necessary to further improve agricultural practices and increase the percentage of organically-cultivated areas.

The biosphere reserve at Schorfheide-Chorin in Brandenburg

Pollutant-related problems are not the only challenges to contend with in surface water. Some rivers and lakes were drastically altered in the past as a result of development measures; returning them to their original state, in order to restore their damaged eco-systems and limit the consequences of flooding is another important challenge. With the exception of the Weser catchment area, all Germany's remaining rivers share their catchment areas with other nations. Accordingly, measures designed to improve the condition of rivers and lakes must be made in consultation with the respective neighboring country.

Many pollutants and nutrients are ultimately carried by the wind and rivers into the seas. Shipping and oil extraction, too, contribute to pollution of the seas, and fisheries are impairing the marine environment. These problems can only be solved through joint action by all states. In this spirit, agreements have been concluded for the protection of the North Sea and the Baltic Sea.

Measures to prevent flooding. According to the Federal Government's guidelines, an environmentally sound flood prevention policy focuses especially on limitation of the sealing of soil, improvement of local capabilities for retention and absorption of precipitation, greatest possible renaturation of rivercourses, as well as safeguarding and enlargement of flood plains. Intense work within the International Commission for the Protection of the River Rhine led to the adoption of a flood action plan in January 1998.

Final disposal of radioactive waste. There are plans to introduce legislation requiring safety reviews at nuclear power stations and restricting disposal to direct final storage. Moreover, the Federal Government has determined that a single final storage facility in deep geologic formations is sufficient for the final storage of all kinds of radioactive waste and that the target date for final storage shall be around the year

2030. Exploration of the salt mine in Gorleben is to be interrupted for reasons pertaining to safety and feasibility and other potential sites in various rock formations are to be examined to determine their suitability. After comparing the results of these studies, one site is to be selected for the prospective storage facility.

Storage of radioactive waste in Morsleben will be discontinued. The plan approval procedure will be limited to shutdown of the facility. It is the declared aim of the Federal Government to require operators of nuclear power stations to create interim storage capacity at the power station or in the vicinity as a matter of principle. Spent nuclear fuels may only be transported if no approved interim storage capacity is available at the power station and the creation of such capacity cannot be demanded of the operator. Interim storage facilities will not be used for final storage.

Radiation protection. On the basis of the Act on the Peaceful Utilization of Atomic Energy and the Protection against its Hazards (Atomic Energy Act), the Radiation Protection Ordinance and the X-Ray Ordinance regulate the safe handling of ionizing rays; stringent provisions protect persons, goods and the environment against damage. The guiding principle is to minimize radiation exposure as much as possible.

About 330,000 people in Germany are engaged in occupations that expose them to radiation, some 240,000 of them in the field of medicine. Their exposure is monitored; the low values registered are indicative of Germany's high standard of radiation protection.

After the reactor accident in Chernobyl, the Act on the Precautionary Protection of the Population against Radiation Exposure was passed and a nationwide early-warning and monitoring system was set up. The measurement networks created for this purpose supply daily data on the presence of radioactivity in the environment and thus make it possible to determine the overall radiological situation in Germany at any time.

Since 1997, protection has also been provided against non-ionizing radiation ("electrosmog") by an ordinance on electromagnetic fields, which specifies limit values for high-frequency and low-frequency electromagnetic radiation for certain permanent installations.

Nature conservation and sustainable use of nature. Of great importance for sustainable development in the area of nature conservation and preservation of biological diversity is the Convention on Biological Diversity signed in Rio de Janeiro in 1992, which has the twofold aim of not only protecting and preserving biological diversity but also providing for sustainable use of its components. Through resolute implementation of this Convention in Germany, the negative impacts on wild animal and plant species and their habitats which have occurred over the last 50 years are to be reduced. At the same time, the loss of plant and animal genetic resources is to be counteracted.

One of the foremost tasks of nature conservation is to safeguard existing natural and near-natural areas, reestablish them where necessary through renaturation measures and link them together to form networks.

Today there are about 5,000 nature reserves comprising roughly 2.3 percent and more than 6,000 landscape protection areas comprising roughly 25 percent of Germany's total area. Another major approach for securing diversity of the species is the adoption of ecological agricultural and forestry methods. Consequently, the Federal Government seeks to increase organic farming methods and the use of other methods with low environmental impact. The criteria for granting EU subsidies will be linked more rigorously to ecological factors. In addition, efforts will be directed towards furthering land protection.

Within the framework of the EU Directive on the conservation of natural habitats as well as wild animals and plants (Flora-Fauna-Habitat Directive), provision has been made for the creation of a European system of networked biotopes ("NATURA 2000") which inter alia will make possible an exchange of genetic material between the individual protected areas. Efforts are under way in Germany's states to establish a network of ecologically valuable areas covering about ten percent of the land area. Germany is also actively involved in the adoption, implementation and elaboration of international nature conservation agreements.

Waste management and soil protection. In October 1996, the Closed Substance Cycle and Waste Management Act came into force. This Act represents a departure from the tradition of waste disposal, focusing instead on the concept of recycling so that raw materials and resources are effectively conserved, low-waste products are developed, and thus in the long term the consumption and production system is restructured into a closed substance cycle. Through a broadened definition of waste it deals with all operations in the production and consumption chain which are of relevance to waste disposal and lays down requirements for waste avoidance, the reuse of waste materials in other products or as a source of energy, as well as environmentally compatible disposal. It zeroes in on the "polluter pays" principle and the concept of product responsibility.

Initiatives on the part of business and industry are to be reinforced by the possibility of having associations and self-governing bodies assume disposal tasks, by the introduction of concept and accounting requirements, and by the institution of specialized waste disposal firms. Moreover, with a view to

Recycling used glass in Velten, Brandenburg

accelerating waste management, regulations will be elaborated for certain wastes.

The principle of product responsibility was legally established for the first time through the Packaging Ordinance, which obligates manufacturers and distributors of packaging materials to take back their products after use and recycle them.

In 1999, 5.7 million tons of packaging material were collected, corresponding to some 78 kilos per person. Meanwhile, further regulations have been introduced for products such as batteries and old cars. Amendments are currently being developed to harmonize laws with EU regulations. An EU regulation for old electronic and electrical devices is also in preparation. The Federal Government sees voluntary self-imposed commitments by those with product responsibility as a possible instrument for supplementing legal regulations. In this context, in 1994, makers of paper used for printing have pledged from the year 2000 to recycle 60 percent of paper.

Collection and processing of biodegradable waste has also boomed: Whereas in 1990 less than one million tons of biodegradable waste were collected separately, by 1997 the figure had already risen to 7.5 million tons. In this area, too, the new version of the "Technical Guidelines to Settlement Waste" contributes to the enhanced processing of biodegradable waste.

Moreover, on the international stage, the Federal Government participates in the "Basle Agreement on the Monitoring of Waste Imports and Exports and Their Disposal". In Germany, a special fund has been set up which can be used to transport back illegally exported waste.

Soil protection. The Federal Government's Soil Protection Concept of 1985 formulated standards for the protection of the environmental medium soil for the very first time. With the Federal Soil Conservation Act of 1998, whose regulations came into force on March 1 1999, the prerequisites were created for effective soil protection as well as the rehabilitation of contaminated soil and waste dumps. The requirements pertaining to soil protection and the rehabilitation of contaminated soil and waste dumps are set out and regulated country-wide in the Federal Government's Act, which has been approved by the Federal Council. Its nationally uniform standards form the basis for efficient action by the competent authorities with a view to permanently maintaining or restoring the soil's productivity in its many different functions, whereby express reference is made to its function as the habitat and source of life for animals, plants and organisms in the soil. In this context measures are to be taken to avert and eliminate hazards to the soil and to protect against future negative impacts on the soil. Thus soil as an environmental medium – like air or water – has been placed under special protection by federal legislation, not only indirectly but also directly.

International cooperation. In organizing an international convention on the environment in Rio de Janeiro, the international community ushered in a process of international cooperation on ecological and development issues. Germany actively supports this process. Two things it calls for are: an institutional strengthening of environmental protection at the United Nations level, and the heeding of ecological considerations by those engaged in world trade. The increasing globalization of flows of commodities necessitates an ecological regulatory framework with global application which also secures environmental protection amidst international competition and prevents dumping of waste. International cooperation on the establishment, recognition and constant improvement of ecological standards and norms must be intensified. To this end, decisions taken at ecological conventions must be gradually yet rigorously implemented. Priority must first be given to issues relating to climate protection, protection of the world's forests and the battle against erosion and desertification. But a high level of international consultation is likewise necessary for the cultivation of the oceans. Over the long term, it will only be possible to satisfy the basic needs of

Solar panels provide a new estate with power

all people by working in harmony with ecological systems and not against them. For this reason, high importance attaches to environmental protection in the framework of Germany's contribution to assisting developing countries. Technologies with a low ecological impact must be made available to the producers in these countries which are only now entering the phase of industrialization. One way in which Germany promotes the transfer of environmental technology is via international ecological fairs, but also through environmental specialists engaged in chambers of commerce abroad.

In 1996, the principle of sustainable development was also anchored in the agreement on the European Union. In particular, it is to be realized by integrating protection of the environment into all other joint EU policies. The scheduled expansion of the EU to incorporate east European nations provides an excellent opportunity to assist these candidates in establishing high ecological standards in their own countries. Assistance will be provided primarily through the establishment of effective ecological administrations by the long-term transfer of environmental specialists (twinning programs).

Further information:
- Bundesministerium für Umwelt, Naturschutz und Reaktorsicherheit
  (German Federal Ministry for the Environment, Nature Conservation and Nuclear Safety)
  Referat Öffentlichkeitsarbeit, 11055 Berlin
  Internet: http://www.bmu.de
  E-mail: oea-1000@bmu.de
- Umweltbundesamt
  (German Federal Environmental Agency)
  Bismarckplatz 1, 14193 Berlin
  Internet: http://www.umweltbundesamt.de
  E-mail: karsten.klenner@uba.de
- Bundesamt für Naturschutz
  (German Federal Office for Nature Conservation)
  Konstantinstrasse 110, 53179 Bonn
  Internet: http://www.BFN.de
  E-mail: pbox-presse@bfn.de
- Bundesamt für Strahlenschutz
  (German Federal Office for Radiation Protection)
  Postfach 101049, 38201 Salzgitter
  Internet: http://www.bfs.de

Energy and raw materials

The Federal Republic has little in the way of raw materials and
energy and is therefore largely dependent upon imports. Two
thirds of its primary energy must be purchased from other
countries. Its dependence on minerals from abroad is also
considerable. For this reason, Germany has long since diversified its sources of energy and raw materials in order to ensure sufficient uninterrupted supplies. Germany has few deposits of oil and ores. Up to one quarter of its natural gas
consumption can be met from domestic sources. It does, however, have large deposits of hard coal, lignite and salt, reserves which will last for many decades. Geological and climatic factors limit its economically exploitable renewable
sources of energy.

Energy supply. With a primary energy consumption of 14,200
petajoules in 1999, Germany is one of the world's largest consumers of energy (see chart, p. 504). Its efforts to conserve
and make rational use of energy have proved successful: Specific energy consumption, i.e. the energy required to generate one unit of gross domestic product, has decreased by
about one third since the beginning of the 1970s and likewise declined by some 13 percent during the 1990s.

Lignite is the principal domestic source of energy in Germany. It
is made available without subsidies in both the eastern and
western parts of the country. The major lignite deposits are
in the Rhineland, southern Brandenburg, Saxony, Saxony-Anhalt and eastern Lower Saxony. Economically recoverable reserves total about 43 billion tons. In 1999, lignite accounted
for some 10 percent of primary energy consumption in Germany.

The main hard coal deposits are in the Ruhr region (North
Rhine-Westphalia) and in the Saarland. Reserves total about
24 billion tons. They cannot, however, be mined competitive-
ly. In 1950 hard coal accounted for 73 percent of the old Fed-

eral Republic's primary energy consumption. By 1999, its share had fallen to around 13 percent.

Oil, too, has lost ground to other sources of energy, largely on account of the oil price explosions in the 1970s. Oil's contribution to energy supply fell from 55 percent in 1973 (compared to only five percent in 1950) to just under 40 percent in 1999. However, this still makes oil Germany's most important energy source, judging by the proportion of primary energy consumption it makes up.

At the end of 1996, the Federal Republic's natural gas reserves were about 382 billion cubic meters. Natural gas is imported from a number of countries, and supplies are secured until well into the next decade. In 1999 natural gas accounted for around 21 percent of primary energy consumption.

Until the start of the 1990s, large amounts of uranium were mined in Germany, primarily in Saxony and Thuringia. The enriched uranium needed for the operation of nuclear power stations is imported. In 1998, nuclear energy accounted for a substantial proportion of the electricity generated by public power stations (about 33 percent). But in June 2000, the Federal Government and major power supply companies signed an agreement under which the use of nuclear energy in Germany will be legally discontinued.

Energy policy. Reliable energy supply is essential for a well-functioning, modern economy. A secure and efficient energy supply as well as environmental protection and resource conservation are the aims of the Federal Government's energy policy.

The opening of the world's markets and the globalization of the economy have changed the general framework conditions for the energy industry as well. Companies are under ever

Wind energy park in North Friesland

greater pressure to adapt, be innovative and minimize costs. This liberalization in the area of energy furnished via supply lines is also leading to the development of electricity and natural gas markets.

Throughout the world it is becoming apparent that as a result of technological progress and burgeoning world trade, it is not so much scarcity or even exhaustion of resources which will be the limiting factor for energy supply in the future but rather the question of what demands can reasonably be placed on the environment.

The energy industry of the Federal Republic of Germany is in private hands. The government's task is to provide a suitable framework, which includes the Energy Management Act, regulations for crisis prevention and the build-up of emergency stocks, and laws to protect the environment.

Since 1973, conditions on international energy markets have changed fundamentally several times. Two sharp increases in the price of oil caused global recessions; then the price dropped rapidly at the end of 1985. The transformations in Central and Eastern Europe and in the former Soviet Union have given a new dimension to East-West cooperation in the utilization of the energy resources of these countries, especially Russia. The Gulf War of 1990-1 once again underscored the uncertainty as to the development of the price of oil, which is still the most important source of energy.

Because of Germany's heavy dependence on imports, not only of oil but also of other commodities, the supply system must remain flexible and adaptable and have access to different sources. This integration in the world's energy markets also affords special opportunities to ensure an efficient energy supply. The oil price crises in the 1970s prompted a significant increase in cooperation in the area of energy policy both within the International Energy Agency and within the European Union. Today the EU has at its disposal a considerable array of instruments to support structural change in the energy sector, to promote the rational use of energy, and to reduce dependence on oil (these include the JOULE/THERMIE, SAVE and ALTENER programs). As part of a comprehensive European strategy for reducing CO_2 emissions, the European Commission has proposed fiscal measures which have the support of the Federal Government.

Germany's energy policy focuses on the following:

- pursuing a free market policy in order to ensure a reliable, economical, efficient and environmentally-friendly supply of energy. The opening of the electricity and natural gas markets will allow the dynamics of competition to play a greater role in these industries. The goal of sustainable development and the commitment to reduce CO_2 emissions necessitate further adjustments in Germany's energy production structures and consumption patterns;

- ensuring an environmentally compatible energy supply. This includes a comprehensive strategy to protect the climate. Voluntary commitments by the parties involved can be appropriate in clearly delineated areas and can be conducive to effective environmental action if the goals are unequivocally defined and verifiable and if sanctions are imposed for failure to meet them;

- stepping up efforts to economize on energy consumption and to promote research on and use of long-term alternative sources of energy, especially those of the renewable kind. By 2010, their share of the energy supply is to be double the present proportion (see chart, p. 504);

- maintaining reliance on a balanced and diversified energy mix. The contribution of German hard coal, however, will decline. Especially as a consequence of unfavorable geological conditions, it is much more expensive than imported coal. In March 1997, the Federal Government, the governments of the coal-mining states of North Rhine-Westphalia and the Saarland, and the coal-mining industry agreed on a financial framework providing for a substantial reduction in public subsidies for the coal-mining industry by the year 2005;

Rotary bucket excavator at the lignite open-cast mine Garzweiler I

Solar energy is one of the power sources of the future

— discontinuing the use of nuclear energy in an orderly fashion on the basis of the agreement reached June 2000 between the Federal Government and the leading energy suppliers. Under the accord, the amount of electricity which may be produced by each of the 19 nuclear plants in Germany is to be defined – based on an agreed standard operating time of 32 calendar years from which the operating time to date is deducted. Once the amount stipulated for the respective nuclear plant has been reached, it must be closed down. In future, alternative energy forms and or energy saving will supply the proportion of energy currently provided by nuclear power. The Federal Government has already paved the way for the development of viable energy supply systems and effective energy-saving measures through such steps as the ecological tax reform, the promotion of renewable energy sources, power/heat co-generating sets, and other energy-saving technologies).

— broadening and intensifying international cooperation in the area of energy policy, especially within the EU but also within the International Energy Agency and within the framework of the energy charter concluded with the countries of Central and Eastern Europe and the newly independent states on the territory of the former Soviet Union.

Raw materials policy. Germany relies largely on imports for its supply of raw materials. Countries of origin include both the commodity-producing countries, which supply ores, concentrates and ferro-alloys, and industrial countries which have the necessary processing industries (foundries, refineries) and can thus market metals and semi-finished products. Growing importance attaches to the recycling of used materials (see the chapter "Environmental protection") and the application of materials research and development, through which the utilization of raw materials can be optimized.

In order to ensure that the Federal Republic of Germany's supply of raw materials is placed on the broadest possible foundation, economic relations with the commodity-producing countries are based above all on the following principles:

— maintaining the efficiency of and further opening the world's commodities markets: For this reason the Federal Government calls upon international bodies to adopt a non-discriminatory framework with regard to raw material policies;

— stabilizing commodity export earnings, especially in the less developed countries, with the aim of ensuring continuous supplies of raw materials;

— accelerating the industrialization process in and facilitating the transfer of technology to the developing countries;

— opening the markets of the industrial countries to imports of manufactures and semi-manufactures from the developing countries;

— promoting the flow of capital to the developing countries and protecting investors from expropriation; and

— exploring new raw material deposits by means of cooperation projects.

Scholarship and research

In recent years, the Nobel Prize winners for chemistry, physics and medicine have included Germans. The 1991 the prize for medicine was awarded to Erwin Neher and Bert Sakmann for their work in the field of cellular biology chemistry, for instance, while in 1989 the prize for physics was shared by Wolfgang Paul and two American colleagues. The prize for chemistry was shared by Johann Deisenhofer, Robert Huber and Hartmut Michel in 1998. Nobel laureates from Germany in 1995 were the developmental biologist Christiane Nüsslein-Volhard (medicine) and the Dutch chemist Paul J. Crutzen, who teaches in Mainz. The nobel prize for medicine was awarded to Günther Blobel, who donated most of the prize money for the reconstruction of the Church of our Lady (Frauenkirche) in Dresden.

Previously, Germany's universities led the world in many areas of scholarship. Up to the Second World War, ten out of 45 Nobel Prizes for physics and 16 out of 40 for chemistry went to Germans. But starting in 1933, the National Socialists drove many of the country's best brains abroad. A good number of them went to the United States, where they were of inestimable value to that country's scientific institutions. Germany had a hard task making up for this brain drain after 1945, and it was a long time before it caught up with the world's leaders in science.

The reunification of Germany has posed a new challenge: building a uniform research environment for the whole country. Today the new states have a competitive research sector consisting of approximately 110 federally-financed research institutions employing about 13,000 people:

— three Helmholtz centers and ten branches;
— 33 institutes of the Gottfried Wilhelm Leibnitz Science Association, (this registered association is comprised of institutes devoted to supraregional projects; they receive half their

funding from the Federation and half from the state in which they are located);

— 18 facilities of the Fraunhofer Society;
— 18 institutes, a subsidiary institute and a research agency of the Max Planck Society and
— 32 national research centers and branches.

Research in the new states focuses especially on new materials, information technologies, microelectronics, biotechnology, environmental research, the geosciences and health research. In many cases, non-university research institutions collaborate with research departments of firms and with higher education institutions. The research sector in the new states has been integrated into numerous European and international programs, cooperation relationships and joint projects.

Concerted efforts are being made to unify the German research sector. For instance, financing innovation-oriented academic research groups at higher education institutions in the new states, has improved the structures for research and provided impetus for innovative inter-university and interdepartmental research projects which also bring in external specialists, some from industry.

Research institutions. Research in the Federal Republic is conducted in three different sectors: by the universities, by public and private non-university and non-industry institutes, and by industry itself (see chart, p. 505). Research by university teachers has a long tradition in Germany. The "unity of research and teaching" has been a pillar of German academic life since Wilhelm von Humboldt reformed the Prussian universities in the early 19th century. The universities are the bedrock of German research. They are the only institutions

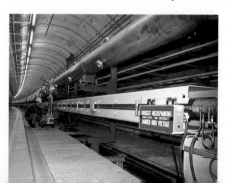

Deutsche Elektronen Synchroton DESY is the national center for basic physical research

whose research embraces all scientific disciplines. Most basic research is done there, and they produce successive generations of scientists, thus ensuring continuity.

Non-university research is primarily an extension of the work done at the universities. For instance, major research projects, especially in the natural sciences, can only be managed by big teams using expensive technology and with heavy financial backing. Such large-scale research is best conducted in the government-funded centers.

A total of 463,000 people in the Federal Republic of Germany have jobs connected with science and research. Well over 50 percent of them are scientists and engineers; the remainder are about half technical staff and half other personnel (such as administrative personnel). In 1998, gross domestic expenditure for research and development totaled more than DM 87 billion (2.3 percent of the gross domestic product). This put Germany in third place among the major industrial states (G7) in gross domestic expenditure for research and development, behind Japan (3.06 percent of GDP)the United States of America (2.79 percent) and France (2.18 percent). The biggest contribution towards expenditure for R&D came from industry (a good DM 54.3 billion). The federal and state governments furnished about DM 15 billion each, and an additional DM 1.5 billion in federal funds were expended for research abroad.

Sponsors of research. In many areas, especially basic scientific research and the humanities, the higher education institutions are the most important sponsors of research and often the prime source of innovation.

Application-oriented basic research is taking on increasing importance. In fields of applied research and development, higher education institutions cooperate with other establishments and industrial laboratories, thus speeding up the practical application of their theoretical findings. The Fachhochschulen, play a decisive role in application-oriented research and are particularly useful contacts and intermediaries for small firms.

Closely linked with the higher education institutions are the academies of science in Düsseldorf, Göttingen, Heidelberg, Leipzig, Mainz, Munich, as well as the Berlin-Brandenburg Academy of Sciences. They are centers of scientific communication and mainly support long-term scholarly projects such as the publication of encyclopedias. The German Academy of the Leopoldina Scientists in Halle is an academic association specializing in the sciences and medicine. Crucial support for academic research comes from the Deutsche Forschungsgemeinschaft (DFG), the largest sponsor after the federal and state governments. It dealt with about 14,000 applications for funds in the area of basic research alone, a record number which reflects in an impressive manner the creativity and capacity for innovation of Germany's universities. The DFG receives its funds from the federal and state governments (in 1998 approximately DM 2.5 billion).

The Max Planck Society for the Advancement of Science is the largest research organization outside the universities. Its more than 80 facilities for highly sophisticated research in Germany are largely financed from public funds furnished by the federal and state governments. It is developing further establishments in the new states. The Max Planck Society engages in basic research which is beyond the scope of higher education institutions or requires particularly large facilities.

The 16 national research centers, which together form the Helmholtz Association of National Research Centres, are another important instrument of government research policy. They receive 90 percent of their funds from the Federation (Federal Ministry of Education and Research) and ten percent from the government of the respective state in which they are located. Their fields of research range from microparticles and aerospace to cancer, environmental and climate research. In 1995, they set themselves a number of goals for the future:

DLR motor test stand for experiments in noise reduction

A cell culture chamber at the Berlin Institute for Genetic Research

- to contribute to securing an energy supply which utilizes politically controversial energy sources as well as solar energy and other alternative energy sources;
- to conduct research conducive to an environment which is not merely "cleaned up", or made "clean" again, but which is not impaired by pollutants in the first place;
- to improve diagnosis and treatment of illnesses such as heart disease, circulatory disorders, cancer and AIDS, where the great breakthrough, however, is yet to be made; and
- to develop new large-scale physicotechnical equipment to explore the microcosmos.

An important link between research and its practical application in industry is the Fraunhofer Society for the Advancement of Applied Research. In its roughly 50 institutes, it carries out commissioned projects in various areas of science and technology, mainly for industry.

Other significant contributions are made by the Federal Republic's major foundations for scholarship and research such as the Fritz Thyssen Foundation and the Volkswagen Foundation. They and the Donors' Association for the Promotion of German Science are much in demand as sponsors of research projects, especially in collaboration with the higher education institutions. The Alexander von Humboldt Foundation, which receives financial support from the Federation, enables foreign scientists to do research in Germany and German scientists to work on similar projects abroad; it also pays for research trips by outstanding foreign scientists.

Around the world, governments are increasingly coming to rely on scientific advice, as political decisions are often related to complex issues which only such experts can unravel. In preparing special reports, investigations and commentaries experts lay the groundwork for practical political decisions. Germany's own such research institutes – referred to as think tanks (after their US forerunners) meanwhile number about

100. Some of them are run privately, others are public enterprises. The most well known of them include:

— the research institute of the German Association for Foreign Policy;
— the Center for Applied Political Research;
— the German Institute for Economic Research;
— the Peace Research Institute; and
— the Wuppertal Institute for Climate, Environment and Energy.

International cooperation. The promotion of international cooperation in the field of research is a major aspect of government policy. In addition to cooperation in international organizations such as the OECD, the promotion of exchanges and direct cooperation between German and foreign scientists (for instance via the German Academic Exchange Service (DAAD) or the Alexander von Humboldt Foundation), there are many other forms of cooperation. Germany has conclud-

Robotics: synchronized movements of artificial and human hands

ed bilateral agreements on scientific and technological cooperation with over 30 countries. It plays an active part in joint research and technology programs within the European Union. Cooperation also extends beyond the territory of the Union, as reflected in the COST program (cooperation with third countries on applied research), the EU's participation in the EUREKA and ESA projects, and the more recent EU-EFTA cooperation under the European Economic Area agreement.

Some of this work at the European level is carried out by institutions with large-scale facilities beyond the means of individual countries. They include the high energy accelerator of the European Organization for Nuclear Research (CERN) in Geneva, the very high flux reactor of the Max von Laue-Paul Langevin Institute (ILL) in Grenoble, and the European Molecular Biology Laboratory (EMBL) in Heidelberg.

The aim of all these programs is to coordinate national research, pool resources in joint projects and hence increase Europe's international competitiveness.

Research policy. Research and the promotion of research in Germany are governed by the freedom of teaching and research as anchored in the Basic Law, by the country's federal structure which divides responsibility between the federal and state governments, and by the demands of industry. It is primarily the scientific institutions themselves who decide what research to undertake and assess the results, especially in the field of basic research. The Science Council, founded in 1957, advises the Federal government and state governments on matters pertaining to thematical and structural development of universities, science and research, as well as university structure. Financed equally by the federal and state governments, it is the most important institute in Germany providing political counseling. It comprises 32 male and female scientists appointed by the German President as well as 22 representatives from the Federal Government and the states. The important contribution the Council has made on matters relating to university and research policy has played a decisive role in the restructuring of universities and research in the new states.

In 1996, the Federal Government submitted the "Report of the Federal Government on Research 1996". In 1998, it presented an update: "Facts and Figures 1998. Update of Report of the

Federal Government on Research 1996". Both reports inform the public and parliament in great detail about the future aims and focuses of its research and technology policy.

Further information:
  – Bundesministerium für Bildung und Forschung
    (German Federal Ministry for Education and Research)
    Heinemannstrasse 2, 53175 Bonn
    Internet: http:// www. bmbf.de
    E-mail: information@bmbf.bund.de

Economic sectors

Industry and its products

The mainstay of the German economy is industry. In 1999, the roughly 48,900 industrial corporations in Germany employed close to 6.4 million people. However, industry's importance has declined markedly in recent years as a result of structural change; its share of the gross value added by all economic sectors fell from 51.7 percent in 1970 (old states) to 25.1 percent in 1999 (Germany as a whole). In the same period the public and private service sectors increased their share considerably.

Public and private services accounted for 21.3 percent of the gross value added in 1999, commerce, gastronomy and the hotel trade and transport 17.4 percent. Financing, renting and corporate service providers make up 29.8 percent. Rapidly expanding branches like information and communications technologies (see chart, p. 506) or fields such as the aerospace industry have failed to compensate for the decline of such traditional branches as textiles and steel.

The great majority of industrial enterprises in Germany are of small or medium size. Only about 1.9 percent of industrial enterprises are large companies with more than 1,000 employees; nearly three quarters are firms with fewer than 100 on the payroll. It is they who make available the majority of training places. However, about 40 percent (2.6 million) of

Presentation of a new printing machine at the "drupa" 2000 trade fair in Düsseldorf

the total work force in the industrial sector are employed by large firms with more than 1,000 employees. All in all, the small group of large companies account for some 51 percent of industry's total turnover. Many of these firms are known throughout the world and have branches or research facilities overseas. They include the carmakers Daimler-Benz, Volkswagen and BMW, the chemical corporations Hoechst, Bayer and BASF, the energy groups E.ON and RWE, the electrical equipment manufacturer Siemens AG, the Bosch Group and Ruhrkohle AG (see chart, p. 506).

After World War II, industry played a crucial part in Germany's economic recovery. A decisive factor in this process was the transition to a market economy in the year 1948. One of the basic principles of the social market economy is entrepreneurial responsibility: It is the entrepreneur himself who must see to his company's growth and ensure that it can adapt to changing circumstances. Government economic policy is largely confined to creating framework conditions conducive to the development of entrepreneurial initiative and to the creation of new jobs. In the Federal Government's view, competition between firms is the best way to keep German industry competitive in the world's markets. It ensures the largest possible number of small and medium-sized firms in the marketplace. The Federal Government therefore aims to improve conditions for the smaller industries and facilitate the establishment of new firms. The following is an outline of the main branches of German industry (see table, p. 505).

Branches of industry. The automobile industry is one of the most important branches of the German economy. Germany is the world's third largest producer of automobiles (after the United States and Japan). Of the 5687 million motor vehicles that were manufactured in the Federal Republic in 1999, 64.6 percent were exported.

The automobile industry has a long tradition in the new states as well. The models produced under the old GDR regime had no chance against international competition after the country was united, and production was phased out. Several large carmakers from western Germany have now opened new plants in Saxony and Thuringia. The western German automobile industry has invested nearly DM 7 billion in the eastern part of the country. Once production is in full swing, about 370,000 cars a year will leave the modern assembly lines there.

The largest number of production facilities in German industry are engaged in mechanical engineering and plant construction. Small and medium-sized firms have always predominated, and it is thanks to their flexibility and technological efficiency that Germany is among the world's leaders in this field. Only about 5.5 percent of the factories have more than 500 employees. These are mainly firms which mass-produce or design and manufacture large, complex facilities. Roughly 83 percent of the companies engaged in mechanical engineering are highly specialized small or medium-sized firms with fewer than 200 employees. As suppliers of high-quality plant and production equipment for industry they play an important role in the economy as a whole. Their range of products is unparalleled: more than 20,000 different products, from consoles, printing machines and agricultural machinery to machine tools. Roughly 68 percent of its turnover is generated by exports. Germany is thus the leading exporter in the world, accounting for 20.4 percent of global trade.

The chemical industry is an important supplier of primary, intermediate and finished products for sectors such as health care,

Producing artificial fibers at Bayer Faser AG in Schongau

Car produc-
tion at the
Volkswagen
factory in
Zwickau

the automobile industry and the construction industry as well as for private consumption in Germany; thanks to its state-of-the-art technology, innovative products and emphasis on research, it plays a leading role worldwide. In addition to the large firms in this branch of German industry, which rank among the world's most important corporations, there are also a multitude of successful small and medium-sized firms. In the new states, the chemical industry has a long tradition. The aim of government policy has been to retain the core of the traditional chemical production regions in the east through a process of restructuring and privatization. In 1999, on a yearly average, about 31,000 people were employed in chemical firms there. The chemical industry is making considerable efforts to improve environmental protection and has assumed a pioneering role in many areas.

The electrical engineering and electronics industry is likewise one of the main branches of industry in Germany. The aero-

Macrolon, a form of plastic, is used among other things in making CDs

Cleaning a
ship's
propeller

space industry, which makes the highest demands of outfitters and component suppliers, has pioneered the introduction of modern technology in many fields. Through its major European cooperation projects (such as Airbus and Ariane) it functions as a motor for cooperation between European industrial firms. German companies have carved out a niche in the field of environmental protection technologies: In 1997, they captured the largest share of world trade (16.5 percent) in this area, placing them second after the United States . Other areas which continue to be of great importance are the food industry, the textile and clothing industry (including the leather goods industry), the metal-producing and metal-processing industry, the mining industry, the precision engineering and optical industry. With an annual turnover of DM 275 billion, tourism represents a significant economic factor. Currently, the total number of people engaged directly in tourism and in related fields including part time and seasonal staff amounts to some 2.8 million. In 1999, the number of overnight stays totaled some 308 million. And over 16 million guests who stayed overnight came from outside Germany. Along with day visitors, they spent some DM 30.7 million in the country.

Competition. It is crucial for Germany's future as an attractive location for business and industry that its firms remain internationally competitive in a global economy which is increasingly driven by technological progress. Only then can the advantages of the international division of labor be fully utilized and jobs and incomes in Germany be safeguarded. To accomplish this, however, business and industry as well as society must be capable of innovation and willing to undergo structural change; firms must concentrate on areas of technological and industrial growth. As a country with high income levels and a high standard of social security but few natural resources, Germany has always had to rely on exports of top

Transporter aircraft for the Airbus – at the ILA 2000 Trade Fair in Berlin

quality, advanced products. Modern technologies, efficient and economical production methods, and efficient company organizational structures form the foundation for the nation's competitiveness.

Many companies, especially those of small and medium size, cannot finance and conduct the preliminary research this necessitates on their own. For this reason they have established a basis for joint "pre-competition" industrial research and technology transfer which affords outstanding opportunities for a broad-based transfer of knowledge. The Federal Government supports these research endeavors through the Confederation of Industrial Research Associations (AiF). The AiF sponsors the Federal Ministry of Economics' PRO INNO promotion program, for example, which supports small and medium-sized companies in a diverse range of cooperation projects in Germany and abroad. In "demonstration centers" or in other firms participating in the initiative "Technologically Oriented Tour and Information Programs" (TOP), moreover, entrepreneurs and executive staff can obtain information from outside their respective fields of activity concerning the application of new technologies, production processes and management procedures and can participate in the exchange of practice-oriented experience.

The chambers of industry and commerce. The Association of German Chambers of Industry and Commerce (DIHT) is the national organization of the 82 German chambers of industry and commerce. All German firms within the country – with the exception of craft and trade enterprises, the independent professions and agricultural operations – are by law members of the chambers of industry and commerce. The chambers represent the interests of regional businesses vis-à-vis the municipalities, the states and the regional government authorities. They function as advisers for their member firms, as knowledgeable providers of information for business and industry. The chambers of industry and commerce are democratically organized and independent of government influence. The Association of German Chambers of Industry and Commerce represents the interests of business and industry at the federal level and before the European Commission in Brussels. It also supports the approximately 110 offices of the German chambers of commerce abroad as well as the offices of delegates and representatives of German business and industry in more than 70 countries all over the world; these provide a wide range of services for small and medium-sized firms in particular to help them compete in foreign markets and thus serve to promote German foreign trade.

Further information:
  — Bundesverband der Deutschen Industrie
    (Federation of German Industries)
    Gustav-Heinemann-Ufer 84-88, 50968 Cologne
    Internet: http://www.bdi-online.de
    E-mail: presse@bdi-online.de
  — Deutscher Industrie- und Handelstag
    (Association of German Chambers of Industry and Commerce)
    Adenauerallee 148, 53113 Bonn
    Internet: http://www.diht.de
    E-mail: diht@bonn.diht.ihk.de

Crafts and trades

Crafts and trades represent the most varied sector of business activity in Germany: Approximately 685,000 independent firms are engaged in 94 crafts and trades. And it is in these firms that some 38 percent of apprentices – currently about 620,000 young people learn their trade. As such, the crafts and trades provide training places which more than fulfil their own requirements, also providing other business sectors with qualified junior staff. In addition, the crafts and trades are one of the most important employers in Germany, contributing some ten percent to gross value added. Rich in tradition, the crafts and trades are today one of industry's most forward-looking sectors. This is reflected not least of all in the mounting use of modern information and communication applications: more than 65 percent of all companies employing between ten and 500 employees meanwhile have their own home page. The National Federation of German Skilled Crafts and Trades (ZDH) is also planning to set up an Internet portal which will make it easier for firms to initiate and conduct business transactions. The EU's expansion to include Central and East European countries will also create opportunities for crafts and trades. Above all, those areas of Germany bordering onto the EU candidates can expect an expansion of business activities. In the Central and East European countries seeking EU entry, much remains to be done in the way of new construction, renovation and infrastructure enhancement. This will create openings for German craft and trade businesses.

State support for the crafts and trades. The Federal Government helps small and medium-sized craft enterprises to maintain and increase their competitiveness fostering small, independent firms by providing them with favorable economic operating conditions. Assistance covers information and further training opportunities, management consultancy and low-interest loans, subsidies for training apprentices in inter-company training centers. Another focus is the promotion of innovation and the transfer of technology to the crafts and trades. The federal and state governments also support new business start-ups through the 1996 Upgrading Training Assistance Act.

Organization of the crafts and trades. Crafts and trades distinguish two types of business: those defined as a fully certified craft business which require a master's examination and those firms similar to a craft or trade which may be operated without a special examination.

The legal framework for operation is provided by the Act for the Regulation of Handicrafts (HwO) dating back to 1953. This Act provides the crafts and trades with a good starting point for maintaining their high standard of performance and productivity amidst the fierce competition engendered by today's global markets.

The last major amendment to the Handicrafts Act which came into force in April 1998 was designed to satisfy consumer expectations of greater crafts and trades skills and improve the standing of the master's examination. Since only holders of the latter qualification may operate a full certified craft businesss, it guarantees specialist, professional standards; further, it ensures commercial and managerial qualifications entitling the holder to run a business independently and train apprenticeships.

Craftsmen in the same craft or trade in a town or county may voluntarily join a guild. At the state level, these guilds are organized in state guild associations. The guilds are above all responsible for vocational training and ongoing education. They can also negotiate collective wage agreements and set

**Baking –
a trade with
a strong
tradition**

Checking the
hydraulics of a
jet engine

up guild health insurance funds for their members. The various guilds in a town or county form the local crafts and trades association. The national organization of the guild associations is the Federal Union of German Handicraft Associations (BFH). The chambers of crafts and trades, which as a rule encompass the territory of an administrative district, are the self-governing bodies of the crafts and trades sector and look after the interests of all the crafts and trades. They maintain the Crafts Register and the Apprentices Register. The chambers belong to the German National Chamber of Crafts (DHKT). The umbrella organization for the guild associations and the chambers of crafts and trades is the National Federation of German Skilled Crafts and Trades (ZDH).

Further information:
— Zentralverband des Deutschen Handwerks
  (National Federation of German Skilled Crafts and Trades)
  Mohrenstrasse 20/21, 10117 Berlin
  Internet: http://www.zdh.de
  E-mail: info@zdh.zdh.de

The independent professions

The independent professions form an important part of the German small and medium-sized business sector. They generate roughly eight percent of the gross domestic product. At the beginning of 2000, there were about 702,000 self-employed persons in the independent professions in Germany. A total of more than 2.7 million people were gainfully employed in this sector, 165,000 of whom were trainees (about 10.5 percent of all trainees). This figure represented approximately 7.5 percent of the entire German work force. The independent professions stand out for the ability to found companies: in 1999 alone, 27,000 new independent businesses were founded. These are concentrated in the following areas:

— independent medical professions (e.g. doctors, dentists, pharmacists and other medical professionals; c. 257,000);
— independent legal and business consultants (e.g. attorneys, tax accountants and notaries, some 191,000);
— independent technical and scientific professions (e.g. architects, engineers, experts and specialists; approx. 122,000); and
— independent professions in the cultural sphere (e.g. artists, journalists, academics and translators, designers; c. 132,000).

Common to all independent professions is the fact that they provide the population and the business community with important services involving advice, assistance, care and representation – properly, on their own responsibility and not under instructions from third parties. Over and above working for their own personal gain, the members of the independent professions are under a special obligation to serve the interests and welfare of society as a whole.

A large proportion of independent professionals are compulsory members of a professional association. The professional associations are self-administered organizations responsible, among other things, for defending the rights of their given

profession. Since 1 July 1995 there has been a separate legal
form – the limited partnership – within which members of
the independent professions (and only these) may join forces.

The independent professions occupy a position in between the
state and its administration, on the one hand, and industry
and trade, on the other. Bordering the former are professionals such as notaries, publicly appointed land surveyors and
publicly appointed and sworn experts, whose work is either
of an official nature or connected with state administrative
activities. The profession of pharmacist borders on the latter,
for instance: Operation of a pharmacy is subject to trade tax,
but the pharmacists themselves are independent
professionals working within the health care system. Many
new professions and fields of activity involving freelance services have developed in recent years.

Independent professions in a process of change. With
Europe growing ever more closer together and global business links increasing, the independent professions must also
adapt accordingly. A key issue in the future will be to think
in terms of new markets. New types of jobs are arising and
the entire nature of gainful employment is changing. For
modern independent professionals, clear mastery of modern
IT and communications technology as well as the ability for
networking are the basis for a business future. Together with
clients or other partners, many independent professionals are
entering the international markets. This process is being fostered by the Internet.

The national professional associations such as the Federal Association of Panel Doctors, the Federal Dental Society, the Federal Chamber of Notaries and the German Tax Accountants Association represent inter alia regional associations or their

Modern
design
requires
computers

Architect Axel Schultes (r.) with a model of the new Chancellor's Office

members as a whole vis-à-vis parliament, authorities and organizations and prepare general guidelines for the exercise of the professions, for further training and continuing education, and for initial training of young professionals. They also keep their members informed on topics which are of relevance to the professions.

Further information:
— Bundesverband der Freien Berufe
   (National Association of Independent Professions)
   Godesberger Allee 54, 53175 Bonn
   Internet: http://www.freie-berufe.de
— Union Freier Berufe e.V.
   (Union of Independent Professions)
   Edelsbergstrasse 8, 80686 München
   E-mail: verband@t-online.de

Agriculture, forestry and fisheries

About half of the Federal Republic's total area of just under 36 million hectares is given over to farming. Like other sectors of the German economy, agriculture has undergone profound structural changes in the past 50 years.

Agriculture. In the old states, the number of farms decreased by about 1.5 million between 1949 and 1999. Increasing mechanization has also saved considerable manpower: In 1950 there were some 1.6 million farms employing just under 3.9 million family workers full time. In 1999, however, there were only 434,000 farms with about 220,000 full-time family employees.

As the number of farms and workers has dwindled, productivity has increased. Whereas in 1950 one farm worker produced enough food for only ten people, in 1999 the number was 124. In spite of this huge growth in productivity, incomes in the agricultural sector have not always kept pace with those in industry.

Family farms still predominate in Germany's western states. In 1999, 85 percent of all farmers worked fewer than 50 hectares (124 acres). In contrast to other Western European countries, 56 percent (1999) are part-time farms, i.e. the main family income comes from activities outside farming.

The chief agricultural products – in terms of sales proceeds – are milk, pork, beef, cereals and sugar beets. In some regions wine, fruits and vegetables as well as other horticultural products play an important role. Horticultural products accounted for 40 percent of the proceeds from plant production.

Especially in the western states, livestock farms are generally small. The factory-type holding is the exception. In 1999, about 96 percent of dairy cows were kept on farms with fewer than 100 animals, and just under 60 percent of fattening pigs (with a live weight of 20 kg or more) on farms keeping fewer than 600 animals. Livestock account for about 60 percent of the proceeds generated by the entire agricultural sector.

The restructuring of agricultural operations in the eastern states is largely complete and has slowed considerably in recent years. In 1999, the number of individual farm enterprises and partnerships rose only slightly, by just under one percent, whereas the number of registered cooperatives declined by two percent. By 1999, well over 30,000 agricultural operations had been established – by splitting up existing farms and setting up new ones – from the 4,650 large cooperatives and state farms that had existed in the former GDR.

Individual farm enterprises retained their importance in the east in 1999. They account for just under four fifths of all agricultural operations but farm less than one quarter of the agricultural area in the eastern states.

The number of partnerships likewise increased slightly in 1999 and has now more than doubled since 1991. These approximately 3,000 partnerships farmed a total of about one fifth of the agricultural area in 1999.

Compared to individual farm enterprises and partnerships, the number of agricultural operations in the form of legal entities changed very little between 1991 and 1999; these roughly 3,000 legal entities farmed more than half of the agricultural area in 1999.

The ownership structure in the Federal Republic's eastern states is fundamentally different from that in the western states. Only about three fourths of the agricultural operations – above all the newly re-established family farms and specialized horticultural enterprises – farm land of their own. On average, 90 percent of the land farmed by all agricultural operations in the new states is leased; in the old states the figure is only 50 percent.

In 1998-9, net incomes in the German agricultural sector were subject to extraordinary pressure. In particular, the drop in pig prices to an all-time low resulted in heavy profit losses for processing firms. Repeatedly, structural deficits in Germany's agricultural sector proved to be an obstacle in the face of ever tougher international competition. Consequently, agricultural policy must ensure that farmers have sufficient freedom to make the necessary entrepreneurial decisions (rationalization, locking into new markets, striking marketing alliance etc.).

Apart from maintaining food supplies, farming in densely populated, highly industrialized Germany has other increasingly important functions, including

— conserving the natural sources of life, especially the diversity of species, the groundwater, the climate and the soil;

— looking after the countryside to provide attractive living, working and recreational areas; and

— ensuring a continuous supply of agricultural ("renewable") raw materials for the chemical-technical sector (industry and commerce) and the energy sector. In 1997, four percent of Germany's arable land was already being utilized for this purpose. The Federal Ministry of Food, Agriculture and Forestry is supporting this alternative form of production through a corresponding promotional concept.

The Common Agricultural Policy (CAP) of the European Community. With the creation of the common agricultural market in the 1960s, important areas of agricultural policy were transferred to the European Community. This applied in particular to market and price policy, foreign trade policy and, to an increasing extent, structural policy.

The Community's objective at the time of its founding was to increase agricultural productivity and thus farmers' incomes, stabilize markets and supply consumers with high-quality foodstuffs at reasonable prices. Much of this was achieved in the subsequent decades. In particular, it was possible to significantly increase agricultural production within a very brief period of time. The supply of important products soon far exceeded demand. Through the introduction of quotas for the product categories milk and sugar, it was possible to limit supply in these categories very early on.

Nevertheless, further measures to ease the strain on the markets were necessary. Fundamental restructuring of the Common Agricultural Policy (CAP) took place in 1992 when the EC passed the agricultural reform. The CAP was subsequently consolidated and expanded by the resolutions pertaining to Agenda 2000. The reform provided for cutbacks in or elimination of the previous market price supports, compensation of the resulting losses in earnings through direct income transfers in the form of acreage premiums.

Harvesting hops in Halltertau, Bavaria

This policy is accompanied – where necessary – by effective measures to restrict production levels. The latter are a clear signal to farmers to cater more to the market. EU member states were also obliged to establish environmental measures in connection with the provisions on support and to sanction infringements against them.

The adoption of Agenda 2000 strengthens and deepens the 1992 reform. In supporting the integral development of rural areas, it attaches central importance to the multi-functional role of agriculture. By placing greater emphasis on market and environmental considerations, the EU has greatly improved its bargaining position with the World Trade Organization (WTO) and can press its case assertively. Agenda 2000 also paves the way for the smooth incorporation of East and Central European nations to the EU.

In spite of continuing difficulties in importing countries, Germany's agriculture and nutrition sectors were able to maintain a high level of exports of farm products in 1999: Products with a total value of DM 43 billion were exported. Imports, on the other hand, amounted to DM 69 billion: The Federal Republic is thus the world's largest importer of agricultural products.

National agricultural policy. The main aim of German agricultural policy is to create a competitive and sustainable economic sector. To enable farms not only to avail themselves of the opportunities offered by the European and international agricultural markets but also to meet their obligations with regard to animal protection and protection of the environment, it is essential that suitable framework conditions are secured for agriculture at international level (WTO agricultural negotiations) and within the EU (further harmonization). Moreover, as in the past, the structural improvement of agricultural and forestry firms must be rigorously pursued. One way this could be achieved would be through the as-

Grape picking on the Wachtelberg, nr. Werder, Brandenburg

sumption of new tasks. Given the limited sales opportunities for food, the social tasks of the agricultural sector assume greater importance. This spectrum might include caring for the man-made landscape, via the production of renewable raw materials, to supplying energy through the operation of plants driven by wind power or powered by biomass. Agricultural policy supports this structural development. Though many decisions on agricultural policy are today taken by the European Union, a few important matters are still in the hands of the national governments. This applies in particular to environmental policy and, to a limited extent, structural policy for the agricultural sector. Although the European Union sets basic conditions in this area, the federal and state governments provide the substance. Together with the states, for instance, financial assistance is provided for investment measures in agricultural operations as well as for land consolidation, village renewal and construction of country roads. In addition, special funds are provided for farms in naturally disadvantaged areas where agriculture is an important economic and social factor.

An environmentally sound agricultural policy is directed towards supporting the sustainable use of natural resources, in order to conserve them for later generations. As in other areas of the economy, laws ensure that the agricultural sector acts in the interests of the environment. The protection of plants is just one example. And with a view to placing as little strain as possible on the eco-systems, well-trained farmers employ methods consistent with "good agricultural practice". Those farmers whose efforts for the environment go beyond this general standard are rewarded in the form of financial assistance programs operated by the EU, federal and state governments. As a result of these environmentally-sound farming programs, one third of Germany's land under cultivation is worked using methods with an especially low environmental impact. These methods range from ecological farming, via conservation of the countryside through to extensive grassland cultivation and contractual environmental protection. Such policy measures will be extended in the future, since they ease the strain on the environment and secure workplaces in rural areas.

A separate social security system tailored to the special needs of the agricultural community has been established for independent farmers and their family members to protect them against the financial consequences of an insured person's illness, need for long-term care, work-related accident, invalidity or death and to ensure their security in old age. This social security system is financed by contributions paid by farmers (about DM 4.7 billion in 1998) and by federal funds (about DM 7 billion in 1998).

Food. Maintenance of a food supply which meets consumers' needs at reasonable prices is the foremost aim of national food policies and is also mandated by the Treaty on European Union. This aim has been achieved in the Federal Republic of Germany for years, as can be seen from the fact that consumers have been spending an increasingly smaller proportion of their income on food. In 1998, it was 15 percent (excluding spirits and tobacco, etc.) compared with 30 percent (in the western states) in 1970.

Germany's markets offer consumers an extraordinarily wide range of foodstuffs to choose from. Controls by producers themselves and legal provisions that are repeatedly adapted in light of the latest scientific knowledge, as well as monitoring of foodstuffs, protect the consumer from hazards to health and fraudulent products and help to improve the quality of foods.

Consumers should be in a position to correctly judge the quality and price of the foods offered for sale and should possess sufficient knowledge of foods and nutrition to choose a balanced diet and avoid illnesses caused by improper nutrition. The Federal Government ensures the flow of necessary information by supporting important consumer information institutions such as the Deutsche Gesellschaft für Ernährung (DGE; German Nutrition Society), the Auswertungs und Informationsdienst für Ernährung, Landwirtschaft und Forsten (AID; Food, Agriculture and Forestry Information Service), as well as the consumer information centers in the individual states. They furnish information on proper nutrition, product quality and prices, the law relating to food and drugs, and storage of private stocks of food.

Protection of animals. A modern, trailblazing Protection of Animals Act has been in effect in Germany since 1972. It stipulates that as a matter of principle, all animals are to be protected from avoidable pain, suffering or harm. New scientific findings prompted significant improvements in the Act in 1986, especially in regard to the use of animals in experiments, the keeping of animals, trade in animals and slaughtering practices. Upon further amendment of the Protection of Animals Act in 1998, additional substantial improvements entered into force. Not only at the national level, however, but also increasingly at the European level, provisions are being drafted for the protection of animals. Germany has ratified the various European conventions for the protection of animals adopted by the Council of Europe.

Within the European Union, directives have been and continue to be issued concerning the keeping of livestock on farms, transportation of animals, use of animals in experiments, and slaughtering practices; these directives are subsequently implemented into national law. Every two years, the Federal Government submits an Animal Protection Report to the German Bundestag detailing developments in the area of animal protection.

Forestry. Almost a third of the Federal Republic's total area – 10.7 million hectares – is covered by forest. The two states with the largest forest area in proportion to their total size are Rhineland-Palatinate and Hesse (about 40 percent), while the one with the lowest proportion of forests is Schleswig-Holstein (about nine percent).

About 40 million cubic meters of solid timber are felled in Germany every year. Considerably less timber is felled than is simultaneously growing back. As a result, wood supplies are now steadily rising. Through deliberate measures to increase deciduous and mixed forests, it has at the same time been possible to strengthen the resistance of tree stocks to damaging environmental influences and to breakage caused by high winds and heavy snow. Deciduous and mixed stands now account for about 60 percent of total forest area.

Forestry is an important profession in Germany, with its many woods

Germany relies on imports in order to meet domestic demand for wood and wood products. Although Germany remains a net importer of wood, as regards semi-finished and finished products, imports greatly exceed exports. Thanks to the constant expansion of external trade, it conducts business with an ever increasing number of nations throughout the world; EU states account for over 60 percent of trading volume.

Forests are important not only as sources of timber but also as recreation areas for the inhabitants of industrial conurbations. Furthermore, they have a beneficial influence on soil, air and climate in that they retard water runoff, weaken the impact of wind, clean the air, and prevent erosion and landslides.

A Forest Preservation and Forestry Promotion Act was enacted in 1975. It stipulates that forest land can only be cleared for other uses with the approval of the state authorities. It also obliges forest owners to employ sustainable cultivation methods and to reforest harvested areas. The foremost aim of German forestry policy is to preserve or restore the extension and natural appearance of the forests, enlarge them where necessary, and permanently ensure their proper management.

Since the beginning of the 1980s, increasing damage to Germany's forests has been detected. People have used the pithy – but inaccurate – term "dying forests" to describe this phenomenon. Within just a few years, damage has become extremely widespread and has afflicted virtually every species of tree. Visible symptoms of this new type of damage are sparse crowns and yellowed leaves and needles. There are various biotic and abiotic causes of this new type of damage, mainly air pollution. Although intensified environmental protection measures to improve the quality of the air have achieved noticeable success, pollution levels in forests and forest soil are still too high. Further efforts at both the national and international level are essential in order to reduce

Shrimp fishing off the North Sea coast

air pollution emitted from industrial installations, power plants, traffic, households and agricultural operations.

The surveys of damage to forests, which date back to 1984, show that the initial pessimistic predictions of swift death of extensive tracts of forest have failed to materialize. What has happened is that forests have seen varying development depending on tree type, region and year. Throughout the country, the overall condition of the forests improved during the 1990s.

Fisheries. The fishing industry, too, has undergone structural changes in recent decades. Coastal countries worldwide have extended their fishing zones to 200 sea miles, with the result that traditional stocks have been decimated by overfishing, chiefly because of the excessive use of modern catching methods. This has greatly reduced the Federal Republic's ocean fishing fleet. Germany's principal fishing areas are the North Sea, the Baltic Sea, and the Atlantic Ocean west of the United Kingdom and around Greenland.

The Federal Republic's only chance of surviving the threat to its fishing industry resulting from the development of international maritime law was within the framework of the European Community. Catch quotas within the EU serve to regulate fishing and safeguard species.

The EC Common Fisheries Policy (CFP) was reviewed in 1992 after ten years, and a new basic regulation was adopted for the next decade. An extrapolation of the previous policy, it focuses in particular on the principle of "relative stability" (i.e. fixed quotas for member states) and on a system of managing fish stocks by establishing annual total catch limits. The aim is to establish an economic and ecological balance between usable marine resources and fishing capacities by protecting stocks and reducing fishing volume. The next review of the CFP is scheduled for 2002. In all probability, it will result in existing principles being upheld.

In 1995, the 4th International Conference on the Protection of the North Sea and the Kyoto International Conference on a Sustainable Contribution of Fisheries to Food Security also addressed the issue of the long-term survival of the fisheries industry. A corresponding conference of the environment ministers and fisheries ministers also took place in Bergen (Norway) in March 1997 within the framework of the International Conference on the Protection of the North Sea. The United Nations and the Food and Agriculture Organization (FAO) have likewise concerned themselves with this subject. In this context – and within the framework of the European Union – the Federal Government advocates an environmentally sound structuring of the fisheries industry in order to ensure its long-term survival.

Further information:
- Bundesministerium für Ernährung, Landwirtschaft und Forsten
  (German Federal Ministry of Food, Agriculture and Forestry)
  Rochusstrasse 1, 53123 Bonn
  Internet: http://www.bml.de
  E-mail: internet@bml.bund.de
- Deutscher Bauernverband e.V.
  (German Farmers' Association)
  Godesberger Allee 142-148, 53175 Bonn
  Internet: http://www.bauernverband.de
  E-mail: DeutscherBauernverband@t-online.de

Commerce

The commercial sector in Germany accounts for some ten percent of gross value added. Well over 4.6 million people – one eighth of the total work force – are meanwhile employed in the approximately 610,000 German Although there has been a marked tendency for companies to merge, most are still in the small or medium-sized category. About half of them employ only one or two persons, and nine tenths of them fewer than ten, usually including the owner and often his or her family members as well.

Wholesale trade. Wholesalers sell commercial goods from manufacturers or foreign markets to retailers, processors or commercial users. Especially retailers obtain consumer durables and non-durables from them. Trade in raw materials, semi-finished goods, scrap and recyclables continues to generate the highest turnover. In 1999, the wholesale trade's turnover totaled more than DM 1 trillion. The 118,000 German wholesalers – including 10,000 domiciled in the east German states – employ 1.2 million people.

Retail trade. The retail trade has undergone a profound structural change in recent decades. Sprawling retail complexes on the edge of town have multiplied. This development is particularly evident in the east German states. As a result, competition has become even stiffer, and profit margins have shrunk accordingly. The trend toward chains has become especially pronounced in the retail grocery trade: The groups with the largest turnover are REWE, Edeka/AVA, Aldi and Metro.

These developments are accompanied by an internationalization of the retail trade: More and more German retailers are stepping up their business activities abroad. Conversely, foreign competitors such as the U.S. corporation Wal-Mart or the French retail group Intermarché are claiming a share of the German market.

In 1999, turnover in the retail trade totaled DM 722 billion (not including pharmacies, filling stations and motor vehicle dealerships). Retail trade turnover thus represented only 30.3 percent of private consumption in 1999; in 1991 the figure was 42 percent. The approximately 4050,000 retailers in Germany have a work force of about 2.837 million. As a consequence of stagnating turnover, about 1.43 million part-time employees were eliminated in 1999.

There are about 60,000 commercial agents and brokers in Germany who together employ well over 135,000. The approximately 55,000 motor vehicle dealerships and filling stations employ more than 520,000 persons.

Increasing motorization and the trend towards more economical bulk buying have favored the spread of hypermarkets, self-service department stores and discount stores, which are becoming ever more popular with consumers. As a result, many small neighborhood retailers have gone out of business. In recent years, however, small and medium-sized retailers have managed to compete with large enterprises by catering for individual tastes, specializing in certain types of products, and offering expert advice and personalized service. They have also increasingly joined forces to cooperate in the areas of purchasing, sales and marketing. The Federal Government supports small and medium-sized retailers through numerous promotional programs and forms of credit. The most important of these are the equity capital assistance loan, the ERP business start-up loan and the ten-percent investment allowance for retailers in downtown areas of cities in Germany's eastern states. A new trend was established in 1999 when retailers started offering delivery services. Markant Südwest, Edeka, SPAR and OTTO Versand, but also many others

Goethe Arcade in Jena, colorfully festooned

Software for Internet vendors

are experimenting with this service. Another major development is the increasing use of the Internet as a means of doing business with many retailers setting up on-line shops. Sales for e-commerce amounted to around DM 3 billion in 1999.

Further information:
- Hauptverband des Deutschen Einzelhandels e.V. (HDE)
  (Head Association of German Retail)
  Am Weidendamm 1a, 10117 Berlin
  Internet: http://www.einzelhandel.de
  E-mail: hde@einzelhandel.de
- Bundesverband des Deutschen Gross- und Aussenhandels e.V.
  (Federation of German Wholesale and Foreign Trade)
  Am Weidendamm 1a, 10117 Berlin
  Internet: http://www.bga.de

Foreign trade

International trade is crucial to the German economy. The Federal Republic has always sought close trade relations with other countries and upheld the principle of an international division of labor. Its trade policy is consistent with this approach. Germany supports further liberalization of trade in a context which accords greater attention to ecological and social priorities in the interest of ensuring sustainable development. By pursuing an outward-looking policy, Germany has achieved the world's second largest foreign trade turnover (after the United States).

External trade. Germany's external trade has been booming for years. According to figures available for 1999 it has posted new records: Exports rose to DM 992.3 billion and imports to DM 867.7 billion, an increase of 3.9 percent and 4.8 percent respectively over the previous year's figures. The German trade surplus fell by DM 2.4 billion to DM 124.6 billion. The economic and financial crises in Asia, Russia and Latin America took their toll, leading to poor first-half figures. But following this stagnation phase, external trade experienced new impetus in the second half of 1999, which sometimes saw two-digit growth rates, a trend repeated early in 2000.

Today, about 24.3 percent of all gainfully employed persons in Germany work directly or indirectly for export; in other words, one in four jobs is dependent on exports. In the case of manufacturing industry the percentage is even higher, for one fourth of this sector's production is exported.

Germany's main exports in 1999 were motor vehicles (DM 191.6 billion), machinery (DM 158.2 billion), chemical products (DM 141.1 billion) and electrical engineering products (DM 123.9 billion).

The Federal Republic's most important imports are motor vehicles (DM 132.1 billion), electrical engineering products (DM 99.7 billion) and machinery (DM 98.7 billion). As a result of its extensive trade relations, Germany is acutely affected by disruptions of world trade and changes in the global economic situation, for these developments have an impact on jobs, investments, profits and standards of living. Thus a stable world economy, free trade and a well-functioning monetary system are crucial prerequisites for the consistently positive development of the German economy (see chart, p. 507).

Trading partners. Germany's most important trading partners are the Western industrialized nations. In 1999, these countries accounted for 77.5 percent of the Federal Republic's exports and 75 percent of its imports.

The progressive economic integration of the European Union (EU) has greatly increased intra-European trade. In 1999, the EU countries accounted for 57.2 percent of Germany's exports and 54.1 percent of its imports.

Germany's most important trading partner continues to be France. In 1999, the Federal Republic exported goods worth approximately DM 112.9 billion to that country, whereas imports from France totaled DM 89.7 billion. The United States has meanwhile become the second largest market for German products, spending DM 100.8 billion in 1997. In terms of Germany's imports, the United States ranks second (DM 71.2 billion) after France, and before the Netherlands and Italy (see chart, p. 507).

In 1999, the Federal Republic posted a further increase in its external trade with the countries of Central and Eastern Europe including the CIS, even though figures were not as impressive as in previous years. Specifically, it imported and exported goods worth a total of DM 192.5 billion (1.8 percent more than in 1998). While exports fell by 5.9 percent in 1999 to DM 97.4 billion, imports increased 11.1 percent to DM 97.4

Hamburg's
container
dockyard

billion. Poland has consolidated its position as Germany's most important trading partner in Eastern Europe: With a trade volume of about DM 42 billion in 1999 (a four percent increase), it ranks ahead of the Czech Republic . The volume of Germany's trade with Russia totaled DM 26.2 billion in 1999 (a fall of 11.3 percent). Dynamic increases were likewise posted in trade with the Czech Republic (up 9.9 percent), and Hungary (up 14.2 percent).

In total, 70 to 75 percent of German foreign trade is with European countries, about 13 percent with the Asia-Pacific region, about ten percent with North America, and about two percent each with Africa and Latin America. Its largest trade imbalance for many years has been with Japan. Whereas Germany imported goods worth DM 42.0 billion from Japan in 1999, Japan spent only DM 20.5 billion in Germany.

Foreign investment. In 1999, German firms invested a total of DM 171.67 billion abroad (net transfer volume). Foreign firms invested DM 96.3 billion in Germany in the same period (after investing only slightly less than DM 38.41 billion in all of 1998). This remarkable rise in investment from abroad, which lowered Germany's negative balance of direct investment to DM 16.3 billion, clearly indicates that foreign investors are finding Germany a more attractive location for business and industry. The pattern of investment follows the global trend: German firms invest primarily in the economies of the European Union and the United States.

This flow of investment is concentrated between the industrial countries; in 1999, the United Kingdom, France, and the United States were the prime destinations for German investment, whereas France, United States and the United Kingdom were the leading sources of foreign investment in Germany. The

service sector and processing industries led all other sectors in terms of the volume of direct investment in both directions.

In the world economy, direct investment is increasingly playing a central role in the globalization of firms and the development of an ever-denser network of economic relations between the world's nations. Competition for mobile capital between nations vying with each other as locations for business and industry has intensified markedly in recent years. According to the 1999 World Investment Report of the United Nations, 92 percent of global direct investment stemmed from industrial countries, which in turn received nearly 72 percent of the influx. Germany thus stands every chance of playing an important role as a supplier and recipient of long-term investment capital in the future as well.

In order to offset possible economic and political risks attaching to investment in developing countries, the Federal Government has introduced special promotional instruments. For instance, it has concluded investment protection and promotion agreements with 124 developing countries, nations in Central and Eastern Europe and countries currently emerging as market economies. To guard against political risks, the Federation also provides financial guarantees for investments in the said countries. The Deutsche Investitions- und Entwicklungsgesellschaft mbH (DEG) founded by the Federation promotes direct investment by German firms in the Third World and in countries currently emerging as market economies. Small and medium-sized German companies receive low-interest loans and grants to help them finance branches in developing countries and the transfer of technology.

Current account. Germany's traditionally large export surpluses occasionally draw criticism abroad. The current ac-

Loading a freight 747 at Frankfurt Airport

count, however, shows that the foreign trade surplus is offset by heavy deficits in the "invisible" service sector. The large amounts spent by German holidaymakers abroad, remittances by foreign workers in Germany to their relatives at home, development assistance, the Federal Republic's contributions to the European Union and other international organizations, and a negative balance of earned and unearned income erode most of the surplus from trade. In fact, Germany's current account initially slipped deeply into the red after unification. The credit balance of DM 79.0 billion in 1990 plunged to a deficit of DM 30 billion in the space of only one year. In 1999, Germany's current account had a negative balance of DM 32.8 billion. Germany is no longer the world's biggest exporter of capital. On the contrary, it has to borrow considerable foreign capital in order to finance economic recovery in the eastern part of the country.

Further information:
  — Bundesverband des Deutschen Gross- und Aussenhandels e.V.
    (Federation of German Wholesale and Foreign Trade)
    Am Weidendamm 1A, 10117 Berlin
    Internet: http://www.bga.de

Money and banking

In accordance with provisions of the Maastricht Treaty, the European Monetary Union commenced on 1 January 1999. Since this date, the unit of currency of the participating countries has been the euro (1 euro = 100 cents). As a sub-unit of the euro, the Deutsche Mark will remain the sole legal tender in Germany for a three-year transitional period until the end of the year 2001. At the start of 2002 the new euro cash is to replace the national banknotes and coins previously in circulation. Since 1 January 1999, however, it has been possible to conduct cashless transactions denominated in euro.

European System of Central Banks (ESCB). In December 1991, it was agreed in the Maastricht Treaty that European economic and monetary union was to be established by 1999 at the latest. Sovereignty in the area of monetary policy was to be transferred to a politically independent European System of Central Banks. At the beginning of May 1998, the European Council resolved that eleven states would initially introduce the common currency. The participating states had to fulfill strict eligibility criteria (stable prices and exchange rates, low interest rates, budgetary discipline) and also commit themselves to continuing to pursue sound financial policies after the commencement of monetary union. On 1 January 1999, the European System of Central Banks assumed sole responsibility for the monetary policy of the participating states. The primary objective pursued by the ESCB is to ensure price stability; all others are secondary. Its most important decision-making body is the Governing Council of the European Central Bank composed of the members of the Executive Board of the ECB and the governors of the national central banks of the participating states.

Accordingly, the Council lays down the guidelines for monetary policy in the eurozone. The current business of the ECB is handled by the Executive Board, composed of the President, the Vice-President and four other members. They are appointed for a single term of no more than eight years. During this time they may not be removed from office. This, too, ensures the independence of the European Central Bank.

The monetary policy instruments at the disposal of the European System of Central Banks essentially correspond to those used by the Deutsche Bundesbank. Regulation of the supply of money in circulation – together with assessment of the other factors contributing to the development of inflation – play a central role. With this monetary strategy the ECSB pursues the twofold aim of ensuring the price stability of the euro and at the same time making available the necessary means to finance economic growth in the monetary union. To this end it relies above all on an open market policy and a minimum reserve policy, as well as standing facilities through which credit institutions can make deposits at the national central banks or satisfy their temporary liquidity needs. By

Euro banknotes

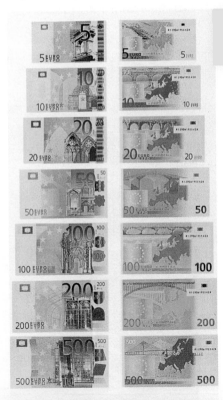

buying securities within the framework of open market operations, the ECSB allows money to flow into the economy; by selling them it withdraws money. The minimum reserves which credit institutions are required to maintain with the ECB are interest-bearing in order to avoid distortion of competition involving countries in which there is no minimum reserve requirement.

The Deutsche Bundesbank. On January 1 1999, the Deutsche Bundesbank became an integral part of the European System of Central Banks (ESCB) consisting of the European Central Bank and the national central banks of EMU Member States.

The most important function of the Bundesbank is to ensure decentralized implementation of the monetary policy centrally formulated by the ECB's Governing Council. The Bundesbank may no longer pursue an independent monetary policy of its own. It still fulfills key functions at the national level in areas

New Year's party on Jan. 1 1999 outside the European Central Bank headquarters in Frankfurt/ Main

such as banking supervision and management of the monetary reserves remaining at the Bundesbank, however, and continues to serve as the Federal Government's "house bank". The Bundesbank will also continue to oversee payment transactions in Germany and conduct issue of the euro banknotes.

The European Economic and Monetary Union is to create monetary stability, low interest rates, sustainable growth and a high level of employment within the Community. Since there will no longer be freely fluctuating exchange rates between the participating states, businesses (especially export firms) will have a more reliable basis on which to plan; tourists will not have to exchange currency, which means their holidays will be cheaper, and consumers will benefit from competition intensified by greater transparency in prices. The dynamism of the European internal market will be boosted, and the European currency can become a more important world reserve currency.

Credit institutions. There are a wide variety of financial institutions in the Federal Republic of Germany. In addition to the largely public savings banks and central savings banks, there are credit cooperatives (Volksbanken and Raiffeisenbanken), private banks, as well as building and loan associations, mortgage banks, central depositaries for securities, and investment trusts. Over the years, however, a concentration process has taken place in the banking sector. Whereas in the 1950s there were just under 14,000 independent credit institutions, by December 1999 the number had shrunk to approximately 3,200. And the trend is unbroken: in 1999, more than 200 cooperative banks merged into larger group institutions.

There are 315 commercial banks (including the "Big Four" – Deutsche Bank, Dresdner Bank, Commerzbank and the HypoVereinsbank), 13 central savings banks , 578 savings banks, the Deutsche Genossenschaftsbank as the central institution of the Volksbanken and Raiffeisenbanken as well as two regional institutions of credit cooperatives, 2,059 credit cooperatives, Deutsche Postbank AG, 30 private and public mortgage banks, 16 credit institutions with special functions, and 33 building and loan associations.

The private commercial banks include large ones that are stock corporations. The central savings banks are the central credit institutions of the public savings banks in the states. As the house banks of the states, they are mainly concerned with regional financing. The overwhelming majority of savings banks are backed by municipalities or associations of municipalities. They are autonomous public enterprises; their guarantor is liable for and must assume their commitments.

The approximately 2,000 local Volksbanken and Raiffeisenbanken with their roughly 16,100 branch banks form the bedrock of the group of cooperative banks. They are legally and financially independent and act on their own responsibility. Within the framework of an interlocking financial system, they receive support for their business activities from the regional institutions of credit cooperatives and from the Deutsche Genossenschaftsbank. On average, each Volksbank or Raiffeisenbank is backed by about 7,900 members.

Mortgage banks give mortgages and municipal loans, financing their lending by issuing mortgage bonds and municipal bonds. Building and loan associations accept the savings deposits of people who want to build or buy their own homes and give them loans for this purpose after a certain percentage of the total contract amount has been saved. Among the credit institutions with special functions is the Development Loan Corporation. It provides investment loans, lends to developing countries and helps finance exports.

The activities of all credit institutions in Germany are supervised by the Federal Banking Supervisory Office in Berlin. If a credit institution runs into financial difficulties, the deposit insurance institutions of the banking trade and statutory compensation funds partially cover savers' losses.

Financial markets. Hardly any other sector of the German economy has grown as vigorously as the financial services sector. The volume of business of Germany's banks rose from DM 4 trillion at the end of 1988 to DM 11.1 trillion at the end of 1999. Whether one looks at savings deposits, stock and security holdings, loans or cashless payments – all the indicators of Germany's financial markets have skyrocketed in the past decade.

In 1999, Germany's stock exchanges registered a turnover of EUR 5.1 trillion (compared with EUR 5.4 trillion in 1998). Approximately 42 percent of this amount was accounted for by fixed-interest bearing securities and the rest by shares (57 percent) and warrants (one percent). The futures market has likewise experienced strong growth since its establishment in 1990. In 1999, contracts totaling EUR 35 trillion were handled. This makes the futures exchange EUREX the largest futures exchange in the world.

Securities trading in Germany is on the one hand conducted decentrally on the secondary market on eight exchanges (Berlin, Bremen, Duesseldorf, Frankfurt am Main, Hamburg, Hanover, Munich and Stuttgart) with the Frankfurt exchange and Xetra accounting for the lion's share of securities trading. On the other hand, a substantial proportion of transactions is conducted as off-exchange trading by telephone and increasingly via electronic trading systems.

On 1 January 1993, the Frankfurter Wertpapierbörse (Frankfurt Stock Exchange) was renamed Deutsche Börse AG. It provides the infrastructure and requisite resources for trading on the Frankfurt Stock Exchange. Together with the Swiss bourse it also operates the futures exchange Eurex which replaced the former German Futures Exchange (DTB). Deutsche Börse AG is today one of the world's foremost providers of bourse and securities services, competing with other major providers, including those in London, Paris and the United States.

Modes of payment. Today nearly every employee has a giro or salary account. In addition, more than 45 million Germans have a Eurocheque card and use this international payment system. Credit cards are also becoming increasingly popular. In 1980, roughly 580,000 people in the Federal Republic were using them; today the number is about 18 million.

For over 20 years it has been possible to withdraw cash from automatic teller machines (ATM). Modern machines now accept a wide variety of domestic and foreign cheque and credit

Advising a client at a bank

cards. Electronic exchange machines at airports and major train stations exchange foreign currencies into Deutsche Mark. The "electronic cash" system introduced in 1990, i.e. cashless payment by cheque card in conjunction with a PIN number, is used at more than 140,000 terminals in Germany, especially in retail stores and gas stations.

At the end of 1996, the money card was introduced, a card with a computer chip storing a specific amount of money which can be used to pay at correspondingly equipped registers. When the amount has been used up, the card can be recharged at the bank or at an ATM. The money card is an "electronic wallet" designed primarily for paying small amounts at retail store checkouts and for use in dispensing machines.

More and more credit institutions are broadening customer contact via phone, PC and fax access. About three million customers now utilize 24-hour telephone banking services; some 6.6 million utilize home banking services via computer.

Further information:
- Bundesverband deutscher Banken e.V.
  (Association of German Banks)
  Burgstasse 28, 10178 Berlin
  Internet: http://www.bdb.de
  E-mail: bankenverband@t-online.de
- Deutscher Sparkassen- und Giroverband e.V.
  (German Savings Banks and Giro Association)
  Simrockstrasse 4, 53113 Bonn
  Internet: http://www.dsgv.de
  E-mail: postmaster@dsgv.de
- Bundesverband der Deutschen Volksbanken und Raiffeisenbanken e.V.
  (Federal Association of German Volksbanken and Raiffeisenbanken)
  Heussallee 5, 53113 Bonn
  Internet: http://www.VRnet.de
  E-mail: BVR.BONN@t-online.de
- Deutsche Börse AG
  Börsenplatz 1, 60313 Frankfurt/Main
  Internet: http://www.exchange.de
- Deutsche Bundesbank
  (German Bundesbank)
  Wilhelm-Epstein-Strasse 14, 60431 Frankfurt/Main
  Internet: http: //www.bundesbank.de
  E-mail: presse-information@bundesbank.de

Traffic and transport

A highly developed transport system is indispensable for a modern industrial society such as Germany. It ensures mobility for the country's inhabitants, gives them a wider choice when selecting their place of work and residence and goes towards creating more equal living conditions. The efficient, flexible operation of industry, crafts and trades and commerce is dependent on a well developed transport network. These factors are all the more important in a country which is as strongly geared towards exports as Germany.

Germany's transport policy faces a number of tough challenges: the development of the internal European market and the EU's expansion to include eastern European countries will increase Germany's role as a major hub of traffic and trade movements at the heart of Europe.

Deutsche Bahn AG. In 1994, Deutsche Bundesbahn and Deutsche Reichsbahn (the railway of the former GDR) were merged and privatized to form Deutsche Bahn AG. Because railways are a very environmentally friendly means of transport, they will remain indispensable for the movement of bulk goods, combined rail/road carriage of goods and passenger transport. Modernization of the railway network is therefore being stepped up and receives considerable financial support from the Federal Government. In 1991, Deutsche Bundesbahn introduced the first high-speed services in the west. The new ICE trains can travel at speeds of up to 280 km/h. In 1998, the high-speed service between Hanover and Berlin began operations. It is anticipated that in 2002, services will be inaugurated on the new high-speed route under construction between Cologne and Frankfurt/Main. Other high-speed rail services integrated into a European network are planned.

Railway connections between the western and eastern German states are being expanded and their efficiency substantially improved. Many of the "German Unity on the Tracks" transport projects have already been realized, closing the gaps between the previously separate railroad networks in east and west.

Further, expansion work is well underway to enhance and improve Berlin's role as a railway hub, in line with the transport requirements of the country's capital. Deutsche Bahn AG is forging ahead with the much-needed modernization of its trains and railway stations. In the next few years, 27 train stations are to be modernized or newly built and linked with shopping and tourism centers.

Over and above this, the entire railway network, currently comprising 380,000 km in length, will undergo modernization work in order to better meet today's requirements. Measures will include steps to increase capacity at bottlenecks, but also improving the economic operation of routes currently underused or only moderately used. Maintenance, renovation and modernization work to track facilities, signal boxes, signaling systems, tunnels and bridges will require ever-larger infusions of cash in future.

The regionalization of short-distance passenger traffic (SPNV), completed on 1 January 1996, is already starting to bear fruit. Under the restructuring of public short-distance passenger traffic (ÖPNV), responsibilities for planning, organization and financing were united in each respective state, to better cater to local demand. This has not only resulted in a better service but has greatly improved efficiency, thereby intensifying competition between transport providers. The Federal Government supports the states by contributing DM 13 billion a year in regionalization funds. This amount will increase owing to the effects of dynamization.

ICE high-speed trains at Kassel's Wilhelmhöhe Station

Since regionalization, responsible associations and transport firms have struck numerous agreements leading to an improvement in short-distance passenger traffic services. For instance, in many states regular services make for better connections to long-distance services and the remaining public transport network. Moreover, previously closed tracks have been re-opened, non-federal trains operate on track belonging to the DB AG, and in many states rolling stock has been replaced. On balance, short-distance passenger traffic services have improved. Responsibility for providing passenger information on the SPNV and ÖPNV services as well as creating suitable information systems is borne by the responsible transport companies. The Federal Government has assisted the DELFI project – the basis for a country-wide travel plan information system as a joint venture of the states and transport firms.

Roads. There are more cars on Germany's roads than ever before. At the start of 2000, there were 50.7 million registered vehicles, including 42.4 million cars. In addition, there are 65 million bicycles.

The network of trunk roads has a total length of about 231,000 km, including more than 11,000 km of autobahns (motorways). In size, therefore, Germany's autobahn network ranks fourth, after the United States, China and Canada. Aside from the situation in the east German states, the main concern at present is to remove bottlenecks and accident black spots and to provide more links with regions with little transport infrastructure. On nearly all of Germany's roads there is a graduated speed limit. On federal highways, for instance, it is 100 km/h, in built-up areas 50 km/h, and in many residential areas just 30 km/h. Speed limits are also in force on much of

Germany's autobahn network. For many people, the car remains an indispensable means of getting to and from work and of enjoying leisure-time pursuits. Rapid goods transport from door to door would not be possible without the use of trucks. The motor vehicle will therefore continue to be one of the principal means of transport.

Research and development in the automobile industry focuses on reducing gasoline consumption and emissions of pollutants. In some areas, road and rail transport do not compete but instead complement each other. One example of this is the "piggyback" system by which trucks are transported over long distances on special railroad flatcars. In container traffic, too, in which the railways are an important link in the transport chain, road and rail work together. This also applies to car-carrying passenger trains.

Road safety is constantly being improved, mainly through modern roads, traffic education, the advance of traffic technology and the construction of cars whose active and passive safety is constantly enhanced to meet the latest technology standards. In spite of increasing mobility and traffic density in the Federal Republic, the number of road fatalities in 1999 (about 7,750) was the lowest on record since the introduction of road traffic accident statistics in 1953. The negative trend has now ended in the east German states, too. Improving road safety remains an ongoing task.

Shipping. As a major exporting and importing country, the Federal Republic of Germany has a merchant fleet of its own comprising some 800 ocean-going vessels. It is one of the safest and most modern fleets in the world. Two thirds of the ships are less than ten years old. Germany is one of the leaders in the field of container and roll-on, roll-off traffic.

Germany's seaports (the largest are Hamburg, Bremen/ Bremerhaven, Wilhelmshaven, Lübeck and Rostock) have been able to hold their own in international competition. They have remained competitive by investing heavily in infrastructure and port facilities, handling over 220 million tons of goods per year. . German ports are "fast ports" in which even large seagoing vessels can be unloaded and reloaded in a short time.

Inland shipping and waterways. Germany has a network of federal waterways covering 23,000 sq. km and 7,300 km of

Frankfurt Airport – the second largest passenger hub in Europe

inland waterways. Though this network on waterways is very wide-meshed, the majority of cities and the most important industrial centers have access to a waterway which contributes considerably to securing their attractiveness as a business location. In addition to their importance for the transport sector, the waterways also play an important role in other business fields, especially for the water industry.

Inland shipping in Germany focuses on the Rhine and its tributaries, which provide large parts of the industry of Central Europe with an efficient infrastructure and access to the seaports in the Rhine's estuary area. Another important transport artery is the West-East waterway link from the Rhine via the West German canal network to Berlin which also allows access to the North and Baltic Seas via the rivers Weser, Elbe and Oder. Some 63 billion ton-kilometers are transported on German waterways every year.

Transporting goods via ship and waterways is a cost-effective, safe and environmentally-friendly method allowing the ideal combination of economy and ecology. The economic factor assumes especial importance when large amounts of goods are to be transported over long distances, dangerous loads are to be ensured safe transport and modern ships can operate to their full capacity. Accordingly, the goods most frequently transported on Germany's inland waterways are bulk goods (building materials, ore, coal, animal feed, steel, wood) or dangerous goods (minerals, chemical products). As part of the trend towards greater use of containers, mixed goods are carried as bulk goods. This has led to the strong expansion of this sector.

Air transport. The strong growth of international air traffic is making heavy demands on the Federal Republic's airports and air traffic control systems. In 1999, 132.5 million passengers were registered at German airports, plus 2.1 million tons of air freight. The country's largest airport is Frankfurt/Main, which is also one of the principal airports in Europe (1999: 45.3 million passengers; 1.4 million tons of air freight). The other international commercial airports in Germany are Berlin-Tegel, Berlin-Tempelhof, Berlin-Schönefeld, Bremen, Cologne/Bonn, Dresden, Duesseldorf, Erfurt, Hamburg, Hanover, Leipzig, Munich, Münster-Osnabrück, Nuremberg, Saarbrücken and Stuttgart. There are also a number of regional airports.

Deutsche Lufthansa AG is one of the leading international airlines. In 1999, it carried about 44 million passengers, using a fleet of around 240 modern aircraft. Every year some 26 million holidaymakers fly with the charter airlines such as Condor, LTU, Hapag-Lloyd and Aero Lloyd etc. More than 120 international airlines maintain regular scheduled flights to German airports, from where there are direct connections to roughly 300 destinations in more than 100 countries.

German airports are operated as private companies. Airport and air safety standards are constantly being updated in order to cope with the heavy congestion in Germany's airspace. Deutsche Lufthansa was privatized in 1994. Since then it has considerably expanded its services by entering into cooperation agreements ("Star Alliance") with foreign carriers.

Forwarding and logistics. In Germany, some four billion tons of goods are transported every year by truck, train, inland and seagoing vessels and airplanes. The forwarding sector generates annual turnover of just under DM 80 billion and employs around 370,000 people. On the whole, it comprises small and medium-sized businesses. Altered demand structures, new production and supply networks, an ever larger diversity of goods and e-commerce have created new flows of commodities requiring organization of entire

Germany's largest letter-sorting center in Hamburg

processes. Logistics firms handle the whole process or assume tasks prior to or following on from production such as assembly or quality control, as well as providing after-installation services. This would not be possible without today's modern information and communication technology.

Postal and courier services. In 1995, the Federal Government began to implement an open-market policy on postal services, which had previously been a monopoly. Since then, competition in this economic sector has increased considerably; in this respect Germany is playing a leading role in Europe. At the end of 1996, more than 100 licensees were already competing with Deutsche Post AG in the area of addressed bulk mail services (Infopost), a segment with an overall volume of some 55 million items. Liberalization of postal services continued when the new Postal Act came into force on 1 January 1998, under the provisions of which Deutsche Post AG's exclusive license for letters weighing up to 200 gm will expire on 31 December 2002.

With some 304,000 employees and a turnover of DM 44 billion (1999), Deutsche Post World Net is the leading logistics company in Europe offering letter mail, express mail, logistics and financial services. Its efficient network of 83 letter mail centers handled some 21 billion items in 1999. Express services cover 227 countries throughout the world.

The market for courier, express and parcel services has already been completely liberalized. Here Deutsche Post commands a roughly 25 percent share, competing with United Parcel Service, Deutscher Paket Dienst, Hermes, DHL and many other providers. The tracking & tracing system has meanwhile established itself as standard for all providers: As soon as an item enters the system it receives a barcode which is subsequently read in at every transport station. This procedure allows constant tracking of the item's location by phone or computer, making it possible to determine when the item will reach the addressee

More than 92,000 new jobs have been created thus far as a result of the emergence of private providers of freight mail and courier services (excluding Deutsche Post). Since 1990, competition has led to a marked increase in turnover and a rise in employment.

Information Technology

Up until 1996, telephone services in Germany were provided exclusively by the Deutsche Bundespost or, later, by Deutsche Telekom AG. 1996 was the year the Telecommunications Act came into force establishing the regulatory framework for liberalization of the telecommunications market as of 1 January 1998. Since then, telecommunications have been deregulated throughout Europe. Following the dissolution of the Federal Ministry of Posts and Telecommunications, a Regulatory Authority for Telecommunications and Posts under the purview of the Federal Ministry of Economics was established to oversee the transition from monopoly structures to a free market. Its main tasks are:

— to control the dominant market role of Deutsche Telekom AG and Deutsche Post AG which previously enjoyed a monopoly;
— to assist the new competitors by creating the necessary equal opportunities in the telecommunications and postal markets;
— to ensure further development on the telecommunications and postal markets.

The Regulatory Authority

— grants licenses for the telecommunications and postal markets;
— manages licenses and telephone numbers;
— investigates matters of radio interference;
— advises citizens on the new regulations and how they affect the newly structured telecommunications and postal markets.

The competitors. Deutsche Telekom AG, whose primary shareholder is still the Federal Republic of Germany, is the largest telecommunications provider in Europe and the third largest carrier in the world. At the end of 1999, the number of telephone connections stood at 47.8 million (including more than 13 million ISDN basic channels). Digitalization of the telecoms network was completed at the end of 1997.

Deutsche Telekom AG is an internationally active company in the telecommunications branch. Europe's largest telecommunications provider and the world's third-largest carrier. As part of the second reform to the postal services, Telekom was transformed into a joint stock company on 1 January 1995. In November 1996 it went public. Deutsche Telekom AG is increasingly expanding its activities abroad. With foreign subsidiaries of its own and offices in Brussels, Paris, London, New York, Moscow, Jakarta, Beijing and Singapore (branch offices in Hong Kong and New Delhi), it is meanwhile represented in the world's major metropolises. In addition, in 1999 it forged ahead with its expansion course in Europe, buying British mobile telephony company One2One and the French fixed-line company Siris. Further, it increased to 100 percent its holdings in Austrian mobile telephony firm max.mobil. Together with Ameritech, it has a majority stake (slightly less than 60 percent) in the Hungarian telecommunications company Matáv. It also maintains other interests in countries including Switzerland, Italy, Poland, the Czech Republic, Croatia, Russia, the Ukraine and in South-East Asia.

Approximately 1,700 other firms are meanwhile registered with the Regulatory Authority for Telecommunications and Posts. They may operate in any branch of the telecommunications sector. In particular, the liberalization of the telephone market has attracted a large number of competitors who have already commenced local, regional or nationwide operations, or are preparing to do so. One bottleneck plaguing Deutsche Telekom AG's competitors in providing telecommunications services is in the area of telephone accesses (subscriber access lines). Here, competitors have the option of using Deutsche Telekom AG's cables against payment of corresponding user

Deutsche Telekom's International Net Management Center

fees or installing their own access lines. This can also be accomplished by means of a wireless local loop.

Above all in large cities, ISDN connections are offered by the major providers such as Mannesmann Arcor, Otelo and MobilCom. In addition, there is an increasing number of regional and local competitors which are publicly or privately owned. They include: NetCologne, Berlikomm, Sonatel, BreisNet, Pulsaar, Gelsennet, SoestCom and many more.

Transformation of the telecommunications sector into a free market has sparked fierce competition among the numerous new providers. Their many different rates are often bewildering to customers. This is especially true in the area of long-distance telephone services, where firms such as otelo, VIAG Intercom, ACC, CNS, EWE, First Telecom, Hutchinson Telecom, Interroute Telecom, Mannesmann Arcor, MobilCom, Talkline, TelDaFax, TelePassport, Tele 2, VEW Telnet and Westcom jostle for shares of the market. Customers have two options: They can either contractually commit themselves to a single provider ("pre-selection") or select the cheapest rate – and thus a different provider – for each individual call ("call-by-call").

Pre-selection equipment and computer software are already available or under development which automatically determine the cheapest rate for a given call and make the connection.

Mobile communications. There are presently about 31 million participants in the digital mobile communications networks in Germany, and the number is currently increasing by several million each year. At the latest by the start of 2001, the number of cell phone subscribers will have surpassed the number of fixed-line connections. In addition to "T-Mobil"

Anyone can now afford modern phone comfort

(9.1 million subscribers, end of 1999) and Vodafone-Mannesmann's "D2 privat" (9.5 million), competitors include E-Plus Mobilfunk ("E1" – RWE, VEBA, BellSouth, Vodafone: 3.5 million) and E2 Mobilfunk (VIAG, British Telecom, Telenor: 280,000). The next generation of mobile communications, UMTS (Universal Mobile Telecommunications System), which is to be introduced throughout Europe by the year 2002 at the latest, will make possible broadband applications as well and will bring the tone quality and transmission speed of mobile communications up to the standard of fixed-network communications. Sending short messages via cell phones is becoming increasingly popular. Messages (known by the acronym SMS = short messaging service) can be up to 160 characters long and can also be sent from a PC to a cell phone (see chart, p. 509).

Services and technical innovations. Since the summer of 1998, it has been possible for telephone customers to be reached both at home and on the road under the same number. This has been achieved by means of "intelligent" structures in the fixed and mobile communications networks which forward the call to wherever the customer happens to be – even to other numbers in the fixed or mobile communications network. In 1999, Deutsche Telekom became the first German company to provide chip cards for electronic signatures which meet the guidelines set out in the German law on signatures. As a result, customers are able, for the first time, to effect legally-binding signatures on electronic documents.

Since the beginning of 1998, it has been possible to obtain "vanity numbers" forming easily remembered combinations of letters. Subsequently, the letters of the alphabet are allocated to certain number keys on the telephone keypad, allowing people to dial names instead of numbers. Technical innovation in the field of telecommunications is leading in the direction of a speech-controlled multimedia terminal affording access to every conceivable form of electronic communication irrespective of time or place.

The telephone is becoming more and more important in the area of direct marketing: Currently, some 1,500 call centers in the Federal Republic of Germany sell goods, furnish information and offer additional services.

Currently in the test phase is the "telephone from the power point" in which existing electricity supply lines are used for telecommunications and Internet access. In addition, a new technology allowing high speed transmission of digital signals via copper wire will soon be ready for implementation. (Representing an advance on ISDN, it is known as ADSL – asymmetric digital subscriber line). Finally, efforts continue to pinpoint the position of cell phones globally, one aim being to use them as electronic orientation devices when driving.

Internet and databases. In the Federal Republic of Germany there is a broad spectrum of electronic information services in which the Internet plays the key role. Numerous firms, organizations and public institutions use the Internet to introduce themselves, offer information, services and opportunities for interaction, sell goods and transact business. More and more companies are utilizing Internet technology to offer information internally (intranet), or to afford business partners secure areas in which to transact business (extranet). The Internet is transforming peoples' lives as did other great inventions of the past such as the railway or telephone. But it is bringing changes at breakneck speed, which fills some with enthusiasm and others with anxiety.

As elsewhere in the world, Germany is also seeing an enormous surge in the number of Internet users. In February 2000, 15.9 million or around 30 percent of the population between the ages of 14 and 69 used the Net. Moreover, it is estimated that by the end of 2000, the number will have exceeded the 20 million mark. Some 70 percent log on from their homes, 36 percent from their offices and 14 percent from their training center. Almost 60 percent of users hold a university degree. Most go on-line several times a week (see chart, p. 509).

The explosive growth of the Internet has led, in Germany, to an appreciable shortfall as regards qualified computer specialists. In response, the Federal Government started the "Schools go Online" campaign: All schools in Germany are to be equipped with an ISDN connection together with the requisite hardware and access software. Simultaneously, teachers, who in many cases had little knowledge of computing to date, are to receive training in the subject. In 1999, the first German chair of e-commerce was set up in Frankfurt/Main.

Those people going on-line for private purposes expect rapid access to encyclopedias, current news, information on upcoming events, consumer information and share prices. They perform "paperwork", effect money transactions, order tickets and book holidays – all from their homes. Around one third of users purchase goods via the Internet: The most popular items are books, followed by computer software and music CDs. Securities trading via the Web has also experienced extraordinary growth. Meanwhile, some 11.5 percent of private shareholders avail themselves of on-line brokerage services.

That said, the Germans do not have that much faith in the Net's data protection and security mechanisms. As the Internet develops at breakneck speed, its advance is accompanied by a noticeable rise in international computer crime. Hackers wreak untold damage the world over with computer viruses. For this reason the federal ministries for the interior and for industry and technology have launched the campaign "Safety in the Internet – Safety in the Information Society" which provides Internet users with detailed information on protection measures they can take.

As regards Internet service providers, T-Online led the field with 8.6 million subscribers in February 2000, followed by AOL with five million, Compuserve with 700,000 and Germany.net with 300,000. Amongst the pure access providers, Yahoo-Online ranked first with 1.3 million users, followed by Freenet (900,000), Mannesmann Arcor (800,000) Viag Interkom (800,000) and otelo (700,000). The most popular search engines are Yahoo, T-Online, AOL, Altavista, Lycos and Fireball.

At the outset of the 21st century, the Internet is something of an information Moloch. One of the great challenges we face is more clearly structuring its services and making the knowl-

Deutsche Lufthansa's traffic operations center in Frankfurt/ Main

edge available via the Net easier to access, more accurate and user-friendly. Picture Video phone connections, interactive adventure TV, video conferences, product presentations per Internet and many more options will be standard features in just a few years from now, in the same way that many newspapers and journals publish an Internet edition which appears ahead of their print version.

Fairs and exhibitions

Germany's fairs have a long tradition. They developed in the early Middle Ages out of markets where people came to trade their wares. They were under the protection of the crowned heads, who granted various towns the right to hold them. On 11 July 1240, for example, Emperor Frederick II granted this privilege to the city of Frankfurt am Main and placed all merchants traveling to the fair under his protection. A privilege from Emperor Maximilian in 1507 made possible the later flourishing of the Leipzig Fair, which had its origins in markets documented as early as 1165.

In Germany, the former comprehensive fair has meanwhile been superseded by specialized fairs for one or more economic sectors. Germany's importance as a location for international fairs is known throughout the world. At present, about two thirds of the 150 leading international specialized fairs are held in Germany. In 1999, some 162,000 exhibitors, including roughly 77,000 from abroad, presented their products and services at 180 international fairs and exhibitions attended by almost ten million visitors. Participating business and industry as a whole spends about DM 11 billion on fairs in Germany.

Today fairs are one of the most important and most efficient marketing tools. Their strength – especially in the age of the Internet – lies in the opportunities they afford for direct personal communication. The proportion of foreign exhibitors at German fairs is continually increasing and in 1999 was almost 48 percent. An expanding range of international goods and services stimulates competition and kindles greater interest on the part of international visitors. Aside from the major events, some 200 regional and many smaller exhibitions take place in Germany every year (see table, p. 510).

The main fair venues. Berlin, Cologne, Duesseldorf, Essen, Frankfurt am Main, Friedrichshafen, Hamburg, Hanover, Leipzig, Munich, Nuremberg and Stuttgart are the main German fair venues. The world's two largest fairs are held in Hanover. The Hanover Fair, founded in 1947, showcases the global spectrum of products for numerous branches of the capital goods industry. In 1999 about 7,700 exhibitors displayed their goods on an area of approximately 270,000 square meters. Hanover is also the venue of "CeBIT", a fair devoted to office, information and telecommunications technologies which emerged from the Hanover Fair in 1986. In 1999, CeBIT attracted roughly 7,400 exhibitors who presented their products on an area of almost 400,000 square meters. Other important fairs held in Hanover are "EMO" (The World of Machine Tools), the International Motor Show (IAA) – Commercial Vehicles, and "LIGNA" (World Fair for Machinery and Equipment for the Wood Industries).

Frankfurt am Main is the venue of the consumer goods fairs "Ambiente" and "Tendence", which focus on table and kitchen decor, gift ideas and home accessories. Frankfurt also hosts the International Motor Show (IAA) – Passenger Cars/Motorcycles and the International Trade Fair Sanitation – Heating – Air Conditioning. Every autumn publishers, booksellers and authors from all over the world meet at the Frankfurt Book Fair.

Cologne, too, is an important venue for fairs such as "ANUGA" (World Food Market), "photokina" (World Fair for Imaging), the International Furniture Fair and specialized fairs for men's clothing, home appliances, hardware and bicycles.

Events in Berlin which attract worldwide attention are the International Green Week Berlin (an agricultural and food exhibition), "ITB Berlin" (International Tourism Exchange), the World of Consumer Electronics and the "ILA – International Aerospace Exhibition".

The world's major auto show: the IAA in Frankfurt/ Main

Munich's
Riem trade
fair complex

Major fairs in Duesseldorf are "drupa" (International Fair Printing and Paper), the International Trade Fair Plastics + Rubber, "MEDICA" (World Forum for Doctors' Surgeries and Hospitals), "interpack" (International Fair for Packaging Machinery, Packaging and Confectionery Machinery) and the international fashion trade fair.

Outstanding fairs in Munich, where a completely new state-of-the-art trade fair complex was opened on the grounds of the former Munich-Riem airport in 1998, are "bauma" (International Trade Fair for Construction Machinery and Equipment and Building Material Machines), "drinktec-interbrau" (World Fair for Beverage Technology), "ispo" (International Trade Fair for Sports Equipment and Fashion) and the International Light Industries and Handicrafts Fair. Specialized fairs for the computer and electronic components industries are attracting increasing attention as well.

Also renowned throughout the world are the International Toy Fair, held every year in Nuremberg, as well as the "Schweißen und Schneiden" (Welding and Cutting Fair) in Essen and the "Schiff, Maschine, Meerestechnik" (Shipbuilding, Mechanical Engineering, Marine Technology Fair) in Hamburg.

German unification has merged two quite different types of trade fair: the decentralized, specialized type organized in cooperation with business and industry in western Germany and the state-controlled type prevalent in the former GDR geared to Leipzig's comprehensive fair. Leipzig has meanwhile developed a new concept focusing on specialized fairs and has built a new exhibition complex, one of the most modern in Europe. Leipzig is also banking on its experience in trade with the countries of Central and Eastern Europe.

Fairs and exhibitions abroad. The growing integration of the world economy makes it increasingly important for German business and industry to participate in foreign trade fairs. Such participation takes the form of joint exhibitions by

EXPO 2000 in Hanover: the German Pavilion

German firms at foreign fairs. In 1997 more than 5,000 German firms participated in fairs abroad with the support of the Federal Government. At regular intervals Germany organizes larger exhibitions abroad in the fields of technology, investment and consumer goods. For instance, a German consumer goods exhibition ("KONSUGERMA") was held for the first time in Shanghai in 1998, while Jakarta was the venue for "TECHNOGERMA" in 1999. Germany participated in the World Exposition in Seville in 1992 and was represented at EXPO '98 in Lisbon.

EXPO 2000. Under the motto "Man – Nature – Technology" EXPO 2000, the first World Expo held in Germany, took place in Hanover from June 1 through Oct. 31, 2000. 155 countries, 17 international organizations and some two dozen globally active corporations took part – a greater number than ever before. Many million visitors were fascinated by the encounters between people and cultures from all over the world, took the opportunity to inform themselves about possible solutions to the global problems of the 21st century, and were truly taken by the presentations by a very many internationally renowned artists and folklore groups.

Further information:
  – Ausstellungs- und Messeausschuss der Deutschen Wirtschaft (AUMA) (German Council of Trade Fairs and Exhibitions)
    Lindenstrasse 8, 50674 Köln
    Internet: http://www.auma-messen.de
    E-mail: info@auma.de

The system of a social market economy

Industrial relations

Of the 36 million gainfully employed persons in the Federal Republic of Germany, 89.3 percent are wage and salary earners, i.e. employees, civil servants, and trainees or apprentices. In addition, there are 3.5 million self-employed, most of whom also have others on the payroll, apart from 311,000 helping family members. Employers include private companies, federal, state and local government authorities, and other public institutions.

Employers and employees cooperate with each other, as they must, but their interests sometimes clash. They then have the right to negotiate collective agreements without interference from the government. The state sets the general conditions by legislation, but it does not lay down how much workers should be paid. This, and many other matters – for example holidays – are left to the "social partners", i.e. the trade unions and employers' associations, to negotiate themselves.

Trade unions. The largest labor organization in the Federal Republic is the Deutscher Gewerkschaftsbund (DGB; German Trade Union Federation) with about 8.04 million members in 11 unions (at the end of 1999; see table, p. 511). DGB unions are based on the industrial association principle: This means that they enroll workers and employees of an entire industrial, commercial or other economic sector (or even several sectors), regardless of the kind of work they do. Thus, a chauffeur and a bookkeeper working in a printing plant, for instance, can both be members of the industrial union IG Medien (Media Union).

Apart from the DGB there are a number of other union organizations. The Deutsche Angestellten-Gewerkschaft (DAG; German Salaried Employees Union) had approximately 462,000 members at the end of 1999. Its members are salaried staff from practically all sectors of the economy. The Deutscher Beamtenbund (DBB; German Civil Servants' Federation), with about 1.2 million members, is the main organization of permanent civil servants which, on account of civil service law, is not involved in collective bargaining and cannot call members out on strike. Otherwise it has all the characteristics of a trade union and has considerable influence. There is also the Christlicher Gewerkschaftsbund Deutschlands (CGB; Christian Trade Union Federation of Germany), which with its affiliated unions, numbers about 305,000 members.

The German trade unions are not connected with any particular party or church. No one can be forced to join a union. The closed shop system (which, according to agreements between employers and unions, allows only union members to be employed) is alien to Germany. The degree of unionization, i.e. the proportion of workers who are members of unions in certain industries, varies greatly but averages less than 50 percent. The unions maintain many colleges and training centers for their members.

Employers' associations. The employers have joined to form regional associations which – like the DGB unions – are based on the principle of "one industry, one association". The central organization of the employers' associations is the Bun-

Employer and employee representatives meet prior to a new round of negotiations

desvereinigung der Deutschen Arbeitgeberverbände (BDA; Confederation of German Employers' Associations). Like the DGB, it does not itself conclude collective agreements but instead functions as a coordinating body, and represents the basic interests of its members. The BDA covers all branches of business – from industry, crafts and trades, commerce, banking and insurance to agriculture and transport.

About 80 percent of entrepreneurs are members of an employers' association – a much larger proportion than in the case of employees. The BDA represents them only in their role as employers, i.e. as negotiating partners of the trade unions. All other interests – taxation or economic policy, for instance – are taken care of by other business organizations such as the Bundesverband der Deutschen Industrie (BDI; Federation of German Industries), the Zentralverband des Deutschen Handwerks (ZDH; National Federation of German Skilled Crafts and Trades) and the Bundesverband des Deutschen Gross- und Aussenhandels (Federation of German Wholesale and Foreign Trade).

Collective agreements. There are two basic types of collective agreements which the unions negotiate with the employers' associations or with individual employers. Wage and salary agreements regulate pay and in most cases are agreed for a short period of time. Framework or general agreements, which as a rule run for several years, regulate conditions of employment such as working hours, holidays, minimum notice, overtime rates, etc. There are also special collective agreements governing specific issues (such as vocational training, supplementary retirement benefits and protection against rationalization measures).

In principle, labor and management can negotiate freely; they must, however, abide by the constitution and the statutes. The average, statutory maximum number of working hours per week is 48, for example, but practically all Germans work fewer than 40 hours a week, and some only 35. Similarly, the law prescribes a minimum paid holiday of 24 working days, but collective agreements generally provide for a holiday of 30 working days (six weeks). Nearly all workers receive additional holiday money and a Christmas bonus on the basis of collective agreements. In many cases, actual wages, salaries and other payments are considerably above collectively agreed rates.

Industrial action. In Germany, industrial action may only be taken in connection with collective wage agreements. It is therefore restricted to those agreements. During the life of a collective agreement, the parties thereto are obligated to maintain industrial peace. This means that industrial action cannot be called on matters covered by agreements still in force. In order to prevent industrial action, in many cases provision has been made for arbitration if the two sides cannot agree. Under the unions' rules, moreover, the members have to be balloted. Only if a qualified majority are in favor may a strike be called.

The workers' right to strike is counterbalanced by the employers' right to lock them out. Within certain limits, lockouts have been upheld by the Federal Labor Court and the Federal Constitutional Court as permissible means of industrial action, but the issue is still controversial. As the state remains neutral in labor disputes, neither strikers nor locked-out workers receive unemployment benefits. Union members receive strike pay from the unions' strike funds for loss of earnings, but non-members get nothing. During a strike, they must either live on their savings or apply for social assistance.

Cooperation. Workers and entrepreneurs are not in opposition to one another all the time, however. They also cooperate in many ways. This is most apparent on the shop floor, but the representatives of both sides' organizations also meet on many other occasions, for example on apprentice examination committees. In the labor courts, which rule on employment disputes, there are lay judges at all levels from both sides. Within the framework of so-called self-government, the management boards and representative assemblies of the social insurance schemes (unemployment insurance, health insurance, accident insurance and pension insurance) are comprised half of employers' representatives and half of employees' representatives ("representatives of the insured"). Politicians also frequently seek the views of the leaders of the two sides' organizations. These, and other forms of cooperation help to foster mutual understanding without blurring the differences between their respective interests.

Works constitution and co-determination. The Works Constitution Act of 1972 defines the regulations for industrial relations at the place of work. It lays down in particular the

right of participation and codetermination of the employees'
representative bodies, the right of the individual employee to
be informed and be heard, as well as the rights of the unions
within the framework of the works constitution.

The works council. The works council represents the interests
of employees vis-à-vis their employers, assesses suggestions
put forward by employees, and passes them on to the employer. The works council shall monitor, among other things,
that the laws, decrees, accident prevention regulations, collective wage agreements concluded, and works-wide agreements are all observed.

Important co-determination rights cover such areas as matters relating to the proper running of the establishment; working
hours (including the introduction of short time or overtime);
holidays; introduction and use of technical devices designed
to monitor the behavior or performance of the employees;
provisions for the prevention of accidents at work, occupational diseases, and for the protection of health on the basis
of legislation or safety regulations. The works council also
has a considerable say in job descriptions, work processes,
the working environment, personnel planning and vocational training. The employer must also consult the works council
before any dismissal. Failure to do so will result in the dismissal being declared null and void.

Co-determination at the managerial level enables employees to
influence company policy through their members on the supervisory board. This co-determination by employees in factories and corporations is a key pillar of the social order in the
Federal Republic of Germany. It rests on the conviction that
democratic legitimation cannot be limited only to government, but must also be effective in all areas of society.

A strike by the Öffentliche Dienste, Transport und Verkehr trade union

Staff discussion on workflow improvement at a car factory

Co-determination in the supervisory board extends to all company activities. Thus the supervisory board, for instance, appoints the members of the management board. It may also revoke their appointment, demand information on all company matters, and render important business decisions, e.g. with regard to major investments or rationalization measures, subject to its approval.

The supervisory boards of companies where co-determination is practiced have to be made up of equal numbers of shareholder and employee representatives. All the employees' members of the supervisory board, i.e. those working in the company and the trade union representatives, are elected by direct ballot or by delegates.

In companies with more than 8,000 employees, the law prescribes elections through delegatesa ballot, but employees may, by a majority vote, opt to be represented by delegates. The employees may, however, reverse this procedure; in other words, they can choose by a majority vote to have a direct ballot.

The shareholders' members of the supervisory board are elected at the firm's respective shareholders' meeting (the "Hauptversammlung" or AGM in the case of stock corporations, the "Gesellschafterversammlung" or partner's meeting in the case of limited liability companies). At the inaugural meeting of the supervisory board, the members elect the chairman and the vice-chairman.

Further information:
— Deutscher Gewerkschaftsbund
  (German Trade Union Federation)
  Hans-Böckler-Strasse 39, 40476 Düsseldorf
  Internet: http://www.dgb.de
  E-mail: info@bundesvorstand.dgb.de
— Deutsche Angestellten-Gewerkschaft
  (German Salaried Employees Union)
  Johannes-Brahms-Platz 1, 20355 Hamburg
  Internet: http://www.dag.de
  E-mail: info@dag.de

– Deutscher Beamtenbund
  (German Civil Servants' Federation)
  Dreizehnmorgenweg 36, 53175 Bonn
  Internet: http://www.dbb.de
  E-mail: http://www.dbb.de/email
– Christlicher Gewerkschaftsbund Deutschlands
  (Christian Trade Union Federation of Germany)
  Konstantinstrasse 13, 53179 Bonn
  Internet: http.://www.dhv-cgb.de/cgb
  E-mail: CGBBonn@t-online.de
– Bundesvereinigung der Deutschen Arbeitgeberverbände
  (Confederation of German Employers' Associations)
  Gustav-Heinemann-Ufer 72, 50968 Cologne
  Internet: http://www.bda-online.de
  E-mail: info@bda-online.de

Social security

Germany's social security system has a long history and its efficiency is legend. Social benefits and services accounted for
33.5 percent of the 1998 gross domestic product. In 1998, total expenditure for social security was about DM 1,272 billion. Just under one third of this was accounted for by pension insurance and one fifth by statutory health insurance.
The state thus meets the requirements of Article 20, para-
graph 1 of the constitution which says that the Federal Republic is a democratic and social federal state. The underlying principles of the social state are solidarity on the one
hand and personal responsibility on the other. To uphold these
principles, the state has enacted extensive social legislation
ranging from sickness, long-term care, accident and old-age
insurance to child benefits, housing supplements and unemployment benefits. It also makes provision for social assistance
to ensure a minimum standard of living (see chart, p. 511).

The history of social insurance. Social insurance in Germany dates from the Middle Ages, when miners first set up
joint funds to support needy colleagues after accidents at
work. But it was not until the late 19th century that the foundations were laid for a comprehensive social insurance
scheme. Impetus for its development was provided by Germany's industrial revolution, which had greatly increased the
number of industrial workers. These workers were virtually
without protection, as their low wages made it impossible for
them to amass any savings to fall back on in the event of illness or accident. Their precarious position became a domestic issue, prompting the Reich Chancellor at the time, Otto
von Bismarck, to introduce progressive social welfare legislation.

Laws enacted in 1883, 1884 and 1889 established three kinds of
compulsory insurance for workers and some groups of
salaried employees which have remained the nucleus of the

German social security system to this very day: health, accident, and pension insurance (which at that time was termed "invalids' insurance"). In 1911, these schemes were merged in the Reich Insurance System, which added pensions for widows and orphans. Also established in 1911, was an independent scheme providing invalidity and old-age insurance for salaried employees. A separate insurance system was introduced for miners in 1923-4. Unemployment insurance was established in 1927, and as from 1939, craftsmen, to the extent that they were not privately insured, were covered by the statutory social insurance scheme as well.

After World War II, the system was greatly extended and improved. In 1957, for instance, a statutory old-age insurance scheme for farmers was introduced, and in that same year pensions in general were indexed, i.e. adjusted in line with the average increase in incomes. As an exception, for the years 2000 and 2001, pensions will be inflation-linked. Further reforms were introduced in 1972 and 1992.

Since 1990, this comprehensive social security system has also benefited pensioners, war victims and disabled persons in the former GDR. The Treaty Establishing a Monetary, Economic and Social Union and the Unification Treaty signed in that year, provided that all citizens in united Germany should have the same benefits after a transitional period.

In 1995, the scope of the social security system was increased to include long-term care insurance, which helps cover the cost of long-term care provided either at home or in institutions.

Health insurance. Nearly everyone in the Federal Republic of Germany has health insurance, whether as compulsory or voluntary members of the statutory health insurance scheme (90 percent of the population) or through private insurance. Under the statutory scheme, insurance is compulsory for all employees up to a certain income level. Voluntary insurance is possible under certain circumstances. The statutory system also covers pensioners, the unemployed, trainees and students, subject to certain conditions. Employees are insured through their respective local, company or guild health insurance fund or through one of the substitute health insurance funds. They are free to choose their health insurance fund regardless of their occupation. In the case of company and guild funds, however, outsiders may only be insured if the respective fund's by-laws provide for this. There are also special health insurance funds for certain occupational groups, such as the seamen's, miners' or farmers' funds. All insured persons have a free choice of panel doctors and dentists. They pay half of the health insurance contributions, and their employers pay the other half. In 1999, the average contribution rate was 13.6 percent for Germany as a whole.

The health insurance fund pays the cost of medical and dental treatment, drugs and medicines, etc. as well as hospitalization and preventive health care. It pays all or part of the cost of necessary curative treatment at a spa. In the event of sickness, employees receive their full wages from their employer for up to six weeks. Some collective agreements provide for a longer period. After that, the statutory health insurance fund provides sickness benefits for up to 78 weeks.

Accident insurance. Protection and assistance after accidents at work and in the case of occupational diseases is provided by the statutory accident insurance scheme. In Germany, all employees and farmers are insured by law against accidents. Other self-employed people can join the insurance scheme voluntarily. Students, schoolchildren and children in day-care establishments are also covered.

The main providers of accident insurance are the employers' liability insurance funds, each of which comprises all the firms in a given trade or industry. Their funds come from contributions paid only by employers. Benefits can be claimed if the occurrence of an event insured against (accident at work, occupational disease) leads to injury, illness or death. Events insured against, also include accidents which occur on the way to and from the place of work. If an insured person sustains accidental injury, the accident insurance fund bears the cost of treatment and pays injury benefits if the person is at the same time unable to work. If the person's working capacity is reduced by at least one fifth or if the insured person dies as a result of the occurrence of an event insured against, the insurance fund pays a pension or a death grant and a pension for surviving dependents, as the case may be. The pensions are adjusted annually. Vocational rehabilitation benefits, under the accident insurance scheme, above all cover retraining measures designed to facilitate the person's reintegration into the work force. The employers' liability insurance funds are furthermore required to issue regulations on prevention of accidents and control of occupational diseases and to monitor their observance.

Pension insurance. The statutory pension insurance scheme is one of the pillars of the Federal Republic of Germany's social security system. It ensures that workers will be able to maintain an adequate standard of living once they have retired.

All wage and salary earners are required by law to be in the scheme. Self-employed persons who are not compulsorily insured by virtue of their membership of certain occupational groups can join voluntarily. Contributions (2000: 19.3 percent of gross earnings) are levied up to a certain income level (DM 8,600 monthly – DM 7,100 in the eastern German states and DM 7,100 in the new states). Employee and employer contributee half each.

The scheme pays old-age pensions and pensions for loss of working capacity as well. After the death of an insured person, the surviving dependents receive a proportion of the pension. There is a "waiting period" governing eligibility for pensions; in other words, the individual must have participated in the insurance scheme for a minimum period of time. As a rule, the old-age pension is payable at the age of 65, but under certain conditions it can be drawn at 63 or 60 (whereby, in the future, the amount of the pension will be reduced as a matter of principle to offset the retiree's earlier – and hence longer – receipt of benefits).

The size of the pension depends primarily on the amount of insured income from employment. The 1992 pension reform gave elderly employees greater flexibility in the transition from working life to retirement. They can now opt for a pen-

Preventative health care – an advantage at any age

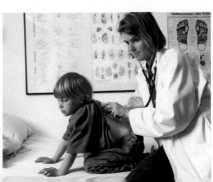

sion, an old-age pension as a part-pension and continue to work part-time. The Act to Promote a Gradual Transition of Elderly Workers into Retirement further broadened the range of options.

Since the 1957 pension reform, the average disposable pension after 45 insured years (basic pension) has risen to about 70 percent of the average worker's net income. Such a pension has, since 1 July 2000, amounted to DM 2,020 in western Germany and DM 1,754 in eastern Germany. The average pension in 1999, owing to interruptions or discontinued payments during professional life, came to DM 1,228 in western Germany and DM 1,342 in eastern Germany. The pensions rise each year in line with wages and salaries; in 2000 and 2001, the pensions will be increased in line with inflation.

Owing to demographic trends, structural adjustments for pensions are necessary in order to secure a stable and social pension system. The German Federal Government's goal with its pension policy is to ensure a balanced spread of the burden for pensions across the generations. The plan is to replace statutory pensions by capital-based old-age provisions.

Paying pensions is not the only purpose of the pension insurance scheme. It also helps to maintain a person's working capacity or to improve or restore that capacity (rehabilitation). Thus it covers the costs and provides support for people who must undergo vocational retraining for health reasons.

Company pensions are a valuable supplement to the statutory scheme. Many companies provide them on a voluntary basis.

Unemployment insurance. As a matter of principle, all employed persons (wage earners, salaried employees, homeworkers and trainees) are insured under the unemployment insurance scheme. Employees and employers each pay half of

Demographic trends mean demand for old-age care will rise sharply

the unemployment insurance contributions. As a rule, persons who become unemployed receive an unemployment benefit in the amount of 60 percent (67 percent if they have at least one child) of their standardized net wages if they were in insurable employment for at least twelve months during the three years prior to the origination of their claim. The length of time that unemployed persons may draw unemployment benefits varies according to age.

Long-term care insurance. Long-term care insurance, which was introduced on 1 January 1995, supplements the existing social safety net in the event that a person requires long-term care. This insurance is compulsory: As a matter of principle, every person insured through a statutory health insurance fund also has long-term care insurance; persons insured through private health insurance funds must take out a private long-term care insurance policy. Long-term care insurance contributions are paid half by employees and half by employers; to offset the burden borne by business and industry, one paid legal holiday (Repentance Day) was eliminated in most of the states. Children who are still entitled to maintenance and spouses with very low incomes or no income at all are insured through the statutory insurance funds at no charge within the framework of the family insurance plan. At present, some 1.86 million people requiring care receive monetary support and other forms of assistance from the care insurance.

Family benefits. In 2000, the monthly child benefit for the first and second child was DM 270 each; the monthly benefit for the third child was DM 300 and DM 350 for each additional child. The tax-free child allowance was DM 3,024 for children up to the end of their 16th year. The tax-exempt allowance is DM 2,400 for children who are of age and are still undergoing education. Since 1986, mothers and fathers have also been entitled to a child-raising benefit for each child of DM 600 per month for a period of 24 months, provided their income does not exceed a certain amount. In addition, mothers or fathers wishing to look after their child themselves can claim up to three years child-raising leave from work during which they cannot be dismissed.

Integration of handicapped. Together with numerous private and public organizations, associations, Church social services, and a large number of voluntary helpers, the Federal Republic of Germany endeavors to enable handicapped persons to lead more-or-less normal lives in the community. The handicapped have a right to assistance as regards

— medical assistance
— vocational-promotion services
— support for school and general social integration
— financial support.

Especially in the case of vocational-promotion measures, a large number of public agencies are at hand: vocational education institutions, vocational assistance agencies, professional training centers, institutions for medical/vocational rehab and workshops for the handicapped. If the degree of handicap (usually ascertained by the official support agencies) is more than 50 percent, the handicapped person receives an ID card for the severely handicapped, which, among other things, guarantees protection at the place of work. All public- and

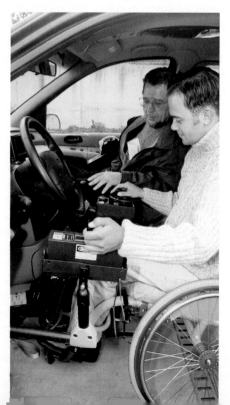

Special equipment enables the severely handicapped to drive

private-sector employers with more than 16 employees are obliged by law to employ a severely handicapped person. If this does not happen, then under the terms of the "Act to Combat Unemployment among the Handicapped" the employers have to pay a levy of a certain ratio.

War victims' benefits and social indemnification for damage to health. Benefits under the social indemnification scheme for damage to health are paid to war victims, members of the armed forces, persons in alternative civilian service, victims of violence, victims of SED injustice, persons suffering from damage caused by vaccines, and other persons for whom the community as a whole has a responsibility to provide. They include a legal entitlement to a pension, which varies in amount according to the severity of the damage to health and is indexed to the general development of wages and salaries, as well as other benefits such as medical and vocational rehabilitation measures. As an exception, for the years 2000 and 2001, pension provisions under the social indemnification law, like pensions under the statutory pension schemes, will be inflation-linked. In the event that a person dies as a result of damage to health, his or her surviving dependents are entitled to survivors' benefits.

Social assistance. Social assistance is provided in the Federal Republic of Germany for people who cannot help themselves and receive no help from others. Under the Social Assistance Act, everybody living in Germany is entitled to social assistance in times of hardship in the form of maintenance grants covering disability, illness or care. This assistance is partly provided by the municipalities and partly by the states. In 1998, social assistance expenditure totaled DM 45 billion.

The health care system

The Federal Republic of Germany has a ramified system of health care backed up by appropriate social services. Although health care is basically the individual's own responsibility, it is also the concern of society as a whole. All people, regardless of their financial or social situation, should have the same chance to maintain or restore their health. Health care in Germany is a decentralized, pluralist and selfgoverning system.

Doctors and hospitals. In 1998, there were about 287,000 doctors in Germany. Medically, therefore, the Germans are among the best cared-for nations in the world. Fewer than half of the nation's doctors are in private practice. The others work in hospitals or administration or are engaged in research. In addition to the 2,030 general hospitals (788 public hospitals, 823 hospitals maintained by independent non-profit organizations and 419 private hospitals) with a total of approximately 534,000 beds, there are 233 other hospital facilities (such as purely day or night clinics). In 1998, about 191,000 beds were also available in 1,395 preventive care or rehabilitation centers.

Safety of pharmaceuticals. The quality, effectiveness and harmlessness of drugs and medicines are tested in accordance with the state marketing authorization procedure spelled out in the Pharmaceuticals Act. This Act also regulates the manufacture of pharmaceuticals, and the prescription requirement as well as the reporting and evaluation of health risks that are observed after authorization. About 90 percent of Germany's more than 82.1 million inhabitants are insured through the statutory health insurance scheme. For persons insured under the statutory health insurance scheme, the costs of the provision of medicines are mainly borne by the health insurance companies; insured persons are charged a co-payment which varies according to the size of the package. Due account is taken of the person's ability to pay: Social clauses ensure that co-payments cause no one financial hardship, and children, adolescents and persons with marginal incomes are exempted from the co-payment requirement altogether as a matter of principle.

Approximately 45,000 marketable drugs are presently available in Germany, more than in any other European country. A dense distribution network consisting of pharmaceutical manufacturers, pharmaceutical wholesalers and pharmacies ensures that people throughout the nation have access to the medicines they need. Thanks to a system of uniform pharmacy retail prices and the provisions of the Drug Price Ordinance, a given medicine may be obtained at any public pharmacy for the same price.

Safety of medical products. Since 1 January 1995, the Medical Devices Act has been in force in the Federal Republic. The European (and thus also German) law concerning medical products serves not only to promote the free movement of goods within the European Economic Area but also (and most importantly) to protect patients, users and third parties. Among the some 400,000 different items classified as medical devices are bandages, condoms, medical instruments, artificial joints, wheelchairs, operating equipment, respirators, radiation equipment, laboratory diagnostic equipment and sterilization equipment for doctors' offices and hospitals. The output value of these medical products totals roughly DM 35 billion. Germany's medical devices industry is the largest in the EU and ranks at the top world-wide, along with those of the United States and Japan.

All medical devices – regardless of their potential risk (classification) – must, by law, meet certain essential requirements. In

Health check-up at a general practitioner's surgery

addition to fulfilling technical, medical and information requirements, manufacturers must supply proof that the devices are suitable for their declared purpose. A risk analysis and a clinical evaluation (and, in some cases, a clinical test as well) must be conducted for each medical device. The benefits must outweigh the risks. Thus all medical devices – regardless of their classification – must meet the same high standard of safety.

Preventive health care. Numerous federal and state institutions as well as private non-profit organizations provide a wide variety of information, courses and advice on health matters. Preventive health care is an important element of the public health care system. The statutory health insurers focus their efforts in this area on:

— Preventive check-ups during pregnancy. Insured women are entitled to medical examinations every four weeks during pregnancy to monitor the health of mother and child.

— Early detection examinations for children and young people. The program for early detection of illness during childhood provides for ten examinations at various ages.

— Health check-ups. Starting at the age of 35, all insured persons can undergo an examination every two years during which their doctor checks especially for signs of the major illnesses characteristic of civilized society such as heart and circulatory disorders, kidney disease and diabetes.

— Preventive cancer check-ups. Insured persons are entitled to an annual examination for early detection of cancer. For women, these examinations begin at the age of 20, for men at the age of 45.

— Preventive dental care for children and young people. Together with kindergartens and schools, the health insurers

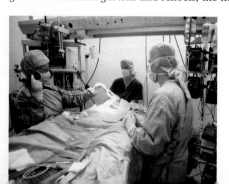

Endoscopic and video-based operations leave few scars

conduct action programs for the prevention of dental problems which target children up to the age of 12. In addition, children and young people between the ages of six and 18 can have a personal dental check-up every six months and, if necessary, receive prophylactic treatment.

The goal of the BZgA Federal Center for Health Education is to ensure more health for citizens. As the specialist agency for promoting health, it devises strategies for health education and prevention and brings these to bear in campaigns and projects. One focus of its work is the health of children and young people. A key item in its information, consultancy and support work is to combat AIDS (acquired immune deficiency syndrome). Since 1987, the Federal Center for Health Education has run an AIDS prevention campaign on behalf of the Federal Government, and this drive has played a key role in minimizing the incidence of new cases of infection with HIV. To date, the Federal Government has made available more than DM 738 million for AIDS prevention measures.

Sick people and their families often need help over and above the medical care provided by the medical profession and hospitals. Of particular importance are comprehensive counseling and the opportunity to discuss their problems with people suffering from the same disease. Opportunities of this kind are afforded by numerous self-help groups, which today have an established place in the nation's health system.

International activities. Germany is a member of all the key international organizations. The World Health Organization (WHO) is the largest international specialist body focusing on health, and is allied with the UN. It has 192 member states. The main goal of the WHO is to contribute to ensuring that all people enjoy the greatest possible state of health. The goal of the Council of Europe is to develop a truly European health policy by making certain all its member states have similar policies on health, a high degree of health prevention, better health education, and promote equal opportunities as regards access to healthcare. The IARC International Cancer Research Center conducts central programs in particular in order to coordinate research work. The OECD is also increasingly concerning itself with health as an issue. Alongside health statistics, which have for years been one of its most important activities, it also presents the economic side to health policy in its investigations and comparative country studies.

The Federal Republic of Germany participates in conventions of the steering committees of the above-mentioned bodies as well as taking part in their main assemblies – through the international sub-section of the Federal Ministry of Health.

Bilateral cooperation with other countries covers the entire spectrum of healthcare, from human medicine to veterinary medicine. Bilateral agreements are reached, cooperation in certain specialist areas devised, and corresponding projects initiated – all with the assistance of other specialist sections of the ministry, other ministries, scientific institutions at the state level, as well as NGOs. Corresponding agreements have been signed with a series of states which are not EU members but with whom Germany cooperates intensively in the field of healthcare: with Poland (1990); Hungary (1990); the USSR (1987), whereby the treaty applies to the successor states to the former USSR; Romania (1987); and China (1980). These agreements lay down the framework for promoting scientific and practical exchanges of information (guest attendance) between German and foreign healthcare institutions; they are, moreover, supplemented by implementation and working programs that define specific cooperation measures.

Further information:
- Bundesministerium für Gesundheit
  (German Federal Ministry of Health)
  Am Propsthof 78a, 53121 Bonn
  Internet: http://www.bmgesundheit.de
  E-mail: poststelle@bmg.bund.de

Consumer protection

The range of goods and services is growing. Every year more than 1,000 new products come onto the market in Germany alone. Since the launching of the European single market on 1 January 1993, the range has become even greater and even more confusing. Products made in Germany compete with goods imported from all over the world. Innovative technologies such as electronic transactions and IT offer opportunities here, but also entail risks for consumers. The latter have a greater choice than ever before. But such a wide variety is a problem for them, too, since they find it increasingly difficult to judge product quality and value for money – or perhaps even safety and potential hazards to health. All too often, buyers are also exposed to dishonest sales methods. Consumer policy consequently plays an important role in the Federal Republic's economic and social order.

The purpose of consumer information is to make the market more transparent and help people make rational decisions on the basis of objective evaluations of quality and price comparisons. Consumers also increasingly need information on claims to compensation for damage or revocation of rights for insurance or loan contracts, money deposits, package travel deals, or when purchasing consumer goods. The consumer organizations also provide information on nutrition and issues pertaining to environmental pollution, and in the areas of building and home living, hobbies, recreational activities, and energy conservation.

Thus, in 1964, the Federal Government, together with the Association of Consumers' Unions (AgV), set up a foundation in Berlin known as "Stiftung Warentest", which tests goods of all kinds from the ballpoint pen to the personal computer as to quality, value for money and compatibility with the environment. Services, too, are tested. This organization meanwhile screens about 1,700 articles in roughly 100 comparative testings each year. Stiftung Warentest only calls upon independent experts and institutes and has earned a good reputation from consumers and manufacturers alike. The latter are glad to advertize the fact that their products have been deemed "good" or "very good" by Stiftung Warentest. The foundation's main publications are the magazine "test", which appears monthly and has a circulation of about 700,000, and the magazine "FINANZtest". Test results are also regularly publicized in some 160 newspapers and periodicals as well as on radio and television.

The public can also seek advice from roughly 350 consumer advice bureaus run by the 16 regional consumer centers, which provide information on the quality and prices of goods and services, and receive financial support from the government. Before parliament introduces new consumer protection legislation, it consults the consumers' unions.

The Association of Consumers' Unions is the national organization of consumer organizations and social policy-oriented member associations. These above all include the consumer centers in the states. The function of the Association of Consumers' Unions is to promote consumer interests and support the consumer information activities of its member organizations. The Association of Consumers' Unions represents the rights and interests of consumers in many political and economic-sector bodies at the national and international level. It cultivates close relations with parliaments and drafts proposals and position papers for legislative initiatives.

Consumer protection has been considerably improved by legislation. The Act on General Terms and Conditions of Contract protects customers from the pitfalls contained in small print; the Consumer Credit Act enables the borrower to cancel a

Comparing ansaphones

loan and requires information to be provided by the lender. The Door-to-Door Sales Contract Cancellation Act governs cancellation of contracts in other specific cases. The Foodstuffs Act protects customers from damaging substances in food, the Travel Contract Act forces operators to fulfill their promises, and the Product Liability Act makes manufacturers liable for flawed products. The Product Safety Act, which entered into force on 1 August 1997, obligates manufacturers and retailers to put safe products into circulation and empowers the competent authorities to take measures to avert dangers posed by defective products. There are also many other laws to protect consumers. They concern such matters as the labeling of foodstuffs, strict criteria for pharmaceutical products, the tolerability of detergents, and price tags on goods in shop windows. The Association of Consumers' Unions and the consumer centers jointly publish brochures, leaflets and other advisory material on all subjects of relevance to consumers.

As the countries of the European Union grow closer together, legislative initiative in the area of consumer protection is also increasingly shifting to the European Union. The Union issues directives which must be converted into national law in the Member States. The European Commission has a Consumers' Consultative Council composed of 20 members. The most important consumer organization at the European level is the European Bureau of Consumers' Unions (BEUC), which represents 30 national consumer organizations.

Protection of consumers from health risks. An important aspect of health policy is the protection of consumers from health risks posed by foodstuffs, articles of daily use, cosmetics and tobacco products. The pertinent statutory regulations are contained in the body of food and veterinary law, which today is largely determined by European Community law.

Harmonization of the national legal provisions of the Member States through European Community law, a process which has meanwhile largely been completed, was the prerequisite for the functioning of a single European internal market. In the internal market, consumer protection and the safeguarding of food quality no longer stop at national borders. Of primary concern to the consumer is the certainty that the food he eats – regardless of where it comes from – is safe and does not pose any hazards to his health.

Like the other Member States of the European Union, Germany has incorporated the European regulations into its national law relating to food production and distribution. The Law on Foods and Commodities provides the main legislative framework; together with the Meat Hygiene Act, the Poultry Hygiene Act and other acts and regulations, it forms a firm foundation for the protection of consumers from health risks posed by foodstuffs, tobacco products, cosmetics and articles of daily use. Implementation of the law is the responsibility of the authorities of the states for the monitoring of the food manufacturing process. The provisions governing the monitoring of the food manufacturing process have likewise been harmonized within the Community to ensure that foodstuffs are inspected similarly in all Member States and that compliance with the standards mandated by law is guaranteed by an official monitoring network which watches over foods from the time they are produced on the farm until they are ready to eat.

Further information:
- Arbeitsgemeinschaft der Verbraucherverbände (AgV)
  (Association of Consumers' Unions)
  Heilsbachstrasse 20, 53123 Bonn
  Internet: http://www.agv.de
  E-mail: mail@agv.de
- Stiftung Warentest
  Lützowplatz 11-13, 10785 Berlin
  Internet: http://www.stiftung-warentest.de
  E-mail: pressestelle@stiftung-warentest.de

Life in society

Women and society

According to the Basic Law, men and women have equal rights. This constitutional rule is absolutely clear, but in practice it has been more a wish than a reality. For this reason, the constitutional and statutory foundations for equality of rights were broadened in 1994. Section 3, subsection 2 now states: "The state fosters equal rights between men and women and works towards eliminating existing disadvantages." Women still do not enjoy the same opportunities as men in society, in politics and at work, however. And this, despite the fact that they are in the majority: In Germany, there are about two million more women than men.

Equality before the law. The principle of equality has only gradually been applied. In 1958, the Act on Equal Rights for Men and Women introduced equal rights for women within the institution of marriage based on a division of roles ("housewife marriage"), as well as equal rights in regard to matrimonial property. This was followed in 1977 by the First Act to Reform the Marriage and Family Law, the aim of which was to introduce the partnership principle in marriage (eliminating the standard "housewife marriage" model) and ensure equal rights for women in regard to marriage and divorce. In divorce cases, the principle of guilt was replaced by the principle of irretrievable breakdown of the marriage; a

The five female ministers in the Federal Cabinet

pension rights adjustment ensured equal division of the pension rights accrued by the spouses during the period of marriage. The Act to Amend the Law Relating to Family Names, which entered into force in April 1994, ensured equality of men and women in respect of the right to the use of a name as well: Preference is no longer unilaterally given to the man's family name. Since July 1997, rape within the institution of marriage has been a punishable offense.

Women in employment. Women represent 42 percent of the workforce in Germany. They generate a large proportion of the tax yield and pay social security contributions totaling billions. Women have become indispensable in business and industry, the health care system, administration and education. Moreover, a high investment is made in their education and training, by women themselves but also by the Federal Government: In 1997, 54.9 percent of pupils obtaining university entrance qualifications were women. Further, in the same year, 46.6 percent of all students in higher education were women. It should also be mentioned that on average, female students get better marks than men. Unfortunately, these figures are still not mirrored in the professional world, especially at middle and top management levels. Women continue to be discriminated against in the world of employment. Specifically, they often experience greater difficulties in finding an apprenticeship and workplace. Above all, in the eastern states, greater numbers of women are affected by unemployment than men. Moreover, women are often employed in jobs which do not match the level of their qualifications and they still do not have adequate access to new technologies and promising new professional fields. And though the principle of "equal pay for equal work" is anchored in the law, on average, women nevertheless earn less than men. It is with a view to countering such unequal opportunities that the Federal Government presented a comprehensive program called "Women and Work". Designed to vigorously pursue equal opportunities for men and women in work and home life, the program focuses on the following goals:

— improving the educational opportunities of young women, above all in the promising professions spawned by the information society;

— increasing women's employment and promotion prospects;

— reducing the disadvantages facing women starting up new firms;

— making it easier to combine family and professional work;

— reducing discrimination in the area of income and wages; and

— raising the proportion of women engaged in research and teaching

Women and family. In 1996, the greater proportion of Germany's population – just under 80 percent – consisted of families with unmarried children (57 percent) or of married couples who were childless or no longer had children in the household (23 percent). No trend towards one-child families is discernible yet. On the contrary: Today, couples starting a family are more likely to have two or more children than in years past. On the other hand, however, more and more couples are choosing not to have any children at all. The Federal Government is aware of the importance of family promotion, as manifest in its legislation providing for the child-raising benefit and child-raising leave. The child-raising benefit of DM 600 per month is paid for the first two years after the birth of each child to those mothers or fathers who care for and raise their newborn child themselves, who do not return to work or do not work full time during that period, and whose annual income does not exceed the stipulated income limits. On 1 January 2001 new legislation governing child-raising benefit comes into force, entitling both parents to apply for child-raising leave simultaneously and spend up to 30 hours a week in part-time work. The aims: to redress the traditional role division between the sexes whereby mothers typically stay at home to look after their children, and address the adverse effects this has on their professional lives. Another advantage is that child-raising periods (three years for each child born in 1992 or later) count towards the parent's pension entitlement. Since 1992, the same applies to time spent taking care of sick family members. This is an important step towards a fair assessment of work in the family compared with gainful activity.

Women in politics. Women have enjoyed the right to vote and the right to stand for election in Germany since 1919. Although the number of politically active women is increasing, it is still much smaller than that of men. Most of the political parties have introduced quotas to increase the number of female representatives on executive committees.

The percentage of women Members of the German Bundestag has risen from 8.4 percent in 1980 to 30.9 percent today. Each Federal Government since 1961 has included at least one woman; in the present Government, five of the 14 federal ministers are women. All state governments have ministers or commissioners for women's affairs. About 1,700 municipalities have created "equality posts" or offices especially for women.

Parallel to the statutory measures to establish equality of the sexes, a strong women's movement has developed in Germany. It vehemently opposes discrimination against women. This movement has emerged outside the existing women's organizations and has been the driving force in setting up more than around 440 centers for battered wives and their children. In 1999, the Federal Government passed an "Action Plan to Fight Violence Against Women", a comprehensive concept designed to overcome all types of violence.

The "women's lobby" is the German Women's Council, the central organization of women's associations. It represents 52 associations with some eleven million members.

Further information:
  — Bundesministerium für Familie, Senioren, Frauen und Jugend
    (German Federal Ministry for Family Affairs, Senior Citizens, Women and
    Young People)
    Glinkastrasse 18-24, 10117 Berlin
    Internet: http://www.bmfsfj.de
    E-mail: poststelle@bmfsfj.bund.de
  — Deutscher Frauenrat
    (German Women's Council)
    Simrockstrasse 5, 53113 Bonn
    Internet: http://www.deutscher-frauenrat.de

Youth

Nearly one in five inhabitants of the Federal Republic (well over 15.9 million) is under 18 years of age. About 10 percent of them are of foreign nationality. Just under one third of the total population (over 25 million) are under 27. For the great majority of them, opportunities in life and future prospects have improved considerably over the past ten years. Especially in the west, most young people are comfortably off in material terms. Their financial prospects have never been better, and they are well supplied with consumer goods. Never before have so many young people traveled as much as they do at present, both at home and abroad. The greatest concern of young people in Germany today is the problem of unemployment.

Topping the list of the ten most popular leisure activities amongst young people – aged between 14 and 29 – is watching TV (89 percent), followed by making phone calls (69 percent). Listening to music scored 67 percent and joint activities with friends 64 percent. Some 38 percent prefer reading books, while for 31 percent the computer provides entertainment; indeed, a computer is the most popular item on young people's shopping lists.

The problem of orientation. As the influence of family, church and neighborhood has declined, the freedom of young people to take matters into their own hands has increased accordingly. This is indicated by longer periods of study, the widening generation gap due to the fact that young people increasingly take their bearings from standards set by their peers, the growing significance of leisure and consumption, and the effects of the mass media. But although this increases the pressure to be more independent, 83 percent of the young people interviewed in western Germany and 89 percent of those interviewed in the east said that when they had personal problems, it was to their parents they first turned for help, viewing the latter as partners rather than figures of authority.

Not all young people meet with understanding for their problems at home or in school, of course. In many cases their links with other persons of responsibility or social groups have been weakened, and very often these groups are rejected by isolated young people. In this situation, they may easily succumb to modes of behavior which pose a danger to them and to the community. These are some of the reasons for the emergence of social and political radicalism. Attacks by young people on foreigners, especially in the east, are evidently not triggered by personal experiences with foreigners, but by fears concerning diminished opportunities as regards life in general and securing job training in particular. These concerns are compounded by an unconsidered mixture of vague, extreme right ideology, a desire for hooligan-like violence and a strong need for recognition at any price coupled with a narrow outlook on life.

The federal and state governments have demonstrated their resolve to pursue suspects with all democratic means and bring them to account. Education and information, however, can play an at least equally important role in the suppression of politically motivated acts of violence, especially given the age of the culprits.

Addressing the problem of right-wing extremism is one of the most urgent tasks the Federal Government has set itself in this legislative period. To this end, it calls for an "Alliance for Democracy and Tolerance" which vigorously upholds, and whose conduct is guided by, the values and guarantees of a social democratic state bound by laws. The Alliance's most important goal is the wholehearted support for the protec-

Fans at a
"Puhdys" con-
cert at Berlin's
Waldbühne

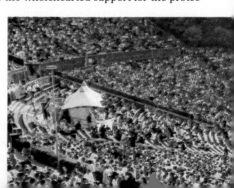

tion and compliance with democratic rules, for respect to be accorded to the dignity of man, for tolerance and solidarity. However, the overwhelming majority of young people no longer have any sympathy whatsoever for xenophobic excesses.

Youth associations and youth organizations. In Germany there are about 90 supraregional youth organizations and associations to which about a quarter of all young people belong. Many of the national associations are affiliated with the German Federal Youth Council, including the Young Protestants Association, the Federation of German Catholic Youth Associations, the trade union youth associations, the state youth associations and the German Boy Scouts Association. The one with the largest membership is the Federation of German Youth Sports Associations.

There are also political youth organizations. Most of the parties in the German Bundestag have youth organizations under their wings which belong to the Council of Political Youth Associations. Youth associations sponsored by the churches, unions, adult education centers, foundations and other educational establishments likewise play an important role in the political education of young people outside of school. They impart knowledge of state and society, European and international political affairs, and socially and politically significant developments in the areas of cultural affairs, economics, science and technology. The aim of political education is to enable young people to make their own judgments concerning social and political events and conflicts, to exercise their own rights and defend their own interests, but also to fulfill their obligations towards, and assume responsibility for, their fellow man, society and the environment. Finally, political edu-

cation is intended to encourage them to play an active role in shaping a free and democratic social and political order.

Cultural youth work. Cultural education is a key element of the education of young people outside of school and thus plays a crucial role in the development of the individual's personality. The Federal Government therefore strives to ensure that children and young people are exposed to and actively involved in the arts and cultural activities at the earliest possible age.

The programs offered in music schools, youth film clubs, theaters, dance groups, libraries, art schools for young people, museums and many other institutions show what a positive impact exposure to the arts and cultural activities can have on the development of young people. In numerous cultural projects, important topics such as ecology, violence and hostility to foreigners are addressed: In the context of these projects, young people are able, independently, to arrive at new insights into existing social conditions and come to realize the importance of peaceful, democratic and cooperative conduct in everyday life.

The Federation of Youth Cultural Associations is an umbrella organization of 48 specialized associations which are active nation-wide. In over 100,000 projects, competitions, workshops, encounters, seminars and meetings, these specialized associations organize and promote cultural youth work at the regional, national and international level. More than 12 million young people participate in these activities each year.

That said, a diminishing interest in politics is evident amongst young people. The reason: many of them feel that the political "circus" portrayed by the mass media bears little relevance to their personal lives. Their attitude towards German politics could best be described as one of "critical awareness". On the whole, young people are not very knowledgeable on the European Union.

Government youth policy. The upbringing of children is primarily the responsibility of parents or guardians. However, the state also assists in their personal and social development so that they can be responsible for themselves and find their proper place at work and in society. The ostracism of violence by caretakers is an important aim of the Federal Government since violence against children is not without consequences for their later development. Victims of violence frequently have low self-esteem, appear indifferent and indulge in aggressive acts, crime and drug abuse. Moreover, children who have suffered violence at home are more likely to be perpetrators of violence themselves. Such considerations prompted the Federal Government to anchor the right to a violence-free upbringing in the German Civil Code in July 2000. Moreover, the Government cares for young people by legislating for their protection and providing them with social assistance and opportunities for voluntary activities. In July 1997, the Federal Government – following up the 1996 Stockholm World Congress against Commercial Sexual Exploitation of Children – published a working program against child abuse, child pornography and sex tourism. This program encompasses a wide range of measures pertaining to information and prevention, the legal sphere, international criminal prosecution and protection of victims. By co-

Youth research programs: school pupils with a solar-cell panel they made

operating with "terre de hommes" and the European Commission, the Federal Government also works to make people sensitive to the rights and protection of children.

As a rule, however, the state allows societies, associations, churches, foundations and other independent institutions to take the lead in providing services for children and young people. There thus emerges a wide range of services which reflect the currents of society and provide a genuine choice for young people and their parents. Germany's federal system, under which responsibilities are delegated as largely as possible to local institutions close to the people, is also manifest in the area of child and youth services. The greater proportion of the funds required is provided by the state and local authorities.

The Federal Government's main channel for implementing its youth policy and promoting youth work is the Federal Child and Youth Plan. Under this plan, DM 192 million is currently being spent to finance the activities of federal youth and child assistance organizations as well as out-of-school projects for young people in areas such as political, social and cultural youth work and international youth exchanges. Support is also given to young people's social education, including the voluntary social year and the voluntary ecological year.

International youth contacts are a bridge of understanding and cooperation across frontiers. International encounters offer young people opportunities for personal enrichment and enable them to grasp complex correlations and understand other cultures. In the context of the Federal Child and Youth Plan, the Federal Government supports more than 3,000 measures in the area of international youth cooperation. In addition, more than 140,000 German and French young

Playing music together at the German-Polish Youth Program's festival

people take part in the roughly 7,000 events sponsored every year by the Franco-German Youth Office, which was founded over 35 years ago. At the beginning of 1993 the German-Polish Youth Office took up its work, which centers on the promotion of bilateral youth movements. In 1999, more than 124,000 young people from Poland and Germany participated in programs sponsored by the German-Polish Youth Office. TANDEM, a coordination office in Regensburg, furnishes information on exchanges between German and Czech young people.

The European Union, too, promotes youth exchanges through the program "Youth for Europe" and enables young people to become intimately acquainted with other countries and cultures through the "European Voluntary Service". Information can be obtained from the International Youth Exchange and Visitors Service of the Federal Republic of Germany.

Further information:
- Deutsch-Französisches Jugendwerk
  (Franco-German Youth Office)
  Rhöndorfer Strasse 23, 53604 Bad Honnef
  Internet: http://www.dfjw.org
  E-mail: info@dfjw.org
- Deutsch-Polnisches Jugendwerk
  (German-Polish Youth Office)
  Friedhofsgasse 2, 14473 Potsdam
  Internet: http://www.dpjw.de
  E-mail: buero@dpjw.org
- TANDEM
  Gutenbergplatz 1a, 93047 Regensburg
- Deutscher Bundesjugendring
  (German Federal Youth Council)
  Haager Weg 44, 53127 Bonn
  Internet : http://www.dbjr.de
  E-mail: info@dbjr.de
- Deutsche Sportjugend
  (Federation of German Youth Sports Associations)
  Otto-Fleck-Schneise 12, 60528 Frankfurt/Main
  Internet: http://www.dsj.de
  E-mail: deutsche-sportjugend@t-online.de
- Bundesvereinigung Kulturelle Jugendbildung
  (Federation of Youth Cultural Associations)
  Küppelstein 34, 42857 Remscheid
  Internet: http://www.bkj.de
  E-mail: info-@bkj.de
- Arbeitsgemeinschaft für Jugendhilfe e.V.
  (Child Welfare Alliance)
  Haager Weg 44, 53127 Bonn
- Bundesarbeitsgemeinschaft Jugendsozialarbeit
  (Federal Association for Socio-educational Provision for Young People)
  Kennedyallee 105-107, 53175 Bonn
  E-mail: BAGJAW@t-online.de

— Arbeitsgemeinschaft der Jungsozialistinnen und Jungsozialisten in der SPD
(Young Socialists in the SPD)
Wilhelmstrasse 140, 10963 Berlin
Internet: http://www.spd.de/jusos/
E-mail: jusos@spd.de
— Junge Union Deutschlands
(Young Christian Democrats of Germany)
Inselstrasse 16, 10179 Berlin
Internet: http://www.junge-union.de
E-mail: ju@junge-union.de
— Grüne Jugend
(Green Alternative Youth Alliance)
Hessische Strasse 10, 10115 Berlin
Internet: http: gajb-bgs@t-online
E-mail: gajb-bgs@t-online.de
— Bundesverband der Jungen Liberalen e.V.
(Federal Association of Young Liberals)
Ackerstrasse 3b, 10115 Berlin
— Internationaler Jugendaustausch und Besucherdienst der Bundesrepublik
Deutschland e.V.
(International Youth Exchange and Visitors Service of the Federal Republic of
Germany)
Hochkreuzallee 20, 53175 Bonn
Internet: http://www.ijab.de
E-mail: ijab-info@ijab.de
— Bundeskonferenz für Erziehungsberatung e.V
(Federal Child Guidance Association)
Herrnstrasse 53, 90763 Fürth,
Internet: http://www.bke.de
E-mail: geschaeftsstelle@bke.de
— Arbeitsgemeinschaft für Erziehungshilfe e.V.
(Child Guidance Associations' Working Party)
Bundesvereinigung (federal confederation)
Gandhistrasse 2, 30559 Hannover
Internet: http://home.t-online.de/home/afet-/
E-mail: afet-@t-online.de

Sports

Sports are a favorite leisure-time activity in Germany. This fact is reflected not only in the popularity of television broadcasts but also in the fact that there are more than 87,000 clubs affiliated with the Deutscher Sportbund (DSB; German Sports Federation). Approximately 27 million people – nearly 25 percent of the entire population – are members of a sports club, and another 12 million do sports independently of a club.

The German Sports Federation. The central sports organization in the Federal Republic of Germany is the German Sports Federation, which embraces 16 regional sports federations and many individual sports associations. In all the various branches, there are approximately 2.6 million people working in an honorary capacity as coaches, trainers, physiotherapists or officials. The western part of the country has a large network of facilities for mass sports and competitive sports. There are, for instance, about 55,000 school and club sports grounds, nearly 35,000 gyms, and over 7,000 indoor and outdoor swimming pools. In the new states, however, there is still a great shortage of facilities for mass sports and an urgent need to renovate existing facilities due to the fact that for decades all the effort went into competition at the highest level.

Sydney 2000: the German four-man pursuit team took the gold medal, setting a new world record

With more than 6.3 million members, the Deutscher Fussball-Bund (DFB; German Football Federation) is by far the largest sports organization in Germany. Soccer is played at thousands of amateur clubs. It is also an immensely popular spectator sport, attracting hundreds of thousands of people to professional games every week during the regular season. The German national soccer team has won the World Cup three times. Sports such as tennis, golf, ice hockey and basketball are enjoying increasing popularity as well.

Sports in the service of the people. Most people who actively participate in sports do so not because they want to become top-notch athletes but rather for the exercise and the pleasure of taking part in a group activity. Sport is beneficial to health, compensates for our sedentary lifestyles in a highly technical world. Year by year, more and more people are attracted to sports, and organized sports are providing ever greater opportunities. At the average club these days, people

At the Olympic Games in Sydney, Thomas Schmidt won the gold medal in white-water canooing

can play soccer, handball, volleyball, basketball, tennis and table-tennis or take part in track and field events. Water sports, too, are very popular, and there are various options for the physically disabled, senior citizens and mothers with small children.

Popular and recreational sports are also promoted by the German Sports Federation's programs. These are currently: "Sports Are More Fun in Clubs", "Sports Clubs. Of Benefit to Everyone" and "Really fit". As part of the Federation's new campaign "Thanks to volunteers in sports", a "Really fit for Sports Program" was offered for various sports disciplines. Every year, millions of sports enthusiasts take part in competitions organized by the Sports Federation. And some 750,000 people a year have their performance in various sports tested, hoping to qualify for a coveted gold, silver or bronze "Sports Badge" awarded by the German Sports Federation.

Top-level sports. Success at modern, top-level sports requires a high degree of personal commitment and access to first-class equipment. Top athletes must not only undergo intensive training. Of equal importance to success are full health care, extensive social support and a certain measure of financial security. National sports centers and Olympic training facilities afford top-notch athletes ideal training conditions as well as the necessary comprehensive back-up support uniting physiotherapy, training theory expertise, emotional support and medical care from doctors who specialize in treating athletes.

In this context, one should mention the Stiftung Deutsche Sporthilfe (Sports Aid Foundation). Established in 1967, it views itself as a social welfare organization providing athletes with a considerable degree of financial support.

Government promotion of sports. Owing to the responsibilities of the Federal Government under the German constitution, government promotion of sports concentrates on top-level competitive sports. However, the constitution also makes provision for federal promotion of outstanding mass sports activities, when the latter serve national interests. In promoting competitive sports, the Government's aim is to place leading German athletes in a position to perform well at international competitions. Considerable state assistance is provided for sports at the municipalities level, at state and national level. The state provides funds for training and competitions, for medical care for top athletes, for training and employment of coaches, for construction of sports facilities and for scientific research pertaining to sports. Owing to its high political prestige, the state has, in recent years, continually increased its funding for competitive sports for the disabled within the scope of its authority and means.

As one of the leading nations in the sports arena, Germany also makes an important contribution to the development of sport both within and outside Europe. Through its special "Golden Plan East" promotion program, the Federal Government participates in the construction of sports facilities for mass sports in the east of the country and the part of Berlin formerly part of the GDR.

Naturally, the Government wishes to lend its support to sporting activities which are free of drugs and other forms of manipulation. Accordingly, additional funds have been set aside for anti-doping research and doping analysis techniques.

Further information:
— Deutscher Sportbund
  (German Sports Federation)
  Otto-Fleck-Schneise 12, 60528 Frankfurt/Main
  Internet: http://www.dsb.de/
  E-mail: dsb@dsb.de

Leisure and holidays

Leisure. Leisure time is the result of a lengthy economic, social
and political development in Germany. By contrast, the annual holiday entitlement for the working population is a 20th-
century achievement. The tradition of leisure time is founded
on the prosperity attained through work. It is socially conced-
ed scope for personal fulfillment which encompasses civil lib-
erties (free disposal of time, freedom of association and freedom to travel) and affords people the opportunity to engage
in activities of their choice.

The amount of leisure time depends on the individual's personal
circumstances and the demands on his or her time imposed
by work and everyday obligations. On average, a German has
three to four hours of free time on weekdays, ten hours of
free time on Saturdays, Sundays and the nine holidays, and
an annual holiday of up to six weeks. Differences between
the eastern and western parts of the country are gradually
disappearing. The average adult thus enjoys nearly 2,500
hours of leisure time per year. German households have long
spent between 10 and 15 percent of their disposable income
on leisure pursuits, generating a total annual turnover of
about DM 440 billion.

Recreational opportunities and personal initiative.
Regardless of whether people are interested in travel, excur-
sions, culture, sports or entertainment, they can choose from
a wide variety of high-quality options for structuring their
leisure time: swimming pools and sports facilities of every
kind, theaters, concert halls and cinemas, libraries and museums, restaurants and camping sites. In addition to utilizing
special recreational facilities, people derive great enjoyment
from the countryside and, increasingly, from the transport infrastructure during the time they are "doing nothing". Germany has a well-developed leisure industry which offers a
broad range of goods and services. The country's recreational

Ballooning –
an impressive
summer sport

infrastructure is also maintained by associations, non-profit organizations and the public sector. More than five million people depend – at least partially – on the leisure industry for their livelihood. The wealth of recreational opportunities attracts visitors, users, guests and buyers and is thus both a source of income for numerous providers as well as an indispensable foundation for the tourism industry. A key prerequisite for most recreational activities is a pleasant and intact environment; providers therefore find themselves obliged to meet ever higher standards.

Each person has his or her own preferences when it comes to structuring leisure time. The most popular recreational activities are watching television, listening to music and reading. Collecting things, artistic pursuits or playing music are also well-liked hobbies. But though Germans largely prefer to spend their leisure time within their own four walls, they also enjoy going out, taking a drive in the car, or riding a motorcycle or a bike. "Automobile-free days" are becoming increasingly popular in Germany. On such days extensive sections of road (for instance, the road between Bingen and Koblenz in the Rhine valley or the "Wine Route" in the Rhineland Palatinate) are only open to bicycles. Many people participate in sports activities, take hikes and work in the garden. At least 12 million Germans devote their free time to helping others through private and volunteer associations and organizations.

Clubs. The extraordinarily wide range of clubs and associations play a particularly important role in the structuring of leisure time in Germany. They number at least 345,000 and have a total membership of 70 million. Nearly one in four Germans is a member of a sports club, and over two million are members of choral societies. There are associations of marksmen, stamp collectors, dog breeders, promoters of local culture, carnivalists, allotment holders and amateur wireless operators, not to mention youth and women's groups. Members pursue their hobbies but socialize as well. Some of these associations also play a role in local politics. People with different party affiliations come together in the marksmen's club or the local historical association, for instance, where they make informal contacts that can affect the life of the community.

The importance of leisure time for people's lives is also the subject of research. The German Leisure Association compiles the results of this research and makes them available to interested parties.

Travel. One fourth of all Germans spend their annual holiday in their own country. In the north visitors are drawn by the North Sea and Baltic Sea coasts and islands as well as by the equable sea climate. Other popular destinations are the lakeland areas in Holstein and Mecklenburg, while those interested in hiking favor the Central Uplands and the Alps. Water sports enthusiasts flock to the many lakes scattered all over the country, whereas those looking for romantic scenery choose the valleys of the Rhine, Main, Mosel, Neckar, Danube, Elbe and Saale rivers.

There are nearly 100 "tourist routes", such as the "German Fairy-Tale Route", the "Romanesque Route" or the "German Wine Route", which take visitors away from the major traffic arteries, opening up the country's traditional landscapes and providing access to a great variety of attractions in idyllic old towns and villages. They lead through regions with breathtaking scenery. The best known among them is the "Romantic Route", which brings to life the Middle Ages, especially in the towns of Rothenburg ob der Tauber, Dinkelsbühl and Nördlingen.

There are plenty of opportunities to meet local people at the countless regional and town fairs, wine festivals and other traditional festivals.

Cuisine and accommodations in the Federal Republic of Germany are of a high standard, ranging from inexpensive rooms on a family farm, in a private home or at a guesthouse to luxury holiday parks and top-class international hotels. For the gourmet there are an increasing number of restaurants which compare favorably with their renowned international

Skiing on the Fellhorn nr. Oberstdorf, Bavaria

counterparts. There is also a wide range of regional specialties. German wines have an excellent reputation throughout the world, and the fact that Germans know a thing or two about brewing beer hardly needs mentioning. The Germans appreciate foreign food as well: Even in the country's smaller towns and villages, visitors will find restaurants featuring international cuisine.

Tourist travel. Germany's well-developed transport network simplifies travel to and throughout the country by rail, road or even waterway. Not only hikers have a wide variety of well-marked routes of all lengths to choose from: Germany is also easily accessible to cyclists, thanks to the many bike paths that have been specially constructed for this purpose. In the east German states, the tourism infrastructure is rapidly being improved. Especially the lakeland and coastal regions of Brandenburg and Mecklenburg-Western Pomerania now offer water sports enthusiasts and nature lovers a multitude of attractive options.

The formalities for foreign visitors are straightforward. Citizens of many countries can now enter Germany as tourists for up to three months without a visa. There are no restrictions on the amount of foreign exchange which may be brought into or taken out of the country.

Germans vacationing abroad tend to favor Spain, Italy and Austria as holiday destinations, followed by Greece, France, the Netherlands and Switzerland. Roughly half of all Germans book an organized holiday through a tour operator. In 1999, Germans spent DM 89 billion on travel abroad.

The German National Tourist Board (GNTB). Designated by the Federal Government as Germany's national marketing organization, the GNTB works world-wide to promote the

Do-it-yourself as a hobby

Hiking in the fall in the Sauerland

Federal Republic as an attractive tourist destination. Its 27 offices and distribution agencies abroad see themselves as professional partners of the tourism industry. They ensure that German tourist offerings are featured in the catalogs of foreign tour organizers. The GNTB's joint stand enables small and medium-sized members of the German tourism industry to participate in important specialized trade fairs and fairs open to the general public. Since January 1, 1999, the GNTB has also been responsible for supra-regional domestic marketing. This new task involves a host of activities since Germany's states represent highly attractive destinations for long and short stays in Europe.

Further information:
- Deutsche Zentrale für Tourismus
  (German National Tourist Board)
  Beethovenstrasse 69, 60325 Frankfurt/Main
  Internet: http://www.deutschland-tourismus.de
  E-mail: info@d-z-t.com
- Deutscher Tourismusverband e.V.
  (German Tourist Industry Association)
  Bertha-von-Suttner-Platz 13, 53111 Bonn
  Internet: http://www.DeutscherTourismusverband.de
  E-mail: DeutscherTourismusverband@t-online.de
- Deutsche Gesellschaft für Freizeit (DGF)
  (German Leisure Association)
  Bahnstrasse 4, 40699 Erkrath
  Internet: http://www.SENIORWEB.UNI-BONN.de
  E-mail: DGFreizeit@t-online.de

Churches and religious communities

More than 55 million people in Germany belong to a Christian church. 27.4 million are Protestants, 27.4 million are Roman Catholics, and a minority belong to other Christian denominations.

There is no state church in Germany. In other words, there are no ties between state and church administrations and hence no control of the churches by the state. The churches and several other religious communities have the status of independent public-law corporations. The relationship between church and state is that of a partnership which is subject to the Basic Law and governed by concordats and agreements. The state finances part of the cost of certain church establishments, such as kindergartens and schools. The churches are empowered to levy taxes on their members, which as a rule, are collected by the state against reimbursement of costs. The clergy are trained mainly at state universities, and the churches have a say in appointments to chairs of theology.

The social and charitable commitment of the churches is an integral part of public life in Germany. Their work is indispensable in hospitals, old people's homes, nursing homes, schools and training centers, and in the provision of counseling and care in all situations in life.

The Evangelical Church in Germany (EKD). The EKD is a community of 24 largely independent Lutheran, Reformed and United regional churches. Church administrative regions are not identical with the territories of Germany's states. The EKD's main legislative body is the Synod, its chief executive body the Council. Member churches participate in the work of the EKD through the Church Conference. The Church Office in Hanover is its central administrative headquarters. The Evangelical Church is a member of the World Council of Churches. It cooperates closely with the Roman Catholic Church.

The Catholic Church. Until 1994, the Catholic Church was divided up into 23 dioceses, five of which were archdioceses. As a result of the reorganization that followed the reunification of Germany, there are now 27 dioceses (seven archdioceses). Germany's bishops and archbishops, more than 70 in all, consult together at the spring and autumn assemblies of the German Bishops' Conference, which has a secretariat in Bonn.

The impetus from the Second Vatican Council for the involvement of the Catholic laity in church affairs is translated into action by elected lay representatives. Together with approximately 140 Catholic associations and institutions, they form the Central Committee of German Catholics. The visits of Pope John Paul II to the Federal Republic in 1980, 1987 and 1996 evoked a tremendous response and stimulated both the ecumenical movement and the dialogue between church and state.

Joint action. Through their dedicated involvement in Germany's social and political development, the two large Christian churches contributed decisively to the restoration of democratic structures after 1945. The churches, in particular the Protestant Church also played an important part in the peaceful revolution in the GDR.

The churches in Germany address the public in many ways, publishing documents on topical issues and other information. Their 1997 joint publication concerning the economic and social situation in Germany, for example, prompted widespread discussion. Worthy of special mention are the two lay movements, the German Catholic Convention and the German Protestant Church Convention, which meet every two years but alternately.

Final service at the Evangelical Annual Convention, Stuttgart, 1999

Charitable works are carried out by Caritas Germany of the Catholic Church and the Social Service Agency of the EKD. Both churches are actively involved in development assistance. The major church aid organizations are funded by voluntary donations. The Protestant "Bread for the World" and the Catholic "Misereor" and "Adveniat" have together collected billions of marks for emergency relief and long-term development measures. In the spring of 1993, the Catholic relief organization "Renovabis" was founded, which sees itself as an action program for solidarity with the countries of Southeastern and Eastern Europe. In 1994, the Protestant churches initiated the annual donation campaign "Hope for Eastern Europe", which is designed to help these countries help themselves.

Other religious communities. A number of other Christian communities are represented in the Federal Republic as well: the Orthodox churches in Germany, the Old Catholic Church and the free churches. The Orthodox churches in Germany have a membership of 1.15 million. After the First Vatican Council of 1870, the Catholic Diocese of Old Catholics in Germany was founded in 1873 by those believers who had been excommunicated as a result of their refusal to accept the dogmas of papal infallibility and papal supremacy in matters of ecclesiastical law. Today the Old Catholic Church has 58 parishes in Germany with a total membership of about 30,000. Among the free churches are the Union of Evangelical Free Churches (Baptist Union), the Union of Free Evangelical Churches, the German Mennonite Church, the Association of Christian Fellowship Mühlheim/Ruhr, the United Methodist Church, the Salvation Army, the Church of the Nazarene, the Union of Pentecostal Free Churches, the Mora-

Episcopal mass at the 750th Anniversary Celebrations of Cologne Cathedral

vian Church and the Seventh-Day Adventists. The Association of Protestant Free Churches in Germany has a membership of more than 280,000.

In 1933, about 530,000 Jews lived in the German Reich. After the National Socialist genocide, only a few thousand people of Jewish origin remained in Germany. Today the Jewish communities have nearly 100,000 members. Many of them have come here in the past few years from the countries of the former Soviet Union. Berlin has the largest Jewish community (more than 11,000 members), followed by Munich (7,200) and Frankfurt/Main (6,600). Overall membership is expected to continue to increase. Since the unification of Germany, Jewish communities with rich traditions in eastern Germany, such as those in Dresden and Leipzig, have once again been able to develop an active community life. The national organization of the Jewish communities is the Central Council of Jews in Germany.

The presence of many foreign workers and their families has greatly increased the importance of religious communities which were previously barely represented in Germany. This is especially the case with Islam. Today, approximately three million Muslims from 41 nations live in the Federal Republic. Turkish Muslims form the largest group, followed by Muslims from former Yugoslavia, the Arab states, and southern and southeastern Asia.

Further information:
  — Kirchenamt der Evangelischen Kirche in Deutschland
    (Church Office of the Evangelical Church in Germany)
    Herrenhäuser Strasse 12, 30419 Hannover
    Internet: http://www.ekd.de
    E-mail: ekd@ekd.de
  — Sekretariat der Deutschen Bischofskonferenz
    (Secretariat of the German Bishops' Conference)
    Kaiserstrasse 163, 53113 Bonn
    Internet: http://www.dbk.de
    E-mail: Pressestelle@dbk.de
  — Zentralrat der Juden in Deutschland
    (Central Council of Jews in Germany)
    Tucholskystrasse 9, 10117 Berlin

Mass media and public opinion

Article 5 of the Basic Law guarantees freedom of opinion and
freedom of the press and also the right to obtain information
from generally accessible sources. There is no censorship. The
International Press Institute in Vienna describes the Federal
Republic as one of the few countries where the state respects
the strong position of a free press.

Diversity of the media. People have a choice of many different and competing media. Daily papers alone sold about 24.6
million copies a day at the end of 1999. More than 230 radio
programs are produced in Germany; over 30 television channels can be received by the average household. At present,
more than 39 million television sets and about 34 million radios are officially registered. On average, Germans over the
age of 14 devote more than 5.5 hours a day to media products: newspapers (30 minutes), the radio (2.5 hours) and television (2.5 hours). Supply is increasing constantly. Only about
one percent of the population are not reached by the media
at all. The great majority regularly use at least two media.

Sources of news. The mass media obtain their material from
news agencies at home and abroad, from their own correspondents and from direct research. The radio and television
networks have offices in all major cities around the world, as
do the large newspapers. A number of news agencies offer
comprehensive coverage of German news. The leading domestic news agency is the Deutsche Presse-Agentur (dpa).
Other news agencies include the Deutscher Depeschendienst
(ddp), the Associated Press (AP), Reuters (rtr) and Agence
France Press (AFP). dpa supplies all German daily newspapers.
AP, rtr and AFP can base their German-language services on
the global networks of their parent companies in the United
States, the United Kingdom and France.

In addition, there are numerous specialized agencies and press
services which cover a virtually unlimited spectrum of sub-

jects. They include the Protestant Press Service (epd), the Catholic News Agency (KNA) and the Sports Information Service (sid). Agencies like the Vereinigte Wirtschaftsdienste (vwd) also provide information for private companies and business organizations.

Various associations, public authorities, parties, companies, etc. have their own press departments which, like outside agencies, keep information flowing to the mass media. This is done by means of news conferences, press releases, mailings, picture services and briefings for journalists.

It is also part of the journalist's daily routine to research topics of his own choosing. Public authorities in the Federal Republic of Germany are required to provide journalists with information within the framework of the law. There are nearly 1,200 accredited correspondents in Bonn and Berlin. They are members of the Federal Press Conference or the Foreign Press Association, both of which are entirely independent of the authorities.

The Press and Information Office of the Federal Government (BPA) acts as an intermediary between the government and the public. The system differs from that of some other countries in that the Government Spokesman is always the guest of the Federal Press Conference when he briefs Bonn's journalists on the policies of the Federal Government. He goes to the press, not vice versa. This also applies to news conferences given by the Federal Chancellor and the federal ministers in conjunction with the Federal Press Conference. The Press and Information Office of the Federal Government is also responsible for keeping the Federal President, the Federal Government and the Bundestag informed about "published opinion" in Germany and abroad. In order to do this,

Chancellor Schröder and Foreign Minister Fischer being "interrogated"

it evaluates the services of 21 news agencies and monitors 59 radio and over 35 television programs from home and abroad.

Public opinion research. In addition to the opinions published in the media and direct contact with the country's citizens, public opinion research is an important instrument for ascertaining the basic attitudes, expectations, hopes and wishes of the public at large. Its advantage lies in the general validity of its findings, provided the surveys use a sufficiently large and representative sample. Its limitations lie in the short-lived nature of its findings: These reflect current moods and trends which may be subject to rapid change.

Public opinion research in Germany is conducted exclusively by private institutes. The Federal Government, the state governments and the political parties team up with these institutes on their surveys. Plurality is important in order to obtain an objective picture of public opinion, for experience has shown that the results of surveys are strongly influenced by the wording of questions and the manner in which they are posed. Here, the public opinion research institutes go their own different ways.

In the case of political opinion research, it has proved particularly informative to ask identically-worded questions again and again at regular intervals. These are reliable indicators of trends because they reveal changes in the public mood over time and thus permit relatively accurate evaluation of current data. Such questions and methods are primarily used to assess the basic attitudes and values of the public at large.

Surveys have shown that people in united Germany are committed to peace and freedom. Specifically, they wish to promote European unification and intensify cooperation especially with the neighboring countries of Eastern Europe. Great importance continues to be attached to Germany's alliance with the United States. The policy of pursuing an equitable balance between the interests of industrial countries and those of developing countries likewise enjoys widespread support in the Federal Republic.

The press

Newspapers enjoy great popularity in the Federal Republic. In terms of the number of newspapers per 1,000 inhabitants, Germany ranks sixth in Europe behind Norway, Finland, Sweden, Switzerland, Austria and the United Kingdom. Some 78 percent of the population read a newspaper every day for an average of 30 minutes. Despite stiff competition from radio and television, newspapers have held their own and kept in step with the times: At the beginning of 2000, 176 newspapers offered online news on the Internet

Local and regional daily newspapers predominate. On workdays 355 newspapers appear in the old and new states. They publish 1,576 local and regional editions in 135 offices. The total circulation is about 24.6 million. "Bild" is the German daily with the largest circulation (4.24 million a day). The editions of "Westdeutsche Allgemeine Zeitung" constitute the biggest-selling subscription paper (see table, p. 512). The large national dailies "Frankfurter Allgemeine Zeitung" and "Die Welt" have smaller circulations but considerable influence on political and business leaders. The same is true of "Süddeutsche Zeitung", "Frankfurter Rundschau", and "Handelsblatt", which have an impact far beyond the regions in which they are published. Other important opinion leaders are the weekly newspapers "Die Zeit", "Die Woche" and the "Rheini-

The press kiosk offer many hundreds of newspapers and magazines

scher Merkur", as well as the news magazines "Der Spiegel" and "Focus". These offer background information, analyses and reports. There are also Sunday newspapers such as "Bild am Sonntag", "Welt am Sonntag", "Sonntag Aktuell" and "Frankfurter Allgemeine Sonntagszeitung". Four Berlin dailies appear seven days a week, as do several daily newspapers in other cities.

Numerous foreign-language newspapers also print a separate edition especially for Germany.

Periodicals. Nearly 10,000 periodicals are published in Germany. Professional and technical journals are the genre with the largest number of publications (3,450). The approximately 1,800 general-interest magazines have a total circulation of 143 million; in addition to the news magazines, periodicals with particularly large circulations include the radio and television magazines, topical illustrated magazines such as "Stern" and "Bunte", and women's magazines. More and more readers are also turning to special-interest publications focusing on a single subject such as tennis, sailing, stock trading, computers or electronic entertainment equipment. Other periodicals include the church magazines, customer magazines (more than 2,300) and free papers. One third of the periodicals market is accounted for by various organizations and associations. The motoring magazine "ADAC-Motorwelt" published by the Allgemeiner Deutscher Automobilclub has a circulation of about 13 million, the largest in Germany. Newspaper stands in the major cities also carry a large selection of foreign newspapers and periodicals.

Press concentration. The number of independent newspapers in Germany has fallen steadily since the mid-1950s. The publishers with the greater financial and technical resources

At the chief editorial desk at Deutsche Presse Agentur in Hamburg

have been able to dominate various regional markets. A large
percentage of the local daily newspapers obtain their material (except for local news) from an outside editorial office. Restructuring has gone hand in hand with technical change
due to the introduction of computers and state-of-the-art
printing technology. Although this has cut production costs,
newspapers are still primarily dependent on advertising for
their economic survival. About 65 percent of revenues are
generated by advertising and about 35 percent by distribution and sales.

The major publishing companies. Economic developments
have led to the formation of large publishing houses. Axel
Springer Verlag AG commands over 20 percent of the daily
newspaper market (due largely to the high circulation of
"Bild"). As regards Sunday papers, Axel Springer AG is almost
without competition with "Welt am Sonntag" and "Bild am
Sonntag". Economic and journalistic power is also concentrat-
ed in the publishing group of the "Westdeutsche Allgemeine
Zeitung", the Süddeutscher Verlag Group, the Verlag M. Du-
Mont Schauberg, the publishing group of the "Frankfurter
Allgemeine Zeitung" and the Holtzbrinck Group. Likewise im-
portant in terms of economic power and journalistic effec-
tiveness are the publishers of periodicals (especially general-
interest magazines), led by the Bauer Verlag Group, Gruner +
Jahr, the Burda Group and the Axel Springer Publishing
Group. The German media corporation with the largest
turnover – and the third-largest media firm in the world – is
Bertelsmann AG, which has global operations.

Press rights. Press rights are governed by the press laws of the
states, which are consistent on basic issues such as the right
of journalists to refuse to disclose their sources of information and the right of persons who have been the subject of
reporting to have a counterstatement published. Print media
are required to exercise due care and to indicate the title and
address of the publication, the date of issue, the names of
the owners and editors, etc. Publishers and journalists exercise self-control through the German Press Council, which
looks into charges of negligence and unethical conduct.
Though its views are not binding, it makes strong use of the
sanction methods open to it, the most severe of which is public censure of the press organ in question.

Further information:
- Bundesverband Deutscher Zeitungsverleger (BDZV)
  (Association of German Newspaper Publishers)
  Riemenschneiderstrasse 10, 53175 Bonn
  Internet: http://www.bdzv.de
  E-mail: bdzv@bdzv.de
- Verband Deutscher Zeitschriftenverleger (VDZ)
  (Association of German Periodical Publishers)
  Winterstrasse 50, 53177 Bonn
  E-mail: info@vdz.de
- Deutscher Journalistenverband (DJV)
  (German Journalists Association)
  Bennauerstrasse 60, 53115 Bonn
  Internet: http://www.djv.de
  E-mail: djv@djv.de
- IG Medien
  (Media Union)
  Friedrichstrasse 15, 70174 Stuttgart
- Deutscher Presserat
  (German Press Council)
  Gerhard-von-Are-Strasse 8, 53111 Bonn
  Internet: http://www.Presserat.de
  E-mail: DeutscherPresserat@compuserve.com

Radio and television

The public broadcasting corporations. In 2000, the Federal Republic had ten regional broadcasting corporations, one broadcasting corporation organized under federal law, the national television network Zweites Deutsches Fernsehen (ZDF) based on an agreement among all Germany's states, and the public corporation DeutschlandRadio.

The largest broadcasting station is Westdeutscher Rundfunk (Cologne) with about 4,400 staff, while the smallest are Ostdeutscher Rundfunk Brandenburg (Potsdam) and Radio Bremen with about 640 and 610 staff respectively.

The others are Bayerischer Rundfunk (Munich), Hessischer Rundfunk (Frankfurt/Main), Norddeutscher Rundfunk (Hamburg), Saarländischer Rundfunk (Saarbrücken), Sender Freies Berlin (Berlin), Südwestrundfunk (Baden-Baden, Mainz, Stuttgart) and Mitteldeutscher Rundfunk (Leipzig). Some of them cater for the states in which they are located; others supply programs for several states. Each broadcasts several radio programs. The regional corporations form the Association of Public Broadcasting Corporations in the Federal Republic of Germany (Arbeitsgemeinschaft der öffentlich-rechtlichen Rundfunkanstalten der Bundesrepublik Deutschland, ARD). Together they operate a nationally transmitted television program called "Erstes Deutsches Fernsehen" (Channel One) for which they all provide material. In addition, they produce their own "Channel Three" TV programs, which can be viewed regionally or in some cases received nationally via satellite or cable. Bayerischer Rundfunk also broadcasts the educational TV program "Alpha".

The Mainz-based Zweites Deutsches Fernsehen transmits the "Channel Two" program nationwide. Aside from its participation in DeutschlandRadio, it is a television-only station, the largest in Europe. Since 1997, ARD and ZDF have also jointly sponsored two specialized public television channels:

"Phoenix", featuring events and documentaries, and "Der Kinderkanal", offering programs for children.

The radio station DeutschlandRadio was founded in 1993 through the transfer of the rights and obligations of the stations Deutschlandfunk and RIAS Berlin. It is jointly financed by ARD and ZDF and is headquartered in Cologne and Berlin. Since 1 January 1994, DeutschlandRadio has been broadcasting two radio programs which focus on information and culture and have no advertising. Deutsche Welle (DW) is the only federal radio station. It is financed largely by federal funds and has a statutory obligation to produce and broadcast radio programs for foreign consumption which give foreign audiences a comprehensive and well-balanced picture of political, cultural and economic life in Germany. Another one of its functions is to present and explain German positions on important issues.

Self-regulation and freedom of broadcasting corporations. Generally speaking, three regulatory bodies are responsible for monitoring and managing Germany's public broadcasting corporations: the Broadcasting Council, the Administrative Council and the corporation's director. As representatives of social groups, members of the Broadcasting Council act in the interests of the general public and monitor the public broadcasting corporations on behalf of the electorate. Members are elected by the state governments or are appointed directly by the political parties, religious communities as well as organizations within the business community and cultural life. Broadcasting Council members advise the corporation director on program content and ensure compliance with the basic regulations governing programs. The Administrative Council determines the budget and monitors the management of the broadcaster. Its members are largely elected by the Broadcasting Council while the latter appoints the director. The director manages the broadcasting corporation in keeping with the resolutions of the broadcasting and administrative councils. Not only is the director responsible for the program, he is also answerable to the public. Public broadcasting corporations are obliged to ensure their programs show no bias towards a particular political opinion and that program content reflects a balanced view. The lack of bias requirement is designed to prevent the one-sided influence of public opinion, but does not affect the right of each individual program director to express his own opinion. However, in allowing diversity of opinion, the public broadcasting corporation must see to it that the various views are presented in a balanced and appropriate manner.

Radio and television programs. Each regional corporation broadcasts several radio programs targeted towards specific audiences. Currently, ARD broadcasters offer over 50 German-language radio programs. These are supplemented by two programs broadcasted nationwide by DeutschlandRadio, providing a broad variety of shows in fields such as current events, politics, regional affairs, entertainment, education, music, sports, drama and opera. Most broadcasters run scientific and literary series as well. Their orchestras and choral groups enrich Germany's cultural life. Finally, special programs for foreign workers are broadcasted in their own languages.

In the nationally transmitted ARD and ZDF television programs, daily news updates, political reporting, home and foreign affairs documentation, television plays, films and entertainment play a big part. For their foreign coverage, both ARD and ZDF maintain extensive correspondent networks and studios of their own in many countries all over the world.

ARD and ZDF also participate in Eurovision's international exchange, mostly for sporting events. They regularly contribute to the news pool of the European Broadcasting Union. ZDF and six other European networks produce films falling under the category of entertainment through the European Film Production Community.

Channel Three television programs are transmitted regionally and also via satellite and cable by the ARD corporations. They focus on regional affairs ranging from politics to cul-

Political talk show "3 zwei eins" broadcast by Hessischer Rundfunk, Frankfurt/ Main

ture. Most of them also regularly broadcast television for schools as well as further education courses at various levels. In addition, ARD and ZDF produce jointly with other European partners the two cultural channels "arte" and "3sat".

Financing. The public broadcasting corporations obtain most of their funds from user fees paid by owners of radios and television sets. ARD and ZDF also depend on income from commercial advertising. Compared with private broadcasters, public broadcasters are allotted very limited time for commercial spots. Television rights, especially for the transmission of sporting events such as soccer or tennis, have become very expensive. As a result, all sports broadcasts – and programs in other sectors as well – are meanwhile sponsored by financially strong companies who are in return permitted to display their company logo on the screen at times other than those allotted for advertising. Broadcasters are obliged to report their projected funding needs to the Commission for the Monitoring and Evaluation of the Financial Requirements of the Broadcasting Corporations. The latter independent body determines the financial requirements according to necessity, efficiency and economy. The state parliaments which make the final decision have only a limited right of examination, owing to the fact that government is duty-bound not to interfere in radio and television.

Private television and radio. The public corporations had to contend with competition on a countrywide scale starting in 1984, when "SAT.1" began operating from Mainz as the first privately financed German television broadcasting company. 1984 also saw the launch "RTL plus Deutschland" (now "RTL", Cologne) whose first broadcasts were made from Luxembourg. Other private broadcasters include "ProSieben",

Thomas Gottschalk's "Wetten dass...?" show – Germany's most popular TV entertainment program

"n-tv", "VOX", "RTL 2", "super RTL", "tm3", "Kabel 1", "Premiere" and "VIVA". RTL and SAT.1 focus primarily on sports, entertainment and feature films but also offer high-caliber political programs. ProSieben concentrates mainly on feature films; DSF is a special-interest channel devoted to transmission of national sporting events; n-tv and N24 are news channels; VIVA offers only music. Super RTL was the first television channel to focus primarily on programs for children. Premiere World is the first pay TV channel in Germany and can only be received via a special decoder.

The programs of private broadcasters are transmitted via satellite and cable and can also be received via terrestrial frequencies. A number of foreign TV programs can be received nationwide via satellite and cable as well. The private television stations are operated by consortia, mostly of media companies. ProSieben, which was transformed into a stock corporation in 1997, is the first German television broadcaster to have its shares traded on the stock exchange. In contrast to the public corporations, private radio and television broadcasters obtain revenue largely from advertising. In 1998, they generated a net advertising turnover of approximately DM 8.0 billion with a work force of about 10,500 permanent employees.

In 1991, there were already 100 private radio stations, but only a few of them offered a full program catering for a whole state; by 1999 their number had increased to about 180. The law requires local radio stations to cater for wide-ranging public tastes. The Federal Constitutional Court has ruled that private radio broadcasters, like the public corporations, may not influence public opinion one-sidedly. Their programs must reflect diversity of opinion to a certain extent. The private broadcasters are subject to legal supervision by the regional media authorities, which are responsible among other things for licensing private broadcasters, monitoring programming and ensuring diversity of opinion. In 1993, the private television broadcasters founded the Freiwillige Selbstkontrolle Fernsehen e.V. (FSF), an organization for the voluntary self-regulation of television within the framework of legal protection for children and young people.

Broadcasting innovation. New technology has considerably changed the broadcasting landscape in Germany. In 1999, about 18 million German households were linked up to the broadband cable network which Deutsche Telekom AG has been laying since 1982. In addition, around three million households have access to cable TV via independent net operators. Programs can also be received directly via satellite with the aid of a parabolic dish antenna. By 1999, roughly 12 million households in Germany had installed dish antennas and could receive signals from geo-stationary satellites. Technological developments, especially the digitalization of transmission technology, have set in motion a process of as yet incalculable dimensions aimed at the melding of telecommunications, information and radio technologies, a process which has spawned special-interest TV, pay TV, video on demand and teleshopping, to name but a few examples.

Both the public and private broadcasting corporations offer "teletext", a service using the normal television signal. 26 German-language teletext channels now appear on the screen on call, offering some 10,000 pages of news, weather reports, tips for consumers, etc. Information on all broadcasters and programs is also posted on the Internet.

Further information:
- Arbeitsgemeinschaft der öffentlich-rechtlichen Rundfunkanstalten der Bundesrepublik Deutschland (ARD)
  (Association of Public Broadcasting Corporations in the Federal Republic of Germany)
  Bertramstrasse 8, 60320 Frankfurt/Main
  Internet: http://www.ard.de
  E-mail: info@ard.de
- Zweites Deutsches Fernsehen (ZDF)
  (German Television Channel Two)
  Postfach 4040, 55100 Mainz
- RTL
  Aachener Strasse 1036, 50858 Cologne
  Internet: http://www.rtl.de
  E-mail: webmaster@rtl.de
- SAT.1
  Oberwallstrasse 6-7, 10117 Berlin
  Internet: http://www.sat1.de
  E-mail: Yasmin.Harow@sat1.de
- Deutsche Welle
  Postfach, 50588 Cologne
  Internet: http://www.dwelle.de
  E-mail: info@dwelle.de
- Verband Privater Rundfunk und Telekommunikation (VPRT) e.V.
  (Association of Private Broadcasters and Telecommunications Companies)
  Burgstrasse 69, 53177 Bonn
  Internet: http://www.vprt.de
  E-mail: vprt@vprt.de
- Freiwillige Selbstkontrolle Fernsehen e.V.
  (Organization for the Voluntary Self-Regulation of Television)
  Rauchstrasse 18, 10787 Berlin

Education and training

Schools

In 1998, 12.7 million pupils received instruction from roughly 720,800 teachers at 52,000 schools in Germany. The Basic Law guarantees everyone the right to self-fulfillment and the right freely to choose his or her school or place of training as well as his or her occupation or profession. It thus follows that the goal of educational policy in the Federal Republic of Germany is to afford every individual the best possible opportunities to receive the kind of education that is commensurate with his or her abilities and interests. As an industrial country that is short of raw materials, Germany is largely dependent on a skilled labor force and therefore invests heavily in education. In 1997, gross public spending alone for schools and higher education institutions (including financial assistance for school pupils and university students) totaled approximately DM 163.9 billion.

Statutory basis. According to Article 7 of the Basic Law, the entire school system is under the supervision of the state. On account of the country's federal structure, that responsibility is shared by the federal and the state governments. Legislation and administration in the field of education predominantly fall within the purview of the states. This is true especially true of the school system, higher education, adult education and continuing education. Common and comparable

basic structures of the states' school systems are ensured
through the "Agreement between the States of the Federal
Republic of Germany for the Standardization of the School
System" of 14 October 1971. This agreement covers such matters as compulsory schooling, organization, recognition of
certificates, etc.

The Standing Conference of the Ministers of Education and Cultural Affairs of the Länder in the Federal Republic of Germany (KMK) has adopted supplementary accords providing
for greater harmonization of the school systems as well as
recognition of certificates awarded by general-education and
vocational schools in all the states. The main task of the KMK
is to ensure mobility for parents within Germany. At the
same time, the Länder intend to provide for more variety in
education in the future.

Compulsory schooling. School attendance is compulsory
from the ages of six to 18, i.e. for 12 years. To satisfy the compulsory schooling requirement, pupils must attend a full-time
school for nine (in some states ten) years and thereafter attend a part-time vocational school (Berufsschule) to satisfy
the compulsory vocational schooling requirement unless they
continue their schooling at a full-time general-education or
vocational secondary school. Attendance at all public schools
is free of charge. Educational materials, especially textbooks,
are also frequently provided free of charge or on loan; when
possession of such materials passes to the pupils, parents may
be required to contribute to the costs on the basis of their income.

The Basic Law also guarantees the right to establish and operate
private schools. If these schools are alternatives to public
schools, they are subject to state approval. Alternative schools

Preparing for
Xmas at a
kindergarten

have no authority to administer examinations and issue report cards and certificates pursuant to the provisions in effect for public schools until they have been awarded state recognition by the educational authorities of the states. Private schools enrich the educational spectrum and receive financial support from the states. More and more pupils in Germany are attending private schools; during the 1998-9 school year, enrollment at the country's 3,793 private general-education and vocational schools totaled about 625,000. 43.2 percent of the pupils attending private general-education schools were enrolled at grammar schools (Gymnasium), 12.7 percent at Free Waldorf Schools and 10.5 percent at private special schools.

Preschool education in Germany is provided in kindergartens, institutions which are not part of the public school system but instead fall under child and youth services. Most of them are run by churches, charitable organizations and municipalities, some by firms or associations. Kindergarten staff focus their efforts on creating a learning environment in a social setting that will further the development of children into responsible members of society. The kindergarten is intended to support and supplement the education and upbringing provided by the family and compensate developmental deficiencies in order to afford children a broad range of opportunities for education and development. Children largely learn through play. As a rule, children attend kindergarten only in the morning. Only some of the kindergartens offer all-day care.

As of January 1996, children have had a legal right to a place in a kindergarten and since January 1999, this right has applied unconditionally. New kindergartens and child care establishments are being constructed so that by the end of 1998, all children in Germany should be able to exercise this legal right. Attendance remains voluntary, however. Parents pay contributions for kindergarten attendance which are graduated according to their income. In 1998, approximately 78 percent of all children in Germany between the ages of three and seven attended kindergartens or day nurseries.

The school system. At the age of six, children enter primary school (Grundschule). In general it lasts four years, in Berlin and Brandenburg six years. In most states, work in the first

Basic Structure of the Educational System in the Federal Republic of Germany

Further education

(general, vocational and scientific further education of all kinds)

further education

Doctorate studies
degree qualifying student for a profession
(ordinary degree, master's degree, state exams for a bachelor's/master's degree)

UNIVERSITY

— University
— technical university/ technical college
— comprehensive university
— teacher training college
— academy of art
— academy of music
— technical college
— technical college for administration

Professional academy | Degree

Diploma qualifying student for a profession	General higher education entrance diploma
VOCATIONAL SCHOOL	**EVENING GRAMMAR SCHOOL/COURSE OF LECTURES**

tertiary education

Diploma as vocational qualification	General entrance qualification for Fachhochschule	Subject-related general entrance require-ment	General higher education entrance diploma	19
			UPPER SECONDARY EDUCATION	
			various school types possible: grammar school, vocational grammar school/technical grammar school, comprehensive school	18
Vocational training in part-time VOCATIONAL SCHOOL and COMPANY (dual system)	**FULL-TIME VOCA-TIONAL SCHOOL**	**VOCA-TIONALLY ORIENTED UPPER SECONDARY SCHOOL**	**VOCATIONAL UPPER SECONDARY SCHOOL**	17
				16
Vocational training year in a school or cooperative				15

secondary education II

Middle school diploma (intermediate school diploma) after ten years. First secondary general school diploma after nine years.

Grade						Age
10	10th grade		**INTER-MEDIATE SCHOOL**		**HIGH SCHOOL**	16
9	**SPECIAL SCHOOL**	**SECONDARY GENERAL SCHOOL**		**COMPREHEN-SIVE SCHOOL**		15
8						14
7						13
6		(Orientation grade dependent on or independent of type of school)				12
5						11
						10

secondary education I

4	**SPECIAL SCHOOL**	**PRIMARY SCHOOL**	9
3			8
2			7
1			6

primary education

	SPECIAL KINDER-GARTEN	**KINDERGARTEN (voluntary)**	5
			4
			3

Elementary education

Grade

Age

two years at school is not graded, but instead assessed in the form of a report giving a detailed description of the individual pupil's progress and weaknesses in specific areas of learning. After primary school, pupils attend one of the other general-education schools offering the first stage of secondary education. Irrespective of the type of school the pupil attends, the fifth and sixth school years constitute a phase of special encouragement, observation and orientation designed to facilitate choices concerning the pupil's further education and fields of emphasis. In most of the states this orientation phase is structured within the framework of the various types of schools; in some, however, it is a separate stage which is independent of school type.

After completing primary school, about one fifth (1998-9) of the children attend the secondary general school (Hauptschule). The secondary general school imparts a basic general education to its pupils. Every pupil at a secondary general school receives instruction primarily in German, mathematics, the natural sciences, the social sciences and one foreign language (usually English) as well as vocational orientation to ease the transition from school to working life. The secondary general school certificate awarded at the end of five or six years is generally used to gain acceptance to vocational training programs offered within the framework of the dual system and opens the door to many occupations in the craft trades and industry for which formal training is required. Graduates of secondary general schools enter a vocational training program and, as part of their training, attend a part-time vocational school (Berufsschule) until at least the age of 18.

The intermediate school (Realschule) is positioned between the secondary general school and the grammar school (Gymnasium) and imparts a more comprehensive general education to its pupils. As a rule, it encompasses six years of schooling, grades 5 through 10, and leads to an intermediate school certificate qualifying the recipient to continue his or her education at upper-level schools such as a full-time vocational school (Berufsfachschule) or a vocationally oriented upper secondary school (Fachoberschule). In 1999, about 40 percent of all school leavers earned an intermediate school certificate.

The grammar school (Gymnasium), which is generally a nine-year secondary school, imparts a comprehensive general education to its pupils. In the upper stage of the grammar school, which encompasses grades 11 through 13, a course system has replaced the conventional classes. There are requirements for individual subjects or groups of subjects, but the wide range of available courses nevertheless affords pupils in the upper stage of the grammar school ample opportunity to individually structure their coursework to emphasize certain fields. Subjects are divided into three general categories: language, literature and art; the social sciences; and mathematics, science and technology. Each of these three categories must be continuously represented among the courses taken by each pupil up through the end of upper secondary instruction, including the Abitur examination. The compulsory coursework also includes religion and sports. Upper secondary instruction at the grammar school concludes with the Abitur examination, which covers four subjects. Upon completing 13 years of schooling and passing the Abitur examination, the pupil is awarded the "certificate of general higher education entrance qualification" (Zeugnis der allgemeinen Hochschulreife). This certificate entitles the recipient to study the subject of his or her choice at a university or equivalent institution.

As a matter of principle, the certificate of higher education entrance qualification or the certificate of Fachhochschule entrance qualification (Fachhochschulreife) is required for admission to a course of study at a higher education institution. Due to the high number of applicants for the limited number of study places, however, nationwide or local admissions restrictions are in effect for some courses of study.

A new course: IT and new media

Advanced-
level art
lessons

Another type of school offering stage I secondary education is
the comprehensive school (Gesamtschule), which as a rule
provides instruction for pupils in grades 5 through 10. Some
comprehensive schools have an upper secondary stage of
their own that is structured along the lines of the upper
stage of the grammar school. The comprehensive school can
take two forms: In the "cooperative" comprehensive school
and the School Center (Schulzentrum), Bremen, the traditional types of schools – secondary general school, intermediate
school and grammar school – exist on the same premises, under joint administration and with curricula so harmonized as
to facilitate pupil transfer from one kind of school to another.
In an "integrated" comprehensive school, by contrast, the
three types of schools are combined into one under a single
administration and all pupils are taught together; beginning
in grade 7, certain subjects are taught in courses structured
according to at least two standards of difficulty geared to the
certificate to be awarded at the end of grade 9 or 10 (secondary general or intermediate school certificate, qualification
to attend upper-stage grammar school classes).

In some states there are other types of schools which combine
the curricula of the secondary general school and the intermediate school. These types of schools include the "regular
schools" in Thuringia, the "middle schools" in Saxony, the
"secondary schools in Saxony-Anhalt, the "integrated intermediate and secondary general schools" in Hamburg, the
"associated intermediate and secondary general schools" in
Hessen and Mecklenburg-West Pommerania, the "regional
schools" in the Rhineland-Palatinate, as well as the "extended
secondary general schools" in the Saarland. Here, the secondary general and intermediate schools are pooled and as of
grade 7 the classes and courses are geared to the certificates.

The certificates they award at the end of grades 9 and 10 are
earned under the same conditions as those awarded by the

other schools offering stage I secondary education and are mutually recognized by all states under the agreement of the Conference of Culture Ministers of 1993 in the version of 1996.

Children and young people with disabilities whose needs cannot be adequately met at general education schools receive instruction at special schools (Sonderschulen). There are special schools for various kinds of disabilities. Some children and young people attend integrated classes at regular schools. The compulsory education requirement applies to the disabled as well, and without restriction.

The "second educational track" offers people a chance to earn school-leaving certificates later in life. Qualified adults who work during the day, for instance, can take coursework at an evening intermediate school to earn an intermediate school certificate or at an evening grammar school to prepare for the Abitur examination. Adults can also prepare for the Abitur examination at full-time adult education colleges.

Teachers. For every type and level of school there are specially trained teachers. All must have completed a course of study at a higher education institution, but the content and duration of such courses vary. Courses of study for primary and secondary general school teachers usually last seven semesters. Longer courses of study generally lasting nine semesters are required for intermediate school, grammar school, special school or vocational school teachers. Upon completion of their course of study, all prospective teachers must pass an initial state examination. This is followed by a period of practical training (usually 24 months), which includes preparatory seminars and practice teaching in schools as well as a second state examination. Teachers at public schools are generally professional civil servants in the service of the states. Most of the teachers in the eastern states of Germany are salaried employees.

Vocational training

After completing school, most young people in Germany (about 70 percent of those born in a given year) enter a course of training offered within the framework of the "dual system" in one of the recognized occupations for which accredited vocational training is required. These are, above all, young people with a secondary general school or intermediate school certificate, but many higher education qualifiers opt for vocational training as well.

The dual system of vocational training. The occupations for which training is provided within the dual system are determined in accordance with the requirements of the job market and in close cooperation between the Federation, the states and both sides of industry. Depending on the occupation, training takes from two to three and a half years. The content is geared to the demands trainees will face later in professional life. Trainees are paid a training allowance. Considerable funds are spent by the state and the companies involved to finance the dual system.

The dual system of vocational training differs in two respects from the purely academic vocational education customary in many other nations:

— Most learning does not take place in schools, but rather in the production facilities or service operations of private business and industry, in a workshop, in a practice of one of the independent professions or in the public service. Trainees are released for specific periods of time to attend a part-time vocational school (Berufsschule), so they are simultaneously vocational school students. Young people receive training three to four days per week at their company, and one to two days per week at the vocational school.

— Training is split between two providers: companies and part-time vocational schools. Responsibilities for vocational training is split as well: On-the-job training is subject to federal law, whereas classroom schooling is the responsibility of the individual states.

Vocational training in firms takes place under conditions and at machines and facilities corresponding to the standard of technology currently in use. Larger firms provide training in their own training workshops and at the workplace. Trainees in smaller enterprises are trained right on the job. Where firms are too highly specialized to be able to impart all the necessary knowledge, they are supported by inter-company training centers. Certain aspects of training may also be taken over by other firms.

The task of instruction at part-time vocational schools is to support and supplement on-the-job training with specialized theoretical training and to broaden young people's general knowledge. Two thirds of classroom instruction is focused on specialized training and one third on general education. The obligation of the trainees to attend part-time vocational school arises out of the education acts of the states.

Vocational training is provided by about 500,000 firms in all branches of business and industry as well as by the independent professions and the public service. About 1.65 million young people are currently receiving training in one of the roughly 356 recognized occupations today for which accredited vocational training is required. Within the employment system, these jobs vary in popularity. Almost 37 percent of boys opt for one of ten preferred occupations, 53 percent in the case of girls. Boys prefer to become automobile mechanics, painters and carbody painters, joiners or electrical fitters while girls' favorite occupations are commercial clerks, business specialists in retail trade, hairdressers and doctor's assistants.

Mechanical engineering trainees at a vocational school

Teaching
workshop for
industrial
mechanics

Training for everyone. All school leavers in Germany should receive training which gives them the best possible vocational qualifications. It is therefore essential that a sufficient number and wide range of training places be made available. Vocational training is open to everyone; within the dual system it is not contingent on particular school-leaving certificates. In both 1999 and 2000, DM 2 billion was spent in initiating the crash program to combat youth unemployment – it endeavors to ensure every young person receives training. The program will be continued in 2001. The dual system has proved its worth in imparting skills to rising generations of specialists and is being further improved. New training occupations are being developed in new fields of employment, and training regulations for existing occupations are being modernized. The number of people trained for new IT and media jobs will increase substantially within the framework of the "Bündnis für Arbeit/Alliance for Jobs" initiative by the business community in response to the shortage of professional IT workers. Moreover, differentiated training options affording new opportunities are to be created for young people whose performance is particularly high or low.

Vocational further training. It is now less true than ever, that learning can stop once vocational training has been concluded. For this reason, the significance of vocational further training is growing. In Germany, there is a differentiated system of further training accommodating a broad range of content, functions and aims. This training is provided by a wide variety of institutions and through different types of financing. The state has a responsibility in terms of social and employment policy to promote further training of those groups of people who are unable to remain afloat in a market economy system on their own. Here, the state has subsidiary obligations. Vocational further training in firms is of particular importance. More than half of all vocational fur-

Commercial
training at
a company

ther training measures are already organized and financed by firms. In addition to learning by integrating people into the work process, it is now possible for individuals to handle their own learning with the help of information and communication technologies. In-company further training is supported and supplemented by a variety of inter-company and non-company organizations and institutions.

Other forms of vocational education. In addition to vocational training within the dual system, vocational education is provided in full-time vocational schools (Berufsfachschulen). These schools prepare young people for a field of employment or provide complete vocational training programs lasting at least one academic year, and specialize in areas such as commerce, social welfare services, home economics and health care. Important providers of vocational further training are the trade and technical schools (Fachschulen). They are open to persons who have already completed a course of vocational training and impart additional specialized knowledge and skills.

Higher education institutions

Germany's oldest higher education institution, the University of Heidelberg, was founded in 1386. Several other universities have also celebrated 500-year jubilees, including Leipzig (founded in 1409) and Rostock (founded in 1419). In the 19th century and in the first half of the 20th century, the educational ideal of German universities was the one pursued by Wilhelm von Humboldt at Berlin University, founded in 1810. The Humboldt type of university was conceived for a relatively small number of students. It was to be a place of pure science where research was done for research's sake and students were not taught primarily with a view to their future professions. This ideal became increasingly unsuited to the requirements of a modern industrial society, however. For this reason, alongside the traditional universities, there consequently emerged technical universities, colleges of education, art and music academies and (especially in the 1970s and 1980s) Fachhochschulen, which were designed to meet the burgeoning demands of research, teaching and promoting new academic and scientific talent. There are now about 350 higher education institutions in Germany, including more than 90 universities and 180 Fachhochschule.

Since 1960, the percentage of a given age group commencing studies at higher education institutions has risen from eight percent to more than 30 percent. In the 1999-2000 winter semester the number of new students was around 291,200, bringing the total enrollment in the same semester to 1,778 million. In addition to teaching, higher education institutions must meet continually growing demand in the area of basic research. According to the constitution, expansion of existing institutions and construction of new ones is a responsibility shared by the national and state governments. This is in order to ensure that higher education institutions form a coherent system in terms of their function, field of specialization, number, size and location by ensuring an adequate and well-balanced range of educational and research places. In west German states, this phase of expanding the number of available study and research positions is largely completed while in the eastern states, special ardor is still required to build up a new higher education structure. The focus of common efforts is now to maintain and strengthen the international competitiveness of Germany's higher education institutions. Consequently, since 1999 the government has increased the necessary financial contributions in order to modernize institutions of tertiary education (DM 2 billion for the year 2000).

Reform of the higher education system. In 1998, the Fourth Amendment to the Framework Act for Higher Education instituted a fundamental overhaul of the higher education system. Through deregulation, a stronger performance orientation and creation of incentives to excel, it aimed to encourage competition and differentiation and thus ensure the international competitiveness of Germany's higher education institutions in the 21st century.

Key elements in this reform are the introduction of a performance-oriented system of financing higher education, an evaluation procedure for research and teaching, a points system for assessing performance to facilitate acquisition and transfer of academic credentials as well as the strengthening of the institutions' obligation to provide student advisory services.

The Fourth Amendment is also intended to move reforms in study forward, thus creating important prerequisites for enhancing the international profile of Germany's higher education institutions. New internationally compatible courses of study and certificates as well as Bachelor and Master degrees

Lecturer and students of economics in a lecture theater

can now be introduced. This will lead to more mobility as well as a shortening of studying time while helping to build modular courses of study with an accompanying credit point system. German higher education institutions can now offer ever more certificates and academic degrees which are in line with internationally recognized standards. Many have already developed new international courses of study leading to acquisition of these new degrees. The 42 internationally oriented courses of study recently introduced with the aid of federal funds are designed to attract both foreign and German applicants. At present, there are more than 450 of these new study courses available for BA or Masters degrees. One foreign language (in most cases English) is also to be used as a language of instruction.

Organization of higher education institutions. All higher education institutions in Germany (apart from a few private and church-owned colleges, the universities of the Federal Armed Forces and the Federal College for Public Administration) belong to the states. The higher education institutions have the right to be self-administered. Within the framework of existing law, each institution draws up its own constitution. It is usually headed by a full-time rector or president who is elected for several years. Self-administration is based on the group participation principle: All groups within the higher education institution – professors, students, assistants and other staff – are entitled and obliged to participate, whereby the form and scope of their participation depends on their qualification, function, responsibility and involvement.

Types of higher education institutions. The mainstays of the tertiary education system are the academic universities and equivalent institutions. Courses of study culminate in a "Magister" or "Diplom" examination or in a "Staatsprüfung" (state examination); since 1998, students have also been able to pursue courses of study leading to a Bachelor's degree or a Master's degree. After that, further qualification up to doctorate level or a second degree is possible. Some courses of study lead only to a Magister degree or a doctorate. The proof of additional academic achievement (Habilitation) required of prospective professors is being changed to international standards.

Another mainstay of the German higher education system is the Fachhochschule, which offers highly practice-related study courses of a scientific nature, especially in the fields of engineering, information technologies, business administration, social work, design, health and therapy. These study courses have traditionally led to a Diplom degree; since 1998 it has also been possible to pursue study courses leading to a Bachelor's degree or a Master's degree. Today nearly every third new student enrolls at a Fachhochschule, where there is a shorter standard period of study and more structuring of the study course than at the universities.

In 1974, the University of Hagen was founded as the first open university in the German-speaking world. In the winter semester of 1999, around 46,800 students were enrolled there and attached to its regional centers, some of which are located in other German-speaking countries as well as in central and eastern European countries. There are other private higher education institutes throughout Germany offering correspondence courses. Conventional higher education institutions are also becoming increasingly involved in correspondence study. Today, computer networking and multimedia open up numerous new options for structuring modern study courses which fit students' needs. These are also increasingly being used to link individual correspondence study modules and multimedia modules, with courses offered at institutions where on-campus attendance is required. In this respect, a number of countries have established organizations offering virtual study possibilities. At the University of Hagen alone there are presently 14,000 students taking such study courses.

Courses of study and students. Government policy has opened higher education study to all strata of the population. In the 1952-3 winter semester, four percent of the new students came from wage-earner families, compared with about 14 percent today. In 1952, 20 percent of all students were women; today the figure is over 45 percent.

The federal and state governments are also strongly interested in having foreigners study in Germany. Approx 174,000 foreign students were enrolled in the 1999 winter semester.

For nearly all courses of study there are recommended curricula and required examinations based on standardized national guidelines. Diploma and Master's courses usually require intermediate examinations. In many fields, students can themselves decide which subjects will be the focus of their studies and which classes they will take. Students at public higher education institutions in the Federal Republic of Germany are not required to pay tuition fees, although certain states charge fees for a second course of study or one that covers a long time period.

Under the Federal Training Assistance Act (BAFöG), students have a legal right to public financial assistance if the funds they need to cover their educational and living expenses are not available from other sources, most notably from their parents' income. During the standard period of study, half of this aid is awarded in the form of a grant and the other half as an interest-free loan that must usually be repaid within five years after the end of the maximum entitlement period. In 1998, 12.6 percent of all students received assistance under the Federal Training Assistance Act. This is a considerable reduction: In 1991 for example, over 24 percent of students were still receiving grants. Payments under this Act are made by the 62 student welfare services, which as a rule are statutory bodies of the states. They are responsible for economic, social, cultural and health care services for students at higher education institutions. The local student welfare services have together formed a national organization, the German Student Welfare Service (DSW). As a new service for prospective foreign students, the DSW now makes service packages available at some 64 higher education institutions which offer room and board as well as social and advisory services at an attractive overall price.

Free admission and limitation of student numbers.
Despite all measures undertaken to cope with the enormous growth in the number of prospective students in the higher education system in the Federal Republic of Germany, nationwide admissions restrictions (numerus clausus) have been necessary for an increasing number of subjects, including some with large enrollments. Capacity is insufficient to meet demand. Study places are usually awarded on the basis of the applicants' Abitur grade average and the "waiting period", the length of time that has elapsed between the Abitur and the application for admission. Some of the study places for

courses of study in which nation-wide admissions restrictions apply are awarded by higher education institutions under a special selection procedure that requires selection interviews as well as the above criteria.

Today, university students still require an average of 12 semesters or six years – almost 10 semesters at higher education institutes – to complete their career qualifications. This is too long compared to the period of study in other countries. They are also commencing studies at an ever older age. Many of them, for example, have completed an apprenticeship or compulsory military or civilian service before pursuing a course of study.

The fact that they begin earning their living comparatively late in life appears to put them at a serious disadvantage vis-à-vis job applicants from other nations – especially in view of constantly increasing international mobility (within the European internal market, for instance).

The situation in the east German states. The reform of higher education in eastern Germany, partly within the framework of the Program for the Renewal of Higher Education and Research in the New Länder (HEP), which cost DM 2.4 billion between 1991 and 1996, has improved the academic range and regional distribution of institutions. There are now 19 universities, two technical institutes, 14 colleges of art and music, 29 general Fachhochschule and eight colleges of public administration in the new states and east Berlin, with a total enrollment of about 337,600 (including Berlin). The HEP have taken significant steps in restructuring teaching and research in higher education institutes in the new states and bringing their programs into line with international standards.

The Association of Rectors and Presidents of Universities and other Higher Education Institutions (HRK) is the body which unites almost all state and state-recognized institutions of higher education in the Federal Republic. Within the HRK, the currently 257 member institutions – represented by their rectors or presidents – work together on all issues relating to the fulfillment of their tasks in research, teaching and study, continuing academic and scientific education, the transfer of technology and knowledge, and international cooperation.

The work of the HRK involves the following:

— promoting cooperation between higher education institutions;
— providing member institutions with information on developments and problems in higher education;
— formulating positions and statements on matters of scientific, academic and higher education policy;
— publicly representing the interests of the member institutions; and
— cultivating international relations.

The German Academic Exchange Service (DAAD). The DAAD (Deutscher Akademischer Austauschdienst) is an organization jointly founded by German institutions of higher education in 1925. Its purpose is to promote relations between higher education institutions in Germany and abroad, especially through exchange schemes. Its programs are open to all countries and all subjects, and benefit both foreigners and Germans. Over 60,000 students world-wide benefitted from the Service in 1999. The DAAD also supports the higher education institutions' international activities, with a number of services such as information programs, publications and advice. Furthermore, the DAAD plays an advisory role in structuring German foreign cultural policy. Its regular members are the higher education institutions represented in the HRK and their student bodies. At the end of 1998, a total of 233 universities, colleges and Fachhochschulen and 128 student bodies from various types of higher education institutions were members of the DAAD.

The DAAD handles the following functions:

— It awards scholarships to foreign and German students, student trainees, young academics, lecturers and professors in

The main building of the Humboldt University in Berlin, which can look back on an auspicious history

order to promote international experience in continuing education and training in the field of higher education and research.

— It arranges and finances long and short-term lectureships at foreign universities and colleges for German academic teaching staff from all disciplines (including junior lecturers for German language, literature and area studies).

— It provides information on study and research opportunities at home and abroad through its publications, oral and written advice to individuals, and by organizing and promoting information visits for foreign and German scientists, scholars and student groups.

— It undertakes international marketing for higher education institutes

— It maintains follow-up contacts with former scholarship holders through a re-invitation program, follow-up meetings and information material e.g. the "DAAD Letter – Hochschule und Ausland"

Further information:
— Hochschulrektorenkonferenz (HRK)
  (Association of Rectors and Presidents of Universities and other Higher Education Institutions in the Federal Republic of Germany)
  Ahrstrasse 39, 53175 Bonn
  Internet: http://www.hrk.de
  E-mail: sekr@hrk.de
— Deutscher Akademischer Austauschdienst (DAAD)
  (German Academic Exchange Service)
  Kennedyallee 50, 53175 Bonn
  Internet: http://www.daad.de
  E-mail: postmaster@daad.de

Adult education

Continuing education is taking on ever greater importance in the overall context of lifelong learning. This is true of both general, continuing education and vocational further training. Political and cultural further education normally fall in the category of general continuing education. The more swiftly knowledge becomes obsolete, the more essential lifelong learning becomes in order to maintain a high level of competence. This is also a principle theme of the Concerted Action in Continuing Education (KAW), which since 1987, has proved its worth as a platform for discussion on the topic of continuing education, and promotes increased cooperation between all the parties involved.

Participation in courses and seminars has increased markedly in Germany in recent years. In 1997, nearly one out of two adults took advantage of opportunities for continuing education, the highest level recorded since surveys were started within the framework of the Continuing Education Reporting System.

Institutional providers of continuing education. A wide range of institutions and organizations provide continuing education in the Federal Republic.

The community adult education centers (Volkshochschulen) are educational establishments without lodging facilities which concentrate exclusively on continuing education. They offer a comprehensive, basic curriculum to interested citizens all over the country, primarily in the area of general continuing education, but increasingly also in the area of vocationally-oriented further training. As a rule, the adult education centers are the further education centers of the municipalities (cities and rural districts); there are now more than 1,000 such centers with numerous branches.

The companies are the most important providers of vocational further training. They offer training in their own company facilities or through cooperation with inter-company further training institutions and other providers.

The private institutes, or commercial further training institutions, are especially active in the areas of vocational retraining, acquisition and expansion of vocational qualifications, computer training, foreign language instruction and course work to obtain formal training qualifications later in life.

The churches focus on areas such as personal growth, issues relating to children's upbringing and schooling, family, society and literature as well as educational assistance relating to life issues, health and relationships.

The higher education institutions, academies and scientific societies offer academic, scientific and specialized further education (often in cooperation with the relevant occupational and professional associations).

The chambers (such as the chambers of industry and commerce, the chambers of crafts and trades, and the chambers of agriculture) as well as the associations and educational organizations of business and industry offer an inter-company framework for vocational training, for purposes of adjustment and promotion. They also administer examinations for recognized qualifications.

The unions concentrate primarily on enabling people to participate actively in political life, and represent workers' interests within companies. In cooperation with the community adult education centers, in the context of the federal association "Work and Life", they also provide broader political and vocational further training.

The charitable associations are particularly concerned with imparting knowledge and skills pertaining to social work, health care and development assistance.

Life is a learning curve – a Berlin course for OAPs

In mid-1999, 215 private institutes of distance learning offered roughly 1,600 correspondence courses (which were not tied to any particular time or place) in the areas of both general continuing education and vocational further training (particularly in commercial and business-oriented subjects). Their curricula, which range from course work towards traditional apprenticeship certificates to guided, self-paced courses of study, also increasingly include the new media.

The federal and state centers for political education offer a wide range of educational events focusing especially on current political issues and basic problems of the democratic state. The same is true of the foundations of the political parties: the Konrad Adenauer Foundation (CDU), the Friedrich Ebert Foundation (SPD), the Friedrich Naumann Foundation (FDP), the Hanns Seidel Foundation (CSU), the Heinrich Böll Foundation (Alliance 90/The Greens) and the Rosa Luxemburg Foundation (PDS).

The schools of the "second educational track" enable adults to acquire school-leaving certificates later in life.

Libraries, museums, socio-cultural centers, independently organized groups, citizens' initiatives, bookstores and other institutions strive to meet specific learning needs outside the framework of the established continuing education organizations.

The public broadcasting networks help to promote the dissemination of information, education and culture with their radio and television programs. The "College of the Air" (Telekolleg) is developed in close cooperation with the adult education centers. Telekolleg means learning in a media system – that is, learning with the aid of TV programs, supplementary written material and direct instruction.

Additional establishments. Of especial importance in adult education are:

Deutsches Institut für Erwachsenenbildung e.V., a non-profit-making, federal-level institution for adult education was set up by the Gottfried Wilhelm Leibniz Scholarly Association. As an institute for scientific service, it organizes adult education which bridges science and practice and provides the basis for practical research and strong scientific development work. The mainstays of the institute's work are service, developmental research, networking and international projects.

The Federal Institute for Vocational Training is legally supervised
by the Federal Ministry of Education and Research and is integrated into the dual system of vocational training (in firms
and part-time vocational schools) and extended vocational
training. It carries out research and development in the area
of vocational training, and furnishes services and advice to
the Federal Government and providers of vocational training.
The Federation and the states work together in the Bund-Länder
Commission for Educational Planning and Research Promotion. The states coordinate their policies in the Standing Conference of the Ministers of Education and Cultural Affairs of
the Länder in the Federal Republic of Germany (KMK).

Further information:
  — Deutsches Institut für Erwachsenenbildung
    (German Institute for Adult Education)
    Hansaallee 150, 60320 Frankfurt/Main
    Internet: http://www.die-frankfurt.de
    E-mail: info@die-frankfurt.de
  — Bundesinstitut für Berufsbildung (BIBB)
    (Federal Institute for Vocational Training)
    Hermann Ehlers Weg 10, 53113 Bonn
    Internet: http://www.bibb.de
    E-mail: Zentrale@bibb.de
  — Bundesministerium für Bildung und Forschung
    (German Federal Ministry of Education and Research)
    Heinemannstrasse 2, 53175 Bonn
    Internet: http://www.bmbf.de
    E-mail: information@bmbf.bund.de
  — Sekretariat der Ständigen Konferenz der Kultusminister der Länder in der Bun-
    desrepublik Deutschland (KMK)
    (Standing Conference of the Ministers of Education and Cultural Affairs of the
    Länder in the Federal Republic of Germany)
    Postbox 2240, 53012 Bonn
    Internet: http://www.kmk.org
    E-mail: eurydice@kmk.de
  — Deutscher Volkshochschul-Verband e.V.
    (German Adult Education Association)
    Obere Wilhelmstrasse 32, 53225 Bonn
    Internet: http://www.dvv-vhs.de
    E-mail: buero@dw-vhs.de
  — Bundeszentrale für politische Bildung
    (Federal Centre for Political Education)
    Berliner Freiheit 7, 53111 Bonn
    Internet: http://www.bpb.de
    E-mail: reichert@bpb.de

Cultural life

Cultural diversity

Cultural federalism. Nowhere is the federal structure of the
Federal Republic more evident than in the cultural sphere.
Germany has never had a cultural metropolis comparable to
Paris in France or London in England. The considerable cultural autonomy of the states has led to the formation of large
and small cultural centers with different profiles. Cultural
and scholarly activity is to be found even in small towns and
communities.

This diversity is apparent, simply from the regional distribution
of the different cultural institutions and activities in Germany. The Deutsche Bibliothek (German Library), a federal
institution, has library facilities in Frankfurt/Main, Leipzig
and Berlin. The Federal Records Office is headquartered in
Koblenz and has branches in a number of cities including
Bayreuth, Berlin, Freiburg im Breisgau and Potsdam. Hamburg has the largest concentration of media; Cologne, Düsseldorf and Kassel are just three of the centers of modern art.
Berlin has the most theaters. The Academies of Science have
their seat in Berlin, Düsseldorf, Göttingen, Heidelberg,
Leipzig, Mainz and Munich. The most prominent museums
are situated in Berlin, Cologne, Frankfurt/Main, Hildesheim,
Munich, Nuremberg and Stuttgart. The two most important
literary archives are in Marbach and Weimar.

The establishment and maintenance of most cultural institutions in Germany is the responsibility of the cities and municipalities. Legislation on cultural matters – with a few exceptions – is the prerogative of the states.

For these reasons, the Federal Republic of Germany has never had a minister for cultural affairs at the federal level. The new Federal Government, however, has appointed a State Minister and Federal Government Commissioner for Cultural Affairs and the Media in the Federal Chancellery. While maintaining the cultural sovereignty of the states, he co-ordinates the Federation's cultural policy duty and federal responsibilities, which were previously distributed among several ministries. He will give impetus to, and be a contact person for the Federation's cultural policy, and see himself as a representative of German culture at the international – and especially European – level. He is particularly committed to supporting cultural projects and institutions in the capital, Berlin, and in the new states.

The German Arts Council. The German Arts Council (GAC) was founded in 1982, as a non-governmental, working commission of organizations and institutions with national significance in the field of cultural and media policy. As of September 1995, the German Arts Council is registered as a non-profit association. The German Arts Council is the umbrella organization of the federal arts associations. It is responsible for the policies and administration of the federal government, the European Union and the states and communities in all matters pertaining to cultural politics. The purpose of the German Arts Council is to discuss cross-disciplinary questions of cultural policy nationwide and on all levels. The German Arts Council has eight specialized sections which in turn

The Buddenbrook House in Lübeck attests to the works of Heinrich and Thomas Mann

embrace more than 190 independent associations and institutions.

Organizations engaged in cultural relations. Cooperation with foreign countries in the field of cultural affairs and international cultural exchanges within the framework of cultural agreements are largely handled by legally independent organizations acting on their own responsibility. They are financed from the budget of the Federal Foreign Office as part of Germany's cultural relations. The most important of them are the Goethe Institute, the German Academic Exchange Service (DAAD), the Alexander von Humboldt Foundation, the Institute for Foreign Relations, and INTER NATIONES.

Further information:
- Deutscher Kulturrat e.V.
  (German Arts Council)
  Weberstrasse 59a, 53113 Bonn
  Internet: http:/www.kulturrat.de
  E-mail: post@kulturrat.de
- Alexander von Humboldt-Stiftung
  (Alexander von Humboldt Foundation)
  Jean-Paul-Strasse 12, 53173 Bonn
  Internet: http://www.avh.de
  E-mail: post@avh.de
- Deutscher Akademischer Austauschdienst (DAAD)
  (German Academic Exchange Service)
  Kennedyallee 50, 53175 Bonn
  Internet: http://www.daad.de
  E-mail: postmaster@daad.de
- Institut für Auslandsbeziehungen
  (Institute for Foreign Relations)
  Charlottenplatz 17, 70173 Stuttgart
  Internet: http://www.ifa.de
  E-mail: info@ifa.de
- INTER NATIONES e.V.
  Kennedyallee 91-103, 53175 Bonn
  Internet: http://www.inter-nationes.de
  E-mail: in-press@inter-nationes.de
- Goethe-Institut e.V.
  (Goethe Institute)
  Helene-Weber-Allee 1, 80637 Munich
  Internet: http://www.goethe.de
  E-mail: zv@goethe.de

Literature

The new beginning after 1945. After the Second World
War, German writers made a new beginning. One cannot,
however, speak of a "zero hour" of German literature, given
the biographical and literary continuity of many authors, the
most prominent of whom in the first half of the century were
Thomas Mann, Gottfried Benn and Bertolt Brecht. A new beginning – for many writers that meant attempting to make
the shocking, in the very sense of the word, nihilistic experience of war and devastation, describable-often by falling
back on foreign models or the thought processes of Existentialism or the Christian tradition. Wolfgang Borchert's drama, "The Outsider" (1947), stories by Heinrich Böll ("The
Train Was on Time", 1949) and Arno Schmidt ("Leviathan",
1949), and lyric poetry by Paul Celan ("Mohn und Gedächt-
nis", 1952), Günter Eich and Peter Huchel are prime examples of this tendency to refrain from directly and realistically
addressing political subjects. They reflect instead upon German guilt and the German defeat using religious or philosophical metaphors. Often the authors picked up the thread
of modernist literature which had been banned for twelve
years under the National Socialists.

Between social criticism and concrete poetry. In the
literature of the 1950s and 1960s, a current rapidly became
discernible which took as its subject the manner in which
people were dealing with the recent past. In many of the
works appearing during those years, criticism of the "economic miracle" of the postwar period was conjoined with endeavors to come to terms with the past. The preoccupation
with swift attainment of a new material prosperity was often
interpreted as flight from responsibility for what had tran-
spired during the National Socialist era. Examples include the
plays and prose of the Swiss natives Friedrich Dürrenmatt
("The Visit", 1956; "The Physicists", 1961) and Max Frisch

("I'm Not Stiller", 1954; "Homo Faber", 1957; "The Firebugs", 1958; "Andorra", 1961). The most significant works by German authors came from the pens of Wolfgang Koeppen ("Das Treibhaus", 1953), Heinrich Böll ("And Never Said a Word", 1953; "The Bread of Those Early Years", 1955; "Billiards at Half-Past Nine", 1959), Siegfried Lenz ("The German Lesson", 1968) and Günter Grass ("The Tin Drum", 1959; "Cat and Mouse", 1961; "Dog Years", 1963). A crucial role was played by "Group 47", a fluctuating group of German-language writers formed by Hans Werner Richter whose annual meetings (which continued until 1967) were both a literary and, as time passed, increasingly political event. Many well-known authors of the period belonged to this group; some of them – most notably Heinrich Böll, who was awarded the 1972 Nobel Prize for Literature – considered it their role to pass moral judgment. In addition to these authors, there were a number of others who, less concerned with interpreting social reality, instead sought to present an (ostensibly) dispassionate picture of it. They included above all Jürgen Becker ("Felder", 1964; "Ränder", 1968), Rolf Dieter Brinkmann ("Keiner weiss mehr", 1968), Alexander Kluge ("Lebensläufe", 1962) and Dieter Wellershoff ("Ein schöner Tag", 1966). Running counter to these currents was the genre of concrete poetry (Max Bense, Eugen Gomringer, Helmut Heissenbüttel, Franz Mon), which attempted to divorce itself completely from content. Here, language itself became literature.

The 68ers. In the mid-1960s, there began a period of radical change in society, not only in the Federal Republic of Germany but also in all the other countries of the West. The student revolts of 1968 marked the clear radicalization of criti-

Günter Grass receives the Nobel Prize for Literature in 1999

Walter
Kempowski

cism of the "silence of the fathers" on the subject of the National Socialist crimes. Aestheticizing tendencies in literature
were branded as attempts to obscure the social and economic
causes of an economic structure which was perceived as unjust. Many authors became social and political activists –
while at the same time refusing to allow themselves to be ap-
propriated for political purposes. Symptomatic of this trend
was the decided opposition of many writers to the Vietnam
War and their support for the new "Ostpolitik" (policy on the
East), which sought to overcome the confrontation between
East and West. Just as typical, however, was the search for a
new role and new forms of literature. The thesis of the
"death of literature" (Hans Magnus Enzensberger) and Peter
Weiss's "Die Ästhetik des Widerstandes" were a radical expression of these new reflections.

Likewise part of this political literature was the documentary
theater (Rolf Hochhuth: "The Deputy", 1963; Heinar Klip-
phardt: "In der Sache J. Robert Oppenheimer", 1964), which
in terms of content and intent, was linked with the genre of
partisan reporting (Günter Wallraff: "Ihr da oben – wir da
unten", 1973) and the literature of the working world.

The artist as a tragic figure? Alongside these currents, a
few loners established themselves as the pre-eminent writers
of their time. The most important works of Arno Schmidt
were "Scenes from the Life of a Faun", 1953; "Das Steinerne
Herz", 1956; "Kühe in Halbtrauer", 1964; "Zettels Traum",
1970; and "Evening Edged in Gold", 1975. Outstanding works
by the Austrian, Thomas Bernhard, include "Frost", 1963;
"Gargoyles", 1967; "The Limeworks", 1970; "Die Ursache",
1975; "Old Masters", 1985; and "Auslöschung. Ein Zerfall",
1986. The works of these two writers represent a serious portrayal, interspersed with irony, of the existence of the artist,
the "man of intellect" in a world of indifference and unimag-
inativeness. Their skepticism, honed on Schopenhauer, sharp-

ened their eye for the comic and the tragic in every human existence.

The Austrian Peter Handke, who was highly regarded at the end of the 1960s, was one of the most influential poets in Germany during the first decade of his career ("Offending the Audience", 1966; "Kaspar", 1968; "The Goalie's Anxiety at the Penalty Kick", 1970; "A Sorrow Beyond Dreams", 1972; "A Moment of True Feeling", 1975). Since the beginning of the 1970s, his literary endeavors have become increasingly solipsistic ("Slow Homecoming", 1979; "Die Abwesenheit", 1987; "Mein Jahr in der Niemandsbucht", 1994).

Literary production. Whereas the 1960s were still full of beginnings, ideas and endeavors to break new ground, the subsequent years appeared to be increasingly marked by exhaustion of artistic devices and potential. The later novels and short stories of the successful authors of the early 1950s and 1960s (Heinrich Böll, Günter Grass, Martin Walser and the Swiss native Max Frisch, to name but a few) frequently lacked the originality and cutting edge characteristic of earlier works; the generation of the 68ers very soon became silent or chose to express themselves in other artistic media (performances, music, film).

A well-known and controversial figure is the literary pundit Marcel Reich-Ranicki, whose reviews and televised discussions have contributed to the positive or negative reception of many contemporary authors. His autobiography "Mein Leben" was at the top of the German bestseller list for months. The diaries of Victor Klemperer, published in 1995, was another very popular book in which the world-class novelist wrote a daily account of his life as a Jew during the era of National Socialism.

Christa Wolf

Literature in the German Democratic Republic (GDR).

Like 1945, the years 1989 and 1990 – the end of "real existing socialism", the GDR and the Soviet Union (in 1991) – marked a profound turning point not only in political history but in the cultural sphere as well. This especially affected the authors who lived in the GDR and who openly professed their conviction that this state – despite all its shortcomings – was the better of the two on German soil.

From the very beginning, literature had taken a different direction in the GDR than in the West. There was neither freedom of information nor freedom of expression, and the opportunities for a free exchange of ideas, texts and persons were extremely limited. An entire country was indoctrinated in the Soviet literary aesthetic of "Socialist Realism". Those who were unwilling to toe this line had no choice but to flee, an option available only until 1961 (construction of the Berlin Wall). Among them was Uwe Johnson ("Speculations About Jacob", 1959; "The Third Book About Achim", 1961; "Two Views", 1965; "Anniversaries", 1970-83).

The works produced in the GDR in the 1950s and 1960s were thus largely conformist "construction" literature, espousing a philosophy of history marked by a tiresome optimism, literature lacking formal innovation or critical confrontation with the 20th-century avantgarde who were largely banned (Franz Kafka, James Joyce, Samuel Beckett, Vladimir Nabokov and many others). Moreover, the fact that reception of nearly all contemporary currents in philosophy – even the thought of Friedrich Nietzsche – was not permitted in the GDR fostered the development of a climate of intellectual mediocrity and ideological uniformity; the only notable exceptions in the field of literature were the works of Heiner Müller ("Die Lohndrücker", 1956; "Philoktet", 1958/64; "Germania Tod in Berlin", 1956/71; "Hamletmaschine", 1977; "Der Auftrag", 1979; "Quartett", 1980) and Christa Wolf ("Divided Heaven", 1963; "The Quest for Christa T.", 1968; "Cassandra", 1983). Even in the final stage of the GDR, literary criticism by individuals such as Christoph Hein, Volker Braun, Ulrich Plenzdorf or Stefan Heym was intermittent and muted. In contrast to literature in nearly all other countries of Soviet-dominated Eastern Europe, literature in the GDR was predominantly affirmative. The most notable prose works and plays by Christa

Wolf and Heiner Müller were admittedly far removed from party allegiance and faith in socialism – at least from the mid-1970s onward – but their models of a different society nevertheless essentially remained deeply rooted in the idea of socialism.

New trends. One of the outstanding authors of the last twenty years is Botho Strauss, whose short stories and novels ("Marlenes Schwester", 1975; "Der junge Mann", 1984), plays ("Die Hypochonder", 1972; "Bekannte Gesichter, gemischte Gefühle", 1974; "Kalldewey, Farce", 1981; "Der Park", 1983) and essays ("Paare, Passanten", 1981; "Wohnen Dämmern Lügen", 1994) make a serious attempt to capture the present at the very moment of its outrageousness by borrowing from mystical images in language and scene sequences.

The end of the political and ideological division of Europe and Germany is still too recent to permit even a tentative answer to the question of how it has influenced or altered German

Ingo Schulze

In 1999, Siegfried Lenz was awarded the City of Frankfurt/Main's Goethe Prize

literature. Günter Grass attempted to assess this radical change in his novel "Ein weites Feld" (1995), but the discussion his work unleashed fizzled as quickly as it had begun. In "Simple Storys" (1998) Ingo Schulze painted a kaleidoscopic portrait of the frequently tragicomic situation of people in the east after the fall of the Wall. Klaus Schlesinger recounted in his short novel "Trug" (2000) a perfect suggestive story of two men in divided Germany. The book demonstrates once again, that important historical events can only become literature after a certain distance has been gained.

Literature prizes. Günter Grass received the 1999 Nobel Prize for Literature because, according to the Swedish Academy, in his words, he "painted the forgotten face of history in brightly dark tones". In the same year, Grass published his short prose collection "Mein Jahrhundert/My Century": Each year carries a short story illustrated with a water color by the artist.

In 1999, Siegfried Lenz received Frankfurt/Main's "Goethe Prize"; the laudatory speech was given by Marcel Reich-Ranicki. The "Friedrich Hölderin Prize" awarded by the city of Bad Homburg went to Reiner Kunze in the same year and Arnold Stadler was awarded the "Georg Büchner Prize" by the German Academy for Language and Poetry. In 1995, this prize was awarded to the Lyricist, Durs Grünbein, born 1962 in Dresden, who was then selected for the Berlin/Brandenburg Academy of Arts, and with his power for words has secured a place for himself amongst the greatest of modern poets.

Philosophical literature. Philosophy in postwar Germany was no less marked by a sharp break and persistent uncertainty than fiction and poetry. One of the most influential German philosophers of this century, Martin Heidegger (1889-1976), who with "Being and Time" (1927) had presented one of the fundamental works of existentialism, became one of the most controversial scholars of the postwar period as a consequence of his occasionally demonstrative affinity for the Nazi "Führer-based" state. Nevertheless, Heidegger's Existentialist approach continued to profoundly influence a broad-based movement in philosophy and all the humanities even after the war. Philosophers such as Karl Jaspers, Hans-Georg Gadamer, Karl Löwith or Jean-Paul Sartre in France developed their theories in elaboration of the philosophy of existentialism.

Another philosophical current associated with the names Ludwig Wittgenstein, Rudolf Carnap and Karl Popper – all divergence of their thought notwithstanding – picked up the thread of positivism. It continued to develop especially in the Anglo-Saxon countries, where it profoundly influenced the Analytic and Linguistic philosophy which became dominant there. Wolfgang Stegmüller was the most influential exponent of these currents in Germany.

From the beginning of the 1960s onward, the influence of the "Frankfurt School" grew in Germany. Its principal exponents in the Federal Republic, Theodor W. Adorno and Max Horkheimer – both Jewish philosophers in the Marxist tradition – had left Germany during the period of Nazi rule, as had Walter Benjamin, Herbert Marcuse and Ernst Bloch. Their theories profoundly influenced the student movements at the end of the 1960s. This school of critical theory turned against both the conservative-apolitical tradition in the wake of existentialism and the tendency of positivism to accept existing conditions as the natural course of events.

Since the 1970s, German philosophy has been increasingly receptive to the Anglo-Saxon tradition – and, conversely, the latter has derived more and more impulses from Continental European thought. The philosophy of Jürgen Habermas, who taught for many years in the United States, is a clear manifestation of this development. It represents an attempt to combine key elements of Continental Western philosophy and those of Anglo-Saxon thought.

The sociologist Niklas Luhmann, distancing himself from Habermas, emphasizes the autonomous developmental inclination of systems such as society, the economy or politics. Philosophical discussion in Germany today focuses especially on ethical questions.

The book trade and libraries

In terms of book production, the Federal Republic ranks third in the world, behind the United Kingdom and China. In 1998, almost 80,000 first and new editions were published in Germany. More than 800,000 titles were available. Several cities are now major publishing centers: Munich, Berlin, Frankfurt am Main, Stuttgart, Cologne and Hamburg.

Publishing houses and retail booksellers. There are over 3,000 publishers in the Federal Republic. 30 of them have an annual turnover of more than DM 100 million, but none of them dominates the market. Many small companies also contribute to the variety of literature available to the public. After World War II, book clubs attracted a wider readership. For example, the Gutenberg Büchergilde book club was set up by the trade union movement.

In 1998, the total turnover of books and journals came to about DM 17.8 billion, an increase of 1.6 percent over the figures for the previous year. Approximately 60 percent of this figure came from retail booksellers through over 5,000 book stores. Over the last few years many book stores have expanded their inventories to offer computer software, audio recordings, as well as gift items. Larger stores features, cafés and Internet access for their customers. Ordering books over the Internet is enjoying increasing popularity these days. Aside from the pharmacies, the book trade is the only branch of commerce in Germany permitted by law to set retail prices. This guarantees that nearly all books are available throughout the whole of Germany at uniform net published prices and that the entire population thus has access to this cultural asset.

The German Publishers & Booksellers Association and book fairs. The professional and trade organization of the book trade is the German Publishers & Booksellers Association in Frankfurt/Main, which was founded 175 years ago in

Leipzig. It brings together companies from all tiers of this branch of industry: publishing houses, firms from the intermediate book trade, and retail booksellers. At the Association's initiative, an exhibition company was founded in 1964 whose primary task is to organize the Frankfurt Book Fair which now takes place every year in October. This fair is the outstanding event of the year for the international book trade, and a large percentage of worldwide rights and license transactions are concluded here. Every year since 1976, the fair has had a different focal theme. In 1994, it was Brazil, in 1995 Austria, in 1996 Ireland, in 1997 Portugal, in 1998 Switzerland and in 1999 the focus was on Hungary (2000 Poland). At the 1997 book fair, more than 6,600 publishing companies from 113 countries exhibited their products. The development of electronic media has taken on great importance in this sector. As a result, the specialty "Electronic Publishing" was introduced at the 1993 Frankfurt Book Fair. The fair culminates in the award of the Peace Prize of the German Book Trade. Among recent prizewinners have been Yehudi Menuhin, Teddy Kollek, Václav Havel, György Konrád, Jorge Semprún, Yaşar Kemal and Martin Walser. In 1999, the prize went to US historian, Fritz Stern, born 1926 in Breslau. The second major book fair is held every spring in Leipzig. It especially serves as an intermediary with the countries of Eastern Europe.

Libraries. Unlike other countries, Germany has no large national library that has existed for centuries. It was not until 1913 that the newly founded Deutsche Bücherei (German Library) in Leipzig brought together all literature written in German under one roof. The division of Germany after World War II led to the foundation of the Deutsche Bibliothek (German Li-

The German book trade – flourishing despite IT

brary) in Frankfurt/Main in 1947. It had the same function in the west as the Leipzig library in the east. Like the Leipzig library, it was founded by the book trade as a copyright library and since 1969, it has been a federal institution.

Under the Unification Treaty of August 1990, the two libraries were merged under the name "Die Deutsche Bibliothek". Die Deutsche Bibliothek is the central archive of all writings in German and the national bibliographical information center of the Federal Republic. Its stocks currently total approximately 14 million volumes. In 1970, the German Music Archive was founded in Berlin as a special section of the Frankfurt Deutsche Bibliothek. Frankfurt is also the home of the German Exile Archive 1933-45. Special sections in Leipzig include the Center for Book Preservation and the German Museum of Books and Writings.

Two of the country's most important academic libraries are the Bayerische Staatsbibliothek (Bavarian State Library) in Munich (more than six million books) and the "Staatsbibliothek zu Berlin – Preussischer Kulturbesitz" in Berlin (about four million books). The state and university libraries likewise have large stocks. In addition to these general libraries, there are specialized libraries such as the Central Medical Library in Cologne. One library with an outstanding reputation is the Herzog August Library in Wolfenbüttel, which has over 660,000 volumes, including 12,000 priceless medieval manuscripts.

In the Federal Republic of Germany there are approximately 13,500 public libraries with more than 129 million volumes. Most of these libraries are maintained by local authorities and churches. Many feature public readings by authors, special events and exhibitions and have thus become centers of

The Oberlausitz Library of Sciences in Görlitz

cultural activity – in many smaller communities the only
such center. They also cater to the special interests of users by
offering special sections for children and young people as
well as music and art libraries. Many cities and communities
operate bookmobiles serving suburban areas and villages.

Further information:
  — Börsenverein des Deutschen Buchhandels e.V.
    (German Publishers & Booksellers Association)
    Grosser Hirschgraben 17-21, 60311 Frankfurt/Main
    Internet: http://www.buchhandel.de
    E-mail: 101513.1345@compuserve.com
  — Deutscher Bibliotheksverband e.V.
    (German Library Association)
    Alt-Moabit 101 A, 10559 Berlin
    Internet: http://www.bdbibl.de/dbv
    E-mail: dbv@dbi-berlin.de

Art

Trends since 1945. After the period of isolation imposed by the National Socialist regime, German artists swiftly ventured into uncharted territory. The young generation of painters and sculptors, some of whom had been soldiers on the front lines, eagerly absorbed what they had been denied by Hitler's dictatorship and the war. Wassily Kandinsky, Oskar Kokoschka, Max Beckmann and Emil Nolde as well as the Expressionists Erich Heckel, Karl Schmidt-Rottluff, Ernst Ludwig Kirchner and Max Pechstein were the outstanding models of the newly evolving art scene. For most of the young artists, Pablo Picasso with his exceedingly complex oeuvre represented the ultimate challenge. Of great import was the confrontation with Surrealism (Max Ernst, Salvador Dalí) and American Abstract Expressionism. But artists such as Roberto Sebastian Matta, Jean Dubuffet, Georges Mathieu, Jean Fautrier and Wols (real name Wolfgang Schulze) likewise furnished important impulses for the art scene in the early years of the Federal Republic.

A number of different groups played a crucial role in the evolution of this art scene. Among them were the "Ecole de Paris", founded in 1940, whose members included Jean Bazaine, Roger Bissière, Maurice Estève, Charles Lapicque, Alfred Manessier, Gustave Singier, Pierre Soulages, Maria Elena Vieira da Silva, Serge Poliakoff, Nicolas de Staël and Hans Hartung; "Cobra" (COpenhagen, BRussels, Amsterdam), founded in 1948, with Asger Jorn, Christian Dotremond, Joseph Noiret, Karel Appel, Constant and Corneille; "junger westen", founded in Recklinghausen in 1948, with Gustav Deppe, Thomas Grochowiak, Ernst Hermanns, Emil Schumacher, Heinrich Siepmann and Hans Werdehausen; "Zen 49", founded in Munich in 1949, whose members included Willi Baumeister, Fritz Winter, Ruprecht Geiger, Gerhard Fietz, Brigitte Meier-Denninghoff, Rolf Cavael and, somewhat later, Joseph Fassbender, Hann Trier, Hubert Berke, Theodor and Woty Werner, Karl Hartung and Hans Uhlmann; and, finally, "Quadriga", founded in Frankfurt/Main in 1953, with K.O. Götz, Otto Greis, Heinz Kreutz and Bernard Schultze.

Art Informel, Beuys and Zero. Parallel to French Tachism, a style of art evolved in the Federal Republic of Germany immediately after World War II under the influence of Surrealism, the "Ecole de Paris" and American Abstract Expressionism. It was a style of art which – miles away from figurative painting or even geometric abstraction – had as its overarching characteristic, an abstract, gesticular and semiautomatic style of painting which is never completely uncontrolled and follows the principle of planned coincidence. The great variety of the German Art Informel is manifest in the works of artists who have long since become internationally renowned: Karl Otto Götz, Bernard Schultze, Fred Thieler, Gerhard Hoehme, Karl Friedrich Dahmen, Emil Schumacher, Peter Brüning and K.R.H. Sonderborg.

At the beginning of the 1950s, nearly all artists of the informal groups sought liberation from the dogmas of representational panel painting. The turn to Art Informel or abstraction unleashed an explosion of creative energies, prompting the evolution of other styles which greatly enriched the postwar art spectrum in the Federal Republic of Germany. These include color field painting, painting through the concrete, dispassionate medium of color as illustrated by the focus of the work of Georg Karl Pfahler (born in 1926), Günter Fruhtrunk (1923-1982) and Lothar Quinte (born in 1923). They also include the environment-related action art of HA Schult (born in 1939) and movements such as the "happening" initiated

Jörg Immendorf in front of a model for his "Giant Oak"

by Wolf Vostell (1932-1998) and the Fluxus activities profoundly influenced by him. Both of the latter are events in which the audience plays an important role, especially in the case of the happening. Fluxus is more theater, performance and self-presentation of the artist-actors.

Here Joseph Beuys (1921-1986) set standards that dwarfed everything else. Even his early drawings dating from the 1940s as well as his objects, sculptures and "actions" reveal that he lived out an unorthodox concept of art which opened up new dimensions and meanings to art. His frequently misunderstood formulas "Art is life, life is art" and "Everyone is an artist", his "actions" with fat and felt, his ideas rooted in the anthroposophical philosophy of Rudolf Steiner, the rigorousness with which he attracted an ever larger following of students at the Düsseldorf Academy of Art – these are but a few striking aspects of the life of Joseph Beuys. With his "extended concept of art" he created an instrument that enabled him to propagate "social sculpture" as the consummation of his philosophy of art.

The Zero group, too, electrified the public early on with happening-type actions. Its chief exponents, Heinz Mack (born in 1931), Otto Piene (born in 1928) and Günther Uecker (born in 1930), represented a type of artist who, after the Holocaust perpetrated by the National Socialists, was no longer interested in following ideologies but rather in creating concrete pictures.

Piene, who is meanwhile world famous, has caused quite a stir everywhere with his fire and smoke pictures and – in a particularly spectacular manner – with his sky events. Mack has received international acclaim for his light steles, light dynamos and Sahara project. Uecker has given people in many

Bernard Schultze – one of the champions of Tachisme

Rebecca Horn
and her
"The Turtle
Sighing Tree"

countries food for thought with his nail objects, sandmills
and expressive instruments of terror.

Socialist Realism. Whereas artists in the Federal Republic of
Germany were able to pick up the thread of existing tradi-
tions and draw on all the new artistic currents in Western Eu-
rope and the United States, their colleagues in the former
German Democratic Republic soon found their hands tied by
the "Socialist Realism" prescribed for them by the regime.
They were permitted to do nothing more than convey a favorable picture of the socialist society and its kind of people.
New trends in this type of painting came largely from the
Leipzig Academy of Art. Among its best-known artists were
Werner Tübke (born in 1929) and Bernhard Heisig (born in
1925), whose monumental paintings, though still tied to historical or social themes, shed the sterility of the style of the
1950s and 1960s.

A.R. Penck (born in 1939), who left the GDR in 1980 and
achieved fame in western Germany, chose idols of the Stone
Age as his theme. With symbols such as crosses and squares
as well as his anarchic figures, he seeks to create a universal
idiom which any person can immediately understand.

The artists of today. Characteristic of the work of Ulrich
Rückriem (born in 1938), are huge dolomite blocks such as
those with which he created the Heinrich Heine Memorial in
Bonn. Jörg Immendorf (born in 1945), is a kind of modern
history painter. In his picture "Café Deutschland", the storm
of history blows the Berlin Wall away. In March 1997, Immendorf was awarded the Mexican "Marco Prize", the world's
largest art prize (US$ 250,000), for his work "Accumulation
2". Anselm Kiefer (born in 1945), shapes massive works of art
from materials such as dust, flower petals, ashes and roots in
his factory-hall studios. "Zweistromland" is the name of a
32-ton sculpture consisting of 200 books made of lead on
shelves eight meters long. He calls his pictures, many of

which are inspired by mythology, "picture bodies" because with his usually untreated materials, he lends sculptured volume to the two-dimensionality of traditional painting.

Rebecca Horn (born in 1944) presents sculptures as "performances" and uses them in her own films. Gerhard Richter (born in 1932), is a master of ambiguity, on the border between representational and abstract art, who skillfully shifts at will from representation reminiscent of the Old Masters to the most extreme forms of abstraction. Georg Baselitz (born in 1938), who has won many awards and gained an international reputation, expresses in his upside-down pictures the misery of the human condition. Of primary importance to him is not that which is portrayed but rather the actual doing and artistic freedom. Markus Lüpertz (born in 1941), the current director of the Düsseldorf Academy of Art, projects a "drunken, rapturous" feeling of life with his "dithyrambic painting". Lüpertz is one of the fathers of the new ("wild") representa-

Katharina Fritsch: "Company at Table" (1988), 32 figures made of polyester, cotton, wood, and fabric (140 x 1,600 x 175 cms), Museum für Moderne Kunst, Frankfurt/Main

tional painting in western Germany, although he has always avoided wild gestures and splurges of color. Sigmar Polke (born in 1941) plays – often ironically – with shifts between different levels in his pictures. He frequently uses printed cloth as a painting surface, employing printing block-like symbols to lend it a significance of its own.

Art promotion and new media. Today, very few painters and sculptors can live solely on the proceeds from the sale of their works. They receive government aid, grants, and assistance from private companies with a keen appreciation for the arts. The Kunstfonds e.V., founded in 1980, helps recognized artists finance ambitious projects. Oases of artistic activity are the artists' colony in Worpswede near Bremen as well as the Villa Massimo and the Villa Romana in Italy. Here scholarship holders can work undisturbed. Business and industry encourage artistic activity as well. For more than 40 years, for instance, the cultural section of the Federation of German Industries has been awarding prizes to painters and sculptors.

The new media of video, computers and telecommunications are being used for artistic purposes as well. The Center for Art and Media in Karlsruhe, the Institute for New Media in Frankfurt/Main and the Academy of Media Arts in Cologne perceive the electronic media as forms of expression which complement traditional forms of painting and sculpture. Video art and interaction between the computer and the observer are the focus of this young art scene.

Architecture and design

Retrospect. German architecture set trends in the first 30 years of the 20th century. The strongest influences came from Weimar and Dessau, where the Bauhaus school was founded in the 1920s, and the style that bears its name evolved. Under the leadership of Walter Gropius (1883-1969) and Ludwig Mies van der Rohe (1886-1969), the Bauhaus style spread to the far corners of the earth. Today, masterpieces of its synthesis of architecture, technology and functionality can be found all over the world.

German contemporary architecture long suffered from the country's difficult situation after 1945. Germany's destroyed cities and towns had to be rebuilt quickly. Millions of people needed inexpensive housing. Architectural quality often took a back seat to a primarily economically oriented functionalism in building and construction which paid little heed to shaping a livable residential and working environment.

In the western part of divided Germany, bitter complaints were increasingly heard as early as the 1960s about the monotonous architecture of satellite townships, the faceless industrial and business districts on the periphery of the cities, and the ill-considered construction marring the inner cities. There was talk of the "bleakness" (Alexander Mitscherlich) of the country's inner cities before an urban development concept focusing on preservation of a city's existing architecture and character was accorded political and social priority in the mid-1970s.

Architectural and urban development sins of at least equal magnitude were committed during this time in the former German Democratic Republic (GDR). Valuable old buildings which had survived the war – most of them located in the inner cities – were razed. The scarce resources earmarked for residential construction were used to build massive precast concrete slab housing developments on the fringes of the cities. With the exception of a few reconstructed buildings (such as the Semper Opera House in Dresden) and new structures, architects had too little opportunity to successfully implement a style of architecture that was in keeping with the times. The necessary materials were in short supply – and skilled professionals often were as well.

Trend-setting contemporary architects. Today Germany has more and more examples of modern innovative architecture which are nevertheless in tune with human needs. Many a superb building still owes its origination to the style and philosophy of the Bauhaus. But more recent trends in architecture have also resulted in the construction of remarkable buildings, such as high-tech buildings in which important functional elements such as elevators, escalators and supply lines have been moved to the outside of the structure, where (often painted different colors) they concurrently serve as decoration. Today, other forms of ornamentation such as capitals, cornices and ornaments in the Art Deco style are being used in a greater variety of ways as eye-catchers in the sense of architecture as art, breaking away from the postulate of architecture as mere fulfillment of function.

Germany's top echelon of architects includes:

— Gottfried Böhm, who in 1986 became the first German to be awarded the Pritzker Architecture Prize;

— Günter Behnisch, who designed not only the buildings and grounds for the 1972 Olympic Games in Munich but also the new plenary chamber of the German Bundestag in Bonn in 1993;

— Frei Otto, who made a name for himself in the fields of flexible suspended roof construction and ecologically oriented building;

— Oswald Mathias Ungers, whose buildings exhibit a severely geometric design;

— Josef Paul Kleihues and Hardt-Waltherr Hämer, who as planning directors of the International Building Exhibition in Berlin have profoundly influenced both the discussion of new architecture (Kleihues) and the treatment of residential units in old buildings (Hämer);

— Volker Staab who set important trends in museum construction with the Munich Pinakothek der Moderne and the Georg Schäfer Museum;

— Axel Schultes, who won the 1993 Berlin "International städte-
baulichen Ideenwettbwerb Spreebogen" and was responsible
for the new Federal Chancellery building (together with
Charlotte Frank).

Outstanding structures. The Federal Republic has some fine
representative buildings. Public clients in particular usually
hold architectural competitions before they decide on the execution of a specific design. These Ideas and Project Competitions are key instruments for promoting architectural quality
in Germany.

Even more than 30 years ago, outstanding structures were produced under these conditions, including the three-sectional
high-rise Thyssen House in Düsseldorf (Helmut Hentrich and
Hubert Petschnigg, 1960). One example of unconventional,
dynamic architecture is the head office of the automobile
manufacturer BMW in Munich with its striking cylindrical
form (Karl Schwanzer, 1972). Another is the Bahlsen building
in Hanover with its interlocking cubist forms (Dieter Bahlo,
Jörn Köhnke, Klaus Stosberg, 1974).

The tent-shaped structures (Günter Behnisch, Fritz Auer, Wolfgang Büxel, Erhard Tränkner, Carlo Weber) designed for the
1972 Olympics in Munich are world famous. These sports facilities are situated in a park which has continued to be a
popular recreational area in the years since the Olympic
Games.

The Philharmonic Hall in Berlin (Hans Scharoun, 1963) features a
vineyard-like, terraced auditorium constructed around the orchestra. A classical ruin was incorporated into Münster's City
Theater (Harald Deilmann, Max von Hausen, Ortwin Rave,
Werner Ruhnau, 1955). The new City Library in Münster – a
two-part structure, one part of which is reminiscent of a ship

**Berlin's new
Jewish
Museum –
brainchild
of Daniel
Libeskind, the
US architect**

Office Building C3 by Arata Isozaki on Potsdamer Platz, Berlin

– attracted considerable attention at the beginning of the 1990s (Julia Bolles-Wilson and Peter Wilson, 1993).

Outstanding museums were created by Hans Döllgast (reconstruction of the Alte Pinakothek in Munich, 1957), Alexander Freiherr von Branca (Neue Pinakothek in Munich, 1981), Hans Hollein (Abteiberg Municipal Museum in Mönchengladbach, 1982), and Peter Busman and Godfrid Haberer (Wallraf-RichartzMuseum/Museum Ludwig in Cologne, 1986).

During the 1980s, the city of Frankfurt/Main erected a "museum mile" along the Main River: the German Architectural Museum (Oswald Mathias Ungers, 1984), the German Cinema Museum (Helge Bofinger, 1984), the Museum of Applied Arts (Richard Meier, 1984), the Museum of Prehistory and Early History (Josef Paul Kleihues, 1989), the Jewish Museum (Ante Josip von Kostelac, 1986) and the German Postal Museum (Behnisch and Partners, 1990). An attraction in the heart of the city of Frankfurt is the "Schirn" Art Gallery (Dietrich Bangert, Bernd Jansen, Stefan Scholz and Axel Schultes, 1985).

The great era of museum construction continued with the completion of three structures in the federal city of Bonn – the Art Center of the Federal Republic of Germany (Gustav Peichl, 1993), the Art Museum (Axel Schultes, 1993) and the Museum of Contemporary German History (Ingeborg and Hartmut Rüdiger, 1994) – as well as the new Hamburg Art Gallery (Oswald Mathias Ungers, 1997). Daniel Libeskind received the German Architecture Prize in 1999 for his design of the Jewish Museum in Berlin. Currently, the Leipzig Museum der Bildenden Künste (Hufnagel, Pütz, Rafaelian), the German Historical Museum in Berlin (Ieoh Ming Pei), the Diözesanmuseum in Cologne (Peter Zumthor), and the new Wallraf Richartz Museum in Cologne (Ungers) are all nearing completion.

An excellent example of how a hospital can blend naturally with the landscape is the Filderklinik in Filderstadt near Stuttgart

(Bockmüller, Weller and Partners, 1975). The Aachen Klinikum (Weber, Brand & Partners, 1988) and the University Clinic in Nuremberg (Joedicke and others, 1993) are prime examples of modern, high-tech architecture.

Since 1945 numerous churches have been built in Germany. Worthy of special mention is the KaiserWilhelm-Gedächtniskirche (Emperor William Memorial Church) in Berlin, which had been destroyed during the Second World War. Egon Eiermann fused the old ruin with a new steel construction with large glass sections (1963). Other remarkable churches are the massive Pilgrimage Church in Neviges (Gottfried Böhm, 1967), the Church of St. Boniface in Dortmund (Emil Steffann, 1954), St. Michael's Church in Frankfurt/Main (Rudolf Schwarz, 1954), St. Pius's Church in Cologne (Joachim Schürmann, 1961), Christ Church in Bochum (Dieter Oesterlen with Werner Schumann, 1959) and the Church of the Reconciliation in Dachau (Helmut Striffler, 1969).

As state and municipal duties increased, state parliaments and town halls needed more room and more sophisticated technical equipment. The State Parliament Building in Düsseldorf (Eller, Meier & Walter, 1992), the Town Hall in Bensberg (Gottfried Böhm, 1964), the Stadthalle in Germering near Munich (Auer & Weber, 1993) and the Music and Congress Hall in Lübeck (von Gerkan, Marg & Partners, 1994) are but a few outstanding examples of the bold self-assurance demonstrated by state and municipal bodies.

The same is true of the impressive new buildings on Potsdamer Platz in Berlin (the Daimler-Chrysler complex, where the architectural team was led by Renzo Piano and the Sony Center designed by Helmut Jahn), as well as for many functional buildings constructed recently, like the Photonikzentrum in

The modernized Kandinsky-Klee Meisterhaus in Dessau, built to plans by Walter Gropius

Berlin-Adlershof (Sauerbruch & Hutton), the "Stadttor" in Dusseldorf (Petzinka, Pink and Partner), the Kunsthalle in Halle (Braun, Köhler & Schlockermann), the Schwimmhalle in Leipzig-Grunau (Behnisch and Partner), the RWE skyscraper in Essen (Ingenhoven) and the Federal Labour Court in Erfurt (Weinmiller & Grossmann). The Hackeschen Höfe (Faust & Weiss) in Berlin are a particularly good example of old buildings which have been successfully renovated.

Despite the great variety and considerable scope of the building tasks shouldered by the public and private sectors, housing construction – which represents more than 50 percent of construction volume – remains the most formidable challenge of the future.

Design. Design has a long tradition in Germany. At the beginning of the 20th century, Peter Behrens (1868-1940) designed products, posters and buildings for the electrical firm AEG. In 1907, the German Labor League was founded for the purpose of promoting the "enrichment of working life through the combined influence of art, industry and the craft trades". The Bauhaus, founded by Walter Gropius (1883-1969) in 1919, which existed from 1919 to 1933, became world famous. The same is true of the Ulm College of Design, which was founded in 1953 by Inge Aicher-Scholl (1917-98), Otl Aicher (1922-91) and Max Bill (1908-94). While it initially followed in the footsteps of the Bauhaus, it soon pursued concepts of its own and set internationally acknowledged standards for design during the 15 years of its existence. It strongly influenced many prominent designers. Otl Aicher, for instance, developed the CI for Deutsche Lufthansa, the "Zweites Deutsches Fernsehen (ZDF)" television network, and the 1972 Olympic Games in Munich. Alexander Neumeister designed the Intercity-Express (ICE) and the Transrapid magnetic levitation train; Hans Gugelot (1920-65) designed the Hamburg elevated train (together with Herbert Lindinger) as well as phonograph equipment and electric razors for the firm Braun.

For many years the name "Braun" was closely linked – especially abroad – with the concept of "German design", which combines functionality with complexity and technology. The Braun design was largely defined by Dieter Rams. Other German firms also set, and still set styles with their products: Wilkhahn in Bad Münder and Vitra in Weil/Rhine for furniture, Lamy for writing implements, and Erco for lamps. Prominent members of the German design scene include Hartmut Esslinger, Erik Spiekermann and Kurt Weidemann.

In the information age, the importance of design in creating new media is assuming an ever greater role. Apart from the aesthetic dimension to deciphering complex information, design plays an important intermediary role between the advances in information technology and the cultural developments in society.

The German Design Council advises and supplies information in matters of design to trade and industry, cultural institutions as well as the public. One of the focusses of its activities is presenting German design outside Germany. On behalf of the Minister of Trade and Industry, it awards the "Federal Prize for Product Design" and the "Federal Prize for Design Promotion" on alternate years.

Apart from the German Design Council, there are a range of other design institutions in Germany. Among the most important are the International Design Center (IDZ) in Berlin, the "designcenter" in Stuttgart and the Design Zentrum Nordrhein-Westfalen in Essen. There are exhibitions with historical and contemporary design features in the Neue Sammlung in Munich, the Neue Museum für Kunst und Design in Nuremberg, the Bauhaus Archive in Berlin, the Vitra Design Museum in Weil/Rhein and the Museum für Künst und Gewerbe in Hamburg. The interests of designers vis-à-vis the political sector and the public are represented by the German Design Forum, which amongst other things constitutes the Design section of the German Arts Council, the umbrella organization of the federal arts associations.

Further information:
  — Bund Deutscher Architekten
    (Federation of German Architects)
    Köpenicker Strasse 48-49, 10179 Berlin
    Internet: http://www.bda.baunetz.de
    E-mail: bda.bs. bn@baunetz.de
  — Deutscher Designertag e.V.
    (German Design Forum)
    Postfach 13 03 33, 20103 Hamburg
    Internet: http://www.designertag.de
  — Rat für Formgebung
    (German Design Council)
    Ludwig-Erhard-Anlage 1, 60327 Frankfurt/Main
    Internet: http://www.euro-design-guide.de
    E-mail: german-design-co@ipf.de

Museums, collections and exhibitions

The large number of museums with different areas of focus has its origin in the social and cultural development of Germany. There are more than 3,000 museums in the Federal Republic: state, municipal, society and private museums; museums of local history and culture; museums of church, diocesan and cathedral treasures; and residential, castle, palace and open-air museums. They have grown up over the centuries out of royal, church and, later, civic collections.

The royal collections were not, however, intended for the erudition of the general public. Rather, they served to prominently display the sovereigns' wealth of treasures and precious objects. Munich, for instance, was an international art center as early as the 16th century in this respect. The Bavarian dukes collected not only works of art but also technical equipment of their time, craftsmen's tools, musical instruments, minerals and exotic items. In the 17th century, the Green Vault of the Saxon rulers in Dresden was probably the largest treasure house in Europe. Its collections eventually grew to fill an art gallery, a salon of mathematics and physics, and a mineralogy museum.

Many wealthy citizens – in keeping with the fashion of the time – also amassed collections of their own. As a result of this passion for collecting, there has come to be a museum in Germany for nearly every field of art and nearly all types of activity. Especially the large museums strive to exhibit as broad a range of their objects as possible. Due to lack of sufficient space, however, nearly all museums are forced to place many objects in storage; these can only be put on public display during special exhibitions.

From Rembrandt and Picasso to tapestries (Kassel), from wine-making equipment (Koblenz) to meteorites (Marburg), from mummies from the moors (Schleswig) to optical instruments (Oberkochen) or the oldest boat in the world reconstructed from original parts (Bremerhaven) – the variety of exhibitions appears limitless.

Art lovers and patrons. Today, Germany's museums, both traditional and modern, try to reach all segments of the population regardless of their level of education. Germans now visit a museum as casually as they used to go to the cinema; long lines form in front of the museum ticket counters when individual exhibits of the works of great classical modern painters are featured. Year in, year out, more than 100 million people visit Germany's museums, which in some major cities have come to form entire ensembles: along the banks of the Main River in Frankfurt, for instance, along the "Museum Mile" in Bonn, or in the capital Berlin, where the Prussian Cultural Heritage Foundation founded in 1951 fills several museums with its collections from Prussian days.

As in the past, wealthy private patrons of the arts have been partly responsible for the current museum boom. Peter Ludwig, one of the best-known, donated many modern works of art to predominantly newly-built museums. The "Ludwig-Forum" in Aachen, housed in a former umbrella factory, focuses, among other things, on art from the former GDR. Ludwig's collection of contemporary French art is on display in the former House of the Teutonic Order in Koblenz.

In Bonn, the Art Center of the Federal Republic of Germany (1993) and the Museum of Contemporary German History (1994) attract thousands of visitors. In Berlin, the Museum of German History presents German history in its entirety, right up to the present time.

A special role is played by museums of cultural history and ethnology. The unparalleled Deutsches Museum in Munich has original items and models depicting, among other things,

Art lessons at the Stuttgart State Gallery

In the Old Masters Gallery at Dresden's Zwinger museum

the world-wide development of technology and science. After renovation work was completed in 2000, the Museum for Communications in Berlin re-opened with an extensive collection of German post and telephone exhibits from over the centuries, while the Germanisches Nationalmuseum in Nuremberg has the largest collection on the history of German art and culture from prehistory to the 20th century. The large number of ethnological museums is attributable to the fact that Germany produced many explorers and scholars who were keenly interested in foreign cultures. In addition to the Berlin museums, the Linden Museum in Stuttgart and the Roemer-Pelizaeus Museum in Hildesheim deserve special mention in this context.

Special exhibitions focus on particular themes. Historical exhibitions such as that on the "Art and Culture of the Carolingian Period" (Paderborn, 1999), or "Emperor Charles V (1500-50) – European Power and Impotence" (Bonn, 2000), stand out as particular crowd-drawers. The exhibition "Kings in Aachen – History and Myth" in the summer of 2000 offered fascinating insights into the traditional Medieval coronations of kings with exhibits from many European museums. A high standard of sophistication and accessibility was set by the exhibition "1848 – Embarking on Freedom", a portrayal of the development of German democracy presented at the Schirn Art Gallery in Frankfurt/Main in 1998. The exhibition "More Light" in Frankfurt, offered a comprehensive overview of art in the Age of Enlightenment in Europe while the Stuttgart Staatsgalerie presented an overview of the works of early impressionist, Camille Pissarro.

The millennium exhibition "Seven Hills – Images and Symbols of the 21st Century" in the Martin Gropius building in Berlin in 2000, offered a futuristic multimedia picture of the coming millennium together with a retrospective on the immortal treasures of the past.

The largest festival of modern art in the world is Kassel's "documenta", which takes place every five years and drew more than 631,000 visitors in 1997.

The great variety of museums. The broad regional distribution of Germany's museums makes them accessible to large numbers of people. There is no central government "museum policy", but museums cooperate with one another in a number of fields, such as restoration and museum security, central documentation and research. These joint activities are coordinated by the Federation of German Museums, established in 1917, to which all Germany's museums belong. The Institut für Museumskunde of the State Museums of Prussian Cultural Heritage in Berlin has similar duties.

Museum architecture, too, shows great variety, ranging from the 19th century art "temples" to such spectacular examples of ultra-modern architecture as the New Museum in Nuremberg which opened on 15 April 2000, the Pinakothek der Moderne in Munich and the two Daniel Libeskind buildings – the Felix Nussbaum House in Osnabruck and the Jewish Museum in Berlin's Mitte district.

Further information:
  — Deutscher Museumsbund
    (Federation of German Museums)
    Lingnerplatz 1, 01069 Dresden
    Internet: http://www.museumsbund.de
    E-mail: Office@museumsbund.de

Theater and Music

The theaters. Germany's theatrical landscape is above all defined by the country's approximately 180 public theaters. These state and municipal theaters, orchestras and regional theaters are complemented by roughly 190 private theaters and more than 30 festival theatres. There are also countless independent groups and amateur theaters. This variety is charactersitic of the German theater scene. Instead of a single "theater capital" which attracts all the talent and all the attention – such as Paris in France, for example – the Federal Republic has a wealth of theaters which are frequently in no way inferior to one other in terms of quality. This great diversity is traditional: In the 17th and 18th centuries, nearly every regional sovereign took great pride in his own court theater and generally spared no expense to ensure that it was well equipped. In the 19th century, under the increasing influence of a prosperous middle class, many towns and cities made the theater a public institution.

The multi-purpose theater offers a broad range of dramatic arts, dance and music theater (operas, operettas, musicals) under one roof. These theaters perform a repertoire of 20 to 30 works in a given season. Each year, approximately ten newly-staged productions enter the repertoire. People thus have an opportunity to become acquainted with many works of drama and music theater in their cities. Supplementing this range of offerings are the puppet theater as well as children's and youth theater, which can be either another branch of the multipurpose theater or an independent operation altogether. The musical theaters, by contrast, perform one and the same piece month after month and year after year, in what is termed en suite operations. Much the same is true especially of the smaller private theaters, which usually perform one piece en suite for several weeks and then go on to present a new production.

The artistic profile of a given theater is largely defined by its ensemble. Building and maintaining this ensemble is consequently of particular importance for the theater. Especially the municipal and state theaters have a permanent staff of actors and actresses, singers and dancers.

The German theater makes its contribution to international cultural exchange and to European integration, above all with festivals such as "Theater der Welt" in Berlin or the "Bonner Biennale". Exchanges of individual productions with theaters in other countries also figure prominently, however, as does collaboration with foreign actors and actresses, singers, dancers, theater managers, conductors, directors, designers, and other artists and craftsmen. The "Theater an der Ruhr" in Mulheim, is a paramount example of this.

The schedule. According to the statistics of the German Theater Association, 5,393 productions of 2,683 works (drama, music theater, dance and puppet theater) were staged in the 1997-8 season. 387 theaters staged more than 92,000 performances. 338 of these works were performed for the very first time or for the first time in the German language. The most popular works that season were:

— opera: "The Magic Flute" (Mozart), "Hänsel und Gretel" (Humperdinck) and "La Bohème" (Puccini)

— operetta: "The Bat" (Strauss), "The Merry Widow" (Lehár) and "Im weissen Rössl" (Benatzky);

— theater: "Threepenny Opera" (Brecht), "Jim Knopf" (Ende) and "Faust" (Goethe)

— dance: "Romeo and Juliet" (Prokofiev), "The Nutcracker" and "Giselle" (Adam)

Apart from the established directors such as Jürgen Flimm, Peter Zadek, Claus Peymann and Peter Stein, a younger generation

Peter Stein directed Goethe's "Faust" at EXPO 2000 – in its entirety at one sitting

of directors is attracting attention with fresh ideas and trail-blazing productions. These include Martin Kušej, Sasha Waltz, Thomas Ostermeier and Thirza Bruncken.

Festivals. The festival calendar for theater lovers includes: the Berlin Theater Encounter in May during which the best German-language productions are introduced, the Ruhrfestspiele in Recklinghausen, also held in May, which showcases classical and modern works for a broad public, and the Euroscene in Leipzig. There are also numerous festival venues whose historical forts, castles and churches offer stunning backdrops for performances by mainly classical authors: Bad Hersfeld, Ludwigsburg, Schwäbisch Hall, Jagsthausen, the Haidplatz in Regensburg, the Wartburg near Eisenach and many more. The Kissinger Summer, the Caldéron Festival in Bamberg and the "Hornberger Schiessen" also enjoy great popularity.

The oldest festival in Germany is the Oberammergau Passion Play, which takes place every ten years in fulfilment of a pledge made in the year of the plague in 1634. The most recent performance was in 2000.

There are more than 100 festivals devoted to music. Every three years in September, Bonn celebrates its International Beethoven Festival; in Augsburg in August and September is the Mozart Summer where concerts are performed in a Rococo ambience. The festival in Eutin celebrates Carl Maria von Weber, whose birthplace it was; In Halle and Göttingen Georg Friedrich Handel is honored while Richard Strauss is celebrated in Munich and Garmisch-Partenkirchen. The Richard Wagner Festival in Bayreuth has been held every year since 1876. In honor of the 250th anniversary of Johann Sebastian Bach's death (28 July) in 2000, more than 500 events were planned in Germany as well, such as the Leipzig Bach Festival and the Thuringian Bach week.

Almost every large city participates in the round of festivals: Munich hosts an Opera Festival (July), Frankfurt/Main the Frankfurt Festival (September), Stuttgart the European Music Festival (August and September) and Berlin the Jazz Festival (November). In addition, Dresden and Potsdam-Sansouci hold music festivals, Erfurt the Summer Concerts in Brühler Garden and Weimar presents its Art Festival. Other highlights include the mdr Music Summer by the Mitteldeutschen Rundfunk, the Rügen Festival featuring Rossini operas and the

The world-
renowned
Bamberg
Symphonic
Orchestra